Everyman, I will go with thee,
and be thy guide

Charles Dickens

HOLIDAY ROMANCE
AND OTHER WRITINGS FOR CHILDREN

A CHILD'S HISTORY OF ENGLAND
With illustrations by
F. W. TOPHAM and MARCUS STONE

HOLIDAY ROMANCE
With illustrations by
G. C. WHITE and JOHN GILBERT

THE LIFE OF OUR LORD

Edited by
GILLIAN AVERY

Series Editor
MICHAEL SLATER
University of London

EVERYMAN
J. M. DENT · LONDON
CHARLES E. TUTTLE
VERMONT

Introduction and other critical apparatus
© J.M. Dent, 1995

First published in Everyman as
A Child's History of England in 1907
This text first published in Everyman in 1995

J.M. Dent
Orion Publishing Group
Orion House, 5 Upper St Martin's Lane,
London WC2H 9EA
and
Charles E. Tuttle Co., Inc.
28 South Main Street,
Rutland, Vermont 05701, USA

Typeset in Sabon by CentraCet Ltd, Cambridge
Printed in Great Britain by
The Guernsey Press Co. Ltd, Guernsey, C. I.

British Library Cataloguing-in-Publication Data
is available upon request.

ISBN 0460 87601 5

CONTENTS

ILLUSTRATIONS

NOTE ON THE AUTHOR,
EDITOR AND SERIES EDITOR

CHARLES DICKENS was born at Portsea, Portsmouth, on 7 February 1812. In 1817 the Dickens family settled in Chatham. These years, 1817–22, were the happiest of Dickens's early life. They came to an end when his father, John Dickens, was recalled to London and the family began its slow slide towards bankruptcy. In February 1824 John Dickens was imprisoned for debt in the Marshalsea and the twelve-year-old Charles was sent to work in a run-down warehouse off the Strand, labelling and packaging bottles of boot blacking. His sense of humiliation and thwarted ambition was acute, and the experience (which may have lasted a year) proved traumatic. His father was discharged from prison later in 1824, under the Insolvent Debtors' Act, and some months later Charles was removed from the warehouse and sent to school. In 1827 he was articled as a solicitor's clerk in Gray's Inn. He learned shorthand, became a reporter at Doctors' Commons and later a skilled reporter of Parliamentary debates. In the years from 1833 to 1836 he wrote a number of short stories and sketches which were published in various journals and collected in *Sketches by Boz* (1836), accompanied with illustrations by George Cruikshank. In April of the same year he married Catherine Hogarth, daughter of a newspaper editor. *Pickwick Papers*, begun in that year as a monthly instalment publication, soon became a great popular success. It was followed by *Oliver Twist* in 1837, *Nicholas Nickleby* in 1838–9 and (in his weekly periodical *Master Humphrey's Clock*) *The Old Curiosity Shop* and *Barnaby Rudge*, 1841. He made a triumphant tour of the United States in 1842 and in the same year published a critical account of his experience there in *American Notes*.

A *Christmas Carol* was published in 1843 and inaugurated the highly successful series of Christmas Books in the 1840s. *Martin Chuzzlewit* appeared in 1843–4 and *Dombey and Son* in 1846–8. *David Copperfield* was completed in 1850, the year in which he founded his own weekly magazine *Household Words*, a characteristically vivacious and imaginative family miscellany, which carried the serialised *Hard Times* in 1854. In that novel, as in its predecessor *Bleak House* (1852–3) and its successor *Little Dorrit* (1855–7), Dickens anatomised and satirised the social and political condition of England. In 1858 he and his wife formally separated and he moved to his new home at Gad's Hill in Kent. In the same year he began his career as a professional public reader of his work, a strenuous enterprise that proved highly lucrative as well as seriously harmful to his health. *A Tale of Two Cities* appeared in 1859 and *Great Expectations* in 1860–1, both serialised in Dickens's successor to *Household Words, All the Year Round*. His last novel to be completed in the old twenty-number monthly format was *Our Mutual Friend* (1864–5). In the winter of 1867–8 he toured the United States with his readings. In 1870 he began *The Mystery of Edwin Drood*, but had completed only half of it when he suffered a stroke at Gad's Hill and died on 9 June.

GILLIAN AVERY is a historian of children's books. *Childhood's Pattern: A Study of the Heroes and Heroines of Children's Fiction 1770–1950* was published in 1975. Her most recent works have been *Behold the Child: American Children and Their Books 1621–1922* (1994) and the opening essay – on children's reading to 1700 – for the *Oxford Illustrated History of Children's Literature* (1995).

MICHAEL SLATER is Professor of Victorian Literature at Birkbeck College (University of London) and a former Editor of *The Dickensian*. He is the author of *Dickens and Women* (1983) and has published a number of other books and articles relating to Dickens, and is the Editor of the *Dent Uniform Edition of Dickens' Journalism*, of which volume 1, *Sketches by Boz and Other Early Papers 1833–9*, appeared in 1994. He has also edited the Everyman edition of *Martin Chuzzlewit* (1994).

CHRONOLOGY OF DICKENS'S LIFE

Year	Age	Life
1812		Born in Portsea, Portsmouth, 7 February
1815	3	Dickens family moves to London
1817	5	Dickens family moves to Chatham
1822	10	Dickens family (now 6 children) moves to London
1824	12	Works at Warren's Blacking. John Dickens (father) in Marshalsea Debtors Prison for a few months
1825	13	Starts school at Wellington House Academy
1827	15	Becomes junior clerk in solicitor's office

CHRONOLOGY OF HIS TIMES

Year	Literary Context	Historical Events
1812	Byron, *Childe Harold* I & II	1811–20 Regency of George, Prince of Wales
		1812–14 War with America
1813	Austen, *Pride and Prejudice*	
	Southey becomes Poet Laureate	
1814	Austen, *Mansfield Park*	
	Scott, *Waverley*	
	Wordsworth, *Excursion*	
1815		Battle of Waterloo
1816	Austen, *Emma*	Spa Fields Riots
1817	Keats, *Poems*	
	Austen dies	
1818	Mary Shelley, *Frankenstein*	
1819	Byron, *Don Juan* I & II	Peterloo Massacre
	Eliot born	The Six Acts
	Whitman born	
1820	Keats, *Lamia . . . and other Poems*	Accession of George IV
		Cato Street Conspiracy
	Flaubert born	
1821	Keats dies	Greek War of Liberation
	De Quincey, *Confessions . . . Opium Eater*	Napoleon dies
1822	Byron, *Vision of Judgement*	Suicide of Castlereagh
	Shelley dies	
1823	Grimm Brothers, *German Popular Stories* (illus. G. Cruikshank)	Agricultural unrest
1824	Byron dies	
1825	Hazlitt, *Spirit of the Age*	Stockton–Darlington railway opens
1826	Disraeli, *Vivian Gray*	
1827	Blake dies	University of London founded

Year   *Age*   *Life*

1829   17   Becomes a freelance reporter at Doctors' Commons
1830   18   Acquires British Museum Reader's Card

1831   19   Falls in love with Maria Beadnell. Appointed Parliamentary
             reporter

1833   21   First story written and published, 'A Dinner at Poplar Walk'

1835   23   Engaged to Catherine Hogarth
1836   24   *Sketches by Boz* published. Marries Catherine. *Pickwick
             Papers* begun
1837   25   *Pickwick Papers* completed. Mary Hogarth (sister-in-law)
             dies. Becomes editor of *Bentley's Miscellany*
1838   26   *Oliver Twist* [dates given for publication of the novels refer
             to completion of their serialisation]

1839   27   *Nicholas Nickleby*
1840   28   Dickens begins *Master Humphrey's Clock*
1841   29   *The Old Curiosity Shop*; *Barnaby Rudge*

1842   30   Visits America (Jan.–Jun.). *American Notes*

1843   31   *A Christmas Carol*

1844   32   Dickens and family stay in Genoa. *Martin Chuzzlewit*; *The
             Chimes*
1845   33   Dickens family returns from Italy. *The Cricket on the Hearth*

1846   34   *Pictures from Italy*. Brief editorship of *Daily News*. *The
             Battle of Life*

Year	Literary Context	Historical Events
1828	Meredith born D. G. Rossetti born	Catholic Emancipation Act
1829	Jerrold, *Black-ey'd Susan*	
1830	Tennyson, *Poems Chiefly Lyrical*	Accession of William IV July Revolution in France Wellington's ministry falls
1831		First cholera epidemic
1832	Carroll born Walter Scott dies	First Reform Bill
1833	Carlyle, *Sartor Resartus* Newman, *Tracts for the Times*	Abolition of slavery throughout British Empire State funding of schools begins
1834	Bulwer-Lytton, *Last Days of Pompeii* Coleridge and Lamb die	Tolpuddle Martyrs New Poor Law
1837	Carlyle, *The French Revolution* Lockhart, *Life of Scott*	Accession of Victoria
1838		Anti-Corn Law League Chartist petitions published London–Birmingham railway opens
1839	Carlyle, *Chartism*	First Factory Inspectors' Report
1840	Hardy born	Penny postage introduced
1841	Carlyle, *Heroes and Hero-Worship*	Peel becomes Prime Minister
1842	Tennyson, *Poems* Browning, *Dramatic Lyrics* Macaulay, *Lays of Ancient Rome*	Chartist riots Report on Sanitary Conditions of Labouring Population
1843	Carlyle, *Past and Present* Ruskin, *Modern Painters* I Wordsworth made Poet Laureate	
1844	Disraeli, *Coningsby* Elizabeth Barrett, *Poems*	Rochdale Pioneers found Co-operative Store
1845	Disraeli, *Sybil*	Railway speculation Newman joins Catholic Church
1846		Repeal of Corn Laws

Year   Age   Life

1848   36   *Dombey and Son. The Haunted Man*

1850   38   Begins his weekly miscellany, *Household Words. David Copperfield*

1851   39   John Dickens dies

1853   41   *Bleak House.* Tours Italy and Switzerland with Wilkie Collins

1854   42   *Hard Times*

1855   43   Meets Maria Beadnell (now Mrs Winter) again. Spends several months in Paris

1856   44   Buys Gad's Hill Place

1857   45   *Little Dorrit.* Meets Ellen Ternan during performances of Wilkie Collins's play *The Frozen Deep*

1858   46   Separates from his wife. Begins professional public readings

Year	Literary Context	Historical Events
1847	Emily Brontë, *Wuthering Heights* Charlotte Brontë, *Jane Eyre* Tennyson, *The Princess*	
1848	Emily Brontë dies Thackeray, *Vanity Fair*	European Revolutions Chartist movement collapses after mass meeting in London Cholera epidemic Pre-Raphaelite Brotherhood founded
1849	Thackeray, *Pendennis* Ruskin, *Seven Lamps of Architecture*	
1850	Tennyson, *In Memoriam* Wordsworth dies Wordsworth, *The Prelude* Kingsley, *Alton Locke*	Pope appoints Catholic bishops to England
1851	Ruskin, *The Stones of Venice* Melville, *Moby-Dick*	Great Exhibition Gold discovered in New South Wales J. M. W. Turner dies
1852	Stowe, *Uncle Tom's Cabin* Thackeray, *Henry Esmond*	Napoleon III becomes Emperor of France Duke of Wellington dies
1853	Charlotte Brontë, *Villette*	Indian Civil Service open to competition
1854	Thoreau, *Walden*	Crimean War begins Newspaper Stamp Duty abolished Palmerston's premiership begins
1855	Browning, *Men and Women* Gaskell, *North and South* Kingsley, *Westward Ho!* Charlotte Brontë dies	
1856	Elizabeth Barrett Browning, *Aurora Leigh* Wilde and Shaw born	End of Crimean War
1857	Trollope, *Barchester Towers* Flaubert, *Madame Bovary*	Indian Mutiny
1858	Eliot, *Scenes of Clerical Life*	Queen Victoria proclaimed Empress of India

Year	Age	Life
1859	47	*A Tale of Two Cities. Household Words* incorporated into new weekly magazine, *All the Year Round*
1861	49	*Great Expectations*
1865	53	*Our Mutual Friend.* Staplehurst railway accident
1867	55	Public readings tour of America (Nov.–May 1868)
1868	56	Begins Farewell Reading Tour
1870	58	Final Farewell Reading in London (March). Begins *The Mystery of Edwin Drood.* Dies 9 June

Year	Literary Context	Historical Events
1859	Tennyson, *Idylls of the King* Darwin, *Origin of Species* Mill, *On Liberty* Smiles, *Self-Help*	Rise of Fenianism in Ireland
1860	Collins, *The Woman in White* Eliot, *The Mill on the Floss*	
1861	Reade, *The Cloister and the Hearth*	Death of Prince Consort American Civil War begins
1862	Mill, *Utilitarianism*	
1863	Kingsley, *Water Babies* Eliot, *Romola* Thackeray dies	Gettysburg Address Slavery abolished in USA
1864	Newman, *Apologia Pro Vita Sua*	
1865	Carroll, *Alice's Adventures in Wonderland* Arnold, *Essays in Criticism*	President Lincoln assassinated Palmerston dies American Civil War ends
1866	Swinburne, *Poems and Ballads* Dostoyevsky, *Crime and Punishment*	First Barnardo Home Atlantic Cable laid
1867	Marx, *Das Kapital*	Disraeli's Reform Bill
1868	Browning, *The Ring and the Book* Collins, *The Moonstone*	Gladstone becomes Prime Minister
1869	Arnold, *Culture and Anarchy* Blackmore, *Lorna Doone*	Suez Canal opens Mill advocates emancipation of women
1870	D. G. Rossetti, *Poems*	Education Act: free public education in Board Schools Franco-Prussian War Fall of Napoleon III

SERIES EDITOR'S PREFACE

The Everyman Dickens is intended to be the most complete edition of Dickens's works so far published. It will be the first paperback edition to provide thorough and coherent coverage of all his shorter fiction as well as his extensive non-fictional writings. In addition to the fifteen novels and the five *Christmas Books*, the Everyman Dickens will include all the Christmas stories from *Household Words* and *All the Year Round*, all other short fiction, the two travel books and all Dickens's writings for children. Four volumes in the series will present the first-ever annotated edition of *Sketches by Boz, The Uncommercial Traveller* and other journalism, a substantial amount of which has been out of print for many years. Each volume will contain all the earliest illustrations to the work or works featured in it, kindly supplied by The Dickens House, and all Dickens's Prefaces.

Every volume will be edited by a specialist in Victorian literature who has a particular interest in the work he or she is dealing with. Where appropriate, explanatory notes will be supplemented by a historical appendix giving more general background information on the text in question.

Throughout the series references to Dickens's published letters will be given as either 'Pilgrim' or 'Nonesuch'. 'Pilgrim' means *The Pilgrim Edition of the Letters of Charles Dickens*, eds. M. House, G. Storey, K. Tillotson *et al* (1965 – in progress), and 'Nonesuch' means *The Letters of Charles Dickens*, ed. W. Dexter, 3 vols (1938), part of the Nonesuch Press Edition of Dickens's Works.

MICHAEL SLATER

INTRODUCTION

In 1888, Edward Salmon, conducting a poll for his book *Juvenile Literature As It Is*, found that Dickens was easily the favourite author of 790 boys. But it is the Dickens of *A Christmas Carol*, *Oliver Twist* and *David Copperfield* that children enjoy and remember; the books he specifically wrote for them have remained little read. Besides, only one of these is fiction – *Holiday Romance*, the linked series of four stories written two years before his death. *The Life of Our Lord*, written in 1846, was intended solely for his family and was not published until 1934. His major work for the young was *A Child's History of England*, the book that most of his critics have combined in deploring.

It is hard to grasp why Dickens should have embarked on this, though less hard to understand why his tone became increasingly irritable as the weary work wound on through thirty-nine episodes in *Household Words*. These began on 25 January 1851 and were not to finish until 10 December 1853. (The work was published in three volumes by Bradbury and Evans between 1852 and 1854.) Even then he only reached 1688, his lame excuse being that 'the events which succeeded the famous Revolution would neither be easily related nor easily understood in such a book as this'.

He had been contemplating such a history at least since 1843, when his eldest son Charley, for whom it was designed, was six. Indeed, he told Douglas Jerrold on 3 May of that year that he was already writing it, for 'I don't know what I should do, if he were to get hold of any conservative or High church notions; and the best way of guarding against any such horrible result, is, I take it, to wring the parrots' necks in his very cradle' (Pilgrim III, 482). (It was entirely characteristic of Dickens to suppose that he could control his children's minds for all time.) However, when he wrote to Miss Burdett-Coutts on 7 August, he spoke of it only as an idea, 'to the end that he may have tender-hearted notions of War and Murder, and may not fix his affections on wrong heros [*sic*], or see the bright side of Glory's sword and know nothing of the rusty one' (Pilgrim III, 539). Nor is any draft of an earlier version of *A Child's History* now known.

Of the children's histories to which he may have been referring the most obviously conservative was the summary that Sarah Trimmer (1741–1810) provided to accompany *A Set of Prints of English History* (?1792), designed to be cut out and hung in the schoolroom. She began with the Romans and finished with George I, and as she was writing during the Napoleonic Wars, when the whole social fabric seemed threatened by the tide of revolution sweeping over Europe, she supported monarchs whenever she could – though she often disapproved of their behaviour. *Mrs Markham's History of England* by Elizabeth Penrose (1780–1837) was on a larger scale. First published in 1823, reissued and enlarged three years later, it was for some forty years the standard history for the young. Though written in the conversational style then popular ('"I shall be very glad, mamma, when you come to a good king"'), it is informal, balanced, clear and also scholarly (most unusually, she identifies her sources). Mrs Penrose had no illusions about 'Glory's sword': 'History is indeed a sad catalogue of human miseries, and one is glad to turn from the horrors of war and bloodshed.' But unlike Dickens, she included not just the deeds of kings, but social and cultural history as well. *Little Arthur's History of England* by Maria Callcott was equally popular. First published in 1835, it went into seventy editions in its first hundred years. As the title suggests, it was designed for small children. Like Dickens, she was fervently patriotic: 'To teach the love of our country is almost a religious duty.' Even so, Callcott is as severe on the monarchs as Dickens himself; the English have rarely admired many of their rulers before Queen Victoria.

Of all these juvenile histories Dickens's is the hardest to follow, partly because he chose to eliminate most dates and all such matters as genealogical tables (though preliminary 'Tables of Reigns' and 'Chronological Tables' were added for volume publication), so that the numbed reader has to struggle with complicated dynastic marriages and claims to the throne without any lifeline to grasp. (Mrs Trimmer, in her much shorter history, had prefaced each chapter with a table of each ruler's family and the marriages within it.) And despite his later affirmation

that his 'faith in The People governed' was 'illimitable' in
contrast to his 'infinitesimal' faith in the people governing (*The
Speeches of Charles Dickens*, ed. K. J. Fielding [1960], p. 407),
and though he did give some account of popular leaders such as
Tyler, Cade and Kett, Hampden and Pym, it is monarchs who
dominate his history. When 'The People' do appear, we rarely
find them doing anything admirable. True, they are often
oppressed, especially in the early reigns, but they are gullible
and easily led, and we watch them, when they are given a free
hand, plunge into looting, pillaging, rape, murder and massacre
– of Danes, Turks, Jews and sometimes just of each other. Or,
as in Henry VIII's time, they slavishly submit to tyranny and
watch the fires of Smithfield burning, 'and not a gentleman of
England raised his hand' (p. 256).

Indeed, violence and macabre detail dominate the narrative.
Almost every page holds *grand guignol* descriptions of torture,
murder, execution, gibbets, burning at the stake. Much blood
flows; most men hate each other and take hideous revenge. It
seems indeed to be an extended version of the gloating account
of Captain Murderer's career in the essay 'Nurse's Stories' (*The
Uncommercial Traveller*). Embellished by characteristic imaginative touches, violent deaths account for many of the more
memorable passages. The body of William II, killed in the New
Forest, is carried in a charcoal-burner's cart to Winchester for
burial, 'shaken and tumbled, with its red beard all whitened
with lime and clotted with blood' (p. 65). The armed tread of
the knights echoes round the dark spaces of Canterbury
Cathedral as they move in on Thomas à Becket, 'and his body
fell upon the pavement, which was dirtied with his blood and
brains' (p. 89). 'Cursing, and swearing, and gnawing his fingers,'
John, having seen his retinue engulfed in the Wash, is carried to
Swinstead Abbey, where all night he lies 'haunted with horrible
fears' (p. 117). 'That night, a horse was led up to the church of
the Grey Friars at Leicester; across whose back was tied, like
some worthless sack, a naked body brought there for burial. It
was the body of the last of the Plantagenet line, King Richard
the Third . . .' (p. 227). Dickens presents his always ferociously
partisan view of personalities with the same power. Henry III is
'a poor old limp court card' (p.126); Henry VIII is 'a swollen,
hideous spectacle, with a great hole in his leg, and so odious to
every sense that it was dreadful to approach him' (p. 257);

James I (whom he always refers to as His Sowship) has 'dull goggle-eyes [which] stared and rolled like an idiot's' (p. 301); James II is 'a gloomy, sullen, bilious sort of man, with a remarkable partiality for the ugliest women in the country' (p. 363).

Apart from Alfred the Great, Dickens reveres only one ruler – Oliver Cromwell. For him, Dickens is prepared to overlook much that he would have castigated in royalty: the massacre at Drogheda, for instance, and Cromwell's high-handed dismissal of Parliament. In the worship of this particular hero, Dickens was echoing Thomas Carlyle – perhaps the only living writer who influenced him. Even so, it is strange that he did not see the irony of his fulminations against Charles I's 'unlawful and despotic' action in dissolving Parliament and ruling without one. And it is stranger still that Dickens of all people, the theatre lover and the creator of Pecksniff, Stiggins and Mrs Clennam, should have missed a chance of a swipe at the Puritans. He conceded that they were 'an uncomfortable sort of people', but his detestation of the Stuarts was so strong that he felt obliged to countenance the latters' opponents.

Violent, prejudiced and jingoistic as it is, *A Child's History* represents, as G. K. Chesterton said in 1907, 'the cock-sure, healthy-minded, essentially manly and essentially ungentlemanly view of history which characterised the Radicals of that particular Radical era'. 'She had a great liking for old customs', Dickens says briskly of Mary Tudor's coronation, 'and she was oiled in the oldest way, and blessed in the oldest way, and done all manner of things to in the oldest way. . . . I hope they did her good' (p. 267). He himself had no use for old customs, or anything that smacked of superstition, and that disposed of the entire pre-Reformation church, which he equated with greed, high living, credulity, ignorance and dirt. The good sense of the English meant that all that nonsense had long been discarded and the Anglo-Saxons now ruled the world. 'Wheresoever that race goes, there, law, and industry, and safety for life and property, and all the great results of steady perseverance, are certain to arise' (p. 28).

What were his sources? No historian himself, he was certainly relying on other potted and popular histories. Frederic Kitton in his 1902 life of Dickens mentions Thomas Keightley's *History of England* (1837–9), which Dickens possessed and annotated, and this has been accepted by most subsequent biographers. If true, it would have been a curious choice. Keightley

(1789–1872) was not a professional historian, but a hack writer who spread himself over a wide range of subjects. (He seems to have been proudest of his *Fairy Mythology*, produced in the wake of the English translation of the Grimm brothers' tales.) The Keightley history was cobbled together from various works, among them – so the preface says – the eight-volume history (1819–30) by the Roman Catholic John Lingard; Keightley aimed to correct Lingard's 'popish views'.

The second work habitually associated with *A Child's History* is *The Pictorial History of England* by 'Charles Knight' (1837–40), which Dickens also possessed. (Knight was, in fact, only the publisher; it was a composite work, of which the principal authors were George L. Craik and Charles Mac-Farlane.) Subtitled 'a history of the people, as well as a history of the kingdom', it would have provided far better material than Keightley. But it is a very long work, of some 9,000 pages, and its arrangement – in sections dealing with religious, cultural, economic, constitutional and political history – is wholly different from Dickens's reign-by-reign account.

The work that Dickens's earlier chapters do seem to be following (tricked out with popular legends and invented dialogue) is David Hume's very popular *History of Great Britain*, published almost a hundred years earlier (1754–61), and it is significant that *A Child's History* finishes, like Hume (and unlike any of the other histories), with the Glorious Revolution. (Dickens did not make use of the sequel to Hume, written by T. G. Smollett, his favourite novelist, which would have taken him down to 1760.) Both histories also start at the same point, with the Druids, who excite much anti-clerical indignation, not only because of their priestly power over the Britons, but also because they 'paid no taxes'.

Most people who write works on subjects of which they know little tend to follow the opinions of the authors they use. But Dickens's facts and his prejudices have an entirely different origin. David Hume, sceptical, conservative and pessimistic, was opposite in temperament to Dickens, who was uninfluenced by his subtle apologia for the Stuarts. Dickens's myth of England is derived rather from T. B. Macaulay (1800–59); or rather, perhaps Macaulay's is the classic expression, by a man of learning and genius, of the myth which mainly dominated mid-Victorian England. The Whig view of history, as expressed by

Macaulay, is a subtle conflation of Protestantism, extreme patriotism and adulation of the Whig aristocracy (here Dickens substituted the people), who set themselves against kings, apparently with the highest motives. It is inherently unhistorical, not because all its facts and principles are wrong, but because it assumes that the present is the ultimate test of the past. Macaulay's doctrine of 'inevitable progress' was intoxicating to a generation that had seen the whole country traversed by railways and had experienced dramatic economic improvement.

A Child's History has never been popular with children. It is too complicated for recreational reading, though some might skim through it for lurid detail; and too subversive (and inaccurate) to be prescribed by pedagogues. Nevertheless, Chesterton thought that this black-and-white account of heroes and villains with its pugnacious ethics was the right approach; it was, he said, a 'child's' history. Only Dickens would have the imaginative ability to lower himself to the nursery floor, so to speak, and remember children's zest for horrors and capacity for unreflecting hatred, but many would doubt whether this was a fair way to teach history.

Holiday Romance is also subversive by the standards of the juvenile fiction of its time. It is a romance in two senses, the second being the ardent devotion of two boys and their brides (who are both less than eight). This *jeu d'esprit* appeared simultaneously (January, March, April, May 1868) in *All the Year Round* and *Our Young Folk* – the latter a children's periodical which had been launched in 1865 by Dickens's Boston publishers, Ticknor and Fields. The firm paid him a phenomenal fee of £1,000, and the instalments came out during the latter months of his 1867–8 American tour. 'I hope the Americans will see the joke of Holiday Romance,' he had written to James Fields in 1867 (Nonesuch III, 539). 'The writing seems to me so like children's, that dull folks (on *any* side of *any* water) might perhaps rate it accordingly!' He added that he had laughed over it so much himself that 'my people here thought I was out of my wits', and that when he had given it to them they had laughed too. However, it did not attract enough attention to be reprinted until this century. The first three stories were published individually in 1912, and the four appeared as a complete entity, 'with decorations by Doris M. Palmer', in 1920; the third and fourth stories ('Captain Boldheart' and 'Mrs Orange') were separately published with illustrations by Robert Stewart Sherriffs in 1948. Only one, 'The Magic Fishbone', which has been used in anthologies and was published as a picture book with illustrations by F. D. Bedford in 1921, is at all well known.

Four children, aged from 'half-past six' to nine, each compose a story. William Tinkling, 'married' to Nettie Ashford 'with a ring (a green one) from Wilkingwater's toy-shop', tells of his desperate efforts to free his bride from the schoolmistresses who oppress her. In Robin Redforth's story, the narrator is a pirate: 'We find him in command of a splendid schooner of one hundred guns, loaded to the muzzle' (p. 418). He captures the Latin grammar master who has done him ill, shows clemency at first and then, discovering the hopelessness of trying to reclaim the man, hangs him at the yard-arm. ('You must try to like the pirate story, for I am very fond of it,' Dickens wrote to John Forster [*Life of Charles Dickens*, Book 8, Chapter 7].) In Part II, Alice Rainbird, aged seven, is the heroine – Princess Alicia – of her own fairy story 'The Magic Fish-bone', in charge of eighteen brothers and sisters whose 'ages varied from seven years to seven months'. (Her happy acceptance of this bounty contrasts with the reactions of the author, apt to say that his wife was 'once again in an uninteresting condition'.) Her father, the king, is as poor and improvident as Dickens's own father, but they get by, thanks to Alicia's resourcefulness and finally with the help of magic. The Good Fairy Grandmarina bestows a suitable princely husband on the princess and tells them of the bliss that lies ahead: '"My dears, you will have thirty-five children"' (p. 417). The last story, 'From the pen of Miss Nettie Ashford', is about a country where 'the grown-up people are obliged to obey the children, and are never allowed to sit up to supper' (p. 428). The children finally decide to send the elders to school for ever and allow them no holidays: 'This was what brought that country to such perfection, and made it such a delightful place to live in' (p. 437).

Holiday Romance was strikingly different from the juvenile fiction of the time, and indeed anticipates much of what was to come later. Little boys passionately in love with little girls had never featured in English children's fiction before. Dickens himself had suffered such pangs (his own *inamorata* had been a peach-faced little creature called Lucy Stroughill), and 'The Second Branch' of his Christmas story 'The Holly-Tree' (1855) had described the elopement of two seven year olds, Mr and Mrs Harry Walmers, junior. Lovesick boys are sometimes found in American stories − in *Tom Sawyer* (1876), for instance, or Thomas Bailey Aldrich's *The Story of a Bad Boy* (1870). But the subject remained a taboo one for English writers until Kenneth Grahame brought it out of the closet in 'Young Adam Cupid' in *The Golden Age* (1895). There is much else in *Holiday Romance* that foreshadows Grahame − the archly ponderous style, for example ('It was when the shades of the next evening but one were beginning to fall, 'ere yet the silver beams of Luna touched the earth . . .' [p. 403]). Above all, there is the division between 'Us' and 'Them' − Them being the clodhopping, tyrannical adults whom Grahame styled 'Olympians' and against whom all sensible children are inexorably at war, when they are not engrossed in their own games and imaginative life, as Dickens's four are. E. Nesbit too might have had *Holiday Romance* in mind when she used a boy narrator in *The Story of the Treasure Seekers* (1899) and *The Wouldbegoods* (1901). Young Oswald Bastable talks very much like Dickens's William Tinkling, who announces that he is the editor of the stories: 'Bob Redforth (he's my cousin and shaking the table on purpose) wanted to be the Editor of it, but I said he shouldn't because he couldn't. *He* has no idea of being an Editor' (p. 399). There is also in Captain Boldheart's buccaneering exploits a foretaste of the pirate games that J. M. Barrie, himself an addict of boys' penny dreadfuls, was to play with the Llewelyn Davies boys and put into *Peter Pan* (1904).

Holiday Romance has a lot of Dickens's own childhood in it and, despite the occasional sentimentality, some genuinely poignant moments, as when Alice Rainbird announces her plans for educating grown-ups to understand children better:

> We will wait − ever constant and true − till the times have got so changed as that everything helps us out, and nothing makes us ridiculous, and the fairies have come back. We will wait − ever constant and true − till we are eighty, ninety, or one hundred. And then the fairies will send *us* children, and we will help them out, poor pretty little creatures, if they pretend ever so much. [p. 406]

The Life of Our Lord was − by many years − Dickens's last published work. In 1849, when he wrote it − without thought of publication − for his own children, his eldest son, Charley, was twelve, and his eighth, Henry Fielding, into whose possession the manuscript eventually passed, was a baby. The widow of the latter, in her preface to the book in April 1934, tells how it remained for forty-seven years in the possession of Dickens's sister-in-law Georgina Hogarth; it then came to Henry, who was 'averse to publishing the work in his own lifetime', and on his death to his widow, who allowed it to be published.

Some easy books look difficult; some difficult books look easy, and this is emphatically one of the second kind. If we take it as a simple paraphrase of the Gospels, we shall find little interest in it, and also miss the point. Dickens's religion is a complex matter, partly because of its claim to be simple, undogmatic and obvious. Dickens may be classified as a Broad Churchman; he had a sitting in his parish church, which he attended occasionally, though he deviated for two or three years to the Unitarian chapel in Little Portland Street. There are two fallacies about the Broad Church, which Dickens would have wished us to accept, and which perhaps he believed himself. One is that since it was theologically vague and unintellectual, it appealed to simple, unintellectual people. Actually, the leading Broad Churchmen were the Queen and all her chaplains; Whig aristocrats; élite headmasters and dons like Thomas Arnold and, later, Mark Pattison and Benjamin Jowett. And the Unitarians were strongly represented among the wealthy commercial classes like the Chamberlains. The poor and uneducated were much more likely to be Methodists, Catholics or evangelical Anglicans, all of whom in varying degrees Dickens disliked and feared.

The second fallacy is that because this religion was 'broad' (i.e. theologically vague), it was irenic. Dickens, we know, was always a hot-tempered man convinced of his own rightness; but the Broad Church in general tended to appeal to militant, angry men capable of great unfairness like Charles Kingsley. Dickens's professions of hostility to 'party spirit' in religion were themselves fierce expressions of it. Indeed, Dickens's temperament sought opposition rather than agreement. In *The Life of Our Lord*, his attitude to sabbatarianism is typical. He tells the Gospel story of Christ healing on the sabbath (Luke 6: 1–11), characteristically omitting the salient point, 'The Son of man is Lord of the sabbath', so that it becomes little more than an impressive act of charity. He doubtless had in mind the sabbatarianism of evangelical Calvinists like Mrs Clennam, so brilliantly attacked in *Little Dorrit*. But when he wrote of his ideal Sunday in the 1836 pamphlet, 'Sunday under Three Heads', it never occurred to him that he agreed in the main with those hated Catholics and High Anglicans that Sunday, as well as being a day of worship, should be a day of rest and rational enjoyment. He was uninterested in his own points of agreement with them and passionate about disagreement.

We would love to know whether Dickens contemplated his account being compared with the Gospels themselves when the children were old enough to have developed a critical spirit. If he had, he might have anticipated the question: 'The Bible says one thing, Papa says the opposite; which is right?' It would arise almost on the first page, when he says that the parents of Jesus were Joseph and Mary. Some of his contemporaries (like Matthew Arnold) believed this because they thought that miracles were impossible. But Dickens's text does not support this view. He has the angel announcing the Birth to the shepherds, the star leading the wise men to Bethlehem, the miraculous calming of the lake, the walking on the water, the Transfiguration and the Resurrection, with the confession of Thomas ('My lord and my God') which must be totally unacceptable to a Unitarian, an . the Ascension. All these episodes are given in fair paraphrase, with no apparent wish to explain away. Indeed, the tone is reverent and (we may easily believe) deeply impressive to the first youthful readers. But as he is rigorously anti-sacramental, he manages to omit the words of consecration from his account of the Last Supper.

For the rest, the main stress is on parables, and works of healing and charity. Dickens was profoundly unsympathetic to those in his time (like the Utilitarians) who attempted to find secular bases for moral principles. For him, the fatherhood of God and the brotherhood of man were inseparable. Though his Christ is more an inspired prophet than the Incarnate Son that he is in Christian orthodoxy, he is yet indispensable. In the novels, his good people are not always obviously religious, though they often are. But the idea that an atheist could be good would have appeared to Dickens a palpable absurdity. For all his wilful theological idiosyncrasies, he is firmly rooted in Christendom.

GILLIAN AVERY

NOTE ON THE TEXTS
AND ILLUSTRATIONS

A *Child's History of England* was apparently mainly dictated by Dickens to his sister-in-law, Georgina Hogarth, and her manuscript seems not to have survived. The manuscript of Chapters 2 and 6 in Dickens's hand are, however, in the Forster Collection at the Victoria and Albert Museum. The *History* was serialised at irregular intervals in *Household Words* between 25 January 1851 and 10 December 1853 and published in three volumes, each with a frontispiece by F. W. Topham (1808–77) in 1852, 1853 and 1854. Marcus Stone (1840–1921) supplied eight illustrations for the Library Edition in 1862, and these are included in this edition. The text is that of the Charles Dickens Edition (1870?), first reprinted by Everyman in 1907.

Holiday Romance was written for an American journal, *Our Young Folks*, published in Boston by Dickens's American publishers, Ticknor and Fields. It appeared in the January, March, April and May 1868 issues with four illustrations by John Gilbert (1817–97) and initial illustrations by G. C. White. It also appeared in *All the Year Round*, vol. 29, on 25 January, 8 February, 14 March and 4 April 1868, and this edition reprints that text with all the illustrations from the American journal. The manuscript is in the Pierpont Morgan Library, New York.

The manuscript of *The Life of Our Lord* is now in the Free Library of Philadelphia, and there is a copy made for the children of Mark Lemon in the Dickens House Museum. It was first published by Associated Newspapers in 1934, which is the text reprinted here.

M.S.

Frontispiece to the Third Volume of the Original Edition

A CHILD'S HISTORY
OF ENGLAND

Details from the Frontispieces to the First and Second Volumes of the
Original Edition

THIS

CHILD'S HISTORY OF ENGLAND

Is Dedicated

TO MY OWN DEAR CHILDREN,

WHOM I HOPE IT MAY HELP, BYE-AND-BYE, TO READ WITH INTEREST
LARGER AND BETTER BOOKS ON THE SAME SUBJECT.

Christmas, 1851

TABLE OF THE REIGNS
BEGINNING WITH KING ALFRED THE GREAT

THE SAXONS

	BEGAN	ENDED	LASTED
The Reign of Alfred the Great	871	901	30 years
The Reign of Edward the Elder	901	925	24 years
The Reign of Athelstan	925	941	16 years
The Reigns of the Six Boy-Kings	941	1016	75 years

THE DANES, AND THE RESTORED SAXONS

The Reign of Canute	1016	1035	19 years
The Reign of Harold Harefoot	1035	1040	5 years
The Reign of Hardicanute	1040	1042	2 years
The Reign of Edward the Confessor	1042	1066	24 years

The Reign of Harold the Second, and the Norman Conquest, were also within the year 1066.

THE NORMANS

The Reign of William the First, called the Conqueror	1066	1087	21 years
The Reign of William the Second, called Rufus	1087	1100	13 years
The Reign of Henry the First, called Fine-Scholar	1100	1135	35 years
The Reigns of Matilda and Stephen	1135	1154	19 years

THE PLANTAGENETS

The Reign of Henry the Second	1154	1189	35 years
The Reign of Richard the First, called the Lion-Heart	1189	1199	10 years
The Reign of John, called Lackland	1199	1216	17 years
The Reign of Henry the Third	1216	1272	56 years
The Reign of Edward the First, called Longshanks	1272	1307	35 years
The Reign of Edward the Second	1307	1327	20 years
The Reign of Edward the Third	1327	1377	50 years

	BEGAN	ENDED	LASTED
The Reign of Richard the Second	1377	1399	22 years
The Reign of Henry the Fourth, } called Bolingbroke	1399	1413	14 years
The Reign of Henry the Fifth	1413	1422	9 years
The Reign of Henry the Sixth	1422	1461	39 years
The Reign of Edward the Fourth	1461	1483	22 years
The Reign of Edward the Fifth	1483	1483	a few weeks
The Reign of Richard the Third	1483	1485	2 years

THE TUDORS

	BEGAN	ENDED	LASTED
The Reign of Henry the Seventh	1485	1509	24 years
The Reign of Henry the Eighth	1509	1547	38 years
The Reign of Edward the Sixth	1547	1553	6 years
The Reign of Mary	1553	1558	5 years
The Reign of Elizabeth	1558	1603	45 years

THE STUARTS

	BEGAN	ENDED	LASTED
The Reign of James the First	1603	1625	22 years
The Reign of Charles the First	1625	1649	24 years

THE COMMONWEALTH

	BEGAN	ENDED	LASTED
The Council of State and Government } by Parliament	1649	1653	4 years
The Protectorate of Oliver Cromwell	1653	1658	5 years
The Protectorate of Richard } Cromwell	1658	1659	7 months
The Council of State and Government } by Parliament, resumed in	1659	1660	13 months

THE STUARTS RESTORED

	BEGAN	ENDED	LASTED
The Reign of Charles the Second	1660	1685	25 years
The Reign of James the Second	1685	1688	3 years

THE REVOLUTION – 1688 (comprised in the concluding chapter)

	BEGAN	ENDED	LASTED
The Reign of William III and Mary II	1689	1695	6 years
The Reign of William the Third		1702	13 years
The Reign of Anne	1702	1714	12 years
The Reign of George the First	1714	1727	13 years
The Reign of George the Second	1727	1760	33 years
The Reign of George the Third	1760	1820	60 years
The Reign of George the Fourth	1820	1830	10 years
The Reign of William the Fourth	1830	1837	7 years
The Reign of Victoria	1837		

CHRONOLOGICAL TABLE AND
TABLE OF CONTENTS

———————

CHAPTER I

Ancient England and the Romans

If you look at a Map of the World, you will see, in the left-hand upper corner of the Eastern Hemisphere, two Islands lying in the sea. They are England and Scotland, and Ireland. England and Scotland form the greater part of these Islands. Ireland is the next in size. The little neighbouring islands, which are so small upon the Map as to be mere dots, are chiefly little bits of Scotland, – broken off, I dare say, in the course of a great length of time, by the power of the restless water.

In the old days, a long, long while ago, before Our Saviour was born on earth and lay asleep in a manger, these Islands were in the same place, and the stormy sea roared round them, just as it roars now. But the sea was not alive, then, with great ships and brave sailors, sailing to and from all parts of the world. It was very lonely. The Islands lay solitary, in the great expanse of water. The foaming waves dashed against their cliffs, and the bleak winds blew over their forests; but the winds and waves brought no adventurers to land upon the Islands, and the savage Islanders knew nothing of the rest of the world, and the rest of the world knew nothing of them.

It is supposed that the Phœnicians, who were an ancient people, famous for carrying on trade, came in ships to these Islands, and found that they produced tin and lead; both very useful things, as you know, and both produced to this very hour upon the sea-coast. The most celebrated tin mines in Cornwall are, still, close to the sea. One of them, which I have seen, is so close to it that it is hollowed out underneath the ocean; and the miners say, that in stormy weather, when they are at work down in that deep place, they can hear the noise of the waves thundering above their heads. So, the Phœnicians, coasting about the Islands, would come, without much difficulty, to where the tin and lead were.

The Phœnicians traded with the Islanders for these metals, and gave the Islanders some other useful things in exchange.

The Islanders were, at first, poor savages, going almost naked, or only dressed in the rough skins of beasts, and staining their bodies, as other savages do, with coloured earths and the juices of plants. But the Phœnicians, sailing over to the opposite coasts of France and Belgium, and saying to the people there, 'We have been to those white cliffs across the water, which you can see in fine weather, and from that country, which is called BRITAIN, we bring this tin and lead,' tempted some of the French and Belgians to come over also. These people settled themselves on the south coast of England, which is now called Kent; and, although they were a rough people too, they taught the savage Britons some useful arts, and improved that part of the Islands. It is probable that other people came over from Spain to Ireland, and settled there.

Thus, by little and little, strangers became mixed with the Islanders, and the savage Britons grew into a wild bold people; almost savage, still, especially in the interior of the country away from the sea where the foreign settlers seldom went; but hardy, brave, and strong.

The whole country was covered with forests, and swamps. The greater part of it was very misty and cold. There were no roads, no bridges, no streets, no houses that you would think deserving of the name. A town was nothing but a collection of straw-covered huts, hidden in a thick wood, with a ditch all round, and a low wall, made of mud, or the trunks of trees placed one upon another. The people planted little or no corn, but lived upon the flesh of their flocks and cattle. They made no coins, but used metal rings for money. They were clever in basket-work, as savage people often are; and they could make a coarse kind of cloth, and some very bad earthenware. But in building fortresses they were much more clever.

They made boats of basket-work, covered with the skins of animals, but seldom, if ever, ventured far from the shore. They made swords, of copper mixed with tin; but, these swords were of an awkward shape, and so soft that a heavy blow would bend one. They made light shields, short pointed daggers, and spears – which they jerked back after they had thrown them at an enemy, by a long strip of leather fastened to the stem. The butt-end was a rattle, to frighten an enemy's horse. The ancient Britons, being divided into as many as thirty or forty tribes, each commanded by its own little king, were constantly fighting with one another, as savage people usually do; and they always fought with these weapons.

They were very fond of horses. The standard of Kent was the picture of a white horse. They could break them in and manage them wonderfully well. Indeed, the horses (of which they had an abundance, though they were rather small) were so well taught in those days, that they can scarcely be said to have improved since; though the men are so much wiser. They understood, and obeyed, every word of command; and would stand still by themselves, in all the din and noise of battle, while their masters went to fight on foot. The Britons could not have succeeded in their most remarkable art, without the aid of these sensible and trusty animals. The art I mean, is the construction and management of war-chariots or cars, for which they have ever been celebrated in history. Each of the best sort of these chariots, not quite breast high in front, and open at the back, contained one man to drive, and two or three others to fight – all standing up. The horses who drew them were so well trained, that they would tear, at full gallop, over the most stony ways, and even through the woods; dashing down their masters' enemies beneath their hoofs, and cutting them to pieces with the blades of swords, or scythes, which were fastened to the wheels, and stretched out beyond the car on each side, for that cruel purpose. In a moment, while at full speed, the horses would stop, at the driver's command. The men within would leap out, deal blows about them with their swords like hail, leap on the horses, on the pole, spring back into the chariots anyhow; and, as soon as they were safe, the horses tore away again.

The Britons had a strange and terrible religion, called the Religion of the Druids. It seems to have been brought over, in very early times indeed, from the opposite country of France, anciently called Gaul, and to have mixed up the worship of the Serpent, and of the Sun and Moon, with the worship of some of the Heathen Gods and Goddesses. Most of its ceremonies were kept secret by the priests, the Druids, who pretended to be enchanters, and who carried magicians' wands, and wore, each of them, about his neck, what he told the ignorant people was a Serpent's egg in a golden case. But it is certain that the Druidical ceremonies included the sacrifice of human victims, the torture of some suspected criminals, and, on particular occasions, even the burning alive, in immense wicker cages, of a number of men and animals together. The Druid Priests had some kind of veneration for the Oak, and for the mistletoe – the same plant that we hang up in houses at Christmas Time now – when its white berries grew upon the Oak. They met together in dark woods, which they called Sacred Groves; and there they instructed, in their mysterious arts, young men who came to them as pupils, and who sometimes stayed with them as long as twenty years.

These Druids built great Temples and altars, open to the sky, fragments of some of which are yet remaining. Stonehenge, on Salisbury Plain, in Wiltshire, is the most extraordinary of these. Three curious stones, called Kits Coty House, on Bluebell Hill, near Maidstone, in Kent, form another. We know, from examination of the great blocks of which such buildings are made, that they could not have been raised without the aid of some ingenious machines, which are common now, but which the ancient Britons certainly did not use in making their own uncomfortable houses. I should not wonder if the Druids, and their pupils who stayed with them twenty years, knowing more than the rest of the Britons, kept the people out of sight while they made these buildings, and then pretended that they built them by magic. Perhaps they had a hand in the fortresses too; at all events, as they were very powerful, and very much believed in, and as they made and executed the laws, and paid no taxes, I don't wonder that they liked their trade. And, as they persuaded the people the more Druids there were, the better off the people would be, I don't wonder that there were a good many of them. But it is pleasant to think that there are no Druids, *now*, who go on in that way, and pretend to carry Enchanters' Wands and Serpents' Eggs – and of course there is nothing of the kind, anywhere.

Such was the improved condition of the ancient Britons, fifty-five years before the birth of Our Saviour, when the Romans, under their great General, Julius Cæsar, were masters of all the rest of the known world. Julius Cæsar had then just conquered Gaul; and hearing, in Gaul, a good deal about the opposite Island with the white cliffs, and about the bravery of the Britons who inhabited it – some of whom had been fetched over to help the Gauls in the war against him – he resolved, as he was so near, to come and conquer Britain next.

So, Julius Cæsar came sailing over to this Island of ours, with eighty vessels and twelve thousand men. And he came from the French coast between Calais and Boulogne, 'because thence was the shortest passage into Britain;' just for the same reason as our steam-boats now take the same track, every day. He expected to conquer Britain easily: but it was not such easy work as he supposed – for the bold Britons fought most bravely; and, what with not having his horse-soldiers with him (for they had been driven back by a storm), and what with having some of his vessels dashed to pieces by a high tide after they were drawn ashore, he ran great risk of being totally defeated. However, for once that the bold Britons beat him, he beat them twice; though not so soundly but that he was very glad to accept their proposals of peace, and go away.

But, in the spring of the next year, he came back; this time, with eight hundred vessels and thirty thousand men. The British tribes chose, as their general-in-chief, a Briton, whom the Romans in their Latin language called CASSIVELLAUNUS, but whose British name is supposed to have been CASWALLON. A brave general he was, and well he and his soldiers fought the Roman army! So well, that whenever in that war the Roman soldiers saw a great cloud of dust, and heard the rattle of the rapid British chariots, they trembled in their hearts. Besides a number of smaller battles, there was a battle fought near Canterbury, in Kent; there was a battle fought near Chertsey, in Surrey; there was a battle fought near a marshy little town in a wood, the capital of that part of Britain which belonged to CASSIVELLAUNUS, and which was probably near what is now Saint Albans, in Hertfordshire. However, brave CASSIVEL-LAUNUS had the worst of it, on the whole; though he and his men always fought like lions. As the other British chiefs were jealous of him, and were always quarrelling with him, and with one another, he gave up, and proposed peace. Julius Cæsar was very glad to grant peace easily, and to go away again with all his remaining ships and men. He had expected to find pearls in Britain, and he may have found a few for anything I know; but, at all events, he found delicious oysters, and I am sure he found tough Britons – of whom, I dare say, he made the same complaint as Napoleon Bonaparte the great French General did, eighteen hundred years afterwards, when he said they were such unreasonable fellows that they never knew when they were beaten. They never *did* know, I believe, and never will.

Nearly a hundred years passed on, and all that time, there was peace in Britain. The Britons improved their towns and mode of life: became more civilised, travelled, and learnt a great deal from the Gauls and Romans. At last, the Roman Emperor, Claudius, sent AULUS PLAUTIUS, a skilful general, with a mighty force, to subdue the Island, and shortly afterwards arrived himself. They did little; and OSTORIUS SCAPULA, another general, came. Some of the British Chiefs of Tribes submitted. Others resolved to fight to the death. Of these brave men, the bravest was CARACTACUS, or CARADOC, who gave battle to the Romans, with his army, among the mountains of North Wales. 'This day,' said he to his soldiers, 'decides the fate of Britain! Your liberty, or your eternal slavery, dates from this hour. Remember your brave ancestors, who drove the great Cæsar himself across the sea!' On hearing these words, his men, with a great shout, rushed upon the Romans. But the strong Roman swords and armour were too much for the weaker British weapons in close conflict. The Britons lost the day. The wife and daughter of the brave CARACTACUS were taken prisoners; his brothers delivered themselves up; he himself was betrayed into the hands of the Romans by his false and base step-mother: and they carried him, and all his family, in triumph to Rome.

But a great man will be great in misfortune, great in prison, great in chains. His noble air, and dignified endurance of distress, so touched the Roman people who thronged the streets to see him, that he and his family were restored to freedom. No one knows whether his great heart broke, and he died in Rome, or whether he ever returned to his own dear country. English oaks have grown up from acorns, and withered away, when they were hundreds of years old – and other oaks have sprung up in their places, and died too, very aged – since the rest of the history of the brave CARACTACUS was forgotten.

Still, the Britons *would not* yield. They rose again and again, and died by thousands, sword in hand. They rose, on every possible occasion. SUETONIUS, another Roman general, came, and stormed the Island of Anglesey (then called MONA), which was supposed to be sacred, and he burnt the Druids in their own wicker cages, by their own fires. But, even while he was in Britain, with his victorious troops, the BRITONS rose. Because BOADICEA, a British queen, the widow of the King of the Norfolk and Suffolk people, resisted the plundering of her property by the Romans who were settled in England, she was scourged, by order of CATUS a Roman officer; and her two daughters were shamefully insulted in her presence, and her husband's relations were made slaves. To avenge this injury, the Britons rose, with all their might and rage. They drove CATUS into Gaul; they laid the Roman possessions waste; they forced the Romans out of London, then a poor little town, but a trading place; they hanged, burnt, crucified, and slew by the sword, seventy thousand Romans in a few days. SUETONIUS strengthened his army, and advanced to give them battle. They strengthened their army, and desperately attacked his, on the field where it was strongly posted. Before the first charge of the Britons was made, BOADICEA, in a war-chariot, with her fair hair streaming in the wind, and her injured daughters lying at her feet, drove among the troops, and cried to them for vengeance on their oppressors, the licentious Romans. The Britons fought to the last; but they were vanquished with great slaughter, and the unhappy queen took poison.

Still, the spirit of the Britons was not broken. When SUETONIUS left the country, they fell upon his troops, and retook the Island of Anglesey. AGRICOLA came, fifteen or twenty years afterwards, and retook it once more and devoted seven years to subduing the country, especially that part of it which is now called SCOTLAND; but, its people, the Caledonians, resisted him at every inch of ground. They fought the bloodiest battles with him; they killed their very wives and children, to prevent his making prisoners of them; they fell, fighting, in such great numbers that certain hills in Scotland are yet supposed to be vast heaps of stones piled up above their graves. HADRIAN came, thirty years afterwards, and still they resisted him. SEVERUS came, nearly a hundred years afterwards, and they worried his great army like dogs, and rejoiced to see them die, by thousands, in the bogs and swamps. CARACALLA, the son and successor of SEVERUS, did the most to conquer them, for a time; but not by force of arms. He knew how little that would do. He yielded up a quantity of land to the Caledonians, and gave the Britons the same privileges as the Romans possessed. There was peace, after this, for seventy years.

Then new enemies arose. They were the SAXONS, a fierce, seafaring people from the countries to the North of the Rhine, the great river of Germany on the banks of which the best grapes grow to make the German wine. They began to come, in pirate ships, to the sea-coast of Gaul and Britain, and to plunder them. They were repulsed by CARAUSIUS, a native either of Belgium or of Britain, who was appointed by the Romans to the command, and under whom the Britons first began to fight upon the sea. But, after this time, they renewed their ravages. A few years more, and the Scots (which was then the name for the people of Ireland), and the Picts, a northern people, began to make frequent plundering incursions into the South of Britain. All these attacks were repeated, at intervals, during two hundred years, and through a long succession of Roman Emperors and chiefs; during all which length of time, the Britons rose against the Romans, over and over again. At last, in the days of the Roman HONORIUS, when the Roman power all over the world was fast declining, and when Rome wanted all her soldiers at home, the Romans abandoned all hope of conquering Britain, and went away. And still, at last, as at first, the Britons rose against them, in their old brave manner; for, a very little while before, they had turned away the Roman magistrates, and declared themselves an independent people.

Five hundred years had passed, since Julius Cæsar's first invasion of the Island, when the Romans departed from it for ever. In the course of that time, although they had been the cause of terrible fighting and bloodshed, they had done much to improve the condition of the Britons. They had made great military roads; they had built forts; they had taught them how to dress, and arm themselves, much better than they had ever known how to do before; they had refined the whole British way of living. AGRICOLA had built a great wall of earth, more than seventy miles long, extending from Newcastle to beyond Carlisle, for the purpose of keeping out the Picts and Scots; HADRIAN had strengthened it; SEVERUS, finding it much in want of repair, had built it afresh of stone. Above all, it was in the Roman time, and by means of Roman ships, that the Christian Religion was first brought into Britain, and its people first taught the great lesson that, to be good in the sight of GOD, they must love their neighbours as themselves, and do unto others as they would be done by. The Druids declared that it was very wicked to believe in any such thing, and cursed all the people who did believe it, very heartily. But, when the people found that they were none the better for the blessings of the

Druids, and none the worse for the curses of the Druids, but, that the sun shone and the rain fell without consulting the Druids at all, they just began to think that the Druids were mere men, and that it signified very little whether they cursed or blessed. After which, the pupils of the Druids fell off greatly in numbers, and the Druids took to other trades.

Thus I have come to the end of the Roman time in England. It is but little that is known of those five hundred years; but some remains of them are still found. Often, when labourers are digging up the ground, to make foundations for houses or churches, they light on rusty money that once belonged to the Romans. Fragments of plates from which they ate, of goblets from which they drank, and of pavement on which they trod, are discovered among the earth that is broken by the plough, or the dust that is crumbled by the gardener's spade. Wells that the Romans sunk, still yield water; roads that the Romans made, form part of our highways. In some old battle-fields, British spear-heads and Roman armour have been found, mingled together in decay, as they fell in the thick pressure of the fight. Traces of Roman camps overgrown with grass, and of mounds that are the burial-places of heaps of Britons, are to be seen in almost all parts of the country. Across the bleak moors of Northumberland, the wall of SEVERUS, overrun with moss and weeds, still stretches, a strong ruin; and the shepherds and their dogs lie sleeping on it in the summer weather. On Salisbury Plain, Stonehenge yet stands: a monument of the earlier time when the Roman name was unknown in Britain, and when the Druids, with their best magic wands, could not have written it in the sands of the wild sea-shore.

CHAPTER 2

Ancient England under the Early Saxons

The Romans had scarcely gone away from Britain, when the Britons began to wish they had never left it. For, the Romans being gone, and the Britons being much reduced in numbers by their long wars, the Picts and Scots came pouring in, over the broken and unguarded wall of SEVERUS, in swarms. They plundered the richest towns, and killed the people; and came back so often for more booty and more slaughter, that the unfortunate Britons lived a life of terror. As if the Picts and Scots were not bad enough on land, the Saxons attacked the islanders by sea; and, as if something more were still wanting to make them miserable, they quarrelled bitterly among themselves as to what prayers they ought to say, and how they ought to say them. The priests, being very angry with one another on these questions, cursed one another in the heartiest manner; and (uncommonly like the old Druids) cursed all the people whom they could not persuade. So, altogether, the Britons were very badly off, you may believe.

They were in such distress, in short, that they sent a letter to Rome entreating help – which they called the Groans of the Britons; and in which they said, 'The barbarians chase us into the sea, the sea throws us back upon the barbarians, and we have only the hard choice left us of perishing by the sword, or perishing by the waves.' But, the Romans could not help them, even if they were so inclined; for they had enough to do to defend themselves against their own enemies, who were then very fierce and strong. At last, the Britons, unable to bear their hard condition any longer, resolved to make peace with the Saxons, and to invite the Saxons to come into their country, and help them to keep out the Picts and Scots.

It was a British Prince named VORTIGERN who took this resolution, and who made a treaty of friendship with HENGIST and HORSA, two Saxon chiefs. Both of these names, in the old Saxon language, signify Horse; for the Saxons, like many other nations in a rough state, were fond of giving men the names of animals, as Horse, Wolf, Bear, Hound. The Indians of North America, – a very inferior people to the Saxons, though – do the same to this day.

HENGIST and HORSA drove out the Picts and Scots; and VORTIGERN, being grateful to them for that service, made no opposition to their settling themselves in that part of England which is called the Isle of Thanet, or to their inviting over more of their countrymen to join them. But HENGIST had a beautiful daughter named ROWENA; and when, at a feast, she filled a golden goblet to the brim with wine, and gave it to VORTIGERN, saying in a sweet voice, 'Dear King, thy health!' the King fell in love with her. My opinion is, that the cunning HENGIST meant him to do so, in order that the Saxons might have greater influence with him; and that the fair ROWENA came to that feast, golden goblet and all, on purpose.

At any rate, they were married; and, long afterwards, whenever the King was angry with the Saxons, or jealous of their encroachments, ROWENA would put her beautiful arms round his neck, and softly say, 'Dear King, they are my people! Be favourable to them, as you loved that Saxon girl who gave you the golden goblet of wine at the feast!' And, really, I don't see how the King could help himself.

Ah! We must all die! In the course of years, VORTIGERN died – he was dethroned, and put in prison, first, I am afraid; and ROWENA died; and generations of Saxons and Britons died; and events that happened during a long, long time, would have been quite forgotten but for the tales and songs of the old Bards, who used to go about from feast to feast, with their white beards, recounting the deeds of their forefathers. Among the histories of which they sang and talked, there was a famous one, concerning the bravery and virtues of KING ARTHUR, supposed to have been a British Prince in those old times. But, whether such a person really lived, or whether there were several persons whose histories came to be confused together under that one name, or whether all about him was invention, no one knows.

I will tell you, shortly, what is most interesting in the early Saxon times, as they are described in these songs and stories of the Bards.

In, and long after, the days of VORTIGERN, fresh bodies of Saxons, under various chiefs, came pouring into Britain. One body, conquering the Britons in the East, and settling there, called their kingdom Essex; another body settled in the West, and called their kingdom Wessex; the Northfolk, or Norfolk people, established themselves in one place; the Southfolk, or Suffolk people, established themselves in another; and gradually seven kingdoms or states arose in England, which were called the Saxon Heptarchy. The poor Britons, falling back before these crowds of fighting men whom they had innocently invited over as friends, retired into Wales and the adjacent country; into Devonshire, and into Cornwall. Those parts of England long remained unconquered. And in Cornwall now – where the sea-coast is very gloomy, steep, and rugged – where, in the dark winter-time, ships have often been wrecked close to the land, and every soul on board has perished – where the winds and waves howl drearily, and split the solid rocks into arches and caverns – there are very ancient ruins, which the people call the ruins of KING ARTHUR'S castle.

Kent is the most famous of the seven Saxon kingdoms, because the Christian religion was preached to the Saxons there (who domineered over the Britons too much, to care for what *they* said about their religion, or anything else) by AUGUSTINE, a monk from Rome. KING ETHELBERT, of Kent, was soon converted; and the moment he said he was a Christian, his courtiers all said *they* were Christians; after which, ten thousand of his subjects said they were Christians too. AUGUSTINE built a little church, close to this King's palace, on the ground now occupied by the beautiful cathedral of Canterbury. SEBERT, the King's nephew, built on a muddy marshy place near London, where there had been a temple to Apollo, a church dedicated to Saint Peter, which is now Westminster Abbey. And, in London itself, on the foundation of a temple to Diana, he built another little church which has risen up, since that old time, to be Saint Paul's.

After the death of ETHELBERT, EDWIN, King of Northumbria, who was such a good king that it was said a woman or child might openly carry a purse of gold, in his reign, without fear, allowed his child to be baptised, and held a great council to consider whether he and his people should all be Christians or not. It was decided that they should be. COIFI, the chief priest of the old religion, made a great speech on the occasion. In this discourse, he told the people that he had found out the old gods to be impostors. 'I am quite satisfied of it,' he said. 'Look at me! I have been serving them all my life, and they have done nothing for me; whereas, if they had been really powerful, they could not have decently done less, in return for all I have done for them, than make my fortune. As they have never made my fortune, I am quite convinced they are impostors!' When this singular priest had finished speaking, he hastily armed himself with sword and lance, mounted a war-horse, rode at a furious gallop in sight of all the people to the temple, and flung his lance against it as an insult. From that time, the Christian religion spread itself among the Saxons, and became their faith.

The next very famous prince was EGBERT. He lived about a

hundred and fifty years afterwards, and claimed to have a better right to the throne of Wessex than BEORTRIC, another Saxon prince who was at the head of that kingdom, and who married EDBURGA, the daughter of OFFA, king of another of the seven kingdoms. This QUEEN EDBURGA was a handsome murderess, who poisoned people when they offended her. One day, she mixed a cup of poison for a certain noble belonging to the court; but her husband drank of it too, by mistake, and died. Upon this, the people revolted, in great crowds; and running to the palace, and thundering at the gates, cried, 'Down with the wicked queen, who poisons men!' They drove her out of the country, and abolished the title she had disgraced. When years had passed away, some travellers came home from Italy, and said that in the town of Pavia they had seen a ragged beggar-woman, who had once been handsome, but was then shrivelled, bent, and yellow, wandering about the streets, crying for bread; and that this beggar-woman was the poisoning English queen. It was, indeed, EDBURGA; and so she died without a shelter for her wretched head.

EGBERT, not considering himself safe in England, in consequence of his having claimed the crown of Wessex (for he thought his rival might take him prisoner and put him to death), sought refuge at the court of CHARLEMAGNE, King of France. On the death of BEORTRIC, so unhappily poisoned by mistake, EGBERT came back to Britain; succeeded to the throne of Wessex; conquered some of the other monarchs of the seven kingdoms; added their territories to his own; and, for the first time, called the country over which he ruled, ENGLAND.

And now, new enemies arose, who, for a long time, troubled England sorely. These were the Northmen, the people of Denmark and Norway, whom the English called the Danes. They were a warlike people, quite at home upon the sea; not Christians; very daring and cruel. They came over in ships, and plundered and burned wheresoever they landed. Once, they beat EGBERT in battle. Once, EGBERT beat them. But, they cared no more for being beaten than the English themselves. In the four following short reigns, of ETHELWULF, and his sons, ETHELBALD, ETHELBERT, and ETHELRED, they came back, over and over again, burning and plundering, and laying England waste. In the last-mentioned reign, they seized EDMUND, King of East England, and bound him to a tree. Then, they proposed to him that he should change his religion; but he, being a good Christian, steadily refused. Upon that, they beat him, made cowardly jests upon him, all defenceless as he was, shot arrows at him, and, finally, struck off his head. It is impossible to say whose head they might have struck off next, but for the death of KING ETHELRED from a wound he had received in fighting against them, and the succession to his throne of the best and wisest king that ever lived in England.

<h2 style="text-align:center">CHAPTER 3</h2>

England under the Good Saxon, Alfred

ALFRED THE GREAT was a young man, three-and-twenty years of age, when he became king. Twice in his childhood, he had been taken to Rome, where the Saxon nobles were in the habit of going on journeys which they supposed to be religious; and, once, he had stayed for some time in Paris. Learning, however, was so little cared for, then, that at twelve years old he had not been taught to read; although, of the sons of KING ETHELWULF, he, the youngest, was the favourite. But he had – as most men who grow up to be great and good are generally found to have had – an excellent mother; and, one day, this lady, whose name was OSBURGA, happened, as she was sitting among her sons, to read a book of Saxon poetry. The art of printing was not known until long and long after that period, and the book, which was written, was what is called 'illuminated,' with beautiful bright letters, richly painted. The brothers admiring it very much, their mother said, 'I will give it to that one of you four princes who first learns to read.' ALFRED sought out a tutor that very day, applied himself to learn with great diligence, and soon won the book. He was proud of it, all his life.

This great king, in the first year of his reign, fought nine battles with the Danes. He made some treaties with them too, by which the false Danes swore they would quit the country. They pretended to consider that they had taken a very solemn oath, in swearing this upon the holy bracelets that they wore, and which were always buried with them when they died; but they cared little for it, for they thought nothing of breaking oaths and treaties too, as soon as it suited their purpose, and coming back again to fight, plunder, and burn, as usual. One fatal winter, in the fourth year of KING ALFRED's reign, they spread themselves in great numbers over the whole of England; and so dispersed and routed the King's soldiers that the King was left alone, and was obliged to disguise himself as a common peasant, and to take refuge in the cottage of one of his cowherds who did not know his face.

Here, KING ALFRED, while the Danes sought him far and near, was left alone one day, by the cowherd's wife, to watch some cakes which she put to bake upon the hearth. But, being at work upon his bow and arrows, with which he hoped to punish the false Danes when a brighter time should come, and thinking deeply of his poor unhappy subjects whom the Danes chased through the land, his noble mind forgot the cakes, and they were burnt. 'What!' said the cowherd's wife, who scolded him well when she came back, and little thought she was scolding the King, 'you will be ready enough to eat them by-and-by, and yet you cannot watch them, idle dog?'

At length, the Devonshire men made head against a new host of Danes who landed on their coast; killed their chief, and captured their flag; on which was represented the likeness of a Raven – a very fit bird for a thievish army like that, I think. The loss of their standard troubled the Danes greatly, for they believed it to be enchanted – woven by the three daughters of one father in a single afternoon – and they had a story among themselves that when they were victorious in battle, the Raven stretched his wings and seemed to fly; and that when they were defeated, he would droop. He had good reason to droop, now, if he could have done anything half so sensible; for, KING ALFRED joined the Devonshire men; made a camp with them on a piece of firm ground in the midst of a bog in Somersetshire; and prepared for a great attempt for vengeance on the Danes, and the deliverance of his oppressed people.

But, first, as it was important to know how numerous those pestilent Danes were, and how they were fortified, KING ALFRED, being a good musician, disguised himself as a glee-man or minstrel, and went, with his harp, to the Danish camp. He played and sang in the very tent of GUTHRUM the Danish leader, and entertained the Danes as they caroused. While he seemed to

Alfred in the Neatherd's Cottage

think of nothing but his music, he was watchful of their tents, their arms, their discipline, everything that he desired to know. And right soon did this great king entertain them to a different tune; for, summoning all his true followers to meet him at an appointed place, where they received him with joyful shouts and tears, as the monarch whom many of them had given up for lost or dead, he put himself at their head, marched on the Danish camp, defeated the Danes with great slaughter, and besieged them for fourteen days to prevent their escape. But, being as merciful as he was good and brave, he then, instead of killing them, proposed peace; on condition that they should altogether depart from that Western part of England, and settle in the East, and that GUTHRUM should become a Christian, in remembrance of the Divine religion which now taught his conqueror, the noble ALFRED, to forgive the enemy who had so often injured him. This, GUTHRUM did. At his baptism, KING ALFRED was his godfather. And GUTHRUM was an honourable chief who well deserved that clemency; for, ever afterwards he was loyal and faithful to the King. The Danes under him were faithful too. They plundered and burned no more, but worked like honest men. They ploughed, and sowed, and reaped, and led good honest English lives. And I hope the children of those Danes played, many a time, with Saxon children in the sunny fields; and that Danish young men fell in love with Saxon girls, and married them; and that English travellers, benighted at the doors of Danish cottages, often went in for shelter until morning; and that Danes and Saxons sat by the red fire, friends, talking of KING ALFRED THE GREAT.

All the Danes were not like these under GUTHRUM; for, after some years, more of them came over, in the old plundering and burning way — among them a fierce pirate of the name of HASTINGS, who had the boldness to sail up the Thames to Gravesend, with eighty ships. For three years, there was a war with these Danes; and there was a famine in the country, too, and a plague, both upon human creatures and beasts. But KING ALFRED, whose mighty heart never failed him, built large ships nevertheless, with which to pursue the pirates on the sea; and he encouraged his soldiers, by his brave example, to fight valiantly against them on the shore. At last, he drove them all away; and then there was repose in England.

As great and good in peace, as he was great and good in war,

KING ALFRED never rested from his labours to improve his people. He loved to talk with clever men, and with travellers from foreign countries, and to write down what they told him, for his people to read. He had studied Latin after learning to read English, and now another of his labours was, to translate Latin books into the English-Saxon tongue, that his people might be interested, and improved by their contents. He made just laws, that they might live more happily and freely; he turned away all partial judges, that no wrong might be done them; he was so careful of their property, and punished robbers so severely, that it was a common thing to say that under the great KING ALFRED, garlands of golden chains and jewels might have hung across the streets, and no man would have touched one. He founded schools; he patiently heard causes himself in his Court of Justice; the great desires of his heart were, to do right to all his subjects, and to leave England better, wiser, happier in all ways, than he found it. His industry in these efforts was quite astonishing. Every day he divided into certain portions, and in each portion devoted himself to a certain pursuit. That he might divide his time exactly, he had wax torches or candles made, which were all of the same size, were notched across at regular distances, and were always kept burning. Thus, as the candles burnt down, he divided the day into notches, almost as accurately as we now divide it into hours upon the clock. But when the candles were first invented, it was found that the wind and draughts of air, blowing into the palace through the doors and windows, and through the chinks in the walls, caused them to gutter and burn unequally. To prevent this, the King had them put into cases formed of wood and white horn. And these were the first lanthorns ever made in England.

All this time, he was afflicted with a terrible unknown disease, which caused him violent and frequent pain that nothing could relieve. He bore it, as he had borne all the troubles of his life, like a brave good man, until he was fifty-three years old; and then, having reigned thirty years, he died. He died in the year nine hundred and one; but, long ago as that is, his fame, and the love and gratitude with which his subjects regarded him, are freshly remembered to the present hour.

In the next reign, which was the reign of EDWARD, surnamed THE ELDER, who was chosen in council to succeed, a nephew of KING ALFRED troubled the country by trying to obtain the throne. The Danes in the East of England took part with this usurper (perhaps because they had honoured his uncle so much, and honoured him for his uncle's sake), and there was hard fighting; but, the King, with the assistance of his sister, gained the day, and reigned in peace for four and twenty years. He gradually extended his power over the whole of England, and so the Seven Kingdoms were united into one.

When England thus became one kingdom, ruled over by one Saxon king, the Saxons had been settled in the country more than four hundred and fifty years. Great changes had taken place in its customs during that time. The Saxons were still greedy eaters and great drinkers, and their feasts were often of a noisy and drunken kind; but many new comforts and even elegances had become known, and were fast increasing. Hangings for the walls of rooms, where, in these modern days, we paste up paper, are known to have been sometimes made of silk, ornamented with birds and flowers in needlework. Tables and chairs were curiously carved in different woods; were sometimes decorated with gold or silver; sometimes even made of those precious metals. Knives and spoons were used at table; golden ornaments were worn – with silk and cloth, and golden tissues and embroideries; dishes were made of gold and silver, brass and bone. There were varieties of drinking-horns, bedsteads, musical instruments. A harp was passed round, at a feast, like the drinking-bowl, from guest to guest; and each one usually sang or played when his turn came. The weapons of the Saxons were stoutly made, and among them was a terrible iron hammer that gave deadly blows, and was long remembered. The Saxons themselves were a handsome people. The men were proud of their long fair hair, parted on the forehead; their ample beards, their fresh complexions, and clear eyes. The beauty of the Saxon women filled all England with a new delight and grace.

I have more to tell of the Saxons yet, but I stop to say this now, because under the GREAT ALFRED, all the best points of the English-Saxon character were first encouraged, and in him first shown. It has been the greatest character among the nations of the earth. Wherever the descendants of the Saxon race have gone, have sailed, or otherwise made their way, even to the remotest regions of the world, they have been patient, persevering, never to be broken in spirit, never to be turned aside from enterprises on which they have resolved. In Europe, Asia, Africa,

America, the whole world over; in the desert, in the forest, on the sea; scorched by a burning sun, or frozen by ice that never melts; the Saxon blood remains unchanged. Wheresoever that race goes, there, law, and industry, and safety for life and property, and all the great results of steady perseverance, are certain to arise.

I pause to think with admiration, of the noble king who, in his single person, possessed all the Saxon virtues. Whom misfortune could not subdue, whom prosperity could not spoil, whose perseverance nothing could shake. Who was hopeful in defeat, and generous in success. Who loved justice, freedom, truth, and knowledge. Who, in his care to instruct his people, probably did more to preserve the beautiful old Saxon language, than I can imagine. Without whom, the English tongue in which I tell this story might have wanted half its meaning. As it is said that his spirit still inspires some of our best English laws, so, let you and I pray that it may animate our English hearts, at least to this — to resolve, when we see any of our fellow-creatures left in ignorance, that we will do our best, while life is in us, to have them taught; and to tell those rulers whose duty it is to teach them, and who neglect their duty, that they have profited very little by all the years that have rolled away since the year nine hundred and one, and that they are far behind the bright example of KING ALFRED THE GREAT.

CHAPTER 4

England under Athelstan and the Six Boy-Kings

ATHELSTAN, the son of Edward the Elder, succeeded that king. He reigned only fifteen years; but he remembered the glory of his grandfather, the great Alfred, and governed England well. He reduced the turbulent people of Wales, and obliged them to pay him a tribute in money, and in cattle, and to send him their best hawks and hounds. He was victorious over the Cornish men, who were not yet quite under the Saxon government. He restored such of the old laws as were good, and had fallen into disuse; made some wise new laws, and took care of the poor

and weak. A strong alliance, made against him by ANLAF a
Danish prince, CONSTANTINE King of the Scots, and the people
of North Wales, he broke and defeated in one great battle, long
famous for the vast numbers slain in it. After that, he had a
quiet reign; the lords and ladies about him had leisure to become
polite and agreeable; and foreign princes were glad (as they have
sometimes been since) to come to England on visits to the
English court.

When Athelstan died, at forty-seven years old, his brother
EDMUND, who was only eighteen, became king. He was the first
of six boy-kings, as you will presently know.

They called him the Magnificent, because he showed a taste
for improvement and refinement. But he was beset by the Danes,
and had a short and troubled reign, which came to a troubled
end. One night, when he was feasting in his hall, and had eaten
much and drunk deep, he saw among the company, a noted
robber named LEOF, who had been banished from England.
Made very angry by the boldness of this man, the King turned
to his cup-bearer, and said, 'There is a robber sitting at the table
yonder, who, for his crimes, is an outlaw in the land – a hunted
wolf, whose life any man may take, at any time. Command that
robber to depart!' 'I will not depart!' said Leof. 'No?' cried the
King. 'No, by the Lord!' said Leof. Upon that the King rose
from his seat, and, making passionately at the robber, and
seizing him by his long hair, tried to throw him down. But the
robber had a dagger underneath his cloak, and, in the scuffle,
stabbed the King to death. That done, he set his back against
the wall, and fought so desperately, that although he was soon
cut to pieces by the King's armed men, and the wall and
pavement were splashed with his blood, yet it was not before he
had killed and wounded many of them. You may imagine what
rough lives the kings of those times led, when one of them could
struggle, half drunk, with a public robber in his own dining-
hall, and be stabbed in presence of the company who ate and
drank with him.

Then succeeded the boy-king EDRED, who was weak and
sickly in body, but of a strong mind. And his armies fought the
Northmen, the Danes, the Norwegians, or the Sea-Kings, as they
were called, and beat them for the time. And, in nine years,
Edred died, and passed away.

Then came the boy-king EDWY, fifteen years of age; but the

real king, who had the real power, was a monk named DUNSTAN – a clever priest, a little mad, and not a little proud and cruel.

Dunstan was then Abbot of Glastonbury Abbey, whither the body of King Edmund the Magnificent was carried, to be buried. While yet a boy, he had got out of his bed one night (being then in a fever), and walked about Glastonbury Church when it was under repair; and, because he did not tumble off some scaffolds that were there, and break his neck, it was reported that he had been shown over the building by an angel. He had also made a harp that was said to play of itself – which it very likely did, as Æolian Harps, which are played by the wind, and are understood now, always do. For these wonders he had been once denounced by his enemies, who were jealous of his favour with the late King Athelstan, as a magician; and he had been waylaid, bound hand and foot, and thrown into a marsh. But he got out again, somehow, to cause a great deal of trouble yet.

The priests of those days were, generally, the only scholars. They were learned in many things. Having to make their own convents and monasteries on uncultivated grounds that were granted to them by the Crown, it was necessary that they should be good farmers and good gardeners, or their lands would have been too poor to support them. For the decoration of the chapels where they prayed, and for the comfort of the refectories where they ate and drank, it was necessary that there should be good carpenters, good smiths, good painters, among them. For their greater safety in sickness and accident, living alone by themselves in solitary places, it was necessary that they should study the virtues of plants and herbs, and should know how to dress cuts, burns, scalds, and bruises, and how to set broken limbs. Accordingly, they taught themselves, and one another, a great variety of useful arts; and became skilful in agriculture, medicine, surgery, and handicraft. And when they wanted the aid of any little piece of machinery, which would be simple enough now, but was marvellous then, to impose a trick upon the poor peasants, they knew very well how to make it; and *did* make it many a time and often, I have no doubt.

Dunstan, Abbot of Glastonbury Abbey, was one of the most sagacious of these monks. He was an ingenious smith, and worked at a forge in a little cell. This cell was made too short to admit of his lying at full length, when he went to sleep – as if *that* did any good to anybody! – and he used to tell the most extraordinary lies about demons and spirits, who, he said, came there to persecute him. For instance, he related that one day when he was at work, the devil looked in at the little window, and tried to tempt him to lead a life of idle pleasure; whereupon, having his pincers in the fire, red hot, he seized the devil by the nose, and put him to such pain, that his bellowings were heard for miles and miles. Some people are inclined to think this nonsense a part of Dunstan's madness (for his head never quite recovered the fever), but I think not. I observe that it induced the ignorant people to consider him a holy man, and that it made him very powerful. Which was exactly what he always wanted.

On the day of the coronation of the handsome boy-king Edwy, it was remarked by ODO, Archbishop of Canterbury (who was a Dane by birth), that the King quietly left the coronation feast, while all the company were there. Odo, much displeased, sent his friend Dunstan to seek him. Dunstan finding him in the company of his beautiful young wife ELGIVA, and her mother ETHELGIVA, a good and virtuous lady, not only grossly abused them, but dragged the young King back into the feasting-hall by force. Some, again, think Dunstan did this because the young King's fair wife was his own cousin, and the monks objected to people marrying their own cousins; but I believe he did it, because he was an imperious, audacious, ill-conditioned priest, who, having loved a young lady himself before he became a sour monk, hated all love now, and everything belonging to it.

The young King was quite old enough to feel this insult. Dunstan had been Treasurer in the last reign, and he soon charged Dunstan with having taken some of the last king's money. The Glastonbury Abbot fled to Belgium (very narrowly escaping some pursuers who were sent to put out his eyes, as you will wish they had, when you read what follows), and his abbey was given to priests who were married; whom he always, both before and afterwards, opposed. But he quickly conspired with his friend, Odo the Dane, to set up the King's young brother, EDGAR, as his rival for the throne; and, not content with this revenge, he caused the beautiful queen Elgiva, though a lovely girl of only seventeen or eighteen, to be stolen from one of the Royal Palaces, branded in the cheek with a red-hot iron, and sold into slavery in Ireland. But the Irish people pitied and

befriended her; and they said, 'Let us restore the girl-queen to
the boy-king, and make the young lovers happy!' and they cured
her of her cruel wound, and sent her home as beautiful as
before. But the villain Dunstan, and that other villain, Odo,
caused her to be waylaid at Gloucester as she was joyfully
hurrying to join her husband, and to be hacked and hewn with
swords, and to be barbarously maimed and lamed, and left to
die. When Edwy the Fair (his people called him so, because he
was so young and handsome) heard of her dreadful fate, he died
of a broken heart; and so the pitiful story of the poor young
wife and husband ends! Ah! Better to be two cottagers in these
better times, than king and queen of England in those bad days,
though never so fair!

Then came the boy-king, EDGAR, called the Peaceful, fifteen
years old. Dunstan, being still the real king, drove all married
priests out of the monasteries and abbeys, and replaced them by
solitary monks like himself, of the rigid order called the Bene-
dictines. He made himself Archbishop of Canterbury, for his
greater glory; and exercised such power over the neighbouring
British princes, and so collected them about the King, that once,
when the King held his court at Chester, and went on the river
Dee to visit the monastery of St John, the eight oars of his boat
were pulled (as the people used to delight in relating in stories
and songs) by eight crowned kings, and steered by the King of
England. As Edgar was very obedient to Dunstan and the
monks, they took great pains to represent him as the best of
kings. But he was really profligate, debauched, and vicious. He
once forcibly carried off a young lady from the convent at
Wilton; and Dunstan, pretending to be very much shocked,
condemned him not to wear his crown upon his head for seven
years – no great punishment, I dare say, as it can hardly have
been a more comfortable ornament to wear, than a stewpan
without a handle. His marriage with his second wife, ELFRIDA,
is one of the worst events of his reign. Hearing of the beauty of
this lady, he dispatched his favourite courtier, ATHELWOLD, to
her father's castle in Devonshire, to see if she were really as
charming as fame reported. Now, she was so exceedingly
beautiful that Athelwold fell in love with her himself, and
married her; but he told the King that she was only rich – not
handsome. The King, suspecting the truth when they came
home, resolved to pay the newly-married couple a visit; and,

suddenly, told Athelwold to prepare for his immediate coming. Athelwold, terrified, confessed to his young wife what he had said and done, and implored her to disguise her beauty by some ugly dress or silly manner, that he might be safe from the King's anger. She promised that she would; but she was a proud woman, who would far rather have been a queen than the wife of a courtier. She dressed herself in her best dress, and adorned herself with her richest jewels; and when the King came, presently, he discovered the cheat. So, he caused his false friend, Athelwold, to be murdered in a wood, and married his widow, this bad Elfrida. Six or seven years afterwards, he died; and was buried, as if he had been all that the monks said he was, in the abbey of Glastonbury, which he – or Dunstan for him – had much enriched.

England, in one part of this reign, was so troubled by wolves, which, driven out of the open country, hid themselves in the mountains of Wales when they were not attacking travellers and animals, that the tribute payable by the Welsh people was forgiven them, on condition of their producing, every year, three hundred wolves' heads. And the Welshmen were so sharp upon the wolves, to save their money, that in four years there was not a wolf left.

Then came the boy-king, EDWARD, called the Martyr, from the manner of his death. Elfrida had a son, named ETHELRED, for whom she claimed the throne; but Dunstan did not choose to favour him, and he made Edward king. The boy was hunting, one day, down in Dorsetshire, when he rode near to Corfe Castle, where Elfrida and Ethelred lived. Wishing to see them kindly, he rode away from his attendants and galloped to the castle gate, where he arrived at twilight, and blew his hunting-horn. 'You are welcome, dear King,' said Elfrida, coming out, with her brightest smiles. 'Pray you dismount and enter.' 'Not so, dear madam,' said the King. 'My company will miss me, and fear that I have met with some harm. Please you to give me a cup of wine that I may drink here, in the saddle, to you and to my little brother, and so ride away with the good speed I have made in riding here.' Elfrida, going in to bring the wine, whispered to an armed servant, one of her attendants, who stole out of the darkening gateway, and crept round behind the King's horse. As the King raised the cup to his lips, saying, 'Health!' to the wicked woman who was smiling on him, and to his innocent brother whose hand she held in hers, and who was only ten years old, this armed man made a spring and stabbed him in the back. He dropped the cup and spurred his horse away; but, soon fainting with loss of blood, drooped from the saddle, and, in his fall, entangled one of his feet in the stirrup. The frightened horse dashed on; trailing his rider's curls upon the ground; dragging his smooth young face through ruts, and stones, and briers, and fallen leaves, and mud; until the hunters, tracking the animal's course by the King's blood, caught his bridle, and released the disfigured body.

Then came the sixth and last of the boy-kings, ETHELRED, whom Elfrida, when he cried out at the sight of his murdered brother riding away from the castle gate, unmercifully beat with a torch which she snatched from one of the attendants. The people so disliked this boy, on account of his cruel mother and the murder she had done to promote him, that Dunstan would not have had him for king, but would have made EDGITHA, the daughter of the dead King Edgar, and of the lady whom he stole out of the convent at Wilton, Queen of England, if she would have consented. But she knew the stories of the youthful kings too well, and would not be persuaded from the convent where she lived in peace; so, Dunstan put Ethelred on the throne, having no one else to put there and gave him the nickname of THE UNREADY – knowing that he wanted resolution and firmness.

At first, Elfrida possessed great influence over the young King, but, as he grew older and came of age, her influence declined. The infamous woman, not having it in her power to do any more evil, then retired from court, and, according to the fashion of the time, built churches and monasteries, to expiate her guilt. As if a church, with a steeple reaching to the very stars, would have been any sign of true repentance for the blood of the poor boy, whose murdered form was trailed at his horse's heels! As if she could have buried her wickedness beneath the senseless stones of the whole world, piled up one upon another, for the monks to live in!

About the ninth or tenth year of this reign, Dunstan died. He was growing old then, but was as stern and artful as ever. Two circumstances that happened in connexion with him, in this reign of Ethelred, made a great noise. Once, he was present at a meeting of the Church, when the question was discussed whether priests should have permission to marry; and, as he sat with his head hung down, apparently thinking about it, a voice seemed to come out of a crucifix in the room, and warn the meeting to be of his opinion. This was some juggling of Dunstan's, and was probably his own voice disguised. But he played off a worse juggle than that, soon afterwards; for, another meeting being held on the same subject, and he and his supporters being seated on one side of a great room, and their opponents on the other, he rose and said, 'To Christ himself, as Judge, do I commit this cause!' Immediately on these words being spoken, the floor where the opposite party sat gave way, and some were killed and many wounded. You may be pretty sure that it had been weakened under Dunstan's direction, and that it fell at Dunstan's signal. *His* part of the floor did not go down. No, no. He was too good a workman for that.

When he died, the monks settled that he was a Saint, and called him Saint Dunstan ever afterwards. They might just as well have settled that he was a coach-horse, and could just as easily have called him one.

Ethelred the Unready was glad enough, I dare say, to be rid of this holy saint; but, left to himself, he was a poor weak king, and his reign was a reign of defeat and shame. The restless Danes, led by SWEYN, a son of the King of Denmark who had quarrelled with his father and had been banished from home, again came into England, and, year after year, attacked and despoiled large towns. To coax these sea-kings away, the weak Ethelred paid them money; but, the more money he paid, the more money the Danes wanted. At first, he gave them ten thousand pounds; on their next invasion, sixteen thousand pounds; on their next invasion, four and twenty thousand pounds: to pay which large sums, the unfortunate English people were heavily taxed. But, as the Danes still came back and wanted more, he thought it would be a good plan to marry into some powerful foreign family that would help him with soldiers. So, in the year one thousand and two, he courted and married Emma, the sister of Richard Duke of Normandy; a lady who was called the Flower of Normandy.

And now, a terrible deed was done in England, the like of which was never done on English ground before or since. On the thirteenth of November, in pursuance of secret instructions sent by the King over the whole country, the inhabitants of every town and city armed, and murdered all the Danes who were their neighbours. Young and old, babies and soldiers, men and women, every Dane was killed. No doubt there were among them many ferocious men who had done the English great wrong, and whose pride and insolence, in swaggering in the houses of the English and insulting their wives and daughters, had become unbearable; but no doubt there were also among them many peaceful Christian Danes who had married English women and become like English men. They were all slain, even to GUNHILDA, the sister of the King of Denmark, married to an English lord; who was first obliged to see the murder of her husband and her child, and then was killed herself.

When the King of the sea-kings heard of this deed of blood, he swore that he would have a great revenge. He raised an army, and a mightier fleet of ships than ever yet had sailed to England; and in all his army there was not a slave or an old man, but every soldier was a free man, and the son of a free man, and in the prime of life, and sworn to be revenged upon the English nation, for the massacre of that dread thirteenth of November, when his countrymen and countrywomen, and the little children whom they loved, were killed with fire and sword. And so, the sea-kings came to England in many great ships, each bearing the flag of its own commander. Golden eagles, ravens, dragons, dolphins, beasts of prey, threatened England from the prows of those ships, as they came onward through the water; and were reflected in the shining shields that hung upon their sides. The ship that bore the standard of the King of the sea-kings was carved and painted like a mighty serpent; and the King in his anger prayed that the Gods in whom he trusted might all desert him, if his serpent did not strike its fangs into England's heart.

And indeed it did. For, the great army landing from the great fleet, near Exeter, went forward, laying England waste, and striking their lances in the earth as they advanced, or throwing them into rivers, in token of their making all the island theirs. In remembrance of the black November night when the Danes were murdered, wheresoever the invaders came, they made the Saxons prepare and spread for them great feasts; and when they had eaten those feasts, and had drunk a curse to England with wild rejoicings, they drew their swords, and killed their Saxon entertainers, and marched on. For six long years they carried on this war: burning the crops, farmhouses, barns, mills, granaries; killing the labourers in the fields; preventing the seed from being sown in the ground; causing famine and starvation; leaving only heaps of ruin and smoking ashes, where they had found rich towns. To crown this misery, English officers and men deserted, and even the favourites of Ethelred the Unready, becoming traitors, seized many of the English ships, turned pirates against their own country, and aided by a storm occasioned the loss of nearly the whole English navy.

There was but one man of note, at this miserable pass, who was true to his country and the feeble King. He was a priest, and a brave one. For twenty days, the Archbishop of Canterbury defended that city against its Danish besiegers; and when a traitor in the town threw the gates open and admitted them, he said, in chains, 'I will not buy my life with money that must be extorted from the suffering people. Do with me what you please!' Again and again, he steadily refused to purchase his release with gold wrung from the poor.

At last, the Danes being tired of this, and being assembled at a drunken merry-making, had him brought into the feasting-hall.

'Now, bishop,' they said, 'we want gold!'

He looked round on the crowd of angry faces; from the shaggy beards close to him, to the shaggy beards against the walls, where men were mounted on tables and forms to see him over the heads of others: and he knew that his time was come.

'I have no gold,' he said.

'Get it, bishop!' they all thundered.

'That, I have often told you I will not,' said he.

They gathered closer round him, threatening, but he stood unmoved. Then, one man struck him; then, another; then a cursing soldier picked up from a heap in a corner of the hall, where fragments had been rudely thrown at dinner, a great ox-bone, and cast it at his face, from which the blood came spurting forth; then, others ran to the same heap, and knocked him down with other bones, and bruised and battered him; until one soldier whom he had baptised (willing, as I hope for the sake of that soldier's soul, to shorten the sufferings of the good man) struck him dead with his battle-axe.

If Ethelred had had the heart to emulate the courage of this noble archbishop, he might have done something yet. But he paid the Danes forty-eight thousand pounds, instead, and gained so little by the cowardly act, that Sweyn soon afterwards came over to subdue all England. So broken was the attachment of the English people, by this time, to their incapable King and their forlorn country which could not protect them, that they welcomed Sweyn on all sides, as a deliverer. London faithfully stood out, as long as the King was within its walls; but, when he sneaked away, it also welcomed the Danes. Then, all was over; and the King took refuge abroad with the Duke of Normandy, who had already given shelter to the King's wife, once the Flower of that country, and to her children.

Still, the English people, in spite of their sad sufferings, could not quite forget the great King Alfred and the Saxon race. When Sweyn died suddenly, in little more than a month after he had been proclaimed King of England, they generously sent to Ethelred, to say that they would have him for their King again, 'if he would only govern them better than he had governed them before.' The Unready, instead of coming himself, sent Edward, one of his sons, to make promises for him. At last, he followed, and the English declared him King. The Danes declared CANUTE, the son of Sweyn, King. Thus, direful war began again, and lasted for three years, when the Unready died. And I know of nothing better that he did, in all his reign of eight and thirty years.

Was Canute to be King now? Not over the Saxons, they said; they must have EDMUND, one of the sons of the Unready, who was surnamed IRONSIDE, because of his strength and stature. Edmund and Canute thereupon fell to, and fought five battles – O unhappy England, what a fighting-ground it was! – and then Ironside, who was a big man, proposed to Canute, who was a little man, that they two should fight it out in single combat. If Canute had been the big man, he would probably have said yes, but, being the little man, he decidedly said no. However, he declared that he was willing to divide the kingdom – to take all that lay north of Watling Street, as the old Roman military road from Dover to Chester was called, and to give Ironside all that lay south of it. Most men being weary of so much bloodshed, this was done. But Canute soon became sole King of England; for Ironside died suddenly within two months. Some think that he was killed, and killed by Canute's orders. No one knows.

CHAPTER 5

England under Canute the Dane

Canute reigned eighteen years. He was a merciless King at first. After he had clasped the hands of the Saxon chiefs, in token of the sincerity with which he swore to be just and good to them in return for their acknowledging him, he denounced and slew many of them, as well as many relations of the late King. 'He who brings me the head of one of my enemies,' he used to say, 'shall be dearer to me than a brother.' And he was so severe in hunting down his enemies, that he must have got together a pretty large family of these dear brothers. He was strongly inclined to kill EDMUND and EDWARD, two children, sons of poor Ironside; but, being afraid to do so in England, he sent them over to the King of Sweden, with a request that the King would be so good as 'dispose of them.' If the King of Sweden had been like many, many other men of that day, he would have had their innocent throats cut; but he was a kind man, and brought them up tenderly.

Normandy ran much in Canute's mind. In Normandy were the two children of the late king – EDWARD and ALFRED by name; and their uncle the Duke might one day claim the crown for them. But the Duke showed so little inclination to do so now, that he proposed to Canute to marry his sister, the widow of The Unready; who, being but a showy flower, and caring for nothing so much as becoming a queen again, left her children and was wedded to him.

Successful and triumphant, assisted by the valour of the English in his foreign wars, and with little strife to trouble him at home, Canute had a prosperous reign, and made many improvements. He was a poet and a musician. He grew sorry, as he grew older, for the blood he had shed at first; and went to Rome in a Pilgrim's dress, by way of washing it out. He gave a great deal of money to foreigners on his journey; but he took it from the English before he started. On the whole, however, he certainly became a far better man when he had no opposition to contend with, and was as great a King as England had known for some time.

The old writers of history relate how that Canute was one day disgusted with his courtiers for their flattery, and how he caused his chair to be set on the sea-shore, and feigned to command the tide as it came up not to wet the edge of his robe, for the land was his; how the tide came up, of course, without regarding him; and how he then turned to his flatterers, and rebuked them, saying, what was the might of any earthly king, to the might of the Creator, who could say unto the sea, 'Thus far shalt thou go, and no farther!' We may learn from this, I think, that a little sense will go a long way in a king; and that courtiers are not easily cured of flattery, nor kings of a liking for it. If the courtiers of Canute had not known, long before, that the King was fond of flattery, they would have known better than to offer it in such large doses. And if they had not known that he was vain of this speech (anything but a wonderful speech it seems to me, if a good child had made it), they would not have been at such great pains to repeat it. I fancy I see them all on the sea-shore together; the King's chair sinking in the sand; the King in a mighty good humour with his own wisdom; and the courtiers pretending to be quite stunned by it!

It is not the sea alone that is bidden to go 'thus far, and no farther.' The great command goes forth to all the kings upon the earth, and went to Canute in the year one thousand and thirty-five, and stretched him dead upon his bed. Beside it, stood his Norman wife. Perhaps, as the King looked his last upon her, he, who had so often thought distrustfully of Normandy, long ago, thought once more of the two exiled Princes in their uncle's court, and of the little favour they could feel for either Danes or Saxons, and of a rising cloud in Normandy that slowly moved towards England.

CHAPTER 6

England under Harold Harefoot, Hardicanute, and Edward the Confessor

CANUTE left three sons, by name SWEYN, HAROLD, and HARDICANUTE; but his Queen, Emma, once the Flower of

Normandy, was the mother of only Hardicanute. Canute had wished his dominions to be divided between the three, and had wished Harold to have England; but the Saxon people in the South of England, headed by a nobleman with great possessions, called the powerful EARL GODWIN (who is said to have been originally a poor cow-boy), opposed this, and desired to have, instead, either Hardicanute, or one of the two exiled Princes who were over in Normandy. It seemed so certain that there would be more bloodshed to settle this dispute, that many people left their homes, and took refuge in the woods and swamps. Happily, however, it was agreed to refer the whole question to a great meeting at Oxford, which decided that Harold should have all the country north of the Thames, with London for his capital city, and that Hardicanute should have all the south. The quarrel was so arranged; and, as Hardicanute was in Denmark troubling himself very little about anything but eating and getting drunk, his mother and Earl Godwin governed the south for him.

They had hardly begun to do so, and the trembling people who had hidden themselves were scarcely at home again, when Edward, the elder of the two exiled Princes, came over from Normandy with a few followers, to claim the English Crown. His mother Emma, however, who only cared for her last son Hardicanute, instead of assisting him, as he expected, opposed him so strongly with all her influence that he was very soon glad to get safely back. His brother Alfred was not so fortunate. Believing in an affectionate letter, written some time afterwards to him and his brother, in his mother's name (but whether really with or without his mother's knowledge is now uncertain), he allowed himself to be tempted over to England, with a good force of soldiers, and landing on the Kentish coast, and being met and welcomed by Earl Godwin, proceeded into Surrey, as far as the town of Guildford. Here, he and his men halted in the evening to rest, having still the Earl in their company; who had ordered lodgings and good cheer for them. But, in the dead of the night, when they were off their guard, being divided into small parties sleeping soundly after a long march and a plentiful supper in different houses, they were set upon by the King's troops, and taken prisoners. Next morning they were drawn out in a line, to the number of six hundred men, and were barbarously tortured and killed; with the exception of every tenth man, who was sold into slavery. As to the wretched Prince

Alfred, he was stripped naked, tied to a horse and sent away into the Isle of Ely, where his eyes were torn out of his head, and where in a few days he miserably died. I am not sure that the Earl had wilfully entrapped him, but I suspect it strongly.

Harold was now King all over England, though it is doubtful whether the Archbishop of Canterbury (the greater part of the priests were Saxons, and not friendly to the Danes) ever consented to crown him. Crowned or uncrowned, with the Archbishop's leave or without it, he was King for four years: after which short reign he died, and was buried; having never done much in life but go a hunting. He was such a fast runner at this, his favourite sport, that the people called him Harold Harefoot.

Hardicanute was then at Bruges, in Flanders, plotting, with his mother (who had gone over there after the cruel murder of Prince Alfred), for the invasion of England. The Danes and Saxons, finding themselves without a King, and dreading new disputes, made common cause, and joined in inviting him to occupy the Throne. He consented, and soon troubled them enough; for he brought over numbers of Danes, and taxed the people so insupportably to enrich those greedy favourites that there were many insurrections, especially one at Worcester, where the citizens rose and killed his tax-collectors; in revenge for which he burned their city. He was a brutal King, whose first public act was to order the dead body of poor Harold Harefoot to be dug up, beheaded, and thrown into the river. His end was worthy of such a beginning. He fell down drunk, with a goblet of wine in his hand, at a wedding-feast at Lambeth, given in honour of the marriage of his standard-bearer, a Dane named TOWED THE PROUD. And he never spoke again.

EDWARD, afterwards called by the monks THE CONFESSOR, succeeded; and his first act was to oblige his mother Emma, who had favoured him so little, to retire into the country; where she died some ten years afterwards. He was the exiled prince whose brother Alfred had been so foully killed. He had been invited over from Normandy by Hardicanute, in the course of his short reign of two years, and had been handsomely treated at court. His cause was now favoured by the powerful Earl Godwin, and he was soon made King. This Earl had been suspected by the people, ever since Prince Alfred's cruel death; he had even been tried in the last reign for the Prince's murder, but had been pronounced not guilty; chiefly, as it was supposed, because of a present he had made to the swinish King, of a gilded ship with a figure-head of solid gold, and a crew of eighty splendidly armed men. It was his interest to help the new King with his power, if the new King would help him against the popular distrust and hatred. So they made a bargain. Edward the Confessor got the Throne. The Earl got more power and more land, and his daughter Editha was made queen; for it was a part of their compact that the King should take her for his wife.

But, although she was a gentle lady, in all things worthy to be beloved – good, beautiful, sensible, and kind – the King from the first neglected her. Her father and her six proud brothers, resenting this cold treatment, harassed the King greatly by exerting all their power to make him unpopular. Having lived so long in Normandy, he preferred the Normans to the English. He made a Norman Archbishop, and Norman Bishops; his great officers and favourites were all Normans; he introduced the Norman fashions and the Norman language; in imitation of the state custom of Normandy, he attached a great seal to his state documents, instead of merely marking them, as the Saxon Kings had done, with the sign of the cross – just as poor people who have never been taught to write, now make the same mark for their names. All this, the powerful Earl Godwin and his six proud sons represented to the people as disfavour shown towards the English; and thus they daily increased their own power, and daily diminished the power of the King.

They were greatly helped by an event that occurred when he had reigned eight years. Eustace, Earl of Bolougne, who had married the King's sister, came to England on a visit. After staying at the court some time, he set forth, with his numerous train of attendants, to return home. They were to embark at Dover. Entering that peaceful town in armour, they took possession of the best houses, and noisily demanded to be lodged and entertained without payment. One of the bold men of Dover, who would not endure to have these domineering strangers jingling their heavy swords and iron corselets up and down his house, eating his meat and drinking his strong liquor, stood in his doorway and refused admission to the first armed man who came there. The armed man drew, and wounded him. The man of Dover struck the armed man dead. Intelligence of what he had done, spreading through the streets to where the Count Eustace and his men were standing by their horses, bridle in hand, they passionately mounted, galloped to the house, surrounded it, forced their way in (the doors and windows being closed when they came up), and killed the man of Dover at his own fireside. They then clattered through the streets, cutting down and riding over men, women, and children. This did not last long, you may believe. The men of Dover set upon them with great fury, killed nineteen of the foreigners, wounded many more, and, blockading the road to the port so that they should not embark, beat them out of the town by the way they had come. Hereupon, Count Eustace rides as hard as man can ride to Gloucester, where Edward is, surrounded by Norman monks and Norman lords. 'Justice!' cries the Count, 'upon the men of Dover, who have set upon and slain my people!' The King sends immediately for the powerful Earl Godwin, who happens to be near; reminds him that Dover is under his government; and orders him to repair to Dover and do military execution on the inhabitants. 'It does not become you,' says the proud Earl in reply, 'to condemn without a hearing those whom you have sworn to protect. I will not do it.'

The King, therefore, summoned the Earl, on pain of banishment and loss of his titles and property, to appear before the court to answer this disobedience. The Earl refused to appear. He, his eldest son Harold, and his second son Sweyn, hastily raised as many fighting men as their utmost power could collect, and demanded to have Count Eustace and his followers surrendered to the justice of the country. The King, in his turn, refused to give them up, and raised a strong force. After some treaty and delay, the troops of the great Earl and his sons began to fall off. The Earl, with a part of his family and abundance of treasure, sailed to Flanders; Harold escaped to Ireland; and the power of the great family was for that time gone in England. But, the people did not forget them.

Then, Edward the Confessor, with the true meanness of a mean spirit, visited his dislike of the once powerful father and sons upon the helpless daughter and sister, his unoffending wife, whom all who saw her (her husband and his monks excepted) loved. He seized rapaciously upon her fortune and her jewels, and allowed her only one attendant, confined her in a gloomy convent, of which a sister of his – no doubt an unpleasant lady after his own heart – was abbess or jailer.

Having got Earl Godwin and his six sons well out of his way, the King favoured the Normans more than ever. He invited over WILLIAM, DUKE OF NORMANDY, the son of that Duke who had received him and his murdered brother long ago, and of a peasant girl, a tanner's daughter, with whom that Duke had fallen in love for her beauty as he saw her washing clothes in a brook. William, who was a great warrior, with a passion for fine horses, dogs, and arms, accepted the invitation; and the Normans in England, finding themselves more numerous than ever when he arrived with his retinue, and held in still greater honour at court than before, became more and more haughty towards the people, and were more and more disliked by them.

The old Earl Godwin, though he was abroad, knew well how the people felt; for, with part of the treasure he had carried away with him, he kept spies and agents in his pay all over England. Accordingly, he thought the time was come for fitting out a great expedition against the Norman-loving King. With it, he sailed to the Isle of Wight, where he was joined by his son Harold, the most gallant and brave of all his family. And so the father and son came sailing up the Thames to Southwark; great numbers of the people declaring for them, and shouting for the English Earl and the English Harold, against the Norman favourites!

The King was at first as blind and stubborn as kings usually have been whensoever they have been in the hands of monks. But the people rallied so thickly round the old Earl and his son, and the old Earl was so steady in demanding without bloodshed the restoration of himself and his family to their rights, that at last the court took the alarm. The Norman Archbishop of Canterbury, and the Norman Bishop of London, surrounded by their retainers, fought their way out of London, and escaped from Essex to France in a fishing-boat. The other Norman favourites dispersed in all directions. The old Earl and his sons (except Sweyn, who had committed crimes against the law) were restored to their possessions and dignities. Editha, the virtuous and lovely Queen of the insensible King, was triumphantly released from her prison, the convent, and once more sat in her chair of state, arrayed in the jewels of which, when she had no champion to support her rights, her cold-blooded husband had deprived her.

The old Earl Godwin did not long enjoy his restored fortune. He fell down in a fit at the King's table, and died upon the third day afterwards. Harold succeeded to his power, and to a far higher place in the attachment of the people than his father had ever held. By his valour he subdued the King's enemies in many bloody fights. He was vigorous against rebels in Scotland – this was the time when Macbeth slew Duncan, upon which event our English Shakespeare, hundreds of years afterwards, wrote his great tragedy; and he killed the restless Welsh King GRIFFITH, and brought his head to England.

What Harold was doing at sea, when he was driven on the French coast by a tempest, is not at all certain; nor does it at all matter. That his ship was forced by a storm on that shore, and that he was taken prisoner, there is no doubt. In those barbarous days, all shipwrecked strangers were taken prisoners, and obliged to pay ransom. So, a certain Count Guy, who was the Lord of Ponthieu where Harold's disaster happened, seized him, instead of relieving him like a hospitable and Christian lord as he ought to have done, and expected to make a very good thing of it.

But Harold sent off immediately to Duke Wiliam of Normandy, complaining of this treatment; and the Duke no sooner heard of it than he ordered Harold to be escorted to the ancient town of Rouen, where he then was, and where he received him as an honoured guest. Now, some writers tell us that Edward the Confessor, who was by this time old and had no children, had made a will, appointing Duke William of Normandy his successor, and had informed the Duke of his having done so. There is no doubt that he was anxious about his successor; because he had even invited over, from abroad, EDWARD THE OUTLAW, a son of Ironside, who had come to England with his wife and three children, but whom the King had strangely refused to see when he did come, and who had died in London suddenly (princes were terribly liable to sudden death in those days), and had been buried in St Paul's Cathedral. The King might possibly have made such a will; or, having always been fond of the Normans, he might have encouraged Norman William to aspire to the English crown, by something that he said to him when he was staying at the English court. But certainly William did now aspire to it; and knowing that Harold would be a powerful rival, he called together a great assembly of his nobles, offered Harold his daughter ADELE in marriage, informed him that he meant on King Edward's death to claim the English crown as his own inheritance, and required Harold then and there to swear to aid him. Harold, being in the Duke's power, took this oath upon the Missal, or Prayer-book. It is a good example of the superstitions of the monks, that this Missal, instead of being placed upon a table, was placed upon a tub; which, when Harold had sworn, was uncovered, and shown to be full of dead men's bones – bones, as the monks pretended, of saints. This was supposed to make Harold's oath a great deal more impressive and binding. As if the great name of the Creator of Heaven and earth could be made more solemn by a knuckle-bone, or a double-tooth, or a finger-nail, of Dunstan!

Within a week or two after Harold's return to England, the dreary old Confessor was found to be dying. After wandering in his mind like a very weak old man, he died. As he had put himself entirely in the hands of the monks when he was alive, they praised him lustily when he was dead. They had gone so far, already, as to persuade him that he could work miracles; and had brought people afflicted with a bad disorder of the skin, to him, to be touched and cured. This was called 'touching for the King's Evil,' which afterwards became a royal custom. You know, however, Who really touched the sick, and healed them; and you know His sacred name is not among the dusty line of human kings.

CHAPTER 7

England under Harold the Second, and Conquered by the Normans

HAROLD was crowned King of England on the very day of the maudlin Confessor's funeral. He had good need to be quick about it. When the news reached Norman William, hunting in his park at Rouen, he dropped his bow, returned to his palace, called his nobles to council, and presently sent ambassadors to Harold, calling on him to keep his oath and resign the Crown. Harold would do no such thing. The barons of France leagued together round Duke William for the invasion of England. Duke William promised freely to distribute English wealth and English lands among them. The Pope sent to Normandy a consecrated banner, and a ring containing a hair which he warranted to have grown on the head of Saint Peter. He blessed the enterprise; and cursed Harold; and requested that the Normans would pay 'Peter's Pence' – or a tax to himself of a penny a year on every house – a little more regularly in future, if they could make it convenient.

King Harold had a rebel brother in Flanders, who was a vassal of HAROLD HARDRADA, King of Norway. This brother, and this Norwegian King, joining their forces against England, with Duke William's help, won a fight in which the English were commanded by two nobles; and then besieged York. Harold, who was waiting for the Normans on the coast at Hastings, with his army, marched to Stamford Bridge, upon the river Derwent to give them instant battle.

He found them drawn up in a hollow circle, marked out by their shining spears. Riding round this circle at a distance, to survey it, he saw a brave figure on horseback, in a blue mantle and a bright helmet, whose horse suddenly stumbled and threw him.

'Who is that man who has fallen?' Harold asked of one of his captains.

'The King of Norway,' he replied.

'He is a tall and stately king,' said Harold, 'but his end is near.'

He added, in a little while, 'Go yonder to my brother, and tell him, if he withdraw his troops, he shall be Earl of Northumberland, and rich and powerful in England.'

The captain rode away and gave the message.

'What will he give to my friend, the King of Norway?' asked the brother.

'Seven feet of earth for a grave,' replied the captain.

'No more?' returned the brother, with a smile.

'The King of Norway, being a tall man, perhaps a little more,' replied the captain.

'Ride back!' said the brother, 'and tell King Harold to make ready for the fight!'

He did so, very soon. And such a fight King Harold led against that force, that his brother, and the Norwegian King, and every chief of note in all their host, except the Norwegian King's son, Olave, to whom he gave honourable dismissal, were left dead upon the field. The victorious army marched to York. As King Harold sat there at the feast, in the midst of all his company, a stir was heard at the doors; and messengers all covered with mire from riding far and fast through broken ground came hurrying in, to report that the Normans had landed in England.

The intelligence was true. They had been tossed about by contrary winds, and some of their ships had been wrecked. A part of their own shore, to which they had been driven back, was strewn with Norman bodies. But they had once more made sail, led by the Duke's own galley, a present from his wife, upon the prow whereof the figure of a golden boy stood pointing towards England. By day, the banner of the three Lions of Normandy, the diverse coloured sails, the gilded vans, the many decorations of this gorgeous ship, had glittered in the sun and sunny water; by night, a light had sparkled like a star at her mast-head. And now, encamped near Hastings, with their leader lying in the old Roman castle of Pevensey, the English retiring in all directions, the land for miles around scorched and smoking, fired and pillaged, was the whole Norman power, hopeful and strong on English ground.

Harold broke up the feast and hurried to London. Within a week, his army was ready. He sent out spies to ascertain the Norman strength. William took them, caused them to be led through his whole camp, and then dismissed. 'The Normans,' said these spies to Harold, 'are not bearded on the upper lip, as we English are, but are shorn. They are priests.' 'My men,' replied Harold, with a laugh, 'will find those priests good soldiers!'

'The Saxons,' reported Duke William's outposts of Norman soldiers, who were instructed to retire as King Harold's army advanced, 'rush on us through their pillaged country with the fury of madmen.'

'Let them come, and come soon!' said Duke William.

Some proposals for a reconciliation were made, but were soon abandoned. In the middle of the month of October, in the year one thousand and sixty-six, the Normans and the English came front to front. All night the armies lay encamped before each other, in a part of the country then called Senlac, now called (in remembrance of them) Battle. With the first dawn of day, they arose. There, in the faint light, were the English on a hill; a wood behind them; in their midst, the Royal banner, representing a fighting warrior, woven in golden thread, adorned with precious stones; beneath the banner, as it rustled in the wind, stood King Harold on foot, with two of his remaining brothers by his side; around them, still and silent as the dead, clustered the whole English army – every soldier covered by his shield, and bearing in his hand his dreaded English battle-axe.

On an opposite hill, in three lines, archers, foot-soldiers, horsemen, was the Norman force. Of a sudden, a great battle-cry, 'God help us!' burst from the Norman lines. The English answered with their own battle-cry, 'God's Rood! Holy Rood!' The Normans then came sweeping down the hill to attack the English.

There was one tall Norman Knight who rode before the Norman army on a prancing horse, throwing up his heavy sword and catching it, and singing of the bravery of his countrymen. An English Knight, who rode out from the English force to meet him, fell by this Knight's hand. Another English Knight rode out, and he fell too. But then a third rode out, and killed the Norman. This was in the first beginning of the fight. It soon raged everywhere.

The English, keeping side by side in a great mass, cared no more for the showers of Norman arrows than if they had been showers of Norman rain. When the Norman horsemen rode against them, with their battle-axes they cut men and horses down. The Normans gave way. The English pressed forward. A cry went forth among the Norman troops that Duke William was killed. Duke William took off his helmet, in order that his face might be distinctly seen, and rode along the line before his men. This gave them courage. As they turned again to face the English, some of their Norman horse divided the pursuing body of the English from the rest, and thus all that foremost portion of the English army fell, fighting bravely. The main body still remaining firm, heedless of the Norman arrows, and with their battle-axes cutting down the crowds of horsemen when they rode up, like forests of young trees, Duke William pretended to retreat. The eager English followed. The Norman army closed again, and fell upon them with great slaughter.

'Still,' said Duke William, 'there are thousands of the English, firm as rocks around their King. Shoot upward, Norman archers, that your arrows may fall down upon their faces!'

The sun rose high, and sank, and the battle still raged. Through all the wild October day, the clash and din resounded in the air. In the red sunset, and in the white moonlight, heaps upon heaps of dead men lay strewn, a dreadful spectacle, all over the ground. King Harold, wounded with an arrow in the eye, was nearly blind. His brothers were already killed. Twenty Norman Knights, whose battered armour had flashed fiery and golden in the sunshine all day long, and now looked silvery in the moonlight, dashed forward to seize the Royal banner from the English Knights and soldiers, still faithfully collected round their blinded King. The King received a mortal wound, and dropped. The English broke and fled. The Normans rallied, and the day was lost.

O what a sight beneath the moon and stars, when lights were shining in the tent of the victorious Duke William, which was pitched near the spot where Harold fell – and he and his knights were carousing, within – and soldiers with torches, going slowly to and fro, without, sought for the corpse of Harold among piles of dead – and the Warrior, worked in golden thread and precious stones, lay low, all torn and soiled with blood – and the three Norman Lions kept watch over the field!

CHAPTER 8

England under William the First, the Norman Conqueror

Upon the ground where the brave Harold fell, William the Norman afterwards founded an abbey, which, under the name of Battle Abbey, was a rich and splendid place through many a troubled year, though now it is a grey ruin overgrown with ivy. But the first work he had to do, was to conquer the English thoroughly; and that, as you know by this time, was hard work for any man.

He ravaged several counties; he burned and plundered many towns; he laid waste scores upon scores of miles of pleasant country; he destroyed innumerable lives. At length STIGAND, Archbishop of Canterbury, with other representatives of the clergy and the people, went to his camp and submitted to him. EDGAR, the insignificant son of Edmund Ironside, was proclaimed King by others, but nothing came of it. He fled to Scotland afterwards, where his sister, who was young and beautiful, married the Scottish King. Edgar himself was not important enough for anybody to care much about him.

On Christmas Day, William was crowned in Westminster Abbey, under the title of WILLIAM THE FIRST; but he is best known as WILLIAM THE CONQUEROR. It was a strange coronation. One of the bishops who performed the ceremony asked the Normans in French, if they would have Duke William for their king? They answered Yes. Another of the bishops put the same question to the Saxons, in English. They too answered Yes, with a loud shout. The noise being heard by a guard of Norman horse-soldiers outside, was mistaken for resistance on the part of the English. The guard instantly set fire to the neighbouring houses, and a tumult ensued; in the midst of which the King, being left alone in the Abbey, with a few priests (and they all being in a terrible fright together), was hurriedly crowned. When the crown was placed upon his head, he swore to govern the English as well as the best of their own monarchs. I dare say you think, as I do, that if we except the Great Alfred, he might pretty easily have done that.

Numbers of the English nobles had been killed in the last disastrous battle. Their estates, and the estates of all the nobles who had fought against him there, King William seized upon, and gave to his own Norman knights and nobles. Many great English families of the present time acquired their English lands in this way, and are very proud of it.

But what is got by force must be maintained by force. These nobles were obliged to build castles all over England, to defend their new property; and, do what he would, the King could neither soothe nor quell the nation as he wished. He gradually introduced the Norman language and the Norman customs; yet, for a long time the great body of the English remained sullen and revengeful. On his going over to Normandy, to visit his subjects there, the oppressions of his half-brother ODO, whom he left in charge of his English kingdom, drove the people mad. The men of Kent even invited over, to take possession of Dover, their old enemy Count Eustace of Boulogne, who had led the fray when the Dover man was slain at his own fireside. The men of Hereford, aided by the Welsh, and commanded by a chief named EDRIC THE WILD, drove the Normans out of their country. Some of those who had been dispossessed of their lands, banded together in the North of England; some, in Scotland; some, in the thick woods and marshes; and whensoever they could fall upon the Normans, or upon the English who had submitted to the Normans, they fought, despoiled, and murdered, like the desperate outlaws that they were. Conspiracies were set on foot for a general massacre of the Normans, like the old massacre of the Danes. In short, the English were in a murderous mood all through the kingdom.

King William, fearing he might lose his conquest, came back, and tried to pacify the London people by soft words. He then set forth to repress the country people by stern deeds. Among the towns which he besieged, and where he killed and maimed the inhabitants without any distinction, sparing none, young or old, armed or unarmed, were Oxford, Warwick, Leicester, Nottingham, Derby, Lincoln, York. In all these places, and in many others, fire and sword worked their utmost horrors, and made the land dreadful to behold. The streams and rivers were discoloured with blood; the sky was blackened with smoke; the fields were wastes of ashes; the waysides were heaped up with dead. Such are the fatal results of conquest and ambition! Although William was a harsh and angry man, I do not suppose that he deliberately meant to work this shocking ruin, when he invaded England. But what he had got by the strong hand, he could only keep by the strong hand, and in so doing he made England a great grave.

Two sons of Harold, by name EDMUND and GODWIN, came over from Ireland, with some ships, against the Normans, but were defeated. This was scarcely done, when the outlaws in the woods so harassed York, that the Governor sent to the King for help. The King despatched a general and a large force to occupy the town of Durham. The Bishop of that place met the general outside the town, and warned him not to enter, as he would be in danger there. The general cared nothing for the warning, and went in with all his men. That night, on every hill within sight of Durham, signal fires were seen to blaze. When the morning dawned, the English, who had assembled in great strength, forced the gates, rushed into the town, and slew the Normans every one. The English afterwards besought the Danes to come and help them. The Danes came, with two hundred and forty ships. The outlawed nobles joined them; they captured York, and drove the Normans out of that city. Then, William bribed the Danes to go away; and took such vengeance on the English, that all the former fire and sword, smoke and ashes, death and ruin, were nothing compared with it. In melancholy songs, and doleful stories, it was still sung and told by cottage fires on winter evenings, a hundred years afterwards, how, in those dreadful days of the Normans, there was not, from the River Humber to the River Tyne, one inhabited village left, nor one cultivated field — how there was nothing but a dismal ruin, where the human creatures and the beasts lay dead together.

The outlaws had, at this time, what they called a Camp of Refuge, in the midst of the fens of Cambridgeshire. Protected by those marshy grounds which were difficult of approach, they lay among the reeds and rushes, and were hidden by the mists that rose up from the watery earth. Now, there also was, at that time, over the sea in Flanders, an Englishman named HERE-WARD, whose father had died in his absence, and whose property had been given to a Norman. When he heard of this wrong that had been done him (from such of the exiled English as chanced to wander into that country), he longed for revenge; and joining the outlaws in their camp of refuge, became their commander. He was so good a soldier, that the Normans supposed him to be aided by enchantment. William, even after he had made a road three miles in length across the Cambridge-shire marshes, on purpose to attack this supposed enchanter, thought it necessary to engage an old lady, who pretended to be a sorceress, to come and do a little enchantment in the royal cause. For this purpose she was pushed on before the troops in a wooden tower; but Hereward very soon disposed of this unfortunate sorceress, by burning her, tower and all. The monks of the convent of Ely near at hand, however, who were fond of good living, and who found it very uncomfortable to have the country blockaded and their supplies of meat and drink cut off, showed the King a secret way of surprising the camp. So Hereward was soon defeated. Whether he afterwards died quietly, or whether he was killed after killing sixteen of the men who attacked him (as some old rhymes relate that he did), I cannot say. His defeat put an end to the Camp of Refuge; and, very soon afterwards, the King, victorious both in Scotland and in England, quelled the last rebellious English noble. He then surrounded himself with Norman lords, enriched by the property of English nobles; had a great survey made of all the land in England, which was entered as the property of its new owners, on a roll called Doomsday Book; obliged the people to put out their fires and candles at a certain hour every night, on the ringing of a bell which was called The Curfew; introduced the Norman dresses and manners; made the Normans masters everywhere, and the English, servants; turned out the English bishops, and put Normans in their places; and showed himself to be the Conqueror indeed.

But, even with his own Normans, he had a restless life. They were always hungering and thirsting for the riches of the English; and the more he gave, the more they wanted. His priests were as greedy as his soldiers. We know of only one Norman who plainly told his master, the King, that he had come with him to England to do his duty as a faithful servant, and that property taken by force from other men had no charms for him. His name was GUILBERT. We should not forget his name, for it is good to remember and to honour honest men.

Besides all these troubles, William the Conqueror was troubled by quarrels among his sons. He had three living. ROBERT, called CURTHOSE, because of his short legs; WILLIAM, called RUFUS or the Red, from the colour of his hair; and HENRY, fond of learning, and called, in the Norman language, BEAUCLERC, or Fine-Scholar. When Robert grew up, he asked of his father the government of Normandy, which he had nominally possessed, as a child, under his mother, MATILDA. The King refusing to grant it, Robert became jealous and discontented; and happening one day, while in this temper, to be ridiculed by his brothers, who threw water on him from a balcony as he was walking before the door, he drew his sword, rushed upstairs, and was only prevented by the King himself from putting them to death. That same night, he hotly departed with some followers from his father's court, and endeavoured to take the Castle of Rouen by surprise. Failing in this, he shut himself up in another Castle in Normandy, which the King besieged, and where Robert one day unhorsed and nearly killed him without knowing who he was. His submission when he discovered his father, and the intercession of the queen and others, reconciled them; but not soundly; for Robert soon strayed abroad, and went from court to court with his complaints. He was a gay, careless, thoughtless fellow, spending all he got on musicians and dancers; but his mother loved him, and often, against the King's command, supplied him with money through a messenger named SAMSON. At length the incensed King swore he would tear out Samson's eyes; and Samson, thinking that his only hope of safety was in becoming a monk, became one, went on such errands no more, and kept his eyes in his head.

All this time, from the turbulent day of his strange coronation, the Conqueror had been struggling, you see, at any cost of cruelty and bloodshed, to maintain what he had seized. All his reign, he struggled still, with the same object ever before him. He was a stern bold man, and he succeeded in it.

He loved money, and was particular in his eating, but he had only leisure to indulge one other passion, and that was his love of hunting. He carried it to such a height that he ordered whole villages and towns to be swept away to make forests for the deer. Not satisfied with sixty-eight Royal Forests, he laid waste an immense district, to form another in Hampshire, called the New Forest. The many thousands of miserable peasants who saw their little houses pulled down, and themselves and children turned into the open country without a shelter, detested him for his merciless addition to their many sufferings; and when, in the twenty-first year of his reign (which proved to be the last), he went over to Rouen, England was as full of hatred against him, as if every leaf on every tree in all his Royal Forests had been a curse upon his head. In the New Forest, his son Richard (for he had four sons) had been gored to death by a Stag; and the people said that this so cruelly-made Forest would yet be fatal to others of the Conqueror's race.

He was engaged in a dispute with the King of France about some territory. While he stayed at Rouen, negotiating with that King, he kept his bed and took medicines: being advised by his physicians to do so, on account of having grown to an unwieldy size. Word being brought to him that the King of France made light of this, and joked about it, he swore in a great rage that he should rue his jests. He assembled his army, marched into the disputed territory, burnt – his old way! – the vines, the crops, and fruit, and set the town of Mantes on fire. But, in an evil hour; for, as he rode over the hot ruins, his horse, setting his hoofs upon some burning embers, started, threw him forward against the pommel of the saddle, and gave him a mortal hurt. For six weeks he lay dying in a monastery near Rouen, and then made his will, giving England to William, Normandy to Robert, and five thousand pounds to Henry. And now, his violent deeds lay heavy on his mind. He ordered money to be given to many English churches and monasteries, and – which was much better repentance – released his prisoners of state, some of whom had been confined in his dungeons twenty years.

It was a September morning, and the sun was rising, when the King was awakened from slumber by the sound of a church bell. 'What bell is that?' he faintly asked. They told him it was the bell of the chapel of Saint Mary. 'I commend my soul,' said he, 'to Mary!' and died.

Think of his name, The Conqueror, and then consider how he lay in death! The moment he was dead, his physicians, priests, and nobles, not knowing what contest for the throne might now take place, or what might happen in it, hastened away, each man for himself and his own property; the mercenary servants of the court began to rob and plunder; the body of the King, in the indecent strife, was rolled from the bed, and lay alone, for hours, upon the ground. O Conqueror, of whom so many great names are proud now, of whom so many great names thought nothing then, it were better to have conquered one true heart, than England!

By-and-by, the priests came creeping in with prayers and candles; and a good knight, named HERLUIN, undertook (which no one else would do) to convey the body to Caen, in Normandy, in order that it might be buried in St Stephen's church there, which the Conqueror had founded. But fire, of which he had made such bad use in his life, seemed to follow him of itself in death. A great conflagration broke out in the town when the body was placed in the church; and those present running out to extinguish the flames, it was once again left alone.

It was not even buried in peace. It was about to be let down, in its Royal robes, into a tomb near the high altar, in presence of a great concourse of people, when a loud voice in the crowd cried out, 'This ground is mine! Upon it, stood my father's house. This King despoiled me of both ground and house to build this church. In the great name of GOD, I here forbid his body to be covered with the earth that is my right!' The priests and bishops present, knowing the speaker's right, and knowing that the King had often denied him justice, paid him down sixty shillings for the grave. Even then, the corpse was not at rest. The tomb was too small, and they tried to force it in. It broke, a dreadful smell arose, the people hurried out into the air, and, for the third time, it was left alone.

Where were the Conqueror's three sons, that they were not at their father's burial? Robert was lounging among minstrels, dancers, and gamesters, in France or Germany. Henry was carrying his five thousand pounds safely away in a convenient chest he had got made. William the Red was hurrying to England, to lay hands upon the Royal treasure and the crown.

CHAPTER 9

England under William the Second, called Rufus

WILLIAM THE RED, in breathless haste, secured the three great forts of Dover, Pevensey, and Hastings, and made with hot speed for Winchester, where the Royal treasure was kept. The treasurer delivering him the keys, he found that it amounted to sixty thousand pounds in silver, besides gold and jewels. Possessed of this wealth, he soon persuaded the Archbishop of Canterbury to crown him, and became William the Second, King of England.

Rufus was no sooner on the throne, than he ordered into prison again the unhappy state captives whom his father had set free, and directed a goldsmith to ornament his father's tomb profusely with gold and silver. It would have been more dutiful in him to have attended the sick Conqueror when he was dying; but England, itself, like this Red King, who once governed it, has sometimes made expensive tombs for dead men whom it treated shabbily when they were alive.

The King's brother, Robert of Normandy, seeming quite content to be only Duke of that country; and the King's other brother, Fine-Scholar, being quiet enough with his five thousand pounds in a chest; the King flattered himself, we may suppose, with the hope of an easy reign. But easy reigns were difficult to have in those days. The turbulent Bishop ODO (who had blessed the Norman army at the Battle of Hastings, and who, I dare say, took all the credit of the victory to himself) soon began, in concert with some powerful Norman nobles, to trouble the Red King.

The truth seems to be that this bishop and his friends, who had lands in England and lands in Normandy, wished to hold both under one Sovereign; and greatly preferred a thoughtless good-natured person, such as Robert was, to Rufus; who, though far from being an amiable man in any respect, was keen, and not to be imposed upon. They declared in Robert's favour, and retired to their castles (those castles were very troublesome to kings) in a sullen humour. The Red King, seeing the Normans thus falling from him, revenged himself upon them by appealing to the English; to whom he made a variety of promises, which he never meant to perform – in particular, promises to soften the cruelty of the Forest Laws; and who, in return, so aided him with their valour, that ODO was besieged in the Castle of Rochester, and forced to abandon it, and to depart from England for ever: whereupon the other rebellious Norman nobles were soon reduced and scattered.

Then, the Red King went over to Normandy, where the people suffered greatly under the loose rule of Duke Robert. The King's object was to seize upon the Duke's dominions. This, the Duke, of course, prepared to resist: and miserable war between the two brothers seemed inevitable, when the powerful nobles on both sides, who had seen so much of war, interfered to prevent it. A treaty was made. Each of the two brothers agreed to give up something of his claims, and that the longer-liver of the two should inherit all the dominions of the other. When they had come to this loving understanding, they embraced and joined their forces against Fine-Scholar; who had bought some territory of Robert with a part of his five thousand pounds, and was considered a dangerous individual in consequence.

St Michael's Mount, in Normandy (there is another St Michael's Mount, in Cornwall, wonderfully like it), was then, as it is now, a strong place perched upon the top of a high rock, around which, when the tide is in, the sea flows, leaving no road to the mainland. In this place, Fine-Scholar shut himself up with his soldiers, and here he was closely besieged by his two brothers. At one time, when he was reduced to great distress for want of water, the generous Robert not only permitted his men to get water, but sent Fine-Scholar wine from his own table; and, on being remonstrated with by the Red King, said 'What! shall we let our own brother die of thirst? Where shall we get another, when he is gone?' At another time, the Red King riding alone on the shore of the bay, looking up at the Castle, was taken by two of Fine-Scholar's men, one of whom was about to kill him, when he cried out, 'Hold, knave! I am the King of England!' The story says that the soldier raised him from the ground respectfully and humbly, and that the King took him into service. The story may or may not be true; but at any rate it is true that Fine-Scholar could not hold out against his united brothers, and that he abandoned Mount St Michael, and wandered about – as poor and forlorn as other scholars have been sometimes known to be.

The Scotch became unquiet in the Red King's time, and were twice defeated – the second time, with the loss of their King, Malcolm, and his son. The Welsh became unquiet too. Against them, Rufus was less successful; for they fought among their native mountains, and did great execution on the King's troops. Robert of Normandy became unquiet too; and, complaining that his brother the King did not faithfully perform his part of their agreement, took up arms, and obtained assistance from the King of France, whom Rufus, in the end, bought off with vast sums of money. England became unquiet too. Lord Mowbray, the powerful Earl of Northumberland, headed a great conspiracy to depose the King, and to place upon the throne, STEPHEN, the Conqueror's near relative. The plot was discovered; all the chief conspirators were seized; some were fined, some were put in prison, some were put to death. The Earl of Northumberland himself was shut up in a dungeon beneath Windsor Castle, where he died, an old man, thirty long years afterwards. The Priests in England were more unquiet than any other class, or power; for the Red King treated them with such small ceremony that he refused to appoint new bishops or archbishops when the old ones died, but kept all the wealth belonging to those offices in his own hands. In return for this, the Priests wrote his life when he was dead, and abused him well. I am inclined to think, myself, that there was little to choose between the Priests and the Red King; that both sides were greedy and designing; and that they were fairly matched.

The Red King was false of heart, selfish, covetous, and mean. He had a worthy minister in his favourite, Ralph, nicknamed – for almost every famous person had a nickname in those rough days – Flambard, or the Firebrand. Once, the King being ill, became penitent, and made ANSELM, a foreign priest and a good man, Archbishop of Canterbury. But he no sooner got well again than he repented of his repentance, and persisted in wrongfully keeping to himself some of the wealth belonging to the archbishopric. This led to violent disputes, which were aggravated by there being in Rome at that time two rival Popes; each of whom declared he was the only real original infallible Pope, who couldn't make a mistake. At last, Anselm, knowing the Red King's character, and not feeling himself safe in England, asked leave to return abroad. The Red King gladly gave it; for he knew that as soon as Anselm was gone, he could begin to store up all the Canterbury money again, for his own use.

By such means, and by taxing and oppressing the English people in every possible way, the Red King became very rich. When he wanted money for any purpose, he raised it by some means or other, and cared nothing for the injustice he did, or the misery he caused. Having the opportunity of buying from Robert the whole duchy of Normandy for five years, he taxed the English people more than ever, and made the very convents sell their plate and valuables to supply him with the means to make the purchase. But he was as quick and eager in putting down revolt as he was in raising money; for, a part of the Norman people objecting – very naturally, I think – to being sold in this way, he headed an army against them with all the speed and energy of his father. He was so impatient that he embarked for Normandy in a great gale of wind. And when the sailors told him it was dangerous to go to sea in such angry weather, he replied, 'Hoist sail and away! Did you ever hear of a king who was drowned?'

You will wonder how it was that even the careless Robert came to sell his dominions. It happened thus. It had long been the custom for many English people to make journeys to Jerusalem, which were called pilgrimages, in order that they might pray beside the tomb of Our Saviour there. Jerusalem belonging to the Turks, and the Turks hating Christianity, these Christian travellers were often insulted and ill-used. The Pilgrims bore it patiently for some time, but at length a remarkable man, of great earnestness and eloquence, called PETER THE HERMIT, began to preach in various places against the Turks, and to declare that it was the duty of good Christians to drive away those unbelievers from the tomb of Our Saviour, and to take possession of it, and protect it. An excitement such as the world had never known before was created. Thousands and thousands of men of all ranks and conditions departed for Jerusalem to make war against the Turks. The war is called in history the first Crusade, and every Crusader wore a cross marked on his right shoulder.

All the Crusaders were not zealous Christians. Among them were vast numbers of the restless, idle, profligate, and adventurous spirits of the time. Some became Crusaders for the love of change; some, in the hope of plunder; some, because they had nothing to do at home; some, because they did what the priests told them; some, because they liked to see foreign countries; some, because they were fond of knocking men about, and would as soon knock a Turk about as a Christian. Robert of Normandy may have been influenced by all these motives; and by a kind desire, besides, to save the Christian Pilgrims from bad treatment in future. He wanted to raise a number of armed men, and to go to the Crusade. He could not do so without money. He had no money; and he sold his dominions to his brother, the Red King, for five years. With the large sum he thus obtained, he fitted out his Crusaders gallantly, and went away to Jerusalem in martial state. The Red King, who made money out of everything, stayed at home, busily squeezing more money out of Normans and English.

After three years of great hardship and suffering – from shipwreck at sea; from travel in strange lands; from hunger, thirst, and fever, upon the burning sands of the desert; and from the fury of the Turks – the valiant Crusaders got possession of Our Saviour's tomb. The Turks were still resisting and fighting bravely, but this success increased the general desire in Europe to join the Crusade. Another great French Duke was proposing to sell his dominions for a term to the rich Red King, when the Red King's reign came to a sudden and violent end.

You have not forgotten the New Forest which the Conqueror made, and which the miserable people whose homes he had laid waste, so hated. The cruelty of the Forest Laws, and the torture and death they brought upon the peasantry, increased this hatred. The poor persecuted country people believed that the New Forest was enchanted. They said that in thunder-storms, and on dark nights, demons appeared, moving beneath the branches of the gloomy trees. They said that a terrible spectre had foretold to Norman hunters that the Red King should be punished there. And now, in the pleasant season of May, when the Red King had reigned almost thirteen years; and a second Prince of the Conqueror's blood – another Richard, the son of Duke Robert – was killed by an arrow in this dreaded Forest; the people said that the second time was not the last, and that there was another death to come.

It was a lonely forest, accursed in the people's hearts for the wicked deeds that had been done to make it; and no man save the King and his Courtiers and Huntsmen, liked to stray there. But, in reality, it was like any other forest. In the spring, the green leaves broke out of the buds; in the summer, flourished heartily, and made deep shades; in the winter, shrivelled and blew down, and lay in brown heaps on the moss. Some trees were stately, and grew high and strong; some had fallen of themselves; some were felled by the forester's axe; some were hollow, and the rabbits burrowed at their roots; some few were struck by lightning, and stood white and bare. There were hill-sides covered with rich fern, on which the morning dew so beautifully sparkled; there were brooks, where the deer went down to drink, or over which the whole herd bounded, flying from the arrows of the huntsmen; there were sunny glades, and solemn places where but little light came through the rustling leaves. The songs of the birds in the New Forest were pleasanter to hear than the shouts of fighting men outside; and even when the Red King and his Court came hunting through its solitudes, cursing loud and riding hard, with a jingling of stirrups and bridles and knives and daggers, they did much less harm there than among the English or Normans, and the stags died (as they lived) far easier than the people.

Upon a day in August, the Red King, now reconciled to his brother, Fine-Scholar, came with a great train to hunt in the New Forest. Fine-Scholar was of the party. They were a merry party, and had lain all night at Malwood-Keep, a hunting-lodge in the forest, where they had made good cheer, both at supper and breakfast, and had drunk a deal of wine. The party

The Finding of the Body of Rufus

dispersed in various directions, as the custom of hunters then was. The King took with him only SIR WALTER TYRREL, who was a famous sportsman, and to whom he had given, before they mounted horse that morning, two fine arrows.

The last time the King was ever seen alive, he was riding with Sir Walter Tyrrel, and their dogs were hunting together.

It was almost night, when a poor charcoal-burner, passing through the forest with his cart, came upon the solitary body of a dead man, shot with an arrow in the breast, and still bleeding. He got it into his cart. It was the body of the King. Shaken and tumbled, with its red beard all whitened with lime and clotted with blood, it was driven in the cart by the charcoal-burner next day to Winchester Cathedral, where it was received and buried.

Sir Walter Tyrrel, who escaped to Normandy, and claimed the protection of the King of France, swore in France that the Red King was suddenly shot dead by an arrow from an unseen hand, while they were hunting together; that he was fearful of being suspected as the King's murderer; and that he instantly set spurs to his horse, and fled to the sea-shore. Others declared that the King and Sir Walter Tyrrel were hunting in company, a little before sunset, standing in bushes opposite one another, when a stag came between them. That the King drew his bow and took aim, but the string broke. That the King then cried, 'Shoot, Walter, in the Devil's name!' That Sir Walter shot. That the arrow glanced against a tree, was turned aside from the stag, and struck the King from his horse, dead.

By whose hand the Red King really fell, and whether that hand despatched the arrow to his breast by accident or by design, is only known to GOD. Some think his brother may have caused him to be killed; but the Red King had made so many enemies, both among priests and people, that suspicion may reasonably rest upon a less unnatural murderer. Men know no more than that he was found dead in the New Forest, which the suffering people had regarded as a doomed ground for his race.

CHAPTER 10

England under Henry the First, called Fine-Scholar

FINE-SCHOLAR, on hearing of the Red King's death, hurried to Winchester with as much speed as Rufus himself had made, to seize the Royal treasure. But the keeper of the treasure, who had been one of the hunting-party in the Forest, made haste to Winchester too, and, arriving there at about the same time, refused to yield it up. Upon this, Fine-Scholar drew his sword, and threatened to kill the treasurer; who might have paid for his fidelity with his life, but that he knew longer resistance to be useless when he found the Prince supported by a company of powerful barons, who declared they were determined to make him King. The treasurer, therefore, gave up the money and jewels of the Crown: and on the third day after the death of the Red King, being a Sunday, Fine-Scholar stood before the high altar in Westminster Abbey, and made a solemn declaration that he would resign the Church property which his brother had seized; that he would do no wrong to the nobles; and that he would restore to the people the laws of Edward the Confessor, with all the improvements of William the Conqueror. So began the reign of KING HENRY THE FIRST.

The people were attached to their new King, both because he had known distresses, and because he was an Englishman by birth and not a Norman. To strengthen this last hold upon them, the King wished to marry an English lady; and could think of no other wife than MAUD THE GOOD, the daughter of the King of Scotland. Although this good Princess did not love the King, she was so affected by the representations the nobles made to her of the great charity it would be in her to unite the Norman and Saxon races, and prevent hatred and bloodshed between them for the future, that she consented to become his wife. After some disputing among the priests, who said that as she had been in a convent in her youth, and had worn the veil of a nun, she could not lawfully be married – against which the Princess stated that her aunt, with whom she had lived in her youth, had indeed sometimes thrown a piece of black stuff over her, but for no other reason than because the nun's veil was the only dress the conquering Normans respected in girl or woman, and not because she had taken the vows of a nun, which she never had – she was declared free to marry, and was made King Henry's Queen. A good Queen she was; beautiful, kind-hearted, and worthy of a better husband than the King.

For he was a cunning and unscrupulous man, though firm and clever. He cared very little for his word, and took any means to gain his ends. All this is shown in his treatment of his brother Robert – Robert, who had suffered him to be refreshed with water, and who had sent him the wine from his own table, when he was shut up, with the crows flying below him, parched with thirst, in the castle on the top of St Michael's Mount, where his Red brother would have let him die.

Before the King began to deal with Robert, he removed and disgraced all the favourites of the late King; who were for the most part base characters, much detested by the people. Flambard, or Firebrand, whom the late King had made Bishop of Durham, of all things in the world, Henry imprisoned in the Tower; but Firebrand was a great joker and a jolly companion, and made himself so popular with his guards that they pretended to know nothing about a long rope that was sent into his prison at the bottom of a deep flagon of wine. The guards took the wine, and Firebrand took the rope; with which, when they were fast asleep, he let himself down from a window in the night, and so got cleverly aboard ship and away to Normandy.

Now Robert, when his brother Fine-Scholar came to the throne, was still absent in the Holy Land. Henry pretended that Robert had been made Sovereign of that country; and he had been away so long, that the ignorant people believed it. But, behold, when Henry had been some time King of England, Robert came home to Normandy; having leisurely returned from Jerusalem through Italy, in which beautiful country he had enjoyed himself very much, and had married a lady as beautiful as itself! In Normandy, he found Firebrand waiting to urge him to assert his claim to the English crown, and declare war against King Henry. This, after great loss of time in feasting and dancing with his beautiful Italian wife among his Norman friends, he at last did.

The English in general were on King Henry's side, though many of the Normans were on Robert's. But the English sailors deserted the King, and took a great part of the English fleet over to Normandy; so that Robert came to invade this country in no foreign vessels, but in English ships. The virtuous Anselm, however, whom Henry had invited back from abroad, and made Archbishop of Canterbury, was steadfast in the King's cause; and it was so well supported that the two armies, instead of fighting, made a peace. Poor Robert, who trusted anybody and everybody, readily trusted his brother, the King; and agreed to go home and receive a pension from England, on condition that all his followers were fully pardoned. This the King very faithfully promised, but Robert was no sooner gone than he began to punish them.

Among them was the Earl of Shrewsbury, who, on being summoned by the King to answer to five-and-forty accusations, rode away to one of his strong castles, shut himself up therein, called around him his tenants and vassals, and fought for his liberty, but was defeated and banished. Robert with all his faults, was so true to his word, that when he first heard of this nobleman having risen against his brother, he laid waste the Earl of Shrewsbury's estates in Normandy, to show the King that he would favour no breach of their treaty. Finding, on better information, afterwards, that the Earl's only crime was having been his friend, he came over to England, in his old thoughtless warm-hearted way, to intercede with the King, and remind him of the solemn promise to pardon all his followers.

This confidence might have put the false King to the blush, but it did not. Pretending to be very friendly, he so surrounded his brother with spies and traps, that Robert, who was quite in his power, had nothing for it but to renounce his pension and escape while he could. Getting home to Normandy, and understanding the King better now, he naturally allied himself with his old friend the Earl of Shrewsbury, who had still thirty castles in that country. This was exactly what Henry wanted. He immediately declared that Robert had broken the treaty, and next year invaded Normandy.

He pretended that he came to deliver the Normans, at their own request, from his brother's misrule. There is reason to fear that his misrule was bad enough; for his beautiful wife had died, leaving him with an infant son, and his court was again so careless, dissipated, and ill-regulated, that it was said he sometimes lay in bed of a day for want of clothes to put on – his attendants having stolen all his dresses. But he headed his army like a brave prince and a gallant soldier, though he had the misfortune to be taken prisoner by King Henry, with four hundred of his Knights. Among them was poor harmless Edgar Atheling, who loved Robert well. Edgar was not important enough to be severe with. The King afterwards gave him a small pension, which he lived upon and died upon, in peace, among the quiet woods and fields of England.

And Robert – poor, kind, generous, wasteful, heedless Robert, with so many faults, and yet with virtues that might have made a better and a happier man – what was the end of him? If the King had had the magnanimity to say with a kind air, 'Brother, tell me, before these noblemen, that from this time you will be my faithful follower and friend, and never raise your hand against me or my forces more!' he might have trusted Robert to the death. But the King was not a magnanimous man. He sentenced his brother to be confined for life in one of the Royal Castles. In the beginning of his imprisonment, he was allowed to ride out, guarded; but he one day broke away from his guard and galloped off. He had the evil fortune to ride into a swamp, where his horse stuck fast and he was taken. When the King heard of it he ordered him to be blinded, which was done by putting a red-hot metal basin on his eyes.

And so, in darkness and in prison, many years, he thought of all his past life, of the time he had wasted, of the treasure he had squandered, of the opportunities he had lost, of the youth he had thrown away, of the talents he had neglected. Sometimes, on fine autumn mornings, he would sit and think of the old hunting parties in the free Forest, where he had been the foremost and the gayest. Sometimes, in the still nights, he would wake, and mourn for the many nights that had stolen past him at the gaming-table; sometimes, would seem to hear, upon the melancholy wind, the old songs of the minstrels; sometimes, would dream, in his blindness, of the light and glitter of the Norman Court. Many and many a time, he groped back, in his fancy, to Jerusalem, where he had fought so well; or, at the head of his brave companions, bowed his feathered helmet to the shouts of welcome greeting him in Italy, and seemed again to walk among the sunny vineyards, or on the shore of the blue sea, with his lovely wife. And then, thinking of her grave, and of his fatherless boy, he would stretch out his solitary arms and weep.

At length, one day, there lay in prison, dead, with cruel and disfiguring scars upon his eyelids, bandaged from his jailer's sight, but on which the eternal Heavens looked down, a worn old man of eighty. He had once been Robert of Normandy. Pity him!

At the time when Robert of Normandy was taken prisoner by his brother, Robert's little son was only five years old. This child was taken, too, and carried before the King, sobbing and crying; for, young as he was, he knew he had good reason to be afraid of his Royal uncle. The King was not much accustomed to pity those who were in his power, but his cold heart seemed for the moment to soften towards the boy. He was observed to make a great effort, as if to prevent himself from being cruel, and ordered the child to be taken away; whereupon a certain Baron, who had married a daughter of Duke Robert's (by name, Helie of Saint Saen), took charge of him, tenderly. The King's gentleness did not last long. Before two years were over, he sent messengers to this lord's Castle to seize the child and bring him away. The Baron was not there at the time, but his servants were faithful, and carried the boy off in his sleep and hid him. When the Baron came home, and was told what the King had done, he took the child abroad, and, leading him by the hand, went from King to King and from Court to Court, relating how the child had a claim to the throne of England, and how his uncle the King, knowing that he had that claim, would have murdered him, perhaps, but for his escape.

The youth and innocence of the pretty little WILLIAM FITZ-ROBERT (for that was his name) made him many friends at that time. When he became a young man, the King of France, uniting with the French Counts of Anjou and Flanders, supported his cause against the King of England, and took many of the King's towns and castles in Normandy. But, King Henry, artful and cunning always, bribed some of William's friends with money, some with promises, some with power. He bought off the Count of Anjou, by promising to marry his eldest son, also named WILLIAM, to the Count's daughter; and indeed the whole trust of this King's life was in such bargains, and he believed (as many another King has done since, and as one King did in France a very little time ago) that every man's truth and honour can be bought at some price. For all this, he was so afraid of William Fitz-Robert and his friends, that for a long time he believed his life to be in danger; and never lay down to sleep, even in his palace surrounded by his guards, without having a sword and buckler at his bedside.

To strengthen his power, the King with great ceremony betrothed his eldest daughter MATILDA, then a child only eight years old, to be the wife of Henry the Fifth, the Emperor of Germany. To raise her marriage-portion, he taxed the English people in a most oppressive manner; then treated them to a great procession, to restore their good humour; and sent Matilda away, in fine state, with the German ambassadors, to be educated in the country of her future husband.

And now his Queen, Maud the Good, unhappily died. It was a sad thought for that gentle lady, that the only hope with which she had married a man whom she had never loved – the hope of reconciling the Norman and English races – had failed. At the very time of her death, Normandy and all France was in arms against England; for, so soon as his last danger was over, King Henry had been false to all the French powers he had promised, bribed, and bought, and they had naturally united against him. After some fighting, however, in which few suffered but the unhappy common people (who always suffered, whatsoever was the matter), he began to promise, bribe, and buy again; and by those means, and by the help of the Pope, who exerted himself to save more bloodshed, and by solemnly declaring, over and over again, that he really was in earnest this time, and would keep his word, the King made peace.

One of the first consequences of this peace was, that the King went over to Normandy with his son Prince William and a great retinue, to have the Prince acknowledged as his successor by the Norman Nobles, and to contract the promised marriage (this was one of the many promises the King had broken) between him and the daughter of the Count of Anjou. Both these things were triumphantly done, with great show and rejoicing; and on the twenty-fifth of November, in the year one thousand one hundred and twenty, the whole retinue prepared to embark at the Port of Barfleur, for the voyage home.

On that day, and at that place, there came to the King, Fitz-Stephen, a sea-captain, and said:

'My liege, my father served your father all his life, upon the sea. He steered the ship with the golden boy upon the prow, in which your father sailed to conquer England. I beseech you to grant me the same office. I have a fair vessel in the harbour here, called The White Ship, manned by fifty sailors of renown. I pray you, Sire, to let your servant have the honour of steering you in The White Ship to England!'

'I am sorry, friend,' replied the King, 'that my vessel is already chosen, and that I cannot (therefore) sail with the son of the man who served my father. But the Prince and all his company shall go along with you, in the fair White Ship, manned by the fifty sailors of renown.'

An hour or two afterwards, the King set sail in the vessel he had chosen, accompanied by other vessels, and, sailing all night with a fair and gentle wind, arrived upon the coast of England in the morning. While it was yet night, the people in some of those ships heard a faint wild cry come over the sea, and wondered what it was.

Now, the Prince was a dissolute, debauched young man of eighteen, who bore no love to the English, and had declared that when he came to the throne he would yoke them to the plough like oxen. He went aboard The White Ship, with one hundred and forty youthful Nobles like himself, among whom were eighteen noble ladies of the highest rank. All this gay company, with their servants and the fifty sailors, made three hundred souls aboard the fair White Ship.

'Give three casks of wine, Fitz-Stephen,' said the Prince, 'to the fifty sailors of renown! My father the King has sailed out of the harbour. What time is there to make merry here, and yet reach England with the rest?'

'Prince,' said Fitz-Stephen, 'before morning, my fifty and The White Ship shall overtake the swiftest vessel in attendance on your father the King, if we sail at midnight!'

Then, the Prince commanded to make merry; and the sailors drank out the three casks of wine; and the Prince and all the noble company danced in the moonlight on the deck of The White Ship.

When, at last, she shot out of the harbour of Barfleur, there was not a sober seaman on board. But the sails were all set, and the oars all going merrily. Fitz-Stephen had the helm. The gay young nobles and the beautiful ladies, wrapped in mantles of various bright colours to protect them from the cold, talked, laughed, and sang. The Prince encouraged the fifty sailors to row harder yet, for the honour of The White Ship.

Crash! A terrific cry broke from three hundred hearts. It was the cry the people in the distant vessels of the King heard faintly on the water. The White Ship had struck upon a rock – was filling – going down!

Fitz-Stephen hurried the Prince into a boat, with some few Nobles. 'Push off,' he whispered; 'and row to land. It is not far, and the sea is smooth. The rest of us must die.'

But, as they rowed away, fast, from the sinking ship, the Prince heard the voice of his sister MARIE, the Countess of Perche, calling for help. He never in his life had been so good as he was then. He cried in an agony, 'Row back at any risk! I cannot bear to leave her!'

They rowed back. As the Prince held out his arms to catch his sister, such numbers leaped in, that the boat was overset. And in the same instant The White Ship went down.

Only two men floated. They both clung to the main yard of the ship, which had broken from the mast, and now supported them. One asked the other who he was? He said, 'I am a nobleman, GODFREY by name, the son of GILBERT DE L'AIGLE. And you?' said he. 'I am BEROLD, a poor butcher of Rouen,' was the answer. Then, they said together, 'Lord, be merciful to us both!' and tried to encourage one another, as they drifted in the cold benumbing sea on that unfortunate November night.

By-and-by, another man came swimming towards them, whom they knew, when he pushed aside his long wet hair, to be Fitz-Stephen. 'Where is the Prince?' said he. 'Gone! Gone!' the two cried together. 'Neither he, nor his brother, nor his sister, nor the King's niece, nor her brother, nor any one of all the brave three hundred, noble or commoner, except we three, has risen above the water!' Fitz-Stephen, with a ghastly face, cried, 'Woe! woe, to me!' and sunk to the bottom.

The other two clung to the yard for some hours. At length the young noble said faintly, 'I am exhausted, and chilled with the cold, and can hold no longer. Farewell, good friend! God preserve you!' So, he dropped and sunk; and of all the brilliant crowd, the poor Butcher of Rouen alone was saved. In the morning, some fishermen saw him floating in his sheep-skin coat, and got him into their boat – the sole relater of the dismal tale.

For three days, no one dared to carry the intelligence to the King. At length, they sent into his presence a little boy, who, weeping bitterly, and kneeling at his feet, told him that The White Ship was lost with all on board. The King fell to the ground like a dead man, and never, never afterwards, was seen to smile.

But he plotted again, and promised again, and bribed and bought again, in his old deceitful way. Having no son to succeed him, after all his pains ('The Prince will never yoke us to the plough, now!' said the English people), he took a second wife – ADELAIS or ALICE, a duke's daughter, and the Pope's niece. Having no more children, however, he proposed to the Barons to swear that they would recognise as his successor, his daughter Matilda, whom, as she was now a widow, he married to the eldest son of the Count of Anjou, GEOFFREY, surnamed PLAN-TAGENET, from a custom he had of wearing a sprig of flowering broom (called Genêt in French) in his cap for a feather. As one false man usually makes many, and as a false King, in particular, is pretty certain to make a false Court, the Barons took the oath about the succession of Matilda (and her children after her), twice over, without in the least intending to keep it. The King was now relieved from any remaining fears of William Fitz-Robert, by his death in the Monastery of St Omer, in France, at twenty-six years old, of a pike-wound in the hand. And as Matilda gave birth to three sons, he thought the succession to the throne secure.

He spent most of the latter part of his life, which was troubled by family quarrels, in Normandy, to be near Matilda. When he had reigned upwards of thirty-five years, and was sixty-seven years old, he died of an indigestion and fever, brought on by eating, when he was far from well, of a fish called Lamprey, against which he had often been cautioned by his physicians. His remains were brought over to Reading Abbey to be buried.

You may perhaps hear the cunning and promise-breaking of King Henry the First, called 'policy' by some people, and 'diplomacy' by others. Neither of these fine words will in the least mean that it was true; and nothing that is not true can possibly be good.

His greatest merit, that I know of, was his love of learning. I should have given him greater credit even for that, if it had been strong enough to induce him to spare the eyes of a certain poet he once took prisoner, who was a knight besides. But he ordered the poet's eyes to be torn from his head, because he had laughed at him in his verses; and the poet, in the pain of that torture, dashed out his own brains against his prison wall. King Henry the First was avaricious, revengeful, and so false, that I suppose a man never lived whose word was less to be relied upon.

CHAPTER II

England under Matilda and Stephen

The King was no sooner dead than all the plans and schemes he had laboured at so long, and lied so much for, crumbled away like a hollow heap of sand. STEPHEN, whom he had never mistrusted or suspected, started up to claim the throne.

Stephen was the son of ADELA, the Conqueror's daughter, married to the Count of Blois. To Stephen, and to his brother HENRY, the late King had been liberal; making Henry Bishop of Winchester, and finding a good marriage for Stephen, and much, enriching him. This did not prevent Stephen from hastily producing a false witness, a servant of the late King, to swear that the King had named him for his heir upon his death-bed. On this evidence the Archbishop of Canterbury crowned him. The new King, so suddenly made, lost not a moment in seizing the Royal treasure, and hiring foreign soldiers with some of it to protect his throne.

If the dead King had even done as the false witness said, he would have had small right to will away the English people, like so many sheep or oxen, without their consent. But he had, in fact, bequeathed all his territory to Matilda; who, supported by ROBERT, Earl of Gloucester, soon began to dispute the crown. Some of the powerful barons and priests took her side; some took Stephen's; all fortified their castles; and again the miserable English people were involved in war, from which they could never derive advantage whosoever was victorious, and in which all parties plundered, tortured, starved, and ruined them.

Five years had passed since the death of Henry the First – and during those five years there had been two terrible invasions by the people of Scotland under their King, David, who was at last defeated with all his army – when Matilda, attended by her brother Robert and a large force, appeared in England to maintain her claim. A battle was fought between her troops and King Stephen's at Lincoln; in which the King himself was taken prisoner, after bravely fighting until his battle-axe and sword were broken, and was carried into strict confinement at Gloucester. Matilda then submitted herself to the Priests, and the Priests crowned her Queen of England.

She did not long enjoy this dignity. The people of London had a great affection for Stephen; many of the Barons considered it degrading to be ruled by a woman; and the Queen's temper was so haughty that she made innumerable enemies. The people of London revolted; and, in alliance with the troops of Stephen, besieged her at Winchester, where they took her brother Robert prisoner, whom, as her best soldier and chief general, she was glad to exchange for Stephen himself, who thus regained his liberty. Then, the long war went on afresh. Once, she was pressed so hard in the Castle of Oxford, in the winter weather when the snow lay thick upon the ground, that her only chance of escape was to dress herself all in white, and, accompanied by no more than three faithful Knights, dressed in like manner that their figures might not be seen from Stephen's camp as they passed over the snow, to steal away on foot, cross the frozen Thames, walk a long distance, and at last gallop away on horseback. All this she did, but to no great purpose then; for her brother dying while the struggle was yet going on, she at last withdrew to Normandy.

In two or three years after her withdrawal her cause appeared in England, afresh, in the person of her son Henry, young Plantagenet, who at only eighteen years of age, was very powerful: not only on account of his mother having resigned all Normandy to him, but also from his having married ELEANOR, the divorced wife of the French King, a bad woman, who had great possessions in France. Louis, the French King, not relishing this arrangement, helped EUSTACE, King Stephen's son, to invade Normandy: but Henry drove their united forces out of that country, and then returned here, to assist his partisans, whom the King was then besieging at Wallingford upon the

Thames. Here, for two days, divided only by the river, the two armies lay encamped opposite to one another – on the eve, as it seemed to all men, of another desperate fight, when the EARL OF ARUNDEL took heart and said 'that it was not reasonable to prolong the unspeakable miseries of two kingdoms to minister to the ambition of two princes.'

Many other noblemen repeating and supporting this when it was once uttered, Stephen and young Plantagenet went down, each to his own bank of the river, and held a conversation across it, in which they arranged a truce; very much to the dissatisfaction of Eustace, who swaggered away with some followers and laid violent hands on the Abbey of St Edmund's-Bury, where he presently died mad. The truce led to a solemn council at Winchester, in which it was agreed that Stephen should retain the crown, on condition of his declaring Henry his successor; that WILLIAM, another son of the King's, should inherit his father's rightful possessions; and that all the Crown lands that Stephen had given away should be recalled, and all the Castles he had permitted to be built demolished. Thus terminated the bitter war, which had now lasted fifteen years, and had again laid England waste. In the next year STEPHEN died, after a troubled reign of nineteen years.

Although King Stephen was, for the time in which he lived, a humane and moderate man, with many excellent qualities; and although nothing worse is known of him than his usurpation of the Crown, which he probably excused to himself by the consideration that King Henry the First was an usurper too – which was no excuse at all; the people of England suffered more in these dread nineteen years, than at any former period even of their suffering history. In the division of the nobility between the two rival claimants of the Crown, and in the growth of what is called the Feudal System (which made the peasants the born vassals and mere slaves of the Barons), every Noble had his strong Castle, where he reigned the cruel king of all the neighbouring people. Accordingly, he perpetrated whatever cruelties he chose. And never were worse cruelties committed upon earth than in wretched England in those nineteen years.

The writers who were living then describe them fearfully. They say that the castles were filled with devils rather than with men; that the peasants, men and women, were put into dungeons for their gold and silver, were tortured with fire and smoke, were hung up by the thumbs, were hung up by the heels with great weights to their heads, were torn with jagged irons, killed with hunger, broken to death in narrow chests filled with sharp-pointed stones, murdered in countless fiendish ways. In England there was no corn, no meat, no cheese, no butter, there were no tilled lands, no harvests. Ashes of burnt towns, and dreary wastes, were all that the traveller, fearful of the robbers who prowled abroad at all hours, would see in a long day's journey; and from sunrise until night, he would not come upon a home.

The clergy sometimes suffered, and heavily too, from pillage, but many of them had castles of their own, and fought in helmet and armour like the barons, and drew lots with other fighting men for their share of booty. The Pope (or Bishop of Rome), on King Stephen's resisting his ambition, laid England under an Interdict at one period of this reign; which means that he allowed no service to be performed in the churches, no couples to be married, no bells to be rung, no dead bodies to be buried. Any man having the power to refuse these things, no matter whether he were called a Pope or a Poulterer, would, of course, have the power of afflicting numbers of innocent people. That nothing might be wanting to the miseries of King Stephen's time, the Pope threw in this contribution to the public store – not very like the widow's contribution, as I think, when Our Saviour sat in Jerusalem over against the Treasury, 'and she threw in two mites, which make a farthing.'

CHAPTER 12

England under Henry the Second

First Part

HENRY PLANTAGENET, when he was but twenty-one years old, quietly succeeded to the throne of England, according to his agreement made with the late King at Winchester. Six weeks after Stephen's death, he and his Queen, Eleanor, were crowned in that city; into which they rode on horseback in great state, side by side, amidst much shouting and rejoicing, and clashing of music, and strewing of flowers.

The reign of King Henry the Second began well. The King had great possessions, and (what with his own rights, and what with those of his wife) was lord of one-third part of France. He was a young man of vigour, ability, and resolution, and immediately applied himself to remove some of the evils which had arisen in the last unhappy reign. He revoked all the grants of land that had been hastily made, on either side, during the late struggles; he obliged numbers of disorderly soldiers to depart from England; he reclaimed all the castles belonging to the Crown; and he forced the wicked nobles to pull down their own castles, to the number of eleven hundred, in which such dismal cruelties had been inflicted on the people. The King's brother, GEOFFREY, rose against him in France, while he was so well employed, and rendered it necessary for him to repair to that country; where, after he had subdued and made a friendly arrangement with his brother (who did not live long), his ambition to increase his possessions involved him in a war with the French King, Louis, with whom he had been on such friendly terms just before, that to the French King's infant daughter, then a baby in the cradle, he had promised one of his little sons in marriage, who was a child of five years old. However, the war came to nothing at last, and the Pope made the two Kings friends again.

Now, the clergy, in the troubles of the last reign, had gone on very ill indeed. There were all kinds of criminals among them – murderers, thieves, and vagabonds; and the worst of the matter was, that the good priests would not give up the bad priests to justice, when they committed crimes, but persisted in sheltering and defending them. The King, well knowing that there could be no peace or rest in England while such things lasted, resolved to reduce the power of the clergy; and, when he had reigned seven years, found (as he considered) a good opportunity for doing so, in the death of the Archbishop of Canterbury. 'I will have for the new Archbishop,' thought the King, 'a friend in whom I can trust, who will help me to humble these rebellious priests, and to have them dealt with, when they do wrong, as other men who do wrong are dealt with.' So, he resolved to make his favourite, the new Archbishop; and this favourite was so extraordinary a man, and his story is so curious, that I must tell you all about him.

Once upon a time, a worthy merchant of London, named GILBERT À BECKET, made a pilgrimage to the Holy Land, and was taken prisoner by a Saracen lord. This lord, who treated him kindly and not like a slave, had one fair daughter, who fell in love with the merchant; and who told him that she wanted to become a Christian, and was willing to marry him if they could fly to a Christian country. The merchant returned her love, until he found an opportunity to escape, when he did not trouble himself about the Saracen lady, but escaped with his servant Richard, who had been taken prisoner along with him, and arrived in England and forgot her. The Saracen lady, who was more loving than the merchant, left her father's house in disguise to follow him, and made her way, under many hardships, to the sea-shore. The merchant had taught her only two English words (for I suppose he must have learnt the Saracen tongue himself, and made love in that language), of which LONDON was one, and his own name, GILBERT, the other. She went among the ships, saying, 'London! London!' over and over again, until the sailors understood that she wanted to find an English vessel that would carry her there; so they showed her such a ship, and she paid for her passage with some of her jewels, and sailed away. Well! The merchant was sitting in his counting-house in London one day, when he heard a great noise in the street; and presently Richard came running in from the warehouse, with his eyes wide open and his breath almost gone, saying, 'Master, master, here is the Saracen lady!' The merchant thought Richard was mad; but Richard said, 'No, master! As I live, the Saracen lady is going up and down the city, calling Gilbert! Gilbert!' Then, he took the merchant by the sleeve, and pointed out at window; and there they saw her among the gables and water-spouts of the dark dirty street, in her foreign dress, so forlorn, surrounded by a wondering crowd, and passing slowly along, calling Gilbert, Gilbert! When the merchant saw her, and thought of the tenderness she had shown him in his captivity, and of her constancy, his heart was moved, and he ran down into the street; and she saw him coming, and with a great cry fainted in his arms. They were married without loss of time, and Richard (who was an excellent man) danced with joy the whole day of the wedding; and they all lived happy ever afterwards.

This merchant and this Saracen lady had one son, THOMAS À BECKET. He it was who became the Favourite of King Henry the Second.

He had become Chancellor, when the King thought of making him Archbishop. He was clever, gay, well educated, brave; had fought in several battles in France; had defeated a French knight in single combat, and brought his horse away as a token of the victory. He lived in a noble palace, he was the tutor of the young Prince Henry, he was served by one hundred and forty knights, his riches were immense. The King once sent him as his ambassador to France; and the French people, beholding in what state he travelled, cried out in the streets, 'How splendid must the King of England be, when this is only the Chancellor!' They had good reason to wonder at the magnificence of Thomas à Becket, for, when he entered a French town, his procession was headed by two hundred and fifty singing boys; then, came his hounds in couples; then, eight waggons, each drawn by five horses driven by five drivers: two of the waggons filled with strong ale to be given away to the people; four, with his gold and silver plate and stately clothes; two, with the dresses of his numerous servants. Then, came twelve horses, each with a monkey on his back; then, a train of people bearing shields and leading fine war-horses splendidly equipped; then, falconers with hawks upon their wrists; then, a host of knights, and gentlemen and priests; then, the Chancellor with his brilliant garments flashing in the sun, and all the people capering and shouting with delight.

The King was well pleased with all this, thinking that it only made himself the more magnificent to have so magnificent a favourite; but he sometimes jested with the Chancellor upon his splendour too. Once, when they were riding together through the streets of London in hard winter weather, they saw a shivering old man in rags. 'Look at the poor object!' said the King. 'Would it not be a charitable act to give that aged man a comfortable warm cloak?' 'Undoubtedly it would,' said Thomas à Becket, 'and you do well, Sir, to think of such Christian duties.' 'Come!' cried the King, 'then give him your cloak!' It was made of rich crimson trimmed with ermine. The King tried to pull it off, the Chancellor tried to keep it on, both were near rolling from their saddles in the mud, when the Chancellor submitted, and the King gave the cloak to the old beggar: much to the beggar's astonishment, and much to the merriment of all the courtiers in attendance. For, courtiers are not only eager to laugh when the King laughs, but they really do enjoy a laugh against a Favourite.

'I will make,' thought King Henry the Second, 'this Chancellor of mine, Thomas à Becket, Archbishop of Canterbury. He will then be the head of the Church, and, being devoted to me, will help me to correct the Church. He has always upheld my power against the power of the clergy, and once publicly told some bishops (I remember), that men of the Church were equally bound to me with men of the sword. Thomas à Becket is the man, of all other men in England, to help me in my great design.' So the King, regardless of all objection, either that he was a fighting man, or a lavish man, or a courtly man, or a man of pleasure, or anything but a likely man for the office, made him Archbishop accordingly.

Now, Thomas à Becket was proud and loved to be famous. He was already famous for the pomp of his life, for his riches, his gold and silver plate, his waggons, horses, and attendants. He could do no more in that way than he had done; and being tired of that kind of fame (which is a very poor one), he longed to have his name celebrated for something else. Nothing, he knew, would render him so famous in the world, as the setting of his utmost power and ability against the utmost power and ability of the King. He resolved with the whole strength of his mind to do it.

He may have had some secret grudge against the King besides. The King may have offended his proud humour at some time or other, for anything I know. I think it likely, because it is a common thing for Kings, Princes, and other great people, to try the tempers of their favourites rather severely. Even the little affair of the crimson cloak must have been anything but a pleasant one to a haughty man. Thomas à Becket knew better than any one in England what the King expected of him. In all his sumptuous life, he had never yet been in a position to disappoint the King. He could take up that proud stand now, as head of the Church; and he determined that it should be written in history, either that he subdued the King, or that the King subdued him.

So, of a sudden, he completely altered the whole manner of his life. He turned off all his brilliant followers, ate coarse food, drank bitter water, wore next his skin sackcloth covered with dirt and vermin (for it was then thought very religious to be very dirty), flogged his back to punish himself, lived chiefly in a little cell, washed the feet of thirteen poor people every day, and looked as miserable as he possibly could. If he had put twelve hundred monkeys on horseback instead of twelve, and had gone in procession with eight thousand waggons instead of eight, he could not have half astonished the people so much as by this great change. It soon caused him to be more talked about as an Archbishop than he had been as a Chancellor.

The King was very angry; and was made still more so, when the new Archbishop, claiming various estates from the nobles as being rightfully Church property, required the King himself, for the same reason, to give up Rochester Castle, and Rochester City too. Not satisfied with this, he declared that no power but himself should appoint a priest to any Church in the part of England over which he was Archbishop; and when a certain gentleman of Kent made such an appointment, as he claimed to have the right to do, Thomas à Becket excommunicated him.

Excommunication was, next to the Interdict I told you of at the close of the last chapter, the great weapon of the clergy. It consisted in declaring the person who was excommunicated, an outcast from the Church and from all religious offices; and in cursing him all over, from the top of his head to the sole of his feet, whether he was standing up, lying down, sitting, kneeling, walking, running, hopping, jumping, gaping, coughing, sneezing, or whatever else he was doing. This unchristian nonsense would of course have made no sort of difference to the person cursed – who could say his prayers at home if he were shut out of church, and whom none but GOD could judge – but for the fears and superstitions of the people, who avoided excommunicated persons, and made their lives unhappy. So, the King said to the new Archbishop, 'Take off this Excommunication from this gentleman of Kent.' To which the Archbishop replied, 'I shall do no such thing.'

The quarrel went on. A priest in Worcestershire committed a most dreadful murder, that aroused the horror of the whole nation. The King demanded to have this wretch delivered up, to be tried in the same court and in the same way as any other murderer. The Archbishop refused, and kept him in the Bishop's prison. The King, holding a solemn assembly in Westminster

Hall, demanded that in future all priests found guilty before their Bishops of crimes against the law of the land should be considered priests no longer, and should be delivered over to the law of the land for punishment. The Archbishop again refused. The King required to know whether the clergy would obey the ancient customs of the country? Every priest there, but one, said, after Thomas à Becket, 'Saving my order.' This really meant that they would only obey those customs when they did not interfere with their own claims; and the King went out of the Hall in great wrath.

Some of the clergy began to be afraid, now, that they were going too far. Though Thomas à Becket was otherwise as unmoved as Westminster Hall, they prevailed upon him, for the sake of their fears, to go to the King at Woodstock, and promise to observe the ancient customs of the country, without saying anything about his order. The King received this submission favourably, and summoned a great council of the clergy to meet at the Castle of Clarendon, by Salisbury. But when the council met, the Archbishop again insisted on the words, 'saving my order;' and he still insisted, though lords entreated him, and priests wept before him and knelt to him, and an adjoining room was thrown open, filled with armed soldiers of the King, to threaten him. At length he gave way, for that time, and the ancient customs (which included what the King had demanded in vain) were stated in writing, and were signed and sealed by the chief of the clergy, and were called the Constitutions of Clarendon.

The quarrel went on, for all that. The Archbishop tried to see the King. The King would not see him. The Archbishop tried to escape from England. The sailors on the coast would launch no boat to take him away. Then, he again resolved to do his worst in opposition to the King, and began openly to set the ancient customs at defiance.

The King summoned him before a great council at Northampton, where he accused him of high treason, and made a claim against him, which was not a just one, for an enormous sum of money. Thomas à Becket was alone against the whole assembly, and the very Bishops advised him to resign his office and abandon his contest with the King. His great anxiety and agitation stretched him on a sick-bed for two days, but he was still undaunted. He went to the adjourned council, carrying a great cross in his right hand, and sat down holding it erect before him. The King angrily retired into an inner room. The whole assembly angrily retired and left him there. But there he sat. The Bishops came out again in a body and renounced him as a traitor. He only said, 'I hear!' and sat there still. They retired again into the inner room, and his trial proceeded without him. By-and-by, the Earl of Leicester, heading the barons, came out to read his sentence. He refused to hear it, denied the power of the court, and said he would refer his cause to the Pope. As he walked out of the hall, with the cross in his hand, some of those present picked up rushes – rushes were strewn upon the floors in those days by way of carpet – and threw them at him. He proudly turned his head, and said that were he not Archbishop, he would chastise those cowards with the sword he had known how to use in bygone days. He then mounted his horse, and rode away, cheered and surrounded by the common people, to whom he threw open his house that night and gave a supper, supping with them himself. That same night he secretly departed from the town; and so, travelling by night and hiding by day, and calling himself 'Brother Dearman,' got away, not without difficulty, to Flanders.

The struggle still went on. The angry King took possession of the revenues of the archbishopric, and banished all the relations and servants of Thomas à Becket, to the number of four hundred. The Pope and the French King both protected him, and an abbey was assigned for his residence. Stimulated by this support, Thomas à Becket, on a great festival day, formally proceeded to a great church crowded with people, and going up into the pulpit publicly cursed and excommunicated all who had supported the Constitutions of Clarendon: mentioning many English noblemen by name, and not distantly hinting at the King of England himself.

When intelligence of this new affront was carried to the King in his chamber, his passion was so furious that he tore his clothes, and rolled like a madman on his bed of straw and rushes. But he was soon up and doing. He ordered all the ports and coasts of England to be narrowly watched, that no letters of Interdict might be brought into the kingdom; and sent messengers and bribes to the Pope's palace at Rome. Meanwhile, Thomas à Becket, for his part, was not idle at Rome, but constantly employed his utmost arts in his own behalf. Thus the contest stood, until there was peace between France and England (which had been for some time at war), and until the two children of the two Kings were married in celebration of it. Then, the French King brought about a meeting between Henry and his old favourite, so long his enemy.

Even then, though Thomas à Becket knelt before the King, he was obstinate and immovable as to those words about his order. King Louis of France was weak enough in his veneration for Thomas à Becket and such men, but this was a little too much for him. He said that à Becket 'wanted to be greater than the saints and better than St Peter,' and rode away from him with the King of England. His poor French Majesty asked à Becket's pardon for so doing, however, soon afterwards, and cut a very pitiful figure.

At last, and after a world of trouble, it came to this. There was another meeting on French ground between King Henry and Thomas à Becket, and it was agreed that Thomas à Becket should be Archbishop of Canterbury, according to the customs of former Archbishops, and that the King should put him in possession of the revenues of that post. And now, indeed, you might suppose the struggle at an end, and Thomas à Becket at rest. No, not even yet. For Thomas à Becket hearing, by some means, that King Henry, when he was in dread of his kingdom being placed under an interdict, had had his eldest son Prince Henry secretly crowned, not only persuaded the Pope to suspend the Archbishop of York who had performed that ceremony, and to excommunicate the Bishops who had assisted at it, but sent a messenger of his own into England, in spite of all the King's precautions along the coast, who delivered the letters of excommunication into the Bishops' own hands. Thomas à Becket then came over to England himself, after an absence of seven years. He was privately warned that it was dangerous to come, and that an ireful knight, named RANULF DE BROC, had threatened that he should not live to eat a loaf of bread in England; but he came.

The common people received him well, and marched about with him in a soldierly way, armed with such rustic weapons as they could get. He tried to see the young prince who had once been his pupil, but was prevented. He hoped for some little support among the nobles and priests, but found none. He made the most of the peasants who attended him, and feasted them, and went from Canterbury to Harrow-on-the-Hill, and from Harrow-on-the-Hill back to Canterbury, and on Christmas Day preached in the Cathedral there, and told the people in his sermon that he had come to die among them, and that it was likely he would be murdered. He had no fear, however – or, if he had any, he had much more obstinacy – for he, then and there, excommunicated three of his enemies, of whom Ranulf de Broc the ireful knight was one.

As men in general had no fancy for being cursed, in their sitting and walking, and gaping and sneezing, and all the rest of it, it was very natural in the persons so freely excommunicated to complain to the King. It was equally natural in the King, who had hoped that this troublesome opponent was at last quieted, to fall into a mighty rage when he heard of these new affronts; and, on the Archbishop of York telling him that he never could hope for rest while Thomas à Becket lived, to cry out hastily before his court, 'Have I no one here who will deliver me from this man?' There were four knights present, who, hearing the King's words, looked at one another, and went out.

The names of these knights were REGINALD FITZURSE, WILLIAM TRACY, HUGH DE MORVILLE, and RICHARD BRITO; three of whom had been in the train of Thomas à Becket in the old days of his splendour. They rode away on horseback, in a very secret manner, and on the third day after Christmas Day arrived at Saltwood House, not far from Canterbury, which belonged to the family of Ranulf de Broc. They quietly collected some followers here, in case they should need any; and proceeding to Canterbury, suddenly appeared (the four knights and twelve men) before the Archbishop, in his own house, at two o'clock in the afternoon. They neither bowed nor spoke, but sat down on the floor in silence, staring at the Archbishop.

Thomas à Becket said, at length, 'What do you want?'

'We want,' said Reginald Fitzurse, 'the excommunication taken from the Bishops, and you to answer for your offences to the King.'

Thomas à Becket defiantly replied, that the power of the clergy was above the power of the King. That it was not for such men as they were, to threaten him. That if he were threatened by all the swords in England, he would never yield.

'Then we will do more than threaten!' said the knights. And

they went out with the twelve men, and put on their armour, and drew their shining swords, and came back.

His servants, in the meantime, had shut up and barred the great gate of the Palace. At first, the knights tried to shatter it with their battle-axes; but, being shown a window by which they could enter, they let the gate alone, and climbed in that way. While they were battering at the door, the attendants of Thomas à Becket had implored him to take refuge in the Cathedral; in which, as a sanctuary or sacred place, they thought the knights would dare to do no violent deed. He told them, again and again, that he would not stir. Hearing the distant voices of the monks singing the evening service, however, he said it was now his duty to attend, and therefore, and for no other reason, he would go.

There was a near way between his Palace and the Cathedral, by some beautiful old cloisters which you may yet see. He went into the Cathedral, without any hurry, and having the Cross carried before him as usual. When he was safely there, his servants would have fastened the door, but he said No! it was the house of God and not a fortress.

As he spoke, the shadow of Reginald Fitzurse appeared in the Cathedral doorway, darkening the little light there was outside, on the dark winter evening. This knight said, in a strong voice, 'Follow me, loyal servants of the King!' The rattle of the armour of the other knights echoed through the Cathedral, as they came clashing in.

It was so dark, in the lofty aisles and among the stately pillars of the church, and there were so many hiding-places in the crypt below and in the narrow passages above, that Thomas à Becket might even at that pass have saved himself if he would. But he would not. He told the monks resolutely that he would not. And though they all dispersed and left him there with no other follower than EDWARD GRYME, his faithful cross-bearer, he was as firm then, as ever he had been in his life.

The knights came on, through the darkness, making a terrible noise with their armed tread upon the stone pavement of the church. 'Where is the traitor?' they cried out. He made no answer. But when they cried, 'Where is the Archbishop?' he said proudly, 'I am here!' and came out of the shade and stood before them.

The knights had no desire to kill him, if they could rid the

King and themselves of him by any other means. They told him he must either fly or go with them. He said he would do neither; and he threw William Tracy off with such force when he took hold of his sleeve, that Tracy reeled again. By his reproaches and his steadiness, he so incensed them, and exasperated their fierce humour, that Reginald Fitzurse, whom he called by an ill name, said, 'Then die!' and struck at his head. But the faithful Edward Gryme put out his arm, and there received the main force of the blow, so that it only made his master bleed. Another voice from among the knights again called to Thomas à Becket to fly; but, with his blood running down his face, and his hands clasped, and his head bent, he commended himself to God, and stood firm. Then they cruelly killed him close to the altar of St Bennet; and his body fell upon the pavement, which was dirtied with his blood and brains.

It is an awful thing to think of the murdered mortal, who had so showered his curses about, lying, all disfigured, in the church, where a few lamps here and there were but red specks on a pall of darkness; and to think of the guilty knights riding away on horseback, looking over their shoulders at the dim Cathedral, and remembering what they had left inside.

Second Part

When the King heard how Thomas à Becket had lost his life in Canterbury Cathedral, through the ferocity of the four Knights, he was filled with dismay. Some have supposed that when the King spoke those hasty words, 'Have I no one here who will deliver me from this man?' he wished, and meant à Becket to be slain. But few things are more unlikely; for, besides that the King was not naturally cruel (though very passionate), he was wise, and must have known full well what any stupid man in his dominions must have known, namely, that such a murder would rouse the Pope and the whole Church against him.

He sent respectful messengers to the Pope, to represent his innocence (except in having uttered the hasty words); and he swore solemnly and publicly to his innocence, and contrived in time to make his peace. As to the four guilty Knights, who fled into Yorkshire, and never again dared to show themselves at Court, the Pope excommunicated them; and they lived miserably for some time, shunned by all their countrymen. At last, they went humbly to Jerusalem as a penance, and there died and were buried.

It happened, fortunately for the pacifying of the Pope, that an opportunity arose very soon after the murder of à Becket, for the King to declare his power in Ireland – which was an acceptable undertaking to the Pope, as the Irish, who had been converted to Christianity by one Patricius (otherwise Saint Patrick) long ago, before any Pope existed, considered that the Pope had nothing at all to do with them, or they with the Pope, and accordingly refused to pay him Peter's Pence, or that tax of a penny a house which I have elsewhere mentioned. The King's opportunity arose in this way.

The Irish were, at that time, as barbarous a people as you can well imagine. They were continually quarrelling and fighting, cutting one another's throats, slicing one another's noses, burning one another's houses, carrying away one another's wives, and committing all sorts of violence. The country was divided into five kingdoms – DESMOND, THOMOND, CONNAUGHT, ULSTER, and LEINSTER – each governed by a separate King, of whom one claimed to be the chief of the rest. Now, one of these Kings, named DERMOND MAC MURROUGH (a wild kind of name, spelt in more than one wild kind of way), had carried off the wife of a friend of his, and concealed her on an island in a bog. The friend resenting this (though it was quite the custom of the country), complained to the chief King, and, with the chief King's help, drove Dermond Mac Murrough out of his dominions. Dermond came over to England for revenge; and offered to hold his realm as a vassal of King Henry, if King Henry would help him to regain it. The King consented to these terms; but only assisted him, then, with what were called Letters Patent, authorising any English subjects who were so disposed, to enter into his services, and aid his cause.

There was, at Bristol, a certain EARL RICHARD DE CLARE, called STRONGBOW; of no very good character; needy and desperate, and ready for anything that offered him a chance of improving his fortunes. There were, in South Wales, two other broken knights of the same good-for-nothing sort, called ROBERT FITZ-STEPHEN and MAURICE FITZ-GERALD. These three, each with a small band of followers, took up Dermond's cause; and it was agreed that if it proved successful, Strongbow should marry Dermond's daughter EVA, and be declared his heir.

The trained English followers of these knights were so superior in all the discipline of battle to the Irish, that they beat them against immense superiority of numbers. In one fight, early in the war, they cut off three hundred heads, and laid them before Mac Murrough; who turned them every one up with his hands, rejoicing, and, coming to one which was the head of a man whom he had much disliked, grasped it by the hair and ears, and tore off the nose and lips with his teeth. You may judge from this, what kind of a gentleman an Irish King in those times was. The captives, all through this war, were horribly treated; the victorious party making nothing of breaking their limbs, and casting them into the sea from the tops of high rocks. It was in the midst of the miseries and cruelties attendant on the taking of Waterford, where the dead lay piled in the streets, and the filthy gutters ran with blood, that Strongbow married Eva. An odious marriage-company those mounds of corpses must have made, I think, and one quite worthy of the young lady's father.

He died, after Waterford and Dublin had been taken, and various successes achieved; and Strongbow became King of Leinster. Now came King Henry's opportunity. To restrain the growing power of Strongbow, he himself repaired to Dublin, as Strongbow's Royal Master, and deprived him of his kingdom, but confirmed him in the enjoyment of great possessions. The King, then, holding state in Dublin, received the homage of nearly all the Irish Kings and Chiefs, and so came home again with a great addition to his reputation as Lord of Ireland, and with a new claim on the favour of the Pope. And now, their reconciliation was completed – more easily and mildly by the Pope, than the King might have expected, I think.

At this period of his reign, when his troubles seemed so few and his prospects so bright, those domestic miseries began which gradually made the King the most unhappy of men, reduced his great spirit, wore away his health, and broke his heart.

He had four sons. HENRY, now aged eighteen – his secret crowning of whom had given such offence to Thomas à Becket; RICHARD, aged sixteen; GEOFFREY, fifteen; and JOHN, his favourite, a young boy whom the courtiers named LACKLAND, because he had no inheritance, but to whom the King meant to give the Lordship of Ireland. All these misguided boys, in their turn, were unnatural sons to him, and unnatural brothers to each other. Prince Henry, stimulated by the French King, and by his bad mother, Queen Eleanor, began the undutiful history.

First, he demanded that his young wife, MARGARET, the French King's daughter, should be crowned as well as he. His father, the King, consented, and it was done. It was no sooner done, than he demanded to have a part of his father's dominions, during his father's life. This being refused, he made off from his father in the night, with his bad heart full of bitterness, and took refuge at the French King's Court. Within a day or two, his brothers Richard and Geoffrey followed. Their mother tried to join them – escaping in man's clothes – but she was seized by King Henry's men, and immured in prison, where she lay, deservedly, for sixteen years. Every day, however, some grasping English noblemen, to whom the King's protection of his people from their avarice and oppression had given offence, deserted him and joined the Princes. Every day he heard some fresh intelligence of the Princes levying armies against him; of Prince Henry's wearing a crown before his own ambassadors at the French Court, and being called the Junior King of England; of all the Princes swearing never to make peace with him, their father, without the consent and approval of the Barons of France. But, with his fortitude and energy unshaken, King Henry met the shock of these disasters with a resolved and cheerful face. He called upon all Royal fathers who had sons, to help him, for his cause was theirs; he hired, out of his riches, twenty thousand men to fight the false French King, who stirred his own blood against him; and he carried on the war with such vigour, that Louis soon proposed a conference to treat for peace.

The conference was held beneath an old wide-spreading green elm-tree, upon a plain in France. It led to nothing. The war recommenced. Prince Richard began his fighting career, by leading an army against his father; but his father beat him and his army back; and thousands of his men would have rued the day in which they fought in such a wicked cause, had not the King received news of an invasion of England by the Scots, and promptly come home through a great storm to repress it. And whether he really began to fear that he suffered these troubles because à Becket had been murdered; or whether he wished to rise in the favour of the Pope, who had now declared à Becket to be a saint, or in the favour of his own people, of whom many believed that even à Becket's senseless tomb could work miracles, I don't know: but the King no sooner landed in England than he went straight to Canterbury; and when he came within sight of the distant Cathedral, he dismounted from his horse, took off his shoes, and walked with bare and bleeding feet to à Becket's grave. There, he lay down on the ground, lamenting, in the presence of many people; and by-and-by he went into the Chapter House, and, removing his clothes from his back and shoulders, submitted himself to be beaten with knotted cords (not beaten very hard, I dare say though) by eighty Priests, one after another. It chanced that on the very day when the King made this curious exhibition of himself, a complete victory was obtained over the Scots; which very much delighted the Priests, who said that it was won because of his great example of repentance. For the Priests in general had found out, since à Becket's death, that they admired him of all things – though they had hated him very cordially when he was alive.

The Earl of Flanders, who was at the head of the base conspiracy of the King's undutiful sons and their foreign friends, took the opportunity of the King being thus employed at home, to lay siege to Rouen, the capital of Normandy. But the King, who was extraordinarily quick and active in all his movements, was at Rouen, too, before it was supposed possible that he could have left England; and there he so defeated the said Earl of Flanders, that the conspirators proposed peace, and his bad sons Henry and Geoffrey submitted. Richard resisted for six weeks; but, being beaten out of castle after castle, he at last submitted too, and his father forgave him.

To forgive these unworthy princes was only to afford them breathing-time for new faithlessness. They were so false, disloyal and dishonourable, that they were no more to be trusted than common thieves. In the very next year, Prince Henry rebelled again, and was again forgiven. In eight years more, Prince Richard rebelled against his elder brother; and Prince Geoffrey infamously said that the brothers could never agree well together, unless they were united against their father. In the very next year after their reconciliation by the King, Prince Henry again rebelled against his father; and again submitted, swearing to be true; and was again forgiven; and again rebelled with Geoffrey.

But the end of this perfidious Prince was come. He fell sick at a French town; and his conscience terribly reproaching him with his baseness, he sent messengers to the King his father, imploring him to come and see him, and to forgive him for the last time on his bed of death. The generous King, who had a royal and forgiving mind towards his children always, would have gone; but this Prince had been so unnatural, that the noblemen about the King suspected treachery, and represented to him that he could not safely trust his life with such a traitor, though his own eldest son. Therefore the King sent him a ring from off his finger as a token of forgiveness; and when the Prince had kissed it, with much grief and many tears, and had confessed to those around him how bad, and wicked, and undutiful a son he had been; he said to the attendant Priests: 'O, tie a rope about my body, and draw me out of bed, and lay me down upon a bed of ashes, that I may die with prayers to God in a repentant manner!' And so he died, at twenty-seven years old.

Three years afterwards, Prince Geoffrey, being unhorsed at a tournament, had his brains trampled out by a crowd of horses passing over him. So, there only remained Prince Richard, and Prince John – who had grown to be a young man now, and had solemnly sworn to be faithful to his father. Richard soon rebelled again, encouraged by his friend the French King, PHILIP THE SECOND (son of Louis, who was dead); and soon submitted and was again forgiven, swearing on the New Testament never to rebel again; and in another year or so, rebelled again; and, in the presence of his father, knelt down on his knee before the King of France; and did the French King homage; and declared that with his aid he would possess himself, by force, of all his father's French dominions.

And yet this Richard called himself a soldier of Our Saviour! And yet this Richard wore the Cross, which the Kings of France and England had both taken, in the previous year, at a brotherly meeting underneath the old wide-spreading elm-tree on the plain, when they had sworn (like him) to devote themselves to a new Crusade, for the love and honour of the Truth!

Sick at heart, wearied out by the falsehood of his sons, and almost ready to lie down and die, the unhappy King who had so long stood firm, began to fail. But the Pope, to his honour, supported him; and obliged the French King and Richard, though successful in fight, to treat for peace. Richard wanted to be crowned King of England, and pretended that he wanted to be married (which he really did not) to the French King's sister, his promised wife, whom King Henry detained in England. King Henry wanted, on the other hand, that the French King's sister should be married to his favourite son, John: the only one of his sons (he said) who had never rebelled against him. At last King Henry, deserted by his nobles one by one, distressed, exhausted, broken-hearted, consented to establish peace.

One final heavy sorrow was reserved for him, even yet. When they brought him the proposed treaty of peace, in writing, as he lay very ill in bed, they brought him also the list of the deserters from their allegiance, whom he was required to pardon. The first name upon this list was John, his favourite son, in whom he had trusted to the last.

'O John! child of my heart!' exclaimed the King, in a great agony of mind. 'O John, whom I have loved the best! O John, for whom I have contended through these many troubles! Have you betrayed me too!' And then he lay down with a heavy groan, and said, 'Now let the world go as it will. I care for nothing more!'

After a time, he told his attendants to take him to the French town of Chinon – a town he had been fond of, during many years. But he was fond of no place now; it was too true that he could care for nothing more upon this earth. He wildly cursed the hour when he was born, and cursed the children whom he left behind him; and expired.

As, one hundred years before, the servile followers of the Court had abandoned the Conqueror in the hour of his death, so they now abandoned his descendant. The very body was stripped, in the plunder of the Royal chamber; and it was not easy to find the means of carrying it for burial to the abbey church of Fontevraud.

Richard was said in after years, by way of flattery, to have the heart of a Lion. It would have been far better, I think, to have had the heart of a Man. His heart, whatever it was, had cause to beat remorsefully within his breast, when he came – as he did – into the solemn abbey, and looked on his dead father's uncovered face. His heart, whatever it was, had been a black and perjured heart, in all its dealings with the deceased King, and more deficient in a single touch of tenderness than any wild beast's in the forest.

There is a pretty story told of this reign, called the story of FAIR ROSAMOND. It relates how the King doted on Fair Rosamond, who was the loveliest girl in all the world; and how he had a beautiful Bower built for her in a Park at Woodstock; and how it was erected in a labyrinth, and could only be found by a clue of silk. How the bad Queen Eleanor, becoming jealous of Fair Rosamond, found out the secret of the clue, and one day, appeared before her, with a dagger and cup of poison, and left her to the choice between those deaths. How Fair Rosamond, after shedding many piteous tears and offering many useless prayers to the cruel Queen, took the poison, and fell dead in the midst of the beautiful bower, while the unconscious birds sang gaily all around her.

Now, there *was* a fair Rosamond, and she was (I dare say) the loveliest girl in all the world, and the King was certainly very fond of her, and the bad Queen Eleanor was certainly made jealous. But I am afraid – I say afraid, because I like the story so much – that there was no bower, no labyrinth, no silken clue, no dagger, no poison. I am afraid fair Rosamond retired to a nunnery near Oxford, and died there, peaceably; her sister-nuns hanging a silken drapery over her tomb, and often dressing it with flowers, in remembrance of the youth and beauty that had enchanted the King when he too was young, and when his life lay fair before him.

It was dark and ended now; faded and gone. Henry Plantagenet lay quiet in the abbey church of Fontevraud, in the fifty-seventh year of his age – never to be completed – after governing England well, for nearly thirty-five years.

CHAPTER 13

England under Richard the First, called the Lion-heart

In the year of our Lord one thousand one hundred and eighty-nine, Richard of the Lion Heart succeeded to the throne of King Henry the Second, whose paternal heart he had done so much to break. He had been, as we have seen, a rebel from his boyhood; but, the moment he became a king against whom others might rebel, he found out that rebellion was a great wickedness. In the heat of this pious discovery, he punished all the leading people who had befriended him against his father. He could scarcely have done anything that would have been a better instance of his real nature, or a better warning to fawners and parasites not to trust in lion-hearted princes.

He likewise put his late father's treasurer in chains, and locked him up in a dungeon from which he was not set free until he had relinquished, not only all the Crown treasure, but all his own money too. So, Richard certainly got the Lion's share of the wealth of this wretched treasurer, whether he had a Lion's heart or not.

He was crowned King of England, with great pomp, at Westminster: walking to the Cathedral under a silken canopy stretched on the tops of four lances, each carried by a great lord. On the day of his coronation, a dreadful murdering of the Jews took place, which seems to have given great delight to numbers of savage persons calling themselves Christians. The King had issued a proclamation forbidding the Jews (who were generally hated, though they were the most useful merchants in England) to appear at the ceremony; but as they had assembled in London from all parts, bringing presents to show their respect for the new Sovereign, some of them ventured down to Westminster Hall with their gifts; which were very readily accepted. It is supposed, now, that some noisy fellow in the crowd, pretending to be a very delicate Christian, set up a howl at this, and struck a Jew who was trying to get in at the Hall door with his present. A riot arose. The Jews who had got into the Hall, were driven forth; and some of the rabble cried out that the new King had commanded the unbelieving race to be put to death. Thereupon the crowd rushed through the narrow streets of the city, slaughtering all the Jews they met; and when they could find no more out of doors (on account of their having fled to their houses, and fastened themselves in), they ran madly about, breaking open all the houses where the Jews lived, rushing in and stabbing or spearing them, sometimes even flinging old people and children out of window into blazing fires they had lighted up below. This great cruelty lasted four-and-twenty hours, and only three men were punished for it. Even they forfeited their lives not for murdering and robbing the Jews, but for burning the houses of some Christians.

King Richard, who was a strong restless burly man, with one idea always in his head, and that the very troublesome idea of breaking the heads of other men, was mightily impatient to go on a Crusade to the Holy Land, with a great army. As great armies could not be raised to go, even to the Holy Land, without a great deal of money, he sold the Crown domains, and even the high offices of State; recklessly appointing noblemen to rule over his English subjects, not because they were fit to govern, but because they could pay high for the privilege. In this way, and by selling pardons at a dear rate, and by varieties of avarice and oppression, he scraped together a large treasure. He then appointed two Bishops to take care of his kingdom in his absence, and gave great powers and possessions to his brother John, to secure his friendship. John would rather have been made Regent of England; but he was a sly man, and friendly to the expedition; saying to himself, no doubt, 'The more fighting, the more chance of my brother being killed; and when he *is* killed, then I become King John!'

Before the newly levied army departed from England, the recruits and the general populace distinguished themselves by astonishing cruelties on the unfortunate Jews: whom, in many large towns, they murdered by hundreds in the most horrible manner.

At York, a large body of Jews took refuge in the Castle, in the absence of its Governor, after the wives and children of many of them had been slain before their eyes. Presently came the Governor, and demanded admission. 'How can we give it thee, O Governor!' said the Jews upon the walls, 'when, if we open the gate by so much as the width of a foot, the roaring crowd behind thee will press in and kill us?'

Upon this, the unjust Governor became angry, and told the people that he approved of their killing those Jews; and a mischievous maniac of a friar, dressed all in white, put himself at the head of the assault, and they assaulted the Castle for three days.

Then said JOCEN, the head-Jew (who was a Rabbi or Priest), to the rest, 'Brethren, there is no hope for us with the Christians who are hammering at the gates and walls, and who must soon break in. As we and our wives and children must die, either by

Christian hands, or by our own, let it be by our own. Let us destroy by fire what jewels and other treasure we have here, then fire the castle, and then perish!'

A few could not resolve to do this, but the greater part complied. They made a blazing heap of all their valuables, and, when those were consumed, set the castle in flames. While the flames roared and crackled around them, and shooting up into the sky, turned it blood-red, Jocen cut the throat of his beloved wife, and stabbed himself. All the others who had wives or children, did the like dreadful deed. When the populace broke in, they found (except the trembling few, cowering in corners, whom they soon killed) only heaps of greasy cinders, with here and there something like part of the blackened trunk of a burnt tree, but which had lately been a human creature, formed by the beneficent hand of the Creator as they were.

After this bad beginning, Richard and his troops went on, in no very good manner, with the Holy Crusade. It was undertaken jointly by the King of England and his old friend Philip of France. They commenced the business by reviewing their forces, to the number of one hundred thousand men. Afterwards, they severally embarked their troops for Messina, in Sicily, which was appointed as the next place of meeting.

King Richard's sister had married the King of this place, but he was dead: and his uncle TANCRED had usurped the crown, cast the Royal Widow into prison, and possessed himself of her estates. Richard fiercely demanded his sister's release, the restoration of her lands, and (according to the Royal custom of the Island) that she should have a golden chair, a golden table, four-and-twenty silver cups, and four-and-twenty silver dishes. As he was too powerful to be successfully resisted, Tancred yielded to his demands; and then the French King grew jealous, and complained that the English King wanted to be absolute in the Island of Messina and everywhere else. Richard, however, cared little or nothing for this complaint; and in consideration of a present of twenty thousand pieces of gold, promised his pretty little nephew ARTHUR, then a child of two years old, in marriage to Tancred's daughter. We shall hear again of pretty little Arthur by-and-by.

This Sicilian affair arranged without anybody's brains being knocked out (which must have rather disappointed him), King Richard took his sister away, and also a fair lady named

BERENGARIA, with whom he had fallen in love in France, and whom his mother, Queen Eleanor (so long in prison, you remember, but released by Richard on his coming to the Throne), had brought out there to be his wife; and sailed with them for Cyprus.

He soon had the pleasure of fighting the King of the Island of Cyprus, for allowing his subjects to pillage some of the English troops who were shipwrecked on the shore; and easily conquering this poor monarch, he seized his only daughter, to be a companion to the lady Berengaria, and put the King himself into silver fetters. He then sailed away again with his mother, sister, wife, and the captive princess; and soon arrived before the town of Acre, which the French King with his fleet was besieging from the sea. But the French King was in no triumphant condition, for his army had been thinned by the swords of the Saracens, and wasted by the plague; and SALADIN, the brave Sultan of the Turks, at the head of a numerous army, was at that time gallantly defending the place from the hills that rise above it.

Wherever the united army of Crusaders went, they agreed in few points except in gaming, drinking, and quarrelling, in a most unholy manner; in debauching the people among whom they tarried, whether they were friends or foes; and in carrying disturbance and ruin into quiet places. The French King was jealous of the English King, and the English King was jealous of the French King, and the disorderly and violent soldiers of the two nations were jealous of one another; consequently, the two Kings could not at first agree, even upon a joint assault on Acre; but when they did make up their quarrel for that purpose, the Saracens promised to yield the town, to give up to the Christians the wood of the Holy Cross, to set at liberty all their Christian captives, and to pay two hundred thousand pieces of gold. All this was to be done within forty days; but, not being done, King Richard ordered some three thousand Saracen prisoners to be brought out in the front of his camp, and there, in full view of their own countrymen, to be butchered.

The French King had no part in this crime; for he was by that time travelling homeward with the greater part of his men; being offended by the overbearing conduct of the English King; being anxious to look after his own dominions; and being ill, besides, from the unwholesome air of that hot and sandy country. King Richard carried on the war without him; and remained in the East, meeting with a variety of adventures, nearly a year and a half. Every night, when his army was on the march, and came to a halt, the heralds cried out three times, to remind all the soldiers of the cause in which they were engaged, 'Save the Holy Sepulchre!' and then all the soldiers knelt and said 'Amen!' Marching or encamping, the army had continually to strive with the hot air of the glaring desert, or with the Saracen soldiers animated and directed by the brave Saladin, or with both together. Sickness and death, battle and wounds, were always among them; but through every difficulty King Richard fought like a giant, and worked like a common labourer. Long and long after he was quiet in his grave, his terrible battle-axe with twenty English pounds of English steel in its mighty head, was a legend among the Saracens; and when all the Saracen and Christian hosts had been dust for many a year, if a Saracen horse started at any object by the wayside, his rider would exclaim, 'What dost thou fear, Fool? Dost thou think King Richard is behind it?'

No one admired this King's renown for bravery more than Saladin himself, who was a generous and gallant enemy. When Richard lay ill of a fever, Saladin sent him fresh fruits from Damascus, and snow from the mountaintops. Courtly messages and compliments were frequently exchanged between them – and then King Richard would mount his horse and kill as many Saracens as he could; and Saladin would mount his, and kill as many Christians as he could. In this way King Richard fought to his heart's content at Arsoof and at Jaffa; and finding himself with nothing exciting to do at Ascalon, except to rebuild, for his own defence, some fortifications there which the Saracens had destroyed, he kicked his ally the Duke of Austria, for being too proud to work at them.

The army at last came within sight of the Holy City of Jerusalem; but, being then a mere nest of jealousy, and quarrelling and fighting, soon retired, and agreed with the Saracens upon a truce for three years, three months, three days, and three hours. Then, the English Christians, protected by the noble Saladin from Saracen revenge, visited Our Saviour's tomb; and then King Richard embarked with a small force at Acre to return home.

But he was shipwrecked in the Adriatic Sea, and was fain to pass through Germany, under an assumed name. Now, there were many people in Germany who had served in the Holy Land under that proud Duke of Austria who had been kicked; and some of them, easily recognising a man so remarkable as King Richard, carried their intelligence to the kicked Duke, who straightway took him prisoner at a little inn near Vienna.

The Duke's master the Emperor of Germany, and the King of France, were equally delighted to have so troublesome a monarch in safe keeping. Friendships which are founded on a partnership in doing wrong, are never true; and the King of France was now quite as heartily King Richard's foe, as he had ever been his friend in his unnatural conduct to his father. He monstrously pretended that King Richard had designed to poison him in the East; he charged him with having murdered, there, a man whom he had in truth befriended; he bribed the Emperor of Germany to keep him close prisoner; and, finally, through the plotting of these two princes, Richard was brought before the German legislature, charged with the foregoing crimes, and many others. But he defended himself so well, that many of the assembly were moved to tears by his eloquence and earnestness. It was decided that he should be treated, during the rest of his captivity, in a manner more becoming his dignity than he had been, and that he should be set free on the payment of a heavy ransom. This ransom the English people willingly raised. When Queen Eleanor took it over to Germany, it was at first evaded and refused. But she appealed to the honour of all the princes of the German Empire in behalf of her son, and appealed so well that it was accepted, and the King released. Thereupon, the King of France wrote to Prince John – 'Take care of thyself. The devil is unchained!'

Prince John had reason to fear his brother, for he had been a traitor to him in his captivity. He had secretly joined the French King; had vowed to the English nobles and people that his brother was dead; and had vainly tried to seize the crown. He was now in France, at a place called Evreux. Being the meanest and basest of men, he contrived a mean and base expedient for making himself acceptable to his brother. He invited the French officers of the garrison in that town to dinner, murdered them all, and then took the fortress. With this recommendation to the good will of a lion-hearted monarch, he hastened to King Richard, fell on his knees before him, and obtained the intercession of Queen Eleanor. 'I forgive him,' said the King, 'and I hope I may forget the injury he has done me, as easily as I know he will forget my pardon.'

While King Richard was in Sicily, there had been trouble in his dominions at home: one of the bishops whom he had left in charge thereof, arresting the other; and making, in his pride and ambition, as great a show as if he were King himself. But the King hearing of it at Messina, and appointing a new Regency, this LONGCHAMP (for that was his name) had fled to France in a woman's dress, and had there been encouraged and supported by the French King. With all these causes of offence against Philip in his mind, King Richard had no sooner been welcomed home by his enthusiastic subjects with great display and splendour, and had no sooner been crowned afresh at Winchester, than he resolved to show the French King that the Devil was unchained indeed, and made war against him with great fury.

There was fresh trouble at home about this time, arising out of the discontents of the poor people, who complained that they were far more heavily taxed than the rich, and who found a spirited champion in WILLIAM FITZ-OSBERT, called LONG-BEARD. He became the leader of a secret society, comprising fifty thousand men; he was seized by surprise; he stabbed the citizen who first laid hands upon him; and retreated, bravely fighting, to a church, which he maintained four days, until he was dislodged by fire, and run through the body as he came out. He was not killed, though; for he was dragged, half dead, at the tail of a horse to Smithfield, and there hanged. Death was long a favourite remedy for silencing the people's advocates; but as we go on with this history, I fancy we shall find them difficult to make an end of, for all that.

The French war, delayed occasionally by a truce, was still in progress when a certain Lord named VIDOMAR, Viscount of Limoges, chanced to find in his ground a treasure of ancient coins. As the King's vassal, he sent the King half of it; but the King claimed the whole. The lord refused to yield the whole. The King besieged the lord in his castle, swore that he would take the castle by storm, and hang every man of its defenders on the battlements.

There was a strange old song in that part of the country, to the effect that in Limoges an arrow would be made by which King Richard would die. It may be that BERTRAND DE GOUR-DON, a young man who was one of the defenders of the castle, had often sung it or heard it sung of a winter night, and remembered it when he saw, from his post upon the ramparts, the King attended only by his chief officer riding below the walls surveying the place. He drew an arrow to the head, took steady aim, said between his teeth, 'Now I pray God speed thee well, arrow!' discharged it, and struck the King in the left shoulder.

Although the wound was not at first considered dangerous, it was severe enough to cause the King to retire to his tent, and direct the assault to be made without him. The castle was taken; and every man of its defenders was hanged, as the King had sworn all should be, except Bertrand de Gourdon, who was reserved until the royal pleasure respecting him should be known.

By this time unskilful treatment had made the wound mortal, and the King knew that he was dying. He directed Bertrand to be brought into his tent. The young man was brought there, heavily chained. King Richard looked at him steadily. He looked, as steadily, at the King.

'Knave!' said King Richard. 'What have I done to thee, that thou shouldest take my life?'

'What hast thou done to me?' replied the young man. 'With thine own hands thou hast killed my father and my two brothers. Myself thou wouldest have hanged. Let me die now, by any torture that thou wilt. My comfort is, that no torture can save thee. Thou too must die; and through me, the world is quit of thee!'

Again the King looked at the young man steadily. Again the young man looked steadily at him. Perhaps some remembrance of his generous enemy Saladin, who was not a Christian, came into the mind of the dying King.

'Youth!' he said, 'I forgive thee. Go unhurt!'

Then, turning to the chief officer who had been riding in his company when he received the wound, King Richard said:

'Take off his chains, give him a hundred shillings, and let him depart.'

He sunk down on his couch, and a dark mist seemed in his weakened eyes to fill the tent wherein he had so often rested, and he died. His age was forty-two; he had reigned ten years. His last command was not obeyed; for the chief officer flayed Bertrand de Gourdon alive, and hanged him.

There is an old tune yet known — a sorrowful air will

sometimes outlive many generations of strong men, and even last longer than battle-axes with twenty pounds of steel in the head – by which this King is said to have been discovered in his captivity. BLONDEL, a favourite Minstrel of King Richard, as the story relates, faithfully seeking his Royal master, went singing it outside the gloomy walls of many foreign fortresses and prisons; until at last he heard it echoed from within a dungeon, and knew the voice, and cried out in ecstasy, 'O Richard, O my King!' You may believe it, if you like; it would be easy to believe worse things. Richard was himself a Minstrel and a Poet. If he had not been a Prince too, he might have been a better man perhaps, and might have gone out of the world with less bloodshed and waste of life to answer for.

CHAPTER 14

England under John, called Lackland

At two-and-thirty years of age, JOHN became King of England. His pretty little nephew ARTHUR had the best claim to the throne; but John seized the treasure, and made fine promises to the nobility, and got himself crowned at Westminster within a few weeks after his brother Richard's death. I doubt whether the crown could possibly have been put upon the head of a meaner coward, or a more detestable villain, if England had been searched from end to end to find him out.

The French King, Philip, refused to acknowledge the right of John to his new dignity, and declared in favour of Arthur. You must not suppose that he had any generosity in feeling for the fatherless boy; it merely suited his ambitious schemes to oppose the King of England. So John and the French King went to war about Arthur.

He was a handsome boy, at that time only twelve years old. He was not born when his father, Geoffrey, had his brains trampled out at the tournament; and, besides the misfortune of never having known a father's guidance and protection, he had the additional misfortune to have a foolish mother (CONSTANCE by name), lately married to her third husband. She took Arthur, upon John's accession, to the French King, who pretended to be very much his friend, and who made him a Knight, and promised him his daughter in marriage; but, who cared so little about him in reality, that finding it his interest to make peace with King John for a time, he did so without the least consideration for the poor little Prince, and heartlessly sacrificed all his interests.

Young Arthur, for two years afterwards, lived quietly; and in the course of that time his mother died. But, the French King then finding it his interest to quarrel with King John again, again made Arthur his pretence, and invited the orphan boy to court. 'You know your rights, Prince,' said the French King, 'and you would like to be a King. Is it not so?' 'Truly,' said Prince Arthur, 'I should greatly like to be a King!' 'Then,' said Philip, 'you shall have two hundred gentlemen who are Knights of mine, and with them you shall go to win back the provinces belonging to you, of which your uncle, the usurping King of England, has taken possession. I myself, meanwhile, will head a force against him in Normandy.' Poor Arthur was so flattered and so grateful that he signed a treaty with the crafty French King, agreeing to consider him his superior Lord, and that the French King should keep for himself whatever he could take from King John.

Now, King John was so bad in all ways, and King Philip was so perfidious, that Arthur, between the two, might as well have been a lamb between a fox and a wolf. But, being so young, he was ardent and flushed with hope; and, when the people of Brittany (which was his inheritance) sent him five hundred more knights and five thousand foot soldiers, he believed his fortune was made. The people of Brittany had been fond of him from his birth, and had requested that he might be called Arthur, in remembrance of that dimly-famous English Arthur, of whom I told you early in this book, whom they believed to have been the brave friend and companion of an old King of their own. They had tales among them about a prophet called MERLIN (of the same old time), who had foretold that their own King should be restored to them after hundreds of years; and they believed that the prophecy would be fulfilled in Arthur; that the time would come when he would rule them with a crown of Brittany upon his head; and when neither King of France nor King of England would have any power over them. When Arthur found himself riding in a glittering suit of armour on a richly capari-soned horse, at the head of his train of knights and soldiers, he began to believe this too, and to consider old Merlin a very superior prophet.

He did not know – how could he, being so innocent and inexperienced? – that his little army was a mere nothing against the power of the King of England. The French King knew it; but the poor boy's fate was little to him, so that the King of England was worried and distressed. Therefore, King Philip went his way into Normandy, and Prince Arthur went his way towards Mirebeau, a French town near Poictiers, both very well pleased.

Prince Arthur went to attack the town of Mirebeau, because his grandmother Eleanor, who has so often made her appearance in this history (and who had always been his mother's enemy), was living there, and because his Knights said, 'Prince, if you can take her prisoner, you will be able to bring the King your uncle to terms!' But she was not to be easily taken. She was old enough by this time – eighty – but she was as full of stratagem as she was full of years and wickedness. Receiving intelligence of young Arthur's approach, she shut herself up in a high tower, and encouraged her soldiers to defend it like men. Prince Arthur with his little army besieged the high tower. King John, hearing how matters stood, came up to the rescue, with *his* army. So here was a strange family-party! The boy-Prince besieging his grandmother, and his uncle besieging him!

This position of affairs did not last long. One summer night King John, by treachery, got his men into the town, surprised Prince Arthur's force, took two hundred of his knights, and seized the Prince himself in his bed. The Knights were put in heavy irons, and driven away in open carts drawn by bullocks, to various dungeons where they were most inhumanly treated, and where some of them were starved to death. Prince Arthur was sent to the castle of Falaise.

One day, while he was in prison at that castle, mournfully thinking it strange that one so young should be in so much trouble, and looking out of the small window in the deep dark wall, at the summer sky and the birds, the door was softly opened, and he saw his uncle the King standing in the shadow of the archway, looking very grim.

'Arthur,' said the King, with his wicked eyes more on the stone floor than on his nephew, 'will you not trust to the gentleness, the friendship, and the truthfulness of your loving uncle?'

'I will tell my loving uncle that,' replied the boy, 'when he does me right. Let him restore to me my kingdom of England, and then come to me and ask the question.'

The King looked at him and went out. 'Keep that boy close prisoner,' said he to the warden of the castle.

Then, the King took secret counsel with the worst of his nobles how the Prince was to be got rid of. Some said, 'Put out his eyes and keep him in prison, as Robert of Normandy was kept.' Others said, 'Have him stabbed.' Others, 'Have him hanged.' Others, 'Have him poisoned.'

King John, feeling that in any case, whatever was done afterwards, it would be a satisfaction to his mind to have those handsome eyes burnt out that had looked at him so proudly while his own royal eyes were blinking at the stone floor, sent certain ruffians to Falaise to blind the boy with red-hot irons. But Arthur so pathetically entreated them, and shed such piteous tears, and so appealed to HUBERT DE BOURG (or BURGH), the warden of the castle, who had a love for him, and was an honourable tender man, that Hubert could not bear it. To his eternal honour he prevented the torture from being performed, and, at his own risk, sent the savages away.

The chafed and disappointed King bethought himself of the stabbing suggestion next, and, with his shuffling manner and his cruel face, proposed it to one William de Bray. 'I am a gentleman and not an executioner,' said William de Bray, and left the presence with disdain.

But it was not difficult for a King to hire a murderer in those days. King John found one for his money, and sent him down to the castle of Falaise. 'On what errand dost thou come?' said Hubert to this fellow. 'To despatch young Arthur,' he returned. 'Go back to him who sent thee,' answered Hubert, 'and say that I will do it!'

King John very well knowing that Hubert would never do it, but that he courageously sent this reply to save the Prince or gain time, despatched messengers to convey the young prisoner to the castle of Rouen.

Arthur was soon forced from the good Hubert – of whom he had never stood in greater need than then – carried away by night, and lodged in his new prison: where, through his grated window, he could hear the deep waters of the river Seine, rippling against the stone wall below.

Arthur and Hubert

One dark night, as he lay sleeping, dreaming perhaps of rescue by those unfortunate gentlemen who were obscurely suffering and dying in his cause, he was roused, and bidden by his jailer to come down the staircase to the foot of the tower. He hurriedly dressed himself and obeyed. When they came to the bottom of the winding stairs, and the night air from the river blew upon their faces, the jailer trod upon his torch and put it out. Then, Arthur, in the darkness, was hurriedly drawn into a solitary boat. And in that boat, he found his uncle and one other man.

He knelt to them, and prayed them not to murder him. Deaf to his entreaties, they stabbed him and sunk his body in the river with heavy stones. When the spring-morning broke, the tower-door was closed, the boat was gone, the river sparkled on its way, and never more was any trace of the poor boy beheld by mortal eyes.

The news of this atrocious murder being spread in England, awakened a hatred of the King (already odious for his many vices, and for his having stolen away and married a noble lady while his own wife was living) that never slept again through his whole reign. In Brittany, the indignation was intense. Arthur's own sister ELEANOR was in the power of John and shut up in a convent at Bristol, but his half-sister ALICE was in Brittany. The people chose her, and the murdered prince's father-in-law, the last husband of Constance, to represent them; and carried their fiery complaints to King Philip. King Philip summoned King John (as the holder of territory in France) to come before him and defend himself. King John refusing to appear, King Philip declared him false, perjured, and guilty; and again made war. In a little time, by conquering the greater part of his French territory, King Philip deprived him of one-third of his domin- ions. And, through all the fighting that took place, King John was always found, either to be eating and drinking, like a gluttonous fool, when the danger was at a distance, or to be running away, like a beaten cur, when it was near.

You might suppose that when he was losing his dominions at this rate, and when his own nobles cared so little for him or his cause that they plainly refused to follow his banner out of England, he had enemies enough. But he made another enemy of the Pope, which he did in this way.

The Archbishop of Canterbury dying, and the junior monks of that place wishing to get the start of the senior monks in the appointment of his successor, met together at midnight, secretly elected a certain REGINALD, and sent him off to Rome to get the Pope's approval. The senior monks and the King soon finding this out, and being very angry about it, the junior monks gave way, and all the monks together elected the Bishop of Norwich, who was the King's favourite. The Pope, hearing the whole story, declared that neither election would do for him, and that *he* elected STEPHEN LANGTON. The monks submitting to the Pope, the King turned them all out bodily, and banished them as traitors. The Pope sent three bishops to the King, to threaten him with an Interdict. The King told the bishops that if any Interdict were laid upon his kingdom, he would tear out the eyes and cut off the noses of all the monks he could lay hold of, and send them over to Rome in that undecorated state as a present for their master. The bishops, nevertheless, soon published the Interdict, and fled.

After it had lasted a year, the Pope proceeded to his next step; which was Excommunication. King John was declared excommunicated, with all the usual ceremonies. The King was so incensed at this, and was made so desperate by the disaffection of his Barons and the hatred of his people, that it is said he even privately sent ambassadors to the Turks in Spain, offering to renounce his religion and hold his kingdom of them if they would help him. It is related that the ambassadors were admitted to the presence of the Turkish Emir through long lines of Moorish guards, and that they found the Emir with his eyes seriously fixed on the pages of a large book, from which he never once looked up. That they gave him a letter from the King containing his proposals, and were gravely dismissed. That presently the Emir sent for one of them, and conjured him, by his faith in his religion, to say what kind of man the King of England truly was? That the ambassador, thus pressed, replied that the King of England was a false tyrant, against whom his own subjects would soon rise. And that this was quite enough for the Emir.

Money being, in his position, the next best thing to men, King John spared no means of getting it. He set on foot another oppressing and torturing of the unhappy Jews (which was quite in his way), and invented a new punishment for one wealthy Jew of Bristol. Until such time as that Jew should produce a certain large sum of money, the King sentenced him to be imprisoned, and, every day, to have one tooth violently wrenched out of his head – beginning with the double teeth. For seven days, the oppressed man bore the daily pain and lost the daily tooth; but, on the eighth, he paid the money. With the treasure raised in such ways, the King made an expedition into Ireland, where some English nobles had revolted. It was one of the very few places from which he did not run away; because no resistance was shown. He made another expedition into Wales – whence he *did* run away in the end: but not before he had got from the Welsh people, as hostages, twenty-seven young men of the best families; every one of whom he caused to be slain in the following year.

To Interdict and Excommunication, the Pope now added his last sentence; Deposition. He proclaimed John no longer King, absolved all his subjects from their allegiance, and sent Stephen Langton and others to the King of France to tell him that, if he would invade England, he should be forgiven all his sins – at least, should be forgiven them by the Pope, if that would do.

As there was nothing that King Philip desired more than to invade England, he collected a great army at Rouen, and a fleet of seventeen hundred ships to bring them over. But the English people, however bitterly they hated the King, were not a people to suffer invasion quietly. They flocked to Dover, where the English standard was, in such great numbers to enrol themselves as defenders of their native land, that there were not provisions for them, and the King could only select and retain sixty thousand. But, at this crisis, the Pope, who had his own reasons for objecting to either King John or King Philip being too powerful, interfered. He entrusted a legate, whose name was PANDOLF, with the easy task of frightening King John. He sent him to the English Camp, from France, to terrify him with exaggerations of King Philip's power, and his own weakness in the discontent of the English Barons and people. Pandolf discharged his commission so well, that King John, in a wretched panic, consented to acknowledge Stephen Langton; to resign his kingdom 'to God, Saint Peter, and Saint Paul' – which meant the Pope; and to hold it, ever afterwards, by the Pope's leave, on payment of an annual sum of money. To this shameful contract he publicly bound himself in the church of the Knights Templars at Dover: where he laid at the legate's feet a part of the tribute, which the legate haughtily trampled upon. But they *do* say, that this was merely a genteel flourish, and that he was afterwards seen to pick it up and pocket it.

There was an unfortunate prophet, of the name of Peter, who had greatly increased King John's terrors by predicting that he would be unknighted (which the King supposed to signify that he would die) before the Feast of the Ascension should be past. That was the day after this humiliation. When the next morning came, and the King, who had been trembling all night, found himself alive and safe, he ordered the prophet – and his son too – to be dragged through the streets at the tails of horses, and then hanged, for having frightened him.

As King John had now submitted, the Pope, to King Philip's great astonishment, took him under his protection, and informed King Philip that he found he could not give him leave to invade England. The angry Philip resolved to do it without his leave; but he gained nothing and lost much; for, the English, commanded by the Earl of Salisbury, went over, in five hundred ships, to the French coast, before the French fleet had sailed away from it, and utterly defeated the whole.

The Pope then took off his three sentences, one after another, and empowered Stephen Langton publicly to receive King John into the favour of the Church again, and to ask him to dinner. The King, who hated Langton with all his might and main – and with reason too, for he was a great and a good man, with whom such a King could have no sympathy – pretended to cry and to be very grateful. There was a little difficulty about settling how much the King should pay as a recompense to the clergy for the losses he had caused them; but, the end of it was, that the superior clergy got a good deal, and the inferior clergy got little or nothing – which has also happened since King John's time, I believe.

When all these matters were arranged, the King in his triumph became more fierce, and false, and insolent to all around him than he had ever been. An alliance of sovereigns against King Philip, gave him an opportunity of landing an army in France; with which he even took a town! But, on the French King's gaining a great victory, he ran away, of course, and made a truce for five years.

And now the time approached when he was to be still further humbled, and made to feel, if he could feel anything, what a wretched creature he was. Of all men in the world, Stephen

Langton seemed raised up by Heaven to oppose and subdue him. When he ruthlessly burnt and destroyed the property of his own subjects, because their Lords, the Barons, would not serve him abroad, Stephen Langton fearlessly reproved and threatened him. When he swore to restore the laws of King Edward, or the laws of King Henry the First, Stephen Langton knew his falsehood, and pursued him through all his evasions. When the Barons met at the abbey of Saint Edmund's-Bury, to consider their wrongs and the King's oppressions, Stephen Langton roused them by his fervid words to demand a solemn charter of rights and liberties from their perjured master, and to swear, one by one, on the High Altar, that they would have it, or would wage war against him to the death. When the King hid himself in London from the Barons, and was at last obliged to receive them, they told him roundly they would not believe him unless Stephen Langton became a surety that he would keep his word. When he took the Cross to invest himself with some interest, and belong to something that was received with favour, Stephen Langton was still immovable. When he appealed to the Pope, and the Pope wrote to Stephen Langton in behalf of his new favourite, Stephen Langton was deaf, even to the Pope himself, and saw before him nothing but the welfare of England and the crimes of the English King.

At Easter-time, the Barons assembled at Stamford, in Lincoln-shire, in proud array, and, marching near to Oxford where the King was, delivered into the hands of Stephen Langton and two others, a list of grievances. 'And these,' they said, 'he must redress, or we will do it for ourselves!' When Stephen Langton told the King as much, and read the list to him, he went half mad with rage. But that did him no more good than his afterwards trying to pacify the Barons with lies. They called themselves and their followers, 'The army of God and the Holy Church.' Marching through the country, with the people throng-ing to them everywhere (except at Northampton, where they failed in an attack upon the castle), they at last triumphantly set up their banner in London itself, whither the whole land, tired of the tyrant, seemed to flock to join them. Seven knights alone, of all the knights in England, remained with the King; who, reduced to this strait, at last sent the Earl of Pembroke to the Barons to say that he approved of everything, and would meet them to sign their charter when they would. 'Then,' said the

Barons, 'let the day be the fifteenth of June, and the place, Runny-Mead.'

On Monday, the fifteenth of June, one thousand two hundred and fourteen, the King came from Windsor Castle, and the Barons came from the town of Staines, and they met on Runny-Mead, which is still a pleasant meadow by the Thames, where rushes grow in the clear water of the winding river, and its banks are green with grass and trees. On the side of the Barons, came the General of their army, ROBERT FITZ-WALTER, and a great concourse of the nobility of England. With the King, came, in all, some four-and-twenty persons of any note, most of whom despised him, and were merely his advisers in form. On that great day, and in that great company, the King signed MAGNA CHARTA – the great charter of England – by which he pledged himself to maintain the Church in its rights; to relieve the Barons of oppressive obligations as vassals of the Crown – of which the Barons, in their turn, pledged themselves to relieve *their* vassals, the people; to respect the liberties of London and all other cities and boroughs; to protect foreign merchants who came to England; to imprison no man without a fair trial; and to sell, delay, or deny justice to none. As the Barons knew his falsehood well, they further required, as their securities, that he should send out of his kingdom all his foreign troops; that for two months they should hold possession of the city of London, and Stephen Langton of the Tower; and that five-and-twenty of their body, chosen by themselves, should be a lawful committee to watch the keeping of the charter, and to make war upon him if he broke it.

All this he was obliged to yield. He signed the charter with a smile, and, if he could have looked agreeable, would have done so, as he departed from the splendid assembly. When he got home to Windsor Castle, he was quite a madman in his helpless fury. And he broke the charter immediately afterwards.

He sent abroad for foreign soldiers, and sent to the Pope for help, and plotted to take London by surprise, while the Barons should be holding a great tournament at Stamford, which they had agreed to hold there as a celebration of the charter. The Barons, however, found him out and put it off. Then, when the Barons desired to see him and tax him with his treachery, he made numbers of appointments with them, and kept none, and shifted from place to place, and was constantly sneaking and skulking about. At last he appeared at Dover, to join his foreign soldiers, of whom numbers came into his pay; and with them he besieged and took Rochester Castle, which was occupied by knights and soldiers of the Barons. He would have hanged them every one; but the leader of the foreign soldiers, fearful of what the English people might afterwards do to him, interfered to save the knights; therefore the King was fain to satisfy his vengeance with the death of all the common men. Then, he sent the Earl of Salisbury, with one portion of his army, to ravage the eastern part of his own dominions, while he carried fire and slaughter into the northern part; torturing, plundering, killing, and inflicting every possible cruelty upon the people; and, every morning, setting a worthy example to his men by setting fire, with his own monster-hands, to the house where he had slept last night. Nor was this all; for the Pope, coming to the aid of his precious friend, laid the kingdom under an Interdict again, because the people took part with the Barons. It did not much matter, for the people had grown so used to it now, that they had begun to think nothing about it. It occurred to them – perhaps to Stephen Langton too – that they could keep their churches open, and ring their bells, without the Pope's permission as well as with it. So, they tried the experiment – and found that it succeeded perfectly.

It being now impossible to bear the country, as a wilderness of cruelty, or longer to hold any terms with such a forsworn outlaw of a King, the Barons sent to LOUIS, son of the French monarch, to offer him the English crown. Caring as little for the Pope's excommunication of him if he accepted the offer, as it is possible his father may have cared for the Pope's forgiveness of his sins, he landed at Sandwich (King John immediately running away from Dover, where he happened to be), and went on to London. The Scottish King, with whom many of the Northern English Lords had taken refuge; numbers of the foreign soldiers, numbers of the Barons, and numbers of the people went over to him every day; – King John, the while, continually running away in all directions. The career of Louis was checked, however, by the suspicions of the Barons, founded on the dying declaration of a French Lord, that when the kingdom was conquered he was sworn to banish them as traitors, and to give their estates to some of his own Nobles. Rather than suffer this, some of the Barons hesitated: others even went over to King John.

It seemed to be the turning-point of King John's fortunes, for, in his savage and murderous course, he had now taken some towns and met with some successes. But, happily for England and humanity, his death was near. Crossing a dangerous quicksand, called the Wash, not very far from Wisbeach, the tide came up and nearly drowned his army. He and his soldiers escaped; but, looking back from the shore when he was safe, he saw the roaring water sweep down in a torrent, overturn the waggons, horses, and men, that carried his treasure, and engulph them in a raging whirlpool from which nothing could be delivered.

Cursing, and swearing, and gnawing his fingers, he went on to Swinstead Abbey, where the monks set before him quantities of pears, and peaches, and new cider – some say poison too, but there is very little reason to suppose so – of which he ate and drank in an immoderate and beastly way. All night he lay ill of a burning fever, and haunted with horrible fears. Next day, they put him in a horse-litter, and carried him to Sleaford Castle, where he passed another night of pain and horror. Next day, they carried him, with greater difficulty than on the day before, to the castle of Newark upon Trent; and there, on the eighteenth of October, in the forty-ninth year of his age, and the seventeenth of his vile reign, was an end of this miserable brute.

CHAPTER 15

England under Henry the Third, called of Winchester

If any of the English Barons remembered the murdered Arthur's sister, Eleanor the fair maid of Brittany, shut up in her convent at Bristol, none among them spoke of her now, or maintained her right to the Crown. The dead Usurper's eldest boy, HENRY by name, was taken by the Earl of Pembroke, the Marshal of England, to the city of Gloucester, and there crowned in great haste when he was only ten years old. As the Crown itself had been lost with the King's treasure, in the raging water, and, as there was no time to make another, they put a circle of plain gold upon his head instead. 'We have been the enemies of this child's father,' said Lord Pembroke, a good and true gentleman, to the few Lords who were present, 'and he merited our ill-will; but the child himself is innocent, and his youth demands our friendship and protection.' Those Lords felt tenderly towards the little boy, remembering their own young children; and they bowed their heads, and said, 'Long live King Henry the Third!'

Next, a great council met at Bristol, revised Magna Charta, and made Lord Pembroke Regent or Protector of England, as the King was too young to reign alone. The next thing to be done, was to get rid of Prince Louis of France, and to win over those English Barons who were still ranged under his banner. He was strong in many parts of England, and in London itself; and he held, among other places, a certain Castle called the Castle of Mount Sorel, in Leicestershire. To this fortress, after some skirmishing and truce-making, Lord Pembroke laid siege. Louis despatched an army of six hundred knights and twenty thousand soldiers to relieve it. Lord Pembroke, who was not strong enough for such a force, retired with all his men. The army of the French Prince, which had marched there with fire and plunder, marched away with fire and plunder, and came, in a boastful swaggering manner, to Lincoln. The town submitted; but the Castle in the town, held by a brave widow lady, named NICHOLA DE CAMVILLE (whose property it was), made such a sturdy resistance, that the French Count in command of the army of the French Prince found it necessary to besiege this Castle. While he was thus engaged, word was brought to him that Lord Pembroke, with four hundred knights, two hundred and fifty men with cross-bows, and a stout force both of horse and foot, was marching towards him. 'What care I?' said the French Count. 'The Englishman is not so mad as to attack me and my great army in a walled town!' But the Englishman did it for all that, and did it – not so madly but so wisely, that he decoyed the great army into the narrow, ill-paved lanes and byways of Lincoln, where its horse-soldiers could not ride in any strong body; and there he made such havoc with them, that the whole force surrendered themselves prisoners, except the Count; who said that he would never yield to any English traitor alive, and accordingly got killed. The end of this victory, which the English called, for a joke, the Fair of Lincoln, was the usual one in those times – the common men were slain without any mercy, and the knights and gentlemen paid ransom and went home.

The wife of Louis, the fair BLANCHE OF CASTILE, dutifully equipped a fleet of eighty good ships, and sent it over from France to her husband's aid. An English fleet of forty ships, some good and some bad, gallantly met them near the mouth of the Thames, and took or sunk sixty-five in one fight. This great loss put an end to the French Prince's hopes. A treaty was made at Lambeth, in virtue of which the English Barons who had remained attached to his cause returned to their allegiance, and it was engaged on both sides that the Prince and all his troops should retire peacefully to France. It was time to go; for war had made him so poor that he was obliged to borrow money from the citizens of London to pay his expenses home.

Lord Pembroke afterwards applied himself to governing the country justly, and to healing the quarrels and disturbances that had arisen among men in the days of the bad King John. He caused Magna Charta to be still more improved, and so amended the Forest Laws that a Peasant was no longer put to death for killing a stag in a Royal Forest, but was only imprisoned. It would have been well for England if it could have had so good a Protector many years longer, but that was not to be. Within three years after the young King's Coronation, Lord Pembroke died; and you may see his tomb, at this day, in the old Temple Church in London.

The Protectorship was now divided. PETER DE ROCHES, whom King John had made Bishop of Winchester, was entrusted with the care of the person of the young sovereign; and the exercise of the Royal authority was confided to EARL HUBERT DE BURGH. These two personages had from the first no liking for each other, and soon became enemies. When the young King was declared of age, Peter de Roches, finding that Hubert increased in power and favour, retired discontentedly, and went abroad. For nearly ten years afterwards Hubert had full sway alone.

But ten years is a long time to hold the favour of a King. This King, too, as he grew up, showed a strong resemblance to his father, in feebleness, inconsistency, and irresolution. The best that can be said of him is that he was not cruel. De Roches coming home again, after ten years, and being a novelty, the King began to favour him and to look coldly on Hubert. Wanting money besides, and having made Hubert rich, he began to dislike Hubert. At last he was made to believe, or pretended to believe, that Hubert had misappropriated some of the Royal treasure; and ordered him to furnish an account of all he had done in his administration. Besides which, the foolish charge was brought against Hubert that he had made himself the King's favourite by magic. Hubert very well knowing that he could never defend himself against such nonsense, and that his old enemy must be determined on his ruin, instead of answering the charges fled to Merton Abbey. Then the King, in a violent passion, sent for the Mayor of London, and said to the Mayor, 'Take twenty thousand citizens, and drag me Hubert de Burgh out of that abbey, and bring him here.' The Mayor posted off to do it, but the Archbishop of Dublin (who was a friend of Hubert's) warning the King that an abbey was a sacred place, and that if he committed any violence there, he must answer for it to the Church, the King changed his mind and called the Mayor back, and declared that Hubert should have four months to prepare his defence, and should be safe and free during that time.

Hubert, who relied upon the King's word, though I think he was old enough to have known better, came out of Merton Abbey upon these conditions, and journeyed away to see his wife: a Scottish Princess who was then at St Edmund's-Bury.

Almost as soon as he had departed from the Sanctuary, his enemies persuaded the weak King to send out one SIR GODFREY DE CRANCUMB, who commanded three hundred vagabonds called the Black Band, with orders to seize him. They came up with him at a little town in Essex, called Brentwood, when he was in bed. He leaped out of bed, got out of the house, fled to the church, ran up to the altar, and laid his hand upon the cross. Sir Godfrey and the Black Band, caring neither for church, altar, nor cross, dragged him forth to the church door, with their drawn swords flashing round his head, and sent for a Smith to rivet a set of chains upon him. When the Smith (I wish I knew his name!) was brought, all dark and swarthy with the smoke of his forge, and panting with the speed he had made; and the Black Band, falling aside to show him the Prisoner, cried with a loud uproar, 'Make the fetters heavy! make them strong!' the

Smith dropped upon his knee – but not to the Black Band – and said, 'This is the brave Earl Hubert de Burgh, who fought at Dover Castle, and destroyed the French fleet, and has done his country much good service. You may kill me, if you like, but I will never make a chain for Earl Hubert de Burgh!'

The Black Band never blushed, or they might have blushed at this. They knocked the Smith about from one to another, and swore at him, and tied the Earl on horseback, undressed as he was, and carried him off to the Tower of London. The Bishops, however, were so indignant at the violation of the Sanctuary of the Church, that the frightened King soon ordered the Black Band to take him back again; at the same time commanding the Sheriff of Essex to prevent his escaping out of Brentwood Church. Well! the Sheriff dug a deep trench all round the church, and erected a high fence, and watched the church night and day; the Black Band and their Captain watched it too, like three hundred and one black wolves. For thirty-nine days, Hubert de Burgh remained within. At length, upon the fortieth day, cold and hunger were too much for him, and he gave himself up to the Black Band, who carried him off, for the second time, to the Tower. When his trial came on, he refused to plead; but at last it was arranged that he should give up all the royal lands which had been bestowed upon him, and should be kept at the Castle of Devizes, in what was called 'free prison,' in charge of four knights appointed by four lords. There, he remained almost a year, until, learning that a follower of his old enemy the Bishop was made Keeper of the Castle, and fearing that he might be killed by treachery, he climbed the ramparts one dark night, dropped from the top of the high Castle wall into the moat, and coming safely to the ground, took refuge in another church. From this place he was delivered by a party of horse despatched to his help by some nobles, who were by this time in revolt against the King, and assembled in Wales. He was finally pardoned and restored to his estates, but he lived privately, and never more aspired to a high post in the realm, or to a high place in the King's favour. And thus end – more happily than the stories of many favourites of Kings – the adventures of Earl Hubert de Burgh.

The nobles, who had risen in revolt, were stirred up to rebellion by the overbearing conduct of the Bishop of Winchester, who, finding that the King secretly hated the Great Charter which had been forced from his father, did his utmost to confirm him in that dislike, and in the preference he showed to foreigners over the English. Of this, and of his even publicly declaring that the Barons of England were inferior to those of France, the English Lords complained with such bitterness, that the King, finding them well supported by the clergy, became frightened for his throne, and sent away the Bishop and all his foreign associates. On his marriage, however, with ELEANOR, a French lady, the daughter of the Count of Provence, he openly favoured the foreigners again; and so many of his wife's relations came over, and made such an immense family-party at court, and got so many good things, and pocketed so much money, and were so high with the English whose money they pocketed, that the bolder English Barons murmured openly about a clause there was in the Great Charter, which provided for the banishment of unreasonable favourites. But, the foreigners only laughed disdainfully, and said, 'What are your English laws to us?'

King Philip of France had died, and had been succeeded by Prince Louis, who had also died after a short reign of three years, and had been succeeded by his son of the same name – so moderate and just a man that he was not the least in the world like a King, as Kings went. ISABELLA, King Henry's mother, wished very much (for a certain spite she had) that England should make war against this King; and, as King Henry was a mere puppet in anybody's hands who knew how to manage his feebleness, she easily carried her point with him. But, the Parliament were determined to give him no money for such a war. So, to defy the Parliament, he packed up thirty large casks of silver – I don't know how he got so much; I dare say he screwed it out of the miserable Jews – and put them aboard ship, and went away himself to carry war into France: accompanied by his mother and his brother Richard, Earl of Cornwall, who was rich and clever. But he only got well beaten and came home.

The good-humour of the Parliament was not restored by this. They reproached the King with wasting the public money to make greedy foreigners rich, and were so stern with him, and so determined not to let him have more of it to waste if they could help it, that he was at his wit's end for some, and tried so shamelessly to get all he could from his subjects, by excuses or by force, that the people used to say the King was the sturdiest beggar in England. He took the Cross, thinking to get some money by that means; but, as it was very well known that he never meant to go on a crusade, he got none. In all his contention, the Londoners were particularly keen against the King, and the King hated them warmly in return. Hating or loving, however, made no difference; he continued in the same condition for nine or ten years, when at last the Barons said that if he would solemnly confirm their liberties afresh, the Parliament would vote him a large sum.

As he readily consented, there was a great meeting held in Westminster Hall, one pleasant day in May, when all the clergy, dressed in their robes and holding every one of them a burning candle in his hand, stood up (the Barons being also there) while the Archbishop of Canterbury read the sentence of excommunication against any man, and all men, who should henceforth, in any way, infringe the Great Charter of the Kingdom. When he had done, they all put out their burning candles with a curse upon the soul of any one, and every one, who should merit that sentence. The King concluded with an oath to keep the Charter, 'As I am a man, as I am a Christian, as I am a Knight, as I am a King!'

It was easy to make oaths, and easy to break them; and the King did both, as his father had done before him. He took to his old courses again when he was supplied with money, and soon cured of their weakness the few who had ever really trusted him. When his money was gone, and he was once more borrowing and begging everywhere with a meanness worthy of his nature, he got into a difficulty with the Pope respecting the Crown of Sicily, which the Pope said he had a right to give away, and which he offered to King Henry for his second son, PRINCE EDMUND. But, if you or I give away what we have not got, and what belongs to somebody else, it is likely that the person to whom we give it, will have some trouble in taking it. It was exactly so in this case. It was necessary to conquer the Sicilian Crown before it could be put upon young Edmund's head. It could not be conquered without money. The Pope ordered the clergy to raise money. The clergy, however, were not so obedient to him as usual; they had been disputing with him for some time about his unjust preference of Italian Priests in England; and they had begun to doubt whether the King's chaplain, whom he allowed to be paid for preaching in seven hundred churches, could possibly be, even by the Pope's favour, in seven hundred places at once. 'The Pope and the King together,' said the Bishop of London, 'may take the mitre off my head; but, if they do, they will find that I shall put on a soldier's helmet. I pay nothing.' The Bishop of Worcester was as bold as the Bishop of London, and would pay nothing either. Such sums as the more timid or more helpless of the clergy did raise were squandered away, without doing any good to the King, or bringing the Sicilian Crown an inch nearer to Prince Edmund's head. The end of the business was, that the Pope gave the Crown to the brother of the King of France (who conquered it for himself), and sent the King of England in, a bill of one hundred thousand pounds for the expenses of not having won it.

The King was now so much distressed that we might almost pity him, if it were possible to pity a King so shabby and ridiculous. His clever brother, Richard, had bought the title of King of the Romans from the German people, and was no longer near him, to help him with advice. The clergy, resisting the very Pope, were in alliance with the Barons. The Barons were headed by SIMON DE MONTFORT, Earl of Leicester, married to King Henry's sister, and, though a foreigner himself, the most popular man in England against the foreign favourites. When the King next met his Parliament, the Barons, led by this Earl, came before him, armed from head to foot, and cased in armour. When the Parliament again assembled, in a month's time, at Oxford, this Earl was at their head, and the King was obliged to consent, on oath, to what was called a Committee of Government: consisting of twenty-four members: twelve chosen by the Barons, and twelve chosen by himself.

But, at a good time for him, his brother Richard came back. Richard's first act (the Barons would not admit him into England on other terms), was to swear to be faithful to the Committee of Government – which he immediately began to oppose with all his might. Then, the Barons began to quarrel among themselves; especially the proud Earl of Gloucester with the Earl of Leicester, who went abroad in disgust. Then, the people began to be dissatisfied with the Barons, because they did not do enough for them. The King's chances seemed so good again at length, that he took heart enough – or caught it from his brother – to tell the Committee of Government that he abolished them – as to his oath, never mind that, the Pope said! – and to seize all the money in the Mint, and to shut himself up in the Tower of London. Here he was joined by his eldest son, Prince Edward; and, from the Tower, he made public a letter of the Pope's to the world in general, informing all men that he had been an excellent and just King for five-and-forty years.

As everybody knew he had been nothing of the sort, nobody cared much for this document. It so chanced that the proud Earl of Gloucester dying, was succeeded by his son; and that his son, instead of being the enemy of the Earl of Leicester, was (for the time) his friend. It fell out, therefore, that these two Earls joined their forces, took several of the Royal Castles in the country, and advanced as hard as they could on London. The London people, always opposed to the King, declared for them with great joy. The King himself remained shut up, not at all gloriously, in the Tower. Prince Edward made the best of his way to Windsor Castle. His mother, the Queen, attempted to follow him by water; but, the people seeing her barge rowing up the river, and hating her with all their hearts, ran to London Bridge, got together a quantity of stones and mud, and pelted the barge as it came through, crying furiously, 'Drown the Witch! Drown her!' They were so near doing it, that the Mayor took the old lady under his protection, and shut her up in St Paul's until the danger was past.

It would require a great deal of writing on my part, and a great deal of reading on yours, to follow the King through his disputes with the Barons, and to follow the Barons through their disputes with one another – so I will make short work of it for both of us, and only relate the chief event that arose out of these quarrels. The good King of France was asked to decide between them. He gave it as his opinion that the King must maintain the Great Charter, and that the Barons must give up the Committee of Government, and all the rest that had been done by the Parliament at Oxford: which the Royalists, or King's party, scornfully called the Mad Parliament. The Barons declared that these were not fair terms, and they would not accept them. Then they caused the great bell of St Paul's to be tolled, for the purpose of rousing up the London people, who armed themselves at the dismal sound and formed quite an army in the streets. I am sorry to say, however, that instead of falling upon the King's party with whom their quarrel was, they fell upon the miserable Jews, and killed at least five hundred of them.

They pretended that some of these Jews were on the King's side, and that they kept hidden in their houses, for the destruction of the people, a certain terrible composition called Greek Fire, which could not be put out with water, but only burnt the fiercer for it. What they really did keep in their houses was money; and this their cruel enemies wanted, and this their cruel enemies took, like robbers and murderers.

The Earl of Leicester put himself at the head of these Londoners and other forces, and followed the King to Lewes in Sussex, where he lay encamped with his army. Before giving the King's forces battle here, the Earl addressed his soldiers, and said that King Henry the Third had broken so many oaths, that he had become the enemy of God, and therefore they would wear white crosses on their breasts, as if they were arrayed, not against a fellow-Christian, but against a Turk. White-crossed accordingly, they rushed into the fight. They would have lost the day – the King having on his side all the foreigners in England: and, from Scotland, JOHN COMYN, JOHN BALIOL, and ROBERT BRUCE, with all their men – but for the impatience of PRINCE EDWARD, who, in his hot desire to have vengeance on the people of London, threw the whole of his father's army into confusion. He was taken prisoner; so was the King; so was the King's brother the King of the Romans; and five thousand Englishmen were left dead upon the bloody grass.

For this success, the Pope excommunicated the Earl of Leicester: which neither the Earl nor the people cared at all about. The people loved him and supported him, and he became the real King; having all the power of the government in his own hands, though he was outwardly respectful to King Henry the Third, whom he took with him wherever he went, like a poor old limp court-card. He summoned a Parliament (in the year one thousand two hundred and sixty-five) which was the first Parliament in England that the people had any real share in electing; and he grew more and more in favour with the people every day, and they stood by him in whatever he did.

Many of the other Barons, and particularly the Earl of Gloucester, who had become by this time as proud as his father, grew jealous of this powerful and popular Earl, who was proud too, and began to conspire against him. Since the battle of Lewes, Prince Edward had been kept as a hostage, and, though he was otherwise treated like a Prince, had never been allowed to go out without attendants appointed by the Earl of Leicester, who watched him. The conspiring Lords found means to propose to him, in secret, that they should assist him to escape, and should make him their leader; to which he very heartily consented.

So, on a day that was agreed upon, he said to his attendants after dinner (being then at Hereford), 'I should like to ride on horseback, this fine afternoon, a little way into the country.' As they, too, thought it would be very pleasant to have a canter in the sunshine, they all rode out of the town together in a gay little troop. When they came to a fine level piece of turf, the Prince fell to comparing their horses one with another, and offering bets that one was faster than another; and the attendants, suspecting no harm, rode galloping matches until their horses were quite tired. The Prince rode no matches himself, but looked on from his saddle, and staked his money. Thus they passed the whole merry afternoon. Now, the sun was setting, and they were all going slowly up a hill, the Prince's horse very fresh and all the other horses very weary, when a strange rider mounted on a grey steed appeared at the top of the hill, and waved his hat. 'What does the fellow mean?' said the attendants one to another. The Prince answered on the instant by setting spurs to his horse, dashing away at his utmost speed, joining the man, riding into the midst of a little crowd of horsemen who were then seen waiting under some trees, and who closed around him; and so he departed in a cloud of dust, leaving the road empty of all but the baffled attendants, who sat looking at one another, while their horses drooped their ears and panted.

The Prince joined the Earl of Gloucester at Ludlow. The Earl of Leicester, with a part of the army and the stupid old King, was at Hereford. One of the Earl of Leicester's sons, Simon de Montfort, with another part of the army, was in Sussex. To prevent these two parts from uniting was the Prince's first object. He attacked Simon de Montfort by night, defeated him, seized his banners and treasure, and forced him into Kenilworth Castle in Warwickshire, which belonged to his family.

His father, the Earl of Leicester, in the meanwhile, not knowing what had happened, marched out of Hereford, with his part of the army and the King, to meet him. He came, on a bright morning in August, to Evesham, which is watered by the pleasant river Avon. Looking rather anxiously across the prospect towards Kenilworth, he saw his own banners advancing; and his face brightened with joy. But, it clouded darkly when he presently perceived that the banners were captured, and in the enemy's hands; and he said, 'It is over. The Lord have mercy on our souls, for our bodies are Prince Edward's!'

He fought like a true Knight, nevertheless. When his horse was killed under him, he fought on foot. It was a fierce battle, and the dead lay in heaps everywhere. The old King, stuck up in a suit of armour on a big war-horse, which didn't mind him at all, and which carried him into all sorts of places where he didn't want to go, got into everybody's way, and very nearly got knocked on the head by one of his son's men. But he managed to pipe out, 'I am Harry of Winchester!' and the Prince, who heard him, seized his bridle, and took him out of peril. The Earl of Leicester still fought bravely, until his best son Henry was killed, and the bodies of his best friends choked his path; and then he fell, still fighting, sword in hand. They mangled his body, and sent it as a present to a noble lady – but a very unpleasant lady, I should think – who was the wife of his worst enemy. They could not mangle his memory in the minds of the faithful people, though. Many years afterwards, they loved him more than ever, and regarded him as a Saint, and always spoke of him as 'Sir Simon the Righteous.'

And even though he was dead, the cause for which he had fought still lived, and was strong, and forced itself upon the King in the very hour of victory. Henry found himself obliged to respect the Great Charter, however much he hated it, and to make laws similar to the laws of the Great Earl of Leicester, and to be moderate and forgiving towards the people at last – even towards the people of London, who had so long opposed him. There were more risings before all this was done, but they were set at rest by these means, and Prince Edward did his best in all things to restore peace. One Sir Adam de Gourdon was the last dissatisfied knight in arms; but, the Prince vanquished him in single combat, in a wood, and nobly gave him his life, and became his friend, instead of slaying him. Sir Adam was not ungrateful. He ever afterwards remained devoted to his generous conqueror.

When the troubles of the Kingdom were thus calmed, Prince Edward and his cousin Henry took the Cross, and went away to the Holy Land, with many English Lords and Knights. Four years afterwards the King of the Romans died, and, next year (one thousand two hundred and seventy-two), his brother the weak King of England died. He was sixty-eight years old then, and had reigned fifty-six years. He was as much of a King in death, as he had ever been in life. He was the mere pale shadow of a King at all times.

CHAPTER 16

England under Edward the First, called Longshanks

It was now the year of our Lord one thousand two hundred and seventy-two; and Prince Edward, the heir to the throne, being away in the Holy Land, knew nothing of his father's death. The Barons, however, proclaimed him King, immediately after the Royal funeral; and the people very willingly consented, since most men knew too well by this time what the horrors of a contest for the crown were. So King Edward the First, called, in a not very complimentary manner, LONGSHANKS, because of the slenderness of his legs, was peacefully accepted by the English Nation.

His legs had need to be strong, however long and thin they were; for they had to support him through many difficulties on the fiery sands of Asia, where his small force of soldiers fainted, died, deserted, and seemed to melt away. But his prowess made light of it, and he said, 'I will go on, if I go on with no other follower than my groom!'

A Prince of this spirit gave the Turks a deal of trouble. He stormed Nazareth, at which place, of all places on earth, I am sorry to relate, he made a frightful slaughter of innocent people; and then he went to Acre, where he got a truce of ten years from the Sultan. He had very nearly lost his life in Acre, through the treachery of a Saracen Noble, called the Emir of Jaffa, who, making the pretence that he had some idea of turning Christian and wanted to know all about that religion, sent a trusty messenger to Edward very often – with a dagger in his sleeve. At last, one Friday in Whitsun week, when it was very hot, and all the sandy prospect lay beneath the blazing sun, burnt up like a great overdone biscuit, and Edward was lying on a couch, dressed for coolness in only a loose robe, the messenger, with his chocolate-coloured face and his bright dark eyes and white teeth, came creeping in with a letter, and kneeled down like a tame tiger. But, the moment Edward stretched out his hand to take the letter, the tiger made a spring at his heart. He was quick, but Edward was quick too. He seized the traitor by his chocolate throat, threw him to the ground, and slew him with the very dagger he had drawn. The weapon had struck Edward in the arm, and although the wound itself was slight, it threatened to be mortal, for the blade of the dagger had been smeared with poison. Thanks, however, to a better surgeon than was often to be found in those times, and to some wholesome herbs, and above all, to his faithful wife, ELEANOR, who devotedly nursed him, and is said by some to have sucked the poison from the wound with her own red lips (which I am very willing to believe), Edward soon recovered and was sound again.

As the King his father had sent entreaties to him to return home, he now began the journey. He had got as far as Italy, when he met messengers who brought him intelligence of the King's death. Hearing that all was quiet at home, he made no haste to return to his own dominions, but paid a visit to the Pope, and went in state through various Italian Towns, where he was welcomed with acclamations as a mighty champion of the Cross from the Holy Land, and where he received presents of purple mantles and prancing horses, and went along in great triumph. The shouting people little knew that he was the last English monarch who would ever embark in a crusade, or that within twenty years every conquest which the Christians had made in the Holy Land at the cost of so much blood, would be won back by the Turks. But all this came to pass.

There was, and there is, an old town standing in a plain in France, called Châlons. When the King was coming towards this place on his way to England, a wily French Lord, called the Count of Châlons, sent him a polite challenge to come with his knights and hold a fair tournament with the Count and *his* knights, and make a day of it with sword and lance. It was represented to the King that the Count of Châlons was not to be trusted, and that, instead of a holiday fight for mere show and in good humour, he secretly meant a real battle, in which the English should be defeated by superior force.

The King, however, nothing afraid, went to the appointed place on the appointed day with a thousand followers. When the Count came with two thousand and attacked the English in earnest, the English rushed at them with such valour that the Count's men and the Count's horses soon began to be tumbled down all over the field. The Count himself seized the King round the neck, but the King tumbled *him* out of his saddle in return for the compliment, and, jumping from his own horse, and standing over him, beat away at his iron armour like a black-smith hammering on his anvil. Even when the Count owned himself defeated and offered his sword, the King would not do him the honour to take it, but made him yield it up to a common soldier. There had been such fury shown in this fight, that it was afterwards called the little Battle of Châlons.

The English were very well disposed to be proud of their King after these adventures; so, when he landed at Dover in the year one thousand two hundred and seventy-four (being then thirty-six years old), and went on to Westminster where he and his good Queen were crowned with great magnificence, splendid rejoicings took place. For the coronation-feast there were pro-vided, among other eatables, four hundred oxen, four hundred sheep, four hundred and fifty pigs, eighteen wild boars, three hundred flitches of bacon, and twenty thousand fowls. The fountains and conduits in the street flowed with red and white wine instead of water; the rich citizens hung silks and cloths of the brightest colours out of their windows to increase the beauty of the show, and threw out gold and silver by whole handfuls to make scrambles for the crowd. In short, there was such eating and drinking, such music and capering, such a ringing of bells and tossing of caps, such a shouting, and singing, and revelling, as the narrow overhanging streets of old London City had not witnessed for many a long day. All the people were merry – except the poor Jews, who, trembling within their houses, and scarcely daring to peep out, began to foresee that they would have to find the money for this joviality sooner or later.

To dismiss this sad subject of the Jews for the present, I am sorry to add that in this reign they were most unmercifully pillaged. They were hanged in great numbers, on accusations of having clipped the King's coin – which all kinds of people had done. They were heavily taxed; they were disgracefully badged; they were, on one day, thirteen years after the coronation, taken up with their wives and children and thrown into beastly prisons, until they purchased their release by paying to the King twelve thousand pounds. Finally, every kind of property belonging to them was seized by the King, except so little as would defray the charge of their taking themselves away into foreign countries. Many years elapsed before the hope of gain induced any of their race to return to England, where they had been treated so heartlessly and had suffered so much.

If King Edward the First had been as bad a king to Christians as he was to Jews, he would have been bad indeed. But he was, in general, a wise and great monarch, under whom the country much improved. He had no love for the Great Charter — few Kings had, through many many years — but he had high qualities. The first bold object which he conceived when he came home, was, to unite under one Sovereign England, Scotland, and Wales; the two last of which countries had each a little king of its own, about whom the people were always quarrelling and fighting, and making a prodigious disturbance — a great deal more than he was worth. In the course of King Edward's reign he was engaged, besides, in a war with France. To make these quarrels clearer, we will separate their histories and take them thus. Wales, first. France, second. Scotland, third.

LLEWELLYN was the Prince of Wales. He had been on the side of the Barons in the reign of the stupid old King, but had afterwards sworn allegiance to him. When King Edward came to the throne, Llewellyn was required to swear allegiance to him also; which he refused to do. The King, being crowned and in his own dominions, three times more required Llewellyn to come and do homage; and three times more Llewellyn said he would rather not. He was going to be married to ELEANOR DE MONTFORT, a young lady of the family mentioned in the last reign; and it chanced that this young lady, coming from France with her youngest brother, EMERIC, was taken by an English ship, and was ordered by the English King to be detained. Upon this, the quarrel came to a head. The King went, with his fleet, to the coast of Wales, where, so encompassing Llewellyn, that he could only take refuge in the bleak mountain region of Snowdon in which no provisions could reach him, he was soon starved into an apology, and into a treaty of peace, and into paying the expenses of the war. The King, however, forgave him some of the hardest conditions of the treaty, and consented to his marriage. And he now thought he had reduced Wales to obedience.

But, the Welsh, although they were naturally a gentle, quiet, pleasant people, who liked to receive strangers in their cottages among the mountains, and to set before them with free hospitality whatever they had to eat and drink, and to play to them on their harps, and sing their native ballads to them, were a people of great spirit when their blood was up. Englishmen, after this affair, began to be insolent in Wales, and to assume the air of masters; and the Welsh pride could not bear it. Moreover, they believed in that unlucky old Merlin, some of whose unlucky old prophecies somebody always seemed doomed to remember when there was a chance of its doing harm; and just at this time some blind old gentleman with a harp and a long white beard, who was an excellent person, but had become of an unknown age and tedious, burst out with a declaration that Merlin had predicted that when English money had become round, a Prince of Wales would be crowned in London. Now, King Edward had recently forbidden the English penny to be cut into halves and quarters for halfpence and farthings, and had actually introduced a round coin; therefore, the Welsh people said this was the time Merlin meant, and rose accordingly.

King Edward had bought over PRINCE DAVID, Llewellyn's brother, by heaping favours upon him; but he was the first to revolt, being perhaps troubled in his conscience. One stormy night, he surprised the Castle of Hawarden, in possession of which an English nobleman had been left; killed the whole garrison, and carried off the nobleman a prisoner to Snowdon. Upon this, the Welsh people rose like one man. King Edward, with his army, marching from Worcester to the Menai Strait, crossed it – near to where the wonderful tubular iron bridge now, in days so different, makes a passage for railway trains – by a bridge of boats that enabled forty men to march abreast. He subdued the Island of Anglesea, and sent his men forward to observe the enemy. The sudden appearance of the Welsh created a panic among them, and they fell back to the bridge. The tide had in the meantime risen and separated the boats; the Welsh pursuing them, they were driven into the sea, and there they sunk, in their heavy iron armour, by thousands. After this victory Llewellyn, helped by the severe winter-weather of Wales, gained another battle; but the King ordering a portion of his English army to advance through South Wales, and catch him between two foes, and Llewellyn bravely turning to meet this new enemy, he was surprised and killed – very meanly, for he was unarmed and defenceless. His head was struck off and sent to London, where it was fixed upon the Tower, encircled with a wreath, some say of ivy, some say of willow, some say of silver, to make it look like a ghastly coin in ridicule of the prediction.

David, however, still held out for six months, though eagerly sought after by the King, and hunted by his own countrymen. One of them finally betrayed him with his wife and children. He was sentenced to be hanged, drawn, and quartered; and from that time this became the established punishment of Traitors in England – a punishment wholly without excuse, as being revolting, vile, and cruel, after its object is dead; and which has no sense in it, as its only real degradation (and that nothing can blot out) is to the country that permits on any consideration such abominable barbarity.

Wales was now subdued. The Queen giving birth to a young prince in the Castle of Carnarvon, the King showed him to the Welsh people as their countryman, and called him Prince of Wales; a title that has ever since been borne by the heir-apparent to the English throne – which that little Prince soon became, by the death of his elder brother. The King did better things for the Welsh than that, by improving their laws and encouraging their trade. Disturbances still took place, chiefly occasioned by the avarice and pride of the English Lords, on whom Welsh lands and castles had been bestowed; but they were subdued, and the country never rose again. There is a legend that to prevent the people from being incited to rebellion by the songs of their bards and harpers, Edward had them all put to death. Some of them may have fallen among other men who held out against the King; but this general slaughter is, I think, a fancy of the harpers themselves, who, I dare say, made a song about it many years afterwards, and sang it by the Welsh firesides until it came to be believed.

The foreign war of the reign of Edward the First arose in this way. The crews of two vessels, one a Norman ship, and the other an English ship, happened to go to the same place in their boats to fill their casks with fresh water. Being rough angry fellows, they began to quarrel, and then to fight – the English with their fists; the Normans with their knives – and, in the fight, a Norman was killed. The Norman crew, instead of revenging themselves upon those English sailors with whom they had quarrelled (who were too strong for them, I suspect), took to their ship again in a great rage, attacked the first English ship they met, laid hold of an unoffending merchant who happened to be on board, and brutally hanged him in the rigging of their own vessel with a dog at his feet. This so enraged the English sailors that there was no restraining them; and whenever, and wherever, English sailors met Norman sailors, they fell upon each other tooth and nail. The Irish and Dutch sailors took part with the English; the French and Genoese sailors helped the Normans; and thus the greater part of the mariners sailing over the sea became, in their way, as violent and raging as the sea itself when it is disturbed.

King Edward's fame had been so high abroad that he had been chosen to decide a difference between France and another foreign power, and had lived upon the Continent three years. At first, neither he nor the French King PHILIP (the good Louis had been dead some time) interfered in these quarrels; but when a fleet of eighty English ships engaged and utterly defeated a Norman fleet of two hundred, in a pitched battle fought round a ship at anchor, in which no quarter was given, the matter became too serious to be passed over. King Edward, as Duke of Guienne, was summoned to present himself before the King of France, at Paris, and answer for the damage done by his sailor subjects. At first, he sent the Bishop of London as his representative, and then his brother EDMUND, who was married to the French Queen's mother. I am afraid Edmund was an easy man, and allowed himself to be talked over by his charming relations, the French court ladies; at all events, he was induced to give up his brother's dukedom for forty days – as a mere form, the French King said, to satisfy his honour – and he was so very much astonished, when the time was out, to find that the French King had no idea of giving it up again, that I should not wonder if it hastened his death: which soon took place.

King Edward was a King to win his foreign dukedom back again, if it could be won by energy and valour. He raised a large army, renounced his allegiance as Duke of Guienne, and crossed the sea to carry war into France. Before any important battle was fought, however, a truce was agreed upon for two years; and in the course of that time, the Pope effected a reconciliation. King Edward, who was now a widower, having lost his affectionate and good wife, Eleanor, married the French King's sister, MARGARET; and the Prince of Wales was contracted to the French King's daughter ISABELLA.

Out of bad things, good things sometimes arise. Out of this hanging of the innocent merchant, and the bloodshed and strife it caused, there came to be established one of the greatest powers that the English people now possess. The preparations for the war being very expensive, and King Edward greatly wanting money, and being very arbitrary in his ways of raising it, some of the Barons began firmly to oppose him. Two of them, in particular, HUMPHREY BOHUN, Earl of Hereford, and ROGER BIGOD, Earl of Norfolk, were so stout against him, that they maintained he had no right to command them to head his forces in Guienne, and flatly refused to go there. 'By Heaven, Sir Earl,' said the King to the Earl of Hereford, in a great passion, 'you shall either go or be hanged!' 'By Heaven, Sir King,' replied the Earl, 'I will neither go nor yet will I be hanged!' and both he and the other Earl sturdily left the court, attended by many Lords. The King tried every means of raising money. He taxed the clergy, in spite of all the Pope said to the contrary; and when they refused to pay, reduced them to submission, by saying Very well, then they had no claim upon the government for protection, and any man might plunder them who would – which a good many men were very ready to do, and very readily did, and which the clergy found too losing a game to be played at long. He seized all the wool and leather in the hands of the merchants, promising to pay for it some fine day; and he set a tax upon the exportation of wool, which was so unpopular among the traders that it was called 'The evil toll.' But all would not do. The Barons, led by those two great Earls, declared any taxes imposed without the consent of Parliament, unlawful; and the Parliament refused to impose taxes, until the King should confirm afresh the two Great Charters, and should solemnly declare in writing, that there was no power in the country to raise money from the people, evermore, but the power of Parliament representing all ranks of the people. The King was very unwilling to diminish his own power by allowing this great privilege in the Parliament; but there was no help for it, and he at last complied. We shall come to another King by-and-by, who might have saved his head from rolling off, if he had profited by his example.

The people gained other benefits in Parliament from the good sense and wisdom of this King. Many of the laws were much improved; provision was made for the greater safety of travellers, and the apprehension of thieves and murderers; the priests were prevented from holding too much land, and so becoming too powerful; and Justices of the Peace were first appointed (though not at first under that name) in various parts of the country.

And now we come to Scotland, which was the great and lasting trouble of the reign of King Edward the First.

About thirteen years after King Edward's coronation, Alexander the Third, the King of Scotland, died of a fall from his horse. He had been married to Margaret, King Edward's sister. All their children being dead, the Scottish crown became the right of a young Princess only eight years old, the daughter of ERIC, King of Norway, who had married a daughter of the deceased sovereign. King Edward proposed, that the Maiden of Norway, as this Princess was called, should be engaged to be married to his eldest son; but, unfortunately, as she was coming over to England she fell sick, and landing on one of the Orkney Islands, died there. A great commotion immediately began in Scotland, where as many as thirteen noisy claimants to the vacant throne started up and made a general confusion.

King Edward being much renowned for his sagacity and justice, it seems to have been agreed to refer the dispute to him. He accepted the trust, and went, with an army, to the Borderland where England and Scotland joined. There, he called upon the Scottish gentlemen to meet him at the Castle of Norham, on the English side of the river Tweed; and to that Castle they came. But, before he would take any step in the business, he required those Scottish gentlemen, one and all, to do homage to him as their superior Lord; and when they hesitated, he said, 'By holy Edward, whose crown I wear, I will have my rights, or I will die in maintaining them!' The Scottish gentlemen, who had not expected this, were disconcerted, and asked for three weeks to think about it.

At the end of the three weeks, another meeting took place, on a green plain on the Scottish side of the river. Of all the competitors for the Scottish throne, there were only two who had any real claim, in right of their near kindred to the Royal Family. These were JOHN BALIOL and ROBERT BRUCE: and the right was, I have no doubt, on the side of John Baliol. At this particular meeting John Baliol was not present, but Robert Bruce was; and on Robert Bruce being formally asked whether he acknowledged the King of England for his superior lord, he answered, plainly and distinctly, Yes, he did. Next day, John Baliol appeared, and said the same. This point settled, some arrangements were made for inquiring into their titles.

The inquiry occupied a pretty long time – more than a year. While it was going on, King Edward took the opportunity of making a journey through Scotland, and calling upon the Scottish people of all degrees to acknowledge themselves his vassals, or be imprisoned until they did. In the meanwhile, Commissioners were appointed to conduct the inquiry, a Parliament was held at Berwick about it, the two claimants were heard at full length, and there was a vast amount of talking. At last, in the great hall of the Castle of Berwick, the King gave judgment in favour of John Baliol: who, consenting to receive his crown by the King of England's favour and permission, was crowned at Scone, in an old stone chair which had been used for ages in the abbey there, at the coronations of Scottish Kings. Then, King Edward caused the great seal of Scotland, used since the late King's death, to be broken in four pieces, and placed in the English Treasury; and considered that he now had Scotland (according to the common saying) under his thumb.

Scotland had a strong will of its own yet, however. King Edward, determined that the Scottish King should not forget he was his vassal, summoned him repeatedly to come and defend himself and his Judges before the English Parliament when appeals from the decisions of Scottish courts of justice were being heard. At length, John Baliol, who had no great heart of his own, had so much heart put into him by the brave spirit of the Scottish people, who took this as a national insult, that he refused to come any more. Thereupon, the King further required him to help him in his war abroad (which was then in progress), and to give up, as security for his good behaviour in future, the three strong Scottish Castles of Jedburgh, Roxburgh, and Berwick. Nothing of this being done; on the contrary, the Scottish people concealing their King among their mountains in the Highlands and showing a determination to resist; Edward marched to Berwick with an army of thirty thousand foot, and four thousand horse; took the Castle and slew its whole garrison, and the inhabitants of the town as well – men, women, and children. LORD WARRENNE, Earl of Surrey, then went on to the Castle of Dunbar, before which a battle was fought, and the whole Scottish army defeated with great slaughter. The victory being complete, the Earl of Surrey was left as guardian of Scotland; the principal offices in that kingdom were given to Englishmen; the more powerful Scottish Nobles were obliged to come and live in England; the Scottish crown and sceptre were brought away; and even the old stone chair was carried off and placed in Westminster Abbey, where you may see it now. Baliol had the Tower of London lent him for a residence, with permission to range about within a circle of twenty miles. Three years afterwards he was allowed to go to Normandy, where he had estates, and where he passed the remaining six years of his life: far more happily, I dare say, than he had lived for a long while in angry Scotland.

Now, there was, in the West of Scotland, a gentleman of small fortune, named WILLIAM WALLACE, the second son of a Scottish knight. He was a man of great size and great strength; he was very brave and daring; when he spoke to a body of his countrymen, he could rouse them in a wonderful manner by the power of his burning words; he loved Scotland dearly, and he hated England with his utmost might. The domineering conduct of the English, who now held the places of trust in Scotland made them as intolerable to the proud Scottish people as they had been, under similar circumstances, to the Welsh; and no man in all Scotland regarded them with so much smothered rage as William Wallace. One day, an Englishman in office, little knowing what he was, affronted *him*. Wallace instantly struck him dead, and taking refuge among the rocks and hills, and there joining with his countryman, SIR WILLIAM DOUGLAS, who was also in arms against King Edward, became the most resolute and undaunted champion of a people struggling for their independence that ever lived upon the earth.

The English Guardian of the Kingdom fled before him, and, thus encouraged, the Scottish people revolted everywhere, and fell upon the English without mercy. The Earl of Surrey, by the King's commands, raised all the power of the Border-counties, and two English armies poured into Scotland. Only one Chief, in the face of those armies, stood by Wallace, who, with a force of forty thousand men, awaited the invaders at a place on the river Forth, within two miles of Stirling. Across the river there was only one poor wooden bridge, called the bridge of Kildean – so narrow, that but two men could cross it abreast. With his eyes upon this bridge, Wallace posted the greater part of his men among some rising grounds, and waited calmly. When the English army came up on the opposite bank of the river, messengers were sent forward to offer terms. Wallace sent them back with a defiance, in the name of the freedom of Scotland. Some of the officers of the Earl of Surrey in command of the English, with *their* eyes also on the bridge, advised him to be discreet and not hasty. He, however, urged to immediate battle by some other officers, and particularly by CRESSINGHAM, King Edward's treasurer, and a rash man, gave the word of command to advance. One thousand English crossed the bridge, two abreast; the Scottish troops were as motionless as stone images. Two thousand English crossed; three thousand, four thousand, five. Not a feather, all this time, had been seen to stir among the Scottish bonnets. Now, they all fluttered. 'Forward, one party, to the foot of the Bridge!' cried Wallace, 'and let no more English cross! The rest, down with me on the five thousand who have come over, and cut them all to pieces.' It was done, in the sight of the whole remainder of the English army, who could give no help. Cressingham himself was killed, and the Scotch made whips for their horses of his skin.

King Edward was abroad at this time, and during the successes on the Scottish side which followed, and which enabled bold Wallace to win the whole country back again, and even to ravage the English borders. But, after a few winter months, the King returned, and took the field with more than his usual energy. One night, when a kick from his horse as they both lay on the ground together broke two of his ribs, and a cry arose that he was killed, he leaped into his saddle, regardless of the pain he suffered, and rode through the camp. Day then appearing, he gave the word (still, of course, in that bruised and aching state) Forward! and led his army on to near Falkirk, where the Scottish forces were seen drawn up on some stony ground, behind a morass. Here, he defeated Wallace and killed fifteen thousand of his men. With the shattered remainder, Wallace drew back to Stirling; but, being pursued, set fire to the town that it might give no help to the English, and escaped. The inhabitants of Perth afterwards set fire to their houses for the same reason, and the King, unable to find provisions, was forced to withdraw his army.

Another ROBERT BRUCE, the grandson of him who had disputed the Scottish crown with Baliol, was now in arms against the King (that elder Bruce being dead), and also JOHN COMYN, Baliol's nephew. These two young men might agree in opposing Edward, but could agree in nothing else, as they were rivals for the throne of Scotland. Probably it was because they knew this, and knew what troubles must arise even if they could hope to get the better of the great English King, that the principal Scottish people applied to the Pope for his interference. The Pope, on the principle of losing nothing for want of trying to get it, very coolly claimed that Scotland belonged to him; but this was a little too much, and the Parliament in a friendly manner told him so.

In the spring time of the year one thousand three hundred and three, the King sent SIR JOHN SEGRAVE, whom he made Governor of Scotland, with twenty thousand men, to reduce the rebels. Sir John was not as careful as he should have been, but encamped at Rosslyn, near Edinburgh, with his army divided into three parts. The Scottish forces saw their advantage; fell on each part separately; defeated each; and killed all the prisoners. Then, came the King himself once more, as soon as a great army could be raised; he passed through the whole north of Scotland, laying waste whatsoever came in his way; and he took up his winter quarters at Dunfermline. The Scottish cause now looked so hopeless, that Comyn and the other nobles made submission and received their pardons. Wallace alone stood out. He was invited to surrender, though on no distinct pledge that his life should be spared; but he still defied the ireful King, and lived among the steep crags of the Highland glens, where the eagles made their nests, and where the mountain torrents roared, and the white snow was deep, and the bitter winds blew round his unsheltered head, as he lay through many a pitch-dark night wrapped up in his plaid. Nothing could break his spirit; nothing could lower his courage; nothing could induce him to forget or to forgive his country's wrongs. Even when the Castle of Stirling, which had long held out, was besieged by the King with every kind of military engine then in use; even when the lead upon cathedral roofs was taken down to help to make them; even when the King, though an old man, commanded in the siege as if he were a youth, being so resolved to conquer; even when the brave garrison (then found with amazement to be not two hundred people, including several ladies) were starved and beaten out and were made to submit on their knees, and with every form of disgrace that could aggravate their sufferings; even then, when there was not a ray of hope in Scotland, William Wallace was as proud and firm as if he had beheld the powerful and relentless Edward laying dead at his feet.

Who betrayed William Wallace in the end, is not quite certain. That he was betrayed — probably by an attendant — is too true. He was taken to the Castle of Dumbarton, under SIR JOHN MENTEITH, and thence to London, where the great fame of his bravery and resolution attracted immense concourses of people to behold him. He was tried in Westminster Hall, with a crown of laurel on his head — it is supposed because he was reported to have said that he ought to wear, or that he would wear, a crown there — and was found guilty as a robber, a murderer, and a traitor. What they called a robber (he said to those who tried him) he was, because he had taken spoil from the King's men. What they called a murderer, he was, because he had slain an insolent Englishman. What they called a traitor, he was not, for he had never sworn allegiance to the King, and had ever scorned to do it. He was dragged at the tails of horses to West Smithfield, and there hanged on a high gallows, torn open before he was dead, be headed and quartered. His head was set upon a pole on London Bridge, his right arm was sent to Newcastle, his left arm to Berwick, his legs to Perth and Aberdeen. But, if King Edward had had his body cut into inches, and had sent every separate inch into a separate town, he could not have dispersed it half so far and wide as his fame. Wallace will be remembered in songs and stories, while there are songs and stories in the English tongue, and Scotland will hold him dear while her lakes and mountains last.

Released from this dreaded enemy, the King made a fairer plan of Government for Scotland, divided the offices of honour among Scottish gentlemen and English gentlemen, forgave past offences, and thought, in his old age, that his work was done.

But he deceived himself. Comyn and Bruce conspired, and made an appointment to meet at Dumfries, in the church of the Minorites. There is a story that Comyn was false to Bruce, and had informed against him to the King; that Bruce was warned of his danger and the necessity of flight, by receiving, one night as he sat at supper, from his friend the Earl of Gloucester, twelve pennies and a pair of spurs; that as he was riding angrily to keep his appointment (through a snow-storm, with his horse's shoes reversed that he might not be tracked), he met an evil-looking serving man, a messenger of Comyn, whom he killed, and concealed in whose dress he found letters that proved Comyn's treachery. However this may be, they were likely enough to quarrel in any case, being hot-headed rivals; and, whatever they quarrelled about, they certainly did quarrel in the church where they met, and Bruce drew his dagger and stabbed Comyn, who fell upon the pavement. When Bruce came out, pale and disturbed, the friends who were waiting for him asked what was the matter? 'I think I have killed Comyn,' said he. 'You only think so?' returned one of them; 'I will make sure!' and going into the church, and finding him alive, stabbed him again and again. Knowing that the King would never forgive this new deed of violence, the party then declared Bruce King of Scotland: got him crowned at Scone – without the chair; and set up the rebellious standard once again.

When the King heard of it he kindled with fiercer anger than he had ever shown yet. He caused the Prince of Wales and two hundred and seventy of the young nobility to be knighted – the trees in the Temple Gardens were cut down to make room for their tents, and they watched their armour all night, according to the old usage: some in the Temple Church: some in West-minster Abbey – and at the public Feast which then took place, he swore, by Heaven, and by two swans covered with gold network which his minstrels placed upon the table, that he would avenge the death of Comyn, and would punish the false Bruce. And before all the company, he charged the Prince his son, in case that he should die before accomplishing his vow, not to bury him until it was fulfilled. Next morning the Prince and the rest of the young Knights rode away to the Border-country to join the English army; and the King, now weak and sick, followed in a horse-litter.

Bruce, after losing a battle and undergoing many dangers and much misery, fled to Ircland where he lay concealed through the winter. That winter, Edward passed in hunting down and executing Bruce's relations and adherents, sparing neither youth nor age, and showing no touch of pity or sign of mercy. In the following spring, Bruce reappeared and gained some victories. In these frays, both sides were grievously cruel. For instance – Bruce's two brothers, being taken captives desperately wounded, were ordered by the King to instant execution. Bruce's friend Sir John Douglas, taking his own castle of Douglas out of the hands of an English Lord, roasted the dead bodies of the slaughtered garrison in a great fire made of every movable within it; which dreadful cookery his men called the Douglas Larder. Bruce, still successful, however, drove the Earl of Pembroke and the Earl of Gloucester into the Castle of Ayr and laid siege to it.

The King, who had been laid up all the winter, but had directed the army from his sick-bed, now advanced to Carlisle, and there, causing the litter in which he had travelled to be placed in the Cathedral as an offering to Heaven, mounted his horse once more, and for the last time. He was now sixty-nine years old, and had reigned thirty-five years. He was so ill, that in four days he could go no more than six miles; still, even at that pace, he went on and resolutely kept his face towards the Border. At length, he lay down at the village of Burgh-upon-Sands; and there, telling those around him to impress upon the Prince that he was to remember his father's vow, and was never to rest until he had thoroughly subdued Scotland, he yielded up his last breath.

CHAPTER 17

England under Edward the Second

KING EDWARD THE SECOND, the first Prince of Wales, was twenty-three years old when his father died. There was a certain favourite of his, a young man from Gascony, named PIERS

GAVESTON, of whom his father had so much disapproved that he had ordered him out of England, and had made his son swear by the side of his sick-bed, never to bring him back. But, the Prince no sooner found himself King, than he broke his oath, as so many other Princes and Kings did (they were far too ready to take oaths), and sent for his dear friend immediately.

Now, this same Gaveston was handsome enough, but was a reckless, insolent, audacious fellow. He was detested by the proud English Lords: not only because he had such power over the King, and made the Court such a dissipated place, but, also, because he could ride better than they at tournaments, and was used, in his impudence, to cut very bad jokes on them; calling one, the old hog; another, the stage-player; another, the Jew; another, the black dog of Ardenne. This was as poor wit as need be, but it made those Lords very wroth; and the surly Earl of Warwick, who was the black dog, swore that the time should come when Piers Gaveston should feel the black dog's teeth.

It was not come yet, however, nor did it seem to be coming. The King made him Earl of Cornwall, and gave him vast riches; and when the King went over to France to marry the French Princess, ISABELLA, daughter of PHILIP LE BEL: who was said to be the most beautiful woman in the world: he made Gaveston, Regent of the Kingdom. His splendid marriage-ceremony in the Church of Our Lady at Boulogne, where there were four Kings and three Queens present (quite a pack of Court Cards, for I dare say the Knaves were not wanting), being over, he seemed to care little or nothing for his beautiful wife; but was wild with impatience to meet Gaveston again.

When he landed at home, he paid no attention to anybody else, but ran into the favourite's arms before a great concourse of people, and hugged him, and kissed him, and called him his brother. At the coronation which soon followed, Gaveston was the richest and brightest of all the glittering company there, and had the honour of carrying the crown. This made the proud Lords fiercer than ever; the people, too, despised the favourite, and would never call him Earl of Cornwall; however much he complained to the King and asked him to punish them for not doing so, but persisted in styling him plain Piers Gaveston.

The Barons were so unceremonious with the King in giving him to understand that they would not bear this favourite, that the King was obliged to send him out of the country. The favourite himself was made to take an oath (more oaths!) that he would never come back, and the Barons supposed him to be banished in disgrace, until they heard that he was appointed Governor of Ireland. Even this was not enough for the besotted King, who brought him home again in a year's time, and not only disgusted the Court and the people by his doting folly, but offended his beautiful wife too, who never liked him afterwards.

He had now the old Royal want – of money – and the Barons had the new power of positively refusing to let him raise any. He summoned a Parliament at York; the Barons refused to make one, while the favourite was near him. He summoned another Parliament at Westminster, and sent Gaveston away. Then, the Barons came, completely armed, and appointed a committee of themselves to correct abuses in the state and in the King's household. He got some money on these conditions, and directly set off with Gaveston to the Border-country, where they spent it in idling away the time, and feasting, while Bruce made ready to drive the English out of Scotland. For, though the old King had even made this poor weak son of his swear (as some say) that he would not bury his bones, but would have them boiled clean in a caldron, and carried before the English army until Scotland was entirely subdued, the second Edward was so unlike the first that Bruce gained strength and power every day.

The committee of Nobles, after some months of deliberation, ordained that the King should henceforth call a Parliament together, once every year, and even twice if necessary, instead of summoning it only when he chose. Further, that Gaveston should once more be banished, and, this time, on pain of death if he ever came back. The King's tears were of no avail; he was obliged to send his favourite to Flanders. As soon as he had done so, however, he dissolved the Parliament, with the low cunning of a mere fool, and set off to the North of England, thinking to get an army about him to oppose the Nobles. And once again he brought Gaveston home, and heaped upon him all the riches and titles of which the Barons had deprived him.

The Lords saw, now, that there was nothing for it but to put the favourite to death. They could have done so, legally, according to the terms of his banishment; but they did so, I am sorry to say, in a shabby manner. Led by the Earl of Lancaster, the King's cousin, they first of all attacked the King and Gaveston at Newcastle. They had time to escape by sea, and the mean King, having his precious Gaveston with him, was quite content to leave his lovely wife behind. When they were comparatively safe, they separated; the King went to York to collect a force of soldiers; and the favourite shut himself up, in the meantime, in Scarborough Castle, overlooking the sea. This was what the Barons wanted. They knew that the Castle could not hold out; they attacked it, and made Gaveston surrender. He delivered himself up to the Earl of Pembroke – that Lord whom he had called the Jew – on the Earl's pledging his faith and knightly word, that no harm should happen to him and no violence be done him.

Now, it was agreed with Gaveston that he should be taken to the Castle of Wallingford, and there kept in honourable custody. They travelled as far as Dedington, near Banbury, where, in the Castle of that place, they stopped for a night to rest. Whether the Earl of Pembroke left his prisoner there, knowing what would happen, or really left him thinking no harm, and only going (as he pretended) to visit his wife, the Countess, who was in the neighbourhood, is no great matter now; in any case, he was bound as an honourable gentleman to protect his prisoner, and he did not do it. In the morning, while the favourite was yet in bed, he was required to dress himself and come down into the court-yard. He did so without any mistrust, but started and turned pale when he found it full of strange armed men. 'I think you know me?' said their leader, also armed from head to foot. 'I am the black dog of Ardenne!'

The time was come when Piers Gaveston was to feel the black dog's teeth indeed. They set him on a mule, and carried him, in mock state and with military music, to the black dog's kennel – Warwick Castle – where a hasty council, composed of some great noblemen, considered what should be done with him. Some were for sparing him, but one loud voice – it was the black dog's bark, I dare say – sounded through the Castle Hall, uttering these words: 'You have the fox in your power. Let him go now, and you must hunt him again.'

They sentenced him to death. He threw himself at the feet of the Earl of Lancaster – the old hog – but the old hog was as savage as the dog. He was taken out upon the pleasant road, leading from Warwick to Coventry, where the beautiful river Avon, by which, long afterwards, WILLIAM SHAKESPEARE was born and now lies buried, sparkled in the bright landscape of the beautiful May-day; and there they struck off his wretched head, and stained the dust with his blood.

When the King heard of this black deed, in his grief and rage he denounced relentless war against his Barons, and both sides were in arms for half a year. But, it then became necessary for them to join their forces against Bruce, who had used the time well while they were divided, and had now a great power in Scotland.

Intelligence was brought that Bruce was then besieging Stirling Castle, and that the Governor had been obliged to pledge himself to surrender it, unless he should be relieved before a certain day. Hereupon, the King ordered the nobles and their fighting-men to meet him at Berwick; but, the nobles cared so little for the King, and so neglected the summons, and lost time, that only on the day before that appointed for the surrender, did the King find himself at Stirling, and even then with a smaller force than he had expected. However, he had, altogether, a hundred thousand men, and Bruce had not more than forty thousand; but, Bruce's army was strongly posted in three square columns, on the ground lying between the Burn or Brook of Bannock and the walls of Stirling Castle.

On the very evening, when the King came up, Bruce did a brave act that encouraged his men. He was seen by a certain HENRY DE BOHUN, an English Knight, riding about before his army on a little horse, with a light battle-axe in his hand, and a crown of gold on his head. This English Knight, who was mounted on a strong war-horse, cased in steel, strongly armed, and able (as he thought) to overthrow Bruce by crushing him with his mere weight, set spurs to his great charger, rode on him, and made a thrust at him with his heavy spear. Bruce parried the thrust, and with one blow of his battle-axe split his skull.

The Scottish men did not forget this, next day when the battle raged. RANDOLPH, Bruce's valiant Nephew, rode, with the small body of men he commanded, into such a host of the English, all shining in polished armour in the sunlight, that they seemed to be swallowed up and lost, as if they had plunged into the sea. But, they fought so well, and did such dreadful execution, that the English staggered. Then came Bruce himself upon them, with all the rest of his army. While they were thus hard pressed and amazed, there appeared upon the hills what they supposed to be a new Scottish army, but what were really only the camp followers, in number fifteen thousand: whom Bruce had taught to show themselves at that place and time. The Earl of Gloucester, commanding the English horse, made a last rush to change the fortune of the day; but Bruce (like Jack the Giant-killer in the story) had had pits dug in the ground, and covered over with turfs and stakes. Into these, as they gave way beneath the weight of the horses, riders and horses rolled by hundreds. The English were completely routed; all their treasure, stores, and engines, were taken by the Scottish men; so many waggons and other wheeled vehicles were seized, that it is related that they would have reached, if they had been drawn out in a line, one hundred and eighty miles. The fortunes of Scotland were, for the time, completely changed; and never was a battle won, more famous upon Scottish ground, than this great battle of BANNOCKBURN.

Plague and famine succeeded in England; and still the power-less King and his disdainful Lords were always in contention. Some of the turbulent chiefs of Ireland made proposals to Bruce, to accept the rule of that country. He sent his brother Edward to them, who was crowned King of Ireland. He afterwards went himself to help his brother in his Irish wars, but his brother was defeated in the end and killed. Robert Bruce, returning to Scotland, still increased his strength there.

As the King's rule had begun in a favourite, so it seemed likely to end in one. He was too poor a creature to rely at all upon himself; and his new favourite was one HUGH LE DESPENSER, the son of a gentleman of ancient family. Hugh was handsome and brave, but he was the favourite of a weak King, whom no man cared a rush for, and that was a dangerous place to hold. The Nobles leagued against him, because the King liked him; and they lay in wait, both for his ruin and his father's. Now, the King had married him to the daughter of the late Earl of Gloucester, and had given both him and his father great possessions in Wales. In their endeavours to extend these, they gave violent offence to an angry Welsh gentleman, named JOHN DE MOWBRAY, and to divers other angry Welsh gentlemen, who resorted to arms, took their castles, and seized their estates. The Earl of Lancaster had first placed the favourite (who was a poor relation of his own) at Court, and he considered his own dignity offended by the preference he received and the honours he acquired; so he, and the Barons who were his friends, joined the Welshmen, marched on London, and sent a message to the King demanding to have the favourite and his father banished. At first, the King unaccountably took it into his head to be spirited, and to send them a bold reply; but when they quartered themselves around Holborn and Clerkenwell, and went down, armed, to the Parliament at Westminster, he gave way, and complied with their demands.

His turn of triumph came sooner than he expected. It arose out of an accidental circumstance. The beautiful Queen, happening to be travelling, came one night to one of the royal castles, and demanded to be lodged and entertained there until morning. The governor of this castle, who was one of the enraged lords, was away, and in his absence, his wife refused admission to the Queen; a scuffle took place among the common men on either side, and some of the royal attendants were killed. The people, who cared nothing for the King, were very angry that their beautiful Queen should be thus rudely treated in her own dominions; and the King, taking advantage of this feeling, besieged the castle, took it, and then called the two Despensers home. Upon this, the confederate lords and the Welshmen went over to Bruce. The King encountered them at Boroughbridge, gained the victory, and took a number of distinguished prisoners; among them, the Earl of Lancaster, now an old man, upon whose destruction he was resolved. This Earl was taken to his own castle of Pontefract, and there tried and found guilty by an unfair court appointed for the purpose; he was not even allowed to speak in his own defence. He was insulted, pelted, mounted on a starved pony without saddle or bridle, carried out, and beheaded. Eight-and-twenty knights were hanged, drawn, and quartered. When the King had despatched this bloody work, and had made a fresh and a long truce with Bruce, he took the Despensers into greater favour than ever, and made the father Earl of Winchester.

One prisoner, and an important one, who was taken at Boroughbridge, made his escape, however, and turned the tide against the King. This was ROGER MORTIMER, always resolutely opposed to him, who was sentenced to death, and placed for safe custody in the Tower of London. He treated his guards to a quantity of wine into which he had put a sleeping potion; and, when they were insensible, broke out of his dungeon, got into a kitchen, climbed up the chimney, let himself down from the roof of the building with a rope-ladder, passed the sentries, got down to the river, and made away in a boat to where servants and horses were waiting for him. He finally escaped to France, where CHARLES LE BEL, the brother of the beautiful Queen, was King. Charles sought to quarrel with the King of England, on pretence of his not having come to do him homage at his coronation. It was proposed that the beautiful Queen should go over to arrange the dispute; she went, and wrote home to the King, that as he was sick and could not come to France himself, perhaps it would be better to send over the young Prince, their son, who was only twelve years old, who could do homage to her brother in his stead, and in whose company she would immediately return. The King sent him: but, both he and the Queen remained at the French Court, and Roger Mortimer became the Queen's lover.

When the King wrote, again and again, to the Queen to come home, she did not reply that she despised him too much to live with him any more (which was the truth), but said she was afraid of the two Despensers. In short, her design was to overthrow the favourites' power, and the King's power, such as it was, and invade England. Having obtained a French force of two thousand men, and being joined by all the English exiles then in France, she landed, within a year, at Orewell, in Suffolk, where she was immediately joined by the Earls of Kent and Norfolk, the King's two brothers; by other powerful noblemen; and lastly, by the first English general who was despatched to check her: who went over to her with all his men. The people of London, receiving these tidings, would do nothing for the King, but broke open the Tower, let out all his prisoners, and threw up their caps and hurrahed for the beautiful Queen.

The King, with his two favourites, fled to Bristol, where he left old Despenser in charge of the town and castle, while he went on with the son to Wales. The Bristol men being opposed to the King, and it being impossible to hold the town with enemies everywhere within the walls, Despenser yielded it up on the third day, and was instantly brought to trial for having traitorously influenced what was called 'the King's mind' – though I doubt if the King ever had any. He was a venerable old man, upwards of ninety years of age, but his age gained no respect or mercy. He was hanged, torn open while he was yet alive, cut up into pieces, and thrown to the dogs. His son was soon taken, tried at Hereford before the same judge on a long series of foolish charges, found guilty, and hanged upon a gallows fifty feet high, with a chaplet of nettles round his head. His poor old father and he were innocent enough of any worse crimes than the crime of having been friends of a King, on whom, as a mere man, they would never have deigned to cast a favourable look. It is a bad crime, I know, and leads to worse; but, many lords and gentlemen – I even think some ladies, too, if I recollect right – have committed it in England, who have neither been given to the dogs, nor hanged up fifty feet high.

The wretched King was running here and there, all this time, and never getting anywhere in particular, until he gave himself up, and was taken off to Kenilworth Castle. When he was safely lodged there, the Queen went to London and met the Parliament. And the Bishop of Hereford, who was the most skilful of her friends, said, What was to be done now? Here was an imbecile, indolent, miserable King upon the throne; wouldn't it be better to take him off, and put his son there instead? I don't know whether the Queen really pitied him at this pass, but she began to cry; so, the Bishop said, Well, my Lords and Gentlemen, what do you think, upon the whole, of sending down to Kenilworth, and seeing if His Majesty (God bless him, and forbid we should depose him!) won't resign?

My Lords and Gentlemen thought it a good notion, so a deputation of them went down to Kenilworth; and there the King came into the great hall of the Castle, commonly dressed in a poor black gown; and when he saw a certain bishop among them, fell down, poor feeble-headed man, and made a wretched spectacle of himself. Somebody lifted him up, and then SIR WILLIAM TRUSSEL, the Speaker of the House of Commons, almost frightened him to death by making him a tremendous speech to the effect that he was no longer a King, and that everybody renounced allegiance to him. After which, SIR THOMAS BLOUNT, the Steward of the Household, nearly finished him, by coming forward and breaking his white wand – which was a ceremony only performed at a King's death. Being asked in this pressing manner what he thought of resigning, the King said he thought it was the best thing he could do. So, he did it, and they proclaimed his son next day.

I wish I could close his history by saying that he lived a harmless life in the Castle and the Castle gardens at Kenilworth, many years – that he had a favourite, and plenty to eat and drink – and, having that, wanted nothing. But he was shamefully humiliated. He was outraged, and slighted, and had dirty water from ditches given him to shave with, and wept and said he would have clean warm water, and was altogether very miserable. He was moved from this castle to that castle, and from that castle to the other castle, because this lord or that lord, or the other lord, was too kind to him: until at last he came to Berkeley Castle, near the River Severn, where (the Lord Berkeley being then ill and absent) he fell into the hands of two black ruffians, called THOMAS GOURNAY and WILLIAM OGLE.

One night – it was the night of September the twenty-first, one thousand three hundred and twenty-seven – dreadful screams were heard, by the startled people in the neighbouring town, ringing through the thick walls of the Castle, and the dark deep night; and they said, as they were thus horribly awakened from their sleep, 'May Heaven be merciful to the King; for those cries forbode that no good is being done to him in his dismal prison!' Next morning he was dead – not bruised, or stabbed, or marked upon the body, but much distorted in the face; and it was whispered afterwards, that those two villians, Gournay and Ogle, had burnt up his inside with a red-hot iron.

If you ever come near Gloucester, and see the centre tower of its beautiful Cathedral, with its four rich pinnacles, rising lightly in the air; you may remember that the wretched Edward the Second was buried in the old abbey of that ancient city, at forty-three years old, after being for nineteen years and a half a perfectly incapable King.

CHAPTER 18

England under Edward the Third

ROGER MORTIMER, the Queen's lover (who escaped to France in the last chapter), was far from profiting by the examples he had had of the fate of favourites. Having, through the Queen's influence, come into possession of the estates of the two Despensers, he became extremely proud and ambitious, and sought to be the real ruler of England. The young King, who was crowned at fourteen years of age with all the usual solemnities, resolved not to bear this, and soon pursued Mortimer to his ruin.

The people themselves were not fond of Mortimer – first, because he was a Royal favourite; secondly, because he was supposed to have helped to make a peace with Scotland which now took place, and in virtue of which the young King's sister Joan, only seven years old, was promised in marriage to David, the son and heir of Robert Bruce, who was only five years old. The nobles hated Mortimer because of his pride, riches, and power. They went so far as to take up arms against him; but were obliged to submit. The Earl of Kent, one of those who did so, but who afterwards went over to Mortimer and the Queen, was made an example of in the following cruel manner:

He seems to have been anything but a wise old earl; and he was persuaded by the agents of the favourite and the Queen, that poor King Edward the Second was not really dead; and thus was betrayed into writing letters favouring his rightful claim to the throne. This was made out to be high treason, and he was tried, found guilty, and sentenced to be executed. They took the poor old lord outside the town of Winchester, and there kept him waiting some three or four hours until they could find somebody to cut off his head. At last, a convict said he would do it, if the government would pardon him in return; and they gave him the pardon; and at one blow he put the Earl of Kent out of his last suspense.

While the Queen was in France, she had found a lovely and good young lady, named Philippa, who she thought would make an excellent wife for her son. The young King married this lady, soon after he came to the throne; and her first child, Edward, Prince of Wales, afterwards became celebrated, as we shall presently see, under the famous title of EDWARD THE BLACK PRINCE.

The young King, thinking the time ripe for the downfall of Mortimer, took counsel with Lord Montacute how he should proceed. A Parliament was going to be held at Nottingham, and that lord recommended that the favourite should be seized by night in Nottingham Castle, where he was sure to be. Now, this, like many other things, was more easily said than done; because, to guard against treachery, the great gates of the Castle were locked every night, and the great keys were carried up-stairs to the Queen, who laid them under her own pillow. But the Castle had a governor, and the governor being Lord Montacute's friend, confided to him how he knew of a secret passage underground, hidden from observation by the weeds and brambles with which it was overgrown; and how, through that passage, the conspirators might enter in the dead of the night, and go straight to Mortimer's room. Accordingly, upon a certain dark night, at midnight, they made their way through this dismal place: startling the rats, and frightening the owls and bats: and came safely to the bottom of the main tower of the Castle, where the King met them, and took them up a profoundly-dark staircase in a deep silence. They soon heard the voice of Mortimer in council with some friends; and bursting into the room with a sudden noise, took him prisoner. The Queen cried out from her bed-chamber, 'Oh, my sweet son, my dear son, spare my gentle Mortimer!' They carried him off, however; and, before the next Parliament, accused him of having made differences between the young King and his mother, and of having brought about the death of the Earl of Kent, and even of the late King; for, as you know by this time, when they wanted to get rid of a man in those old days, they were not particular of what they accused him. Mortimer was found guilty of all this, and was sentenced to be hanged at Tyburn. The King shut his mother up in genteel confinement, where she passed the rest of her life; and now he became King in earnest.

The first effort he made was to conquer Scotland. The English lords who had lands in Scotland, finding that their rights were not respected under the late peace, made war on their own account: choosing for their general, Edward, the son of John Baliol, who made such a vigorous fight, that in less than two months he won the whole Scottish Kingdom. He was joined, when thus triumphant, by the King and Parliament; and he and the King in person besieged the Scottish forces in Berwick. The whole Scottish army coming to the assistance of their countrymen, such a furious battle ensued, that thirty thousand men are said to have been killed in it. Baliol was then crowned King of Scotland, doing homage to the King of England; but little came of his successes after all, for the Scottish men rose against him, within no very long time, and David Bruce came back within ten years and took his kingdom.

France was a far richer country than Scotland, and the King had a much greater mind to conquer it. So, he let Scotland alone, and pretended that he had a claim to the French throne in right of his mother. He had, in reality, no claim at all; but that mattered little in those times. He brought over to his cause many little princes and sovereigns, and even courted the alliance of the people of Flanders – a busy, working community, who had very small respect for kings, and whose head man was a brewer. With such forces as he raised by these means, Edward invaded France; but he did little by that, except run into debt in carrying on the war to the extent of three hundred thousand pounds. The next year he did better; gaining a great sea-fight in the harbour of Sluys. This success, however, was very short-lived, for the Flemings took fright at the siege of Saint Omer and ran away, leaving their weapons and baggage behind them. Philip, the French King, coming up with his army, and Edward being very anxious to decide the war, proposed to settle the difference by single combat with him, or by a fight of one hundred knights on each side. The French King said, he thanked him; but being very well as he was, he would rather not. So, after some skirmishing and talking, a short peace was made.

It was soon broken by King Edward's favouring the cause of John, Earl of Montford; a French nobleman, who asserted a claim of his own against the French King, and offered to do homage to England for the Crown of France, if he could obtain it through England's help. This French lord, himself, was soon defeated by the French King's son, and shut up in a tower in Paris; but his wife, a courageous and beautiful woman, who is said to have had the courage of a man, and the heart of a lion, assembled the people of Brittany, where she then was; and, showing them her infant son, made many pathetic entreaties to them not to desert her and their young Lord. They took fire at this appeal, and rallied round her in the strong castle of Hennebon. Here she was not only besieged without by the French under Charles de Blois, but was endangered within by a dreary old bishop, who was always representing to the people what horrors they must undergo if they were faithful – first from famine, and afterwards from fire and sword. But this noble lady, whose heart never failed her, encouraged her soldiers by her own example; went from post to post like a great general; even mounted on horseback fully armed, and, issuing from the castle by a by-path, fell upon the French camp, set fire to the tents, and threw the whole force into disorder. This done, she got safely back to Hennebon again, and was received with loud shouts of joy by the defenders of the castle, who had given her up for lost. As they were now very short of provisions, however, and as they could not dine off enthusiasm, and as the old bishop was always saying, 'I told you what it would come to!' they began to lose heart, and to talk of yielding the castle up. The brave Countess retiring to an upper room and looking with great grief out to sea, where she expected relief from England, saw, at this very time, the English ships in the distance, and was relieved and rescued! Sir Walter Manning, the English commander, so admired her courage, that, being come into the castle with the English knights, and having made a feast there, he assaulted the French by way of dessert, and beat them off triumphantly. Then he and the knights came back to the castle with great joy; and the Countess who had watched them from a high tower, thanked them with all her heart, and kissed them every one.

This noble lady distinguished herself afterwards in a sea-fight with the French off Guernsey, when she was on her way to England to ask for more troops. Her great spirit roused another lady, the wife of another French lord (whom the French King very barbarously murdered), to distinguish herself scarcely less. The time was fast coming, however, when Edward, Prince of Wales, was to be the great star of this French and English war.

It was in the month of July, in the year one thousand three hundred and forty-six, when the King embarked at Southampton for France, with an army of about thirty thousand men in all, attended by the Prince of Wales and by several of the chief nobles. He landed at La Hogue in Normandy; and, burning and destroying as he went, according to custom, advanced up the left bank of the River Seine, and fired the small towns even close to Paris; but, being watched from the right bank of the river by the French King and all his army, it came to this at last, that Edward found himself, on Saturday the twenty-sixth of August, one thousand three hundred and forty-six, on a rising ground behind the little French village of Crecy, face to face with the French King's force. And, although the French King had an enormous army – in number more than eight times his – he there resolved to beat him or be beaten.

The young Prince, assisted by the Earl of Oxford and the Earl of Warwick, led the first division of the English army; two other great Earls led the second; and the King, the third. When the morning dawned, the King received the sacrament, and heard prayers, and then, mounted on horseback with a white wand in his hand, rode from company to company, and rank to rank, cheering and encouraging both officers and men. Then the whole army breakfasted, each man sitting on the ground where he had stood; and then they remained quietly on the ground with their weapons ready.

Up came the French King with all his great force. It was dark and angry weather; there was an eclipse of the sun; there was a thunder-storm, accompanied with tremendous rain; the frightened birds flew screaming above the soldiers' heads. A certain captain in the French army advised the French King, who was by no means cheerful, not to begin the battle until the morrow. The King, taking this advice, gave the word to halt. But, those behind not understanding it, or desiring to be foremost with the rest, came pressing on. The roads for a great distance were covered with this immense army, and with the common people from the villages, who were flourishing their rude weapons, and making a great noise. Owing to these circumstances, the French army advanced in the greatest confusion; every French lord doing what he liked with his own men, and putting out the men of every other French lord.

Now, their King relied strongly upon a great body of cross-bowmen from Genoa; and these he ordered to the front to begin the battle, on finding that he could not stop it. They shouted once, they shouted twice, they shouted three times, to alarm the English archers; but, the English would have heard them shout three thousand times and would have never moved. At last the cross-bowmen went forward a little, and began to discharge their bolts; upon which, the English let fly such a hail or arrows, that the Genoese speedily made off — for their cross-bows, besides being heavy to carry, required to be wound up with a handle, and consequently took time to re-load; the English, on the other hand, could discharge their arrows almost as fast as the arrows could fly.

When the French King saw the Genoese turning, he cried out to his men to kill those scoundrels, who were doing harm instead of service. This increased the confusion. Meanwhile the

English archers, continuing to shoot as fast as ever, shot down great numbers of the French soldiers and knights; whom certain sly Cornish-men and Welsh-men, from the English army, creeping along the ground, despatched with great knives.

The Prince and his division were at this time so hard-pressed, that the Earl of Warwick sent a message to the King, who was overlooking the battle from a windmill, beseeching him to send more aid.

'Is my son killed?' said the King.

'No, sire, please God,' returned the messenger.

'Is he wounded?' said the King.

'No, sire.'

'Is he thrown to the ground?' said the King.

'No, sire, not so; but, he is very hard-pressed.'

'Then,' said the King, 'go back to those who sent you, and tell them I shall send no aid; because I set my heart upon my son proving himself this day a brave knight, and because I am resolved, please God, that the honour of a great victory shall be his!'

These bold words, being reported to the Prince and his division, so raised their spirits, that they fought better than ever. The King of France charged gallantly with his men many times; but it was of no use. Night closing in, his horse was killed under him by an English arrow, and the knights and nobles who had clustered thick about him early in the day, were now completely scattered. At last, some of his few remaining followers led him off the field by force, since he would not retire of himself, and they journeyed away to Amiens. The victorious English, lighting their watch-fires, made merry on the field, and the King, riding to meet his gallant son, took him in his arms, kissed him, and told him that he had acted nobly, and proved himself worthy of the day and of the crown. While it was yet night, King Edward was hardly aware of the great victory he had gained; but, next day, it was discovered that eleven princes, twelve hundred knights, and thirty thousand common men lay dead upon the French side. Among these was the King of Bohemia, an old blind man; who, having been told that his son was wounded in the battle, and that no force could stand against the Black Prince, called to him two knights, put himself on horseback between them, fastened the three bridles together, and dashed in among the English, where he was presently slain. He bore as his crest three white ostrich feathers, with the motto *Ich dien*, signifying in English 'I serve.' This crest and motto were taken by the Prince of Wales in remembrance of that famous day, and have been borne by the Prince of Wales ever since.

Five days after this great battle, the King laid siege to Calais. This siege – ever afterwards memorable – lasted nearly a year. In order to starve the inhabitants out, King Edward built so many wooden houses for the lodgings of his troops, that it is said their quarters looked like a second Calais suddenly sprung around the first. Early in the siege, the governor of the town drove out what he called the useless mouths, to the number of seventeen hundred persons, men and women, young and old. King Edward allowed them to pass through his lines, and even fed them, and dismissed them with money; but, later in the siege, he was not so merciful – five hundred more, who were afterwards driven out, dying of starvation and misery. The garrison were so hard-pressed at last, that they sent a letter to King Philip, telling him that they had eaten all the horses, all the dogs, and all the rats and mice that could be found in the place; and, that if he did not relieve them, they must either surrender to the English, or eat one another. Philip made one effort to give them relief; but they were so hemmed in by the English power, that he could not succeed, and was fain to leave the place. Upon this they hoisted the English flag, and surrendered to King Edward. 'Tell your general,' said he to the humble messengers who came out of the town, 'that I require to have sent here, six of the most distinguished citizens, bare-legged, and in their shirts, with ropes about their necks; and let those six men bring with them the keys of the castle and the town.'

When the Governor of Calais related this to the people in the Market-place, there was great weeping and distress; in the midst of which, one worthy citizen, named Eustace de Saint Pierre, rose up and said, that if the six men required were not sacrificed, the whole population would be; therefore, he offered himself as the first. Encouraged by this bright example, five other worthy citizens rose up one after another, and offered themselves to save the rest. The Governor, who was too badly wounded to be able to walk, mounted a poor old horse that had not been eaten, and conducted these good men to the gate, while all the people cried and mourned.

Edward received them wrathfully, and ordered the heads of

The Intercession of Queen Philippa for the Citizens of Calais the whole six to be struck off. However, the good Queen fell upon her knees, and besought the King to give them up to her. The King replied, 'I wish you had been somewhere else; but I cannot refuse you.' So she had them properly dressed, made a feast for them, and sent them back with a handsome present, to the great rejoicing of the whole camp. I hope the people of Calais loved the daughter to whom she gave birth soon afterwards, for her gentle mother's sake.

Now came that terrible disease, the Plague, into Europe, hurrying from the heart of China; and killed the wretched people – especially the poor – in such enormous numbers, that one-half of the inhabitants of England are related to have died of it. It killed the cattle, in great numbers, too; and so few working men remained alive, that there were not enough left to till the ground.

After eight years of differing and quarrelling, the Prince of Wales again invaded France with an army of sixty thousand men. He went through the south of the country, burning and plundering wheresoever he went; while his father, who had still the Scottish war upon his hands, did the like in Scotland, but was harassed and worried in his retreat from that country by the Scottish men, who repaid his cruelties with interest.

The French King, Philip, was now dead, and was succeeded by his son John. The Black Prince, called by that name from the colour of the armour he wore to set off his fair complexion, continuing to burn and destroy in France, roused John into determined opposition; and so cruel had the Black Prince been in his campaign, and so severely had the French peasants suffered, that he could not find one who, for love, or money, or the fear of death, would tell him what the French King was doing, or where he was. Thus it happened that he came upon the French King's forces, all of a sudden, near the town of Poitiers, and found that the whole neighbouring country was occupied by a vast French army. 'God help us!' said the Black Prince, 'we must make the best of it.'

So, on a Sunday morning, the eighteenth of September, the Prince – whose army was now reduced to ten thousand men in all – prepared to give battle to the French King, who had sixty thousand horse alone. While he was so engaged, there came riding from the French camp, a Cardinal, who had persuaded John to let him offer terms, and try to save the shedding of

Christian blood. 'Save my honour,' said the Prince to this good priest, 'and save the honour of my army, and I will make any reasonable terms.' He offered to give up all the towns, castles, and prisoners, he had taken, and to swear to make no war in France for seven years; but, as John would hear of nothing but his surrender, with a hundred of his chief knights, the treaty was broken off, and the Prince said quietly – 'God defend the right; we shall fight to-morrow.'

Therefore, on the Monday morning, at break of day, the two armies prepared for battle. The English were posted in a strong place, which could only be approached by one narrow lane, skirted by hedges on both sides. The French attacked them by this lane; but were so galled and slain by English arrows from behind the hedges, that they were forced to retreat. Then went six hundred English bowmen round about, and, coming upon the rear of the French army, rained arrows on them thick and fast. The French knights, thrown into confusion, quitted their banners and dispersed in all directions. Said Sir John Chandos to the Prince, 'Ride forward, noble Prince, and the day is yours. The King of France is so valiant a gentleman, that I know he will never fly, and may be taken prisoner.' Said the Prince to this, 'Advance, English banners, in the name of God and St George!' and on they pressed until they came up with the French King, fighting fiercely with his battle-axe, and, when all his nobles had forsaken him, attended faithfully to the last by his youngest son Philip, only sixteen years of age. Father and son fought well, and the King had already two wounds in his face, and had been beaten down, when he at last delivered himself to a banished French knight, and gave him his right-hand glove in token that he had done so.

The Black Prince was generous as well as brave, and he invited his royal prisoner to supper in his tent, and waited upon him at table, and, when they afterwards rode into London in a gorgeous procession, mounted the French King on a fine cream-coloured horse, and rode at his side on a little pony. This was all very kind, but I think it was, perhaps, a little theatrical too, and has been made more meritorious than it deserved to be; especially as I am inclined to think that the greatest kindness to the King of France would have been not to have shown him to the people at all. However, it must be said, for these acts of politeness, that in course of time, they did much to soften the horrors of war and the passions of conquerors. It was a long, long time before the common soldiers began to have the benefit of such courtly deeds; but they did at last; and thus it is possible that a poor soldier who asked for quarter at the battle of Waterloo, or any other such great fight, may have owed his life indirectly to Edward the Black Prince.

At this time there stood in the Strand, in London, a palace called the Savoy, which was given up to the captive King of France and his son for their residence. As the King of Scotland had now been King Edward's captive for eleven years too, his success was, at this time, tolerably complete. The Scottish business was settled by the prisoner being released under the title of Sir David, King of Scotland, and by his engaging to pay a large ransom. The state of France encouraged England to propose harder terms to that country, where the people rose against the unspeakable cruelty and barbarity of its nobles; where the nobles rose in turn against the people; where the most frightful outrages were committed on all sides; and where the insurrection of the peasants, called the insurrection of the Jacquerie, from Jacques, a common Christian name among the country people of France, awakened terrors and hatreds that have scarcely yet passed away. A treaty called the Great Peace, was at last signed, under which King Edward agreed to give up the greater part of his conquests, and King John to pay, within six years, a ransom of three million crowns of gold. He was so beset by his own nobles and courtiers for having yielded to these conditions – though they could help him to no better – that he came back of his own will to his old palace-prison of the Savoy, and there died.

There was a Sovereign of Castile at that time, called PEDRO THE CRUEL, who deserved the name remarkably well; having committed, among other cruelties, a variety of murders. This amiable monarch being driven from his throne for his crimes, went to the province of Bordeaux, where the Black Prince – now married to his cousin JOAN, a pretty widow – was residing, and besought his help. The Prince, who took to him much more kindly than a prince of such fame ought to have taken to such a ruffian, readily listened to his fair promises, and agreeing to help him, sent secret orders to some troublesome disbanded soldiers of his and his father's, who called themselves the Free Companions, and who had been a pest to the French people, for some time, to aid this Pedro. The Prince, himself, going into Spain to head the army of relief, soon set Pedro on his throne again – where he no sooner found himself, than, of course, he behaved like the villain he was, broke his word without the least shame, and abandoned all the promises he had made to the Black Prince.

Now, it had cost the Prince a good deal of money to pay soldiers to support this murderous King; and finding himself, when he came back disgusted to Bordeaux, not only in bad health, but deeply in debt, he began to tax his French subjects to pay his creditors. They appealed to the French King, CHARLES; war again broke out; and the French town of Limoges, which the Prince had greatly benefited, went over to the French King. Upon this he ravaged the province of which it was the capital; burnt, and plundered, and killed in the old sickening way; and refused mercy to the prisoners, men, women, and children taken in the offending town, though he was so ill and so much in need of pity himself from Heaven, that he was carried in a litter. He lived to come home and make himself popular with the people and Parliament, and he died on Trinity Sunday, the eighth of June, one thousand three hundred and seventy-six, at forty-six years old.

The whole nation mourned for him as one of the most renowned and beloved princes it had ever had; and he was buried with great lamentations in Canterbury Cathedral. Near to the tomb of Edward the Confessor, his monument, with his figure, carved in stone, and represented in the old black armour, lying on its back, may be seen at this day, with an ancient coat of mail, a helmet, and a pair of gauntlets hanging from a beam above it, which most people like to believe were once worn by the Black Prince.

King Edward did not outlive his renowned son, long. He was old, and one Alice Perrers, a beautiful lady, had contrived to make him so fond of her in his old age, that he could refuse her nothing, and made himself ridiculous. She little deserved his love, or – what I dare say she valued a great deal more – the jewels of the late Queen, which he gave her among other rich presents. She took the very ring from his finger on the morning of the day when he died, and left him to be pillaged by his faithless servants. Only one good priest was true to him, and attended him to the last.

Besides being famous for the great victories I have related, the reign of King Edward the Third was rendered memorable in better ways, by the growth of architecture and the erection of Windsor Castle. In better ways still, by the rising up of WICK-LIFFE, originally a poor parish priest: who devoted himself to exposing, with wonderful power and success, the ambition and corruption of the Pope, and of the whole church of which he was the head.

Some of those Flemings were induced to come to England in this reign too, and to settle in Norfolk, where they made better woollen cloths than the English had ever had before. The Order of the Garter (a very fine thing in its way, but hardly so important as good clothes for the nation) also dates from this period. The King is said to have picked up a lady's garter at a ball, and to have said, *Honi soit qui mal y pense* – in English, 'Evil be to him who evil thinks of it.' The courtiers were usually glad to imitate what the King said or did, and hence from a slight incident the Order of the Garter was instituted, and became a great dignity. So the story goes.

CHAPTER 19

England under Richard the Second

RICHARD, son of the Black Prince, a boy eleven years of age, succeeded to the Crown under the title of King Richard the Second. The whole English nation were ready to admire him for the sake of his brave father. As to the lords and ladies about the Court, they declared him to be the most beautiful, the wisest, and the best – even of princes – whom the lords and ladies about the Court, generally declare to be the most beautiful, the wisest, and the best of mankind. To flatter a poor boy in this base manner was not a very likely way to develop whatever good was in him; and it brought him to anything but a good or happy end.

The Duke of Lancaster, the young King's uncle – commonly called John of Gaunt, from having been born at Ghent, which the common people so pronounced – was supposed to have some thoughts of the throne himself; but, as he was not popular, and the memory of the Black Prince was, he submitted to his nephew.

The war with France being still unsettled, the Government of England wanted money to provide for the expenses that might arise out of it; accordingly a certain tax, called the Poll-tax, which had originated in the last reign, was ordered to be levied on the people. This was a tax on every person in the kingdom, male and female, above the age of fourteen, of three groats (or three fourpenny pieces) a year; clergymen were charged more, and only beggars were exempt.

I have no need to repeat that the common people of England had long been suffering under great oppression. They were still the mere slaves of the lords of the land on which they lived, and were on most occasions harshly and unjustly treated. But, they had begun by this time to think very seriously of not bearing quite so much; and, probably, were emboldened by that French insurrection I mentioned in the last chapter.

The people of Essex rose against the Poll-tax, and being severely handled by the government officers, killed some of them. At this very time one of the tax-collectors, going his rounds from house to house, at Dartford in Kent came to the cottage of one WAT, a tiler by trade, and claimed the tax upon his daughter. Her mother, who was at home, declared that she was under the age of fourteen; upon that, the collector (as other collectors had already done in different parts of England) behaved in a savage way, and brutally insulted Wat Tyler's daughter. The daughter screamed, the mother screamed. Wat the Tiler, who was at work not far off, ran to the spot, and did what any honest father under such provocation might have done – struck the collector dead at a blow.

Instantly the people of that town uprose as one man. They made Wat Tyler their leader; they joined with the people of Essex, who were in arms under a priest called JACK STRAW; they took out of prison another priest named JOHN BALL; and gathering in numbers as they went along, advanced, in a great confused army of poor men, to Blackheath. It is said that they wanted to abolish all property, and to declare all men equal. I do not think this very likely; because they stopped the travellers on the roads and made them swear to be true to King Richard and the people. Nor were they at all disposed to injure those who had done them no harm, merely because they were of high station; for, the King's mother, who had to pass through their camp at Blackheath, on her way to her young son, lying for safety in the Tower of London, had merely to kiss a few dirty-faced rough-bearded men who were noisily fond of royalty, and so got away in perfect safety. Next day the whole mass marched on to London Bridge.

There was a drawbridge in the middle, which WILLIAM WALWORTH the Mayor caused to be raised to prevent their coming into the city; but they soon terrified the citizens into lowering it again, and spread themselves, with great uproar, over the streets. They broke open the prisons; they burned the papers in Lambeth Palace; they destroyed the DUKE OF LANCAS-TER'S Palace, the Savoy, in the Strand, said to be the most beautiful and splendid in England; they set fire to the books and documents in the Temple; and made a great riot. Many of these outrages were committed in drunkenness; since those citizens, who had well-filled cellars, were only too glad to throw them open to save the rest of their property; but even the drunken rioters were very careful to steal nothing. They were so angry with one man, who was seen to take a silver cup at the Savoy Palace, and put it in his breast, that they drowned him in the river, cup and all.

The young King had been taken out to treat with them before they committed these excesses; but, he and the people about him were so frightened by the riotous shouts, that they got back to the Tower in the best way they could. This made the insurgents bolder; so they went on rioting away, striking off the heads of those who did not, at a moment's notice, declare for King Richard and the people; and killing as many of the unpopular persons whom they supposed to be their enemies as they could by any means lay hold of. In this manner they passed one very violent day, and then proclamation was made that the King would meet them at Mile-end, and grant their requests.

The rioters went to Mile-end to the number of sixty thousand, and the King met them there, and to the King the rioters peaceably proposed four conditions. First, that neither they, nor their children, nor any coming after them, should be made slaves any more. Secondly, that the rent of land should be fixed at a certain price in money, instead of being paid in service. Thirdly, that they should have liberty to buy and sell in all markets and public places, like other free men. Fourthly, that they should be pardoned for past offences. Heaven knows, there was nothing very unreasonable in these proposals! The young King deceitfully pretended to think so, and kept thirty clerks up, all night, writing out a charter accordingly.

Now, Wat Tyler himself wanted more than this. He wanted the entire abolition of the forest laws. He was not at Mile-end with the rest, but, while that meeting was being held, broke into the Tower of London and slew the archbishop and the treasurer, for whose heads the people had cried out loudly the day before. He and his men even thrust their swords into the bed of the Princess of Wales while the Princess was in it, to make certain that none of their enemies were concealed there.

So, Wat and his men still continued armed, and rode about the city. Next morning, the King with a small train of some sixty gentlemen – among whom was WALWORTH the Mayor – rode into Smithfield, and saw Wat and his people at a little distance. Says Wat to his men, 'There is the King. I will go speak with him, and tell him what we want.'

Straightway Wat rode up to him, and began to talk. 'King,' says Wat, 'dost thou see all my men there?'

'Ah,' says the King. 'Why?'

'Because,' says Wat, 'they are all at my command, and have sworn to do whatever I bid them.'

Some declared afterwards that as Wat said this, he laid his hand on the King's bridle. Others declared that he was seen to play with his own dagger. I think, myself, that he just spoke to the King like a rough, angry man as he was, and did nothing more. At any rate he was expecting no attack, and preparing for no resistance, when Walworth the Mayor did the not very valiant deed of drawing a short sword and stabbing him in the throat. He dropped from his horse, and one of the King's people speedily finished him. So fell Wat Tyler. Fawners and flatterers made a mighty triumph of it, and set up a cry which will occasionally find an echo to this day. But Wat was a hard-working man, who had suffered much, and had been foully outraged; and it is probable that he was a man of much higher nature and a much braver spirit than any of the parasites who exulted then, or have exulted since, over his defeat.

Seeing Wat down, his men immediately bent their bows to avenge his fall. If the young King had not had presence of mind at that dangerous moment, both he and the Mayor to boot, might have followed Tyler pretty fast. But the King riding up to the crowd, cried out that Tyler was a traitor, and that he would be their leader. They were so taken by surprise, that they set up a great shouting, and followed the boy until he was met at Islington by a large body of soldiers.

The end of this rising was the then usual end. As soon as the King found himself safe, he unsaid all he had said, and undid all he had done; some fifteen hundred of the rioters were tried (mostly in Essex) with great rigour, and executed with great cruelty. Many of them were hanged on gibbets, and left there as a terror to the country people; and, because their miserable friends took some of the bodies down to bury, the King ordered the rest to be chained up – which was the beginning of the barbarous custom of hanging in chains. The King's falsehood in this business makes such a pitiful figure, that I think Wat Tyler appears in history as beyond comparison the truer and more respectable man of the two.

Richard was now sixteen years of age, and married Anne of Bohemia, an excellent princess, who was called 'the good Queen Anne.' She deserved a better husband; for the King had been fawned and flattered into a treacherous, wasteful, dissolute, bad young man.

There were two Popes at this time (as if one were not enough!), and their quarrels involved Europe in a great deal of trouble. Scotland was still troublesome too; and at home there was much jealousy and distrust, and plotting and counter-plotting, because the King feared the ambition of his relations, and particularly of his uncle, the Duke of Lancaster, and the duke had his party against the King, and the King had his party against the duke. Nor were these home troubles lessened when the duke went to Castile to urge his claim to the crown of that kingdom; for then the Duke of Gloucester, another of Richard's uncles, opposed him, and influenced the Parliament to demand the dismissal of the King's favourite ministers. The King said in reply, that he would not for such men dismiss the meanest servant in his kitchen. But, it had begun to signify little what a King said when a Parliament was determined; so Richard was at last obliged to give way, and to agree to another Government of the kingdom, under a commission of fourteen nobles, for a year. His uncle of Gloucester was at the head of this commission, and, in fact, appointed everybody composing it.

Having done all this, the King declared as soon as he saw an opportunity that he had never meant to do it, and that it was all illegal; and he got the judges secretly to sign a declaration to that effect. The secret oozed out directly, and was carried to the Duke of Gloucester. The Duke of Gloucester, at the head of forty thousand men, met the King on his entering into London to enforce his authority; the King was helpless against him; his favourites and ministers were impeached and were mercilessly executed. Among them were two men whom the people regarded with very different feelings; one, Robert Tresilian, Chief Justice, who was hated for having made what was called 'the bloody circuit' to try the rioters; the other, Sir Simon Burley, an honourable knight, who had been the dear friend of the Black Prince, and the governor and guardian of the King. For this gentleman's life the good Queen even begged of Gloucester on her knees; but Gloucester (with or without reason) feared and hated him, and replied, that if she valued her husband's crown, she had better beg no more. All this was done under what was called by some the wonderful – and by others, with better reason, the merciless – Parliament.

But Gloucester's power was not to last for ever. He held it for only a year longer; in which year the famous battle of Otterbourne, sung in the old ballad of Chevy Chase, was fought. When the year was out, the King, turning suddenly to Gloucester, in the midst of a great council said, 'Uncle, how old am I?' 'Your highness,' returned the Duke, 'is in your twenty-second year.' 'Am I so much?' said the King; 'then I will manage my own affairs! I am much obliged to you, my good lords, for your past services, but I need them no more.' He followed this up, by appointing a new Chancellor and a new Treasurer, and announced to the people that he had resumed the Government. He held it for eight years without opposition. Through all that time, he kept his determination to revenge himself some day upon his uncle Gloucester, in his own breast.

At last the good Queen died, and then the King, desiring to take a second wife, proposed to his council that he should marry Isabella, of France, the daughter of Charles the Sixth; who, the French courtiers said (as the English courtiers had said of Richard), was a marvel of beauty and wit, and quite a phenomenon – of seven years old. The council were divided about this marriage, but it took place. It secured peace between England and France for a quarter of a century; but it was strongly opposed to the prejudices of the English people. The Duke of Gloucester, who was anxious to take the occasion of making himself popular, declaimed against it loudly, and this at length decided the King to execute the vengeance he had been nursing so long.

He went with a gay company to the Duke of Gloucester's house, Pleshey Castle, in Essex, where the Duke, suspecting nothing, came out into the court-yard to receive his royal visitor. While the King conversed in a friendly manner with the Duchess, the Duke was quietly seized, hurried away, shipped for Calais, and lodged in the castle there. His friends, the Earls of Arundel and Warwick, were taken in the same treacherous manner, and confined to their castles. A few days after, at Nottingham, they were impeached of high treason. The Earl of Arundel was condemned and beheaded, and the Earl of Warwick was banished. Then, a writ was sent by a messenger to the Governor of Calais, requiring him to send the Duke of Gloucester over to be tried. In three days he returned an answer that he could not do that, because the Duke of Gloucester had died in prison. The Duke was declared a traitor, his property was confiscated to the King, a real or pretended confession he had made in prison to one of the Justices of the Common Pleas was produced against him, and there was an end of the matter. How the unfortunate duke died, very few cared to know. Whether he really died naturally; whether he killed himself; whether, by the King's order, he was strangled, or smothered between two beds (as a serving-man of the Governor's named Hall, did afterwards declare), cannot be discovered. There is not much doubt that he was killed, somehow or other, by his nephew's orders. Among the most active nobles in these proceedings were the King's cousin, Henry Bolingbroke, whom the King had made Duke of Hereford to smooth down the old family quarrels, and some others: who had in the family-plotting times done just such acts themselves as they now condemned in the duke. They seem to have been a corrupt set of men; but such men were easily found about the court in such days.

The people murmured at all this, and were still very sore about the French marriage. The nobles saw how little the King cared for law, and how crafty he was, and began to be somewhat afraid of themselves. The King's life was a life of continued feasting and excess; his retinue, down to the meanest servants, were dressed in the most costly manner, and caroused at his tables, it is related, to the number of ten thousand persons every day. He himself, surrounded by a body of ten thousand archers, and enriched by a duty on wool which the Commons had granted him for life, saw no danger of ever being otherwise than powerful and absolute, and was as fierce and haughty as a King could be.

He had two of his old enemies left, in the persons of the Dukes of Hereford and Norfolk. Sparing these no more than the others, he tampered with the Duke of Hereford until he got him to declare before the Council that the Duke of Norfolk had lately held some treasonable talk with him, as he was riding near Brentford; and that he had told him, among other things, that he could not believe the King's oath – which nobody could, I should think. For this treachery he obtained a pardon, and the Duke of Norfolk was summoned to appear and defend himself. As he denied the charge and said his accuser was a liar and a traitor, both noblemen, according to the manner of those times, were held in custody, and the truth was ordered to be decided by wager of battle at Coventry. This wager of battle meant that whosoever won the combat was to be considered in the right; which nonsense meant in effect, that no strong man could ever be wrong. A great holiday was made; a great crowd assembled, with much parade and show; and the two combatants were about to rush at each other with their lances, when the King, sitting in a pavilion to see fair, threw down the truncheon he carried in his hand, and forbade the battle. The Duke of Hereford was to be banished for ten years, and the Duke of Norfolk was to be banished for life. So said the King. The Duke of Hereford went to France, and went no farther. The Duke of Norfolk made a pilgrimage to the Holy Land, and afterwards died at Venice of a broken heart.

Faster and fiercer, after this, the King went on in his career. The Duke of Lancaster, who was the father of the Duke of Hereford, died soon after the departure of his son; and, the King, although he had solemnly granted to that son leave to inherit his father's property, if it should come to him during his banishment, immediately seized it all, like a robber. The judges were so afraid of him, that they disgraced themselves by declaring this theft to be just and lawful. His avarice knew no bounds. He outlawed seventeen counties at once, on a frivolous pretence, merely to raise money by way of fines for misconduct. In short, he did as many dishonest things as he could; and cared so little for the discontent of his subjects – though even the spaniel favourites began to whisper to him that there was such a thing as discontent afloat – that he took that time, of all others, for leaving England and making an expedition against the Irish.

He was scarcely gone, leaving the DUKE OF YORK Regent in his absence, when his cousin, Henry of Hereford, came over from France to claim the rights of which he had been so monstrously deprived. He was immediately joined by the two great Earls of Northumberland and Westmoreland; and his uncle, the Regent, finding the King's cause unpopular, and the disinclination of the army to act against Henry, very strong, withdrew with the Royal forces towards Bristol. Henry, at the head of an army, came from Yorkshire (where he had landed) to London and followed him. They joined their forces – how they brought that about, is not distinctly understood – and proceeded to Bristol Castle, whither three noblemen had taken the young Queen. The castle surrendering, they presently put those three noblemen to death. The Regent then remained there, and Henry went on to Chester.

All this time, the boisterous weather had prevented the King from receiving intelligence of what had occurred. At length it was conveyed to him in Ireland, and he sent over the EARL OF SALISBURY, who, landing at Conway, rallied the Welshmen, and waited for the King a whole fortnight; at the end of that time the Welshmen, who were perhaps not very warm for him in the beginning, quite cooled down and went home. When the King did land on the coast at last, he came with a pretty good power, but his men cared nothing for him, and quickly deserted. Supposing the Welshmen to be still at Conway, he disguised himself as a priest, and made for that place in company with his two brothers and some few of their adherents. But, there were no Welshmen left – only Salisbury and a hundred soldiers. In this distress, the King's two brothers, Exeter and Surrey, offered to go to Henry to learn what his intentions were. Surrey, who was true to Richard, was put into prison. Exeter, who was false, took the royal badge, which was a hart, off his shield, and assumed the rose, the badge of Henry. After this, it was pretty plain to the King what Henry's intentions were, without sending any more messengers to ask.

The fallen King, thus deserted – hemmed in on all sides, and pressed with hunger – rode here and rode there, and went to this castle, and went to that castle, endeavouring to obtain some provisions, but could find none. He rode wretchedly back to Conway, and there surrendered himself to the Earl of Northumberland, who came from Henry, in reality to take him prisoner, but in appearance to offer terms; and whose men were hidden not far off. By this earl he was conducted to the castle of Flint, where his cousin Henry met him, and dropped on his knee as if he were still respectful to his sovereign.

'Fair cousin of Lancaster,' said the King, 'you are very welcome' (very welcome, no doubt; but he would have been more so, in chains or without a head).

'My lord,' replied Henry, 'I am come a little before my time; but, with your good pleasure, I will show you the reason. Your people complain with some bitterness, that you have ruled them rigorously for two-and-twenty years. Now, if it please God, I will help you to govern them better in future.'

'Fair cousin,' replied the abject King, 'since it pleaseth you, it pleaseth me mightily.'

After this, the trumpets sounded, and the King was stuck on a wretched horse, and carried prisoner to Chester, where he made to issue a proclamation, calling a Parliament. From Chester he was taken on towards London. At Lichfield he tried to escape by getting out of a window and letting himself down into a garden; it was all in vain, however, and he was carried on and shut up in the Tower, where no one pitied him, and where the whole people, whose patience he had quite tired out, reproached him without mercy. Before he got there, it is related, that his very dog left him and departed from his side to lick the hand of Henry.

The day before the Parliament met, a deputation went to this wrecked King, and told him that he had promised the Earl of Northumberland at Conway Castle to resign the crown. He said he was quite ready to do it, and signed a paper in which he renounced his authority and absolved his people from their allegiance to him. He had so little spirit left that he gave his royal ring to his triumphant cousin Henry with his own hand, and said, that if he could have had leave to appoint a successor, that same Henry was the man of all others whom he would have named. Next day, the Parliament assembled in Westminster Hall, where Henry sat at the side of the throne, which was empty and covered with a cloth of gold. The paper just signed by the King was read to the multitude amid shouts of joy, which were echoed through all the streets; when some of the noise had died away, the King was formally deposed. Then Henry arose, and, making the sign of the cross on his forehead and breast, challenged the realm of England as his right; the archbishops of Canterbury and York seated him on the throne.

The multitude shouted again, and the shouts re-echoed throughout all the streets. No one remembered, now, that Richard the Second had ever been the most beautiful, the wisest, and the best of princes; and he now made living (to my thinking) a far more sorry spectacle in the Tower of London, than Wat Tyler had made, lying dead, among the hoofs of the royal horses in Smithfield.

The Poll-tax died with Wat. The Smiths to the King and Royal Family, could make no chains in which the King could hang the people's recollection of him; so the Poll-tax was never collected.

CHAPTER 20

England under Henry the Fourth, called Bolingbroke

During the last reign, the preaching of Wickliffe against the pride and cunning of the Pope and all his men, had made a great noise in England. Whether the new King wished to be in favour with the priests, or whether he hoped, by pretending to be very religious, to cheat Heaven itself into the belief that he was not an usurper, I don't know. Both suppositions are likely enough. It is certain that he began his reign by making a strong show against the followers of Wickliffe, who were called Lollards, or heretics – although his father, John of Gaunt, had been of that way of thinking, as he himself had been more than suspected of being. It is no less certain that he first established in England the detestable and atrocious custom, brought from abroad, of burning those people as a punishment for their opinions. It was the importation into England of one of the practices of what was called the Holy Inquisition: which was the most *un*holy and the most infamous tribunal that ever disgraced mankind, and made men more like demons than followers of Our Saviour.

No real right to the crown, as you know, was in this King. Edward Mortimer, the young Earl of March – who was only eight or nine years old, and who was descended from the Duke of Clarence, the elder brother of Henry's father – was, by succession, the real heir to the throne. However, the King got his son declared Prince of Wales; and, obtaining possession of the young Earl of March and his little brother, kept them in confinement (but not severely) in Windsor Castle. He then required the Parliament to decide what was to be done with the deposed King, who was quiet enough, and who only said that he hoped his cousin Henry would be 'a good lord' to him. The Parliament replied that they would recommend his being kept in some secret place where the people could not resort, and where his friends could not be admitted to see him. Henry accordingly passed this sentence upon him, and it now began to be pretty clear to the nation that Richard the Second would not live very long.

It was a noisy Parliament, as it was an unprincipled one, and the Lords quarrelled so violently among themselves as to which of them had been loyal and which disloyal, and which consistent and which inconsistent, that forty gauntlets are said to have been thrown upon the floor at one time as challenges to as many battles: the truth being that they were all false and base together, and had been, at one time with the old King, and at another time with the new one, and seldom true for any length of time to any one. They soon began to plot again. A conspiracy was formed to invite the King to a tournament at Oxford, and then to take him by surprise and kill him. This murderous enterprise, which was agreed upon at secret meetings in the house of the Abbot of Westminster, was betrayed by the Earl of Rutland – one of the conspirators. The King, instead of going to the tournament or staying at Windsor (where the conspirators suddenly went, on finding themselves discovered, with the hope of seizing him), retired to London, proclaimed them all traitors, and advanced upon them with a great force. They retired into the west of England, proclaiming Richard King; but, the people rose against them, and they were all slain. Their treason hastened the death of the deposed monarch. Whether he was killed by hired assassins, or whether he was starved to death, or whether he refused food on hearing of his brothers being killed (who were in that plot), is very doubtful. He met his death somehow; and his body was publicly shown at St Paul's Cathedral with only the lower part of the face uncovered. I can scarcely doubt that he was killed by the King's orders.

The French wife of the miserable Richard was now only ten years old; and, when her father, Charles of France, heard of her misfortunes and of her lonely condition in England, he went mad: as he had several times done before, during the last five or six years. The French Dukes of Burgundy and Bourbon took up the poor girl's cause, without caring much about it, but on the chance of getting something out of England. The people of Bordeaux, who had a sort of superstitious attachment to the memory of Richard, because he was born there, swore by the Lord that he had been the best man in all his kingdom – which was going rather far – and promised to do great things against the English. Nevertheless, when they came to consider that they, and the whole people of France were ruined by their own nobles, and that the English rule was much the better of the two, they cooled down again; and the two dukes, although they were very great men, could do nothing without them. Then, began negotiations between France and England for the sending home to Paris of the poor little Queen with all her jewels and her fortune of two hundred thousand francs in gold. The King was quite willing to restore the young lady, and even the jewels; but he said he really could not part with the money. So, at last she was safely deposited at Paris without her fortune, and then the Duke of Burgundy (who was cousin to the French King) began to quarrel with the Duke of Orleans (who was brother to the French King) about the whole matter; and those two dukes made France even more wretched than ever.

As the idea of conquering Scotland was still popular at home, the King marched to the river Tyne and demanded homage of the King of that country. This being refused, he advanced to Edinburgh, but did little there; for, his army being in want of provisions, and the Scotch being very careful to hold him in check without giving battle, he was obliged to retire. It is to his immortal honour that in this sally he burnt no villages and slaughtered no people, but was particularly careful that his army should be merciful and harmless. It was a great example in those ruthless times.

A war among the border people of England and Scotland went on for twelve months, and then the Earl of Northumberland, the nobleman who had helped Henry to the crown, began to rebel against him – probably because nothing that Henry could do for him would satisfy his extravagant expectations. There was a certain Welsh gentleman, named OWEN GLENDOWER, who had been a student in one of the Inns of Court, and had afterwards been in the service of the late King, whose Welsh property was taken from him by a powerful lord related to the present King, who was his neighbour. Appealing for redress, and getting none, he took up arms, was made an outlaw, and declared himself sovereign of Wales. He pretended to be a magician; and not only were the Welsh people stupid enough to believe him, but, even Henry believed him too; for, making three expeditions into Wales, and being three times driven back by the wildness of the country, the bad weather, and the skill of Glendower, he thought he was defeated by the Welshman's magic arts. However, he took Lord Grey and Sir Edmund Mortimer, prisoners, and allowed the relatives of Lord Grey to ransom him, but would not extend such favour to Sir Edmund Mortimer. Now, Henry Percy, called HOTSPUR, son of the Earl of Northumberland, who was married to Mortimer's sister, is supposed to have taken offence at this; and, therefore, in conjunction with his father and some others, to have joined Owen Glendower, and risen against Henry. It is by no means clear that this was the real cause of the conspiracy; but perhaps it was made the pretext. It was formed, and was very powerful; including SCROOP, Archbishop of York, and the EARL OF DOUGLAS, a powerful and brave Scottish nobleman. The King was prompt and active, and the two armies met at Shrewsbury.

There were about fourteen thousand men in each. The old Earl of Northumberland being sick, the rebel forces were led by his son. The King wore plain armour to deceive the enemy; and four noblemen, with the same object, wore the royal arms. The rebel charge was so furious, that every one of those gentlemen were killed, the royal standard was beaten down, and the young

Prince of Wales was severely wounded in the face. But he was one of the bravest and best soldiers that ever lived, and he fought so well, and the King's troops were so encouraged by his bold example, that they rallied immediately, and cut the enemy's forces all to pieces. Hotspur was killed by an arrow in the brain, and the rout was so complete that the whole rebellion was struck down by this one blow. The Earl of Northumberland surrendered himself soon after hearing of the death of his son, and received a pardon for all his offences.

There were some lingerings of rebellion yet: Owen Glendower being retired to Wales, and a preposterous story being spread among the ignorant people that King Richard was still alive. How they could have believed such nonsense it is difficult to imagine; but they certainly did suppose that the Court fool of the late King, who was something like him, was he, himself; so that it seemed as if, after giving so much trouble to the country in his life, he was still to trouble it after his death. This was not the worst. The young Earl of March and his brother were stolen out of Windsor Castle. Being retaken, and being found to have been spirited away by one Lady Spencer, she accused her own brother, that Earl of Rutland who was in the former conspiracy and was now Duke of York, of being in the plot. For this he was ruined in fortune, though not put to death; and then another plot arose among the old Earl of Northumberland, some other lords, and that same Scroop, Archbishop of York, who was with the rebels before. These conspirators caused a writing to be posted on the church doors, accusing the King of a variety of crimes; but, the King being eager and vigilant to oppose them, they were all taken, and the Archbishop was executed. This was the first time that a great churchman had been slain by the law in England; but the King was resolved that it should be done, and done it was.

The next most remarkable event of this time was the seizure, by Henry, of the heir to the Scottish throne – James, a boy of nine years old. He had been put aboard-ship by his father, the Scottish King Robert, to save him from the designs of his uncle, when, on his way to France, he was accidentally taken by some English cruisers. He remained a prisoner in England for nineteen years, and became in his prison a student and a famous poet.

With the exception of occasional troubles with the Welsh and with the French, the rest of King Henry's reign was quiet enough. But, the King was far from happy, and probably was troubled in his conscience by knowing that he had usurped the crown, and had occasioned the death of his miserable cousin. The Prince of Wales, though brave and generous, is said to have been wild and dissipated, and even to have drawn his sword on GASCOIGNE, the Chief Justice of the King's Bench, because he was firm in dealing impartially with one of his dissolute companions. Upon this the Chief Justice is said to have ordered him immediately to prison; the Prince of Wales is said to have submitted with a good grace; and the King is said to have exclaimed, 'Happy is the monarch who has so just a judge, and a son so willing to obey the laws.' This is all very doubtful, and so is another story (of which Shakespeare has made beautiful use), that the Prince once took the crown out of his father's chamber as he was sleeping, and tried it on his own head.

The King's health sank more and more, and he became subject to violent eruptions on the face and to bad epileptic fits, and his spirits sank every day. At last, as he was praying before the shrine of St Edward at Westminster Abbey, he was seized with a terrible fit, and was carried into the Abbot's chamber, where he presently died. It had been foretold that he would die at Jerusalem, which certainly is not, and never was, Westminster. But, as the Abbot's room had long been called the Jerusalem chamber, people said it was all the same thing, and were quite satisfied with the prediction.

The King died on the 20th of March, 1413, in the forty-seventh year of his age, and the fourteenth of his reign. He was buried in Canterbury Cathedral. He had been twice married, and had, by his first wife, a family of four sons and two daughters. Considering his duplicity before he came to the throne, his unjust seizure of it, and above all, his making that monstrous law for the burning of what the priests call heretics, he was a reasonably good king, as kings went.

CHAPTER 21

England under Henry the Fifth

First Part

The Prince of Wales began his reign like a generous and honest man. He set the young Earl of March free; he restored their estates and their honours to the Percy family, who had lost them by their rebellion against his father; he ordered the imbecile and unfortunate Richard to be honourably buried among the Kings of England; and he dismissed all his wild companions, with assurances that they would not want, if they would resolve to be steady, faithful, and true.

It is much easier to burn men than to burn their opinions; and those of the Lollards were spreading every day. The Lollards were represented by the priests – probably falsely for the most part – to entertain treasonable designs against the new King; and Henry, suffering himself to be worked upon by these representations, sacrificed his friend Sir John Oldcastle, the Lord Cobham, to them, after trying in vain to convert him by arguments. He was declared guilty, as the head of the sect, and sentenced to the flames; but he escaped from the Tower before the day of execution (postponed for fifty days by the King himself), and summoned the Lollards to meet him near London on a certain day. So the priests told the King, at least. I doubt whether there was any conspiracy beyond such as was got up by their agents. On the day appointed, instead of five-and-twenty thousand men, under the command of Sir John Oldcastle, in the meadows of St Giles, the King found only eighty men, and no Sir John at all. There was, in another place, an addle-headed brewer, who had gold trappings to his horses, and a pair of gilt spurs in his breast – expecting to be made a knight next day by Sir John, and so to gain the right to wear them – but there was no Sir John, nor did anybody give information respecting him, though the King offered great rewards for such intelligence. Thirty of these unfortunate Lollards were hanged and drawn immediately, and were then burnt, gallows and all; and the various prisons in and around London were crammed full of others. Some of these unfortunate men made various confessions of treasonable designs; but, such confessions were easily got, under torture and the fear of fire, and are very little to be trusted. To finish the sad story of Sir John Oldcastle at once, I may mention that he escaped into Wales, and remained there safely, for years. When discovered by Lord Powis, it is very doubtful if he would have been taken alive – so great was the old soldier's bravery – if a miserable old woman had not come behind him and broken his legs with a stool. He was carried to London in a horse-litter, was fastened by an iron chain to a gibbet, and so roasted to death.

To make the state of France as plain as I can in a few words, I should tell you that the Duke of Orleans, and the Duke of Burgundy, commonly called 'John without fear,' had had a grand reconciliation of their quarrel in the last reign, and had appeared to be quite in a heavenly state of mind. Immediately after which, on a Sunday, in the public streets of Paris, the Duke of Orleans was murdered by a party of twenty men, set on by the Duke of Burgundy – according to his own deliberate confession. The widow of King Richard had been married in France to the eldest son of the Duke of Orleans. The poor mad King was quite powerless to help her, and the Duke of Burgundy became the real master of France. Isabella dying, her husband (Duke of Orleans since the death of his father) married the daughter of the Count of Armagnac, who, being a much abler man than his young son-in-law, headed his party; thence called after him Armagnacs. Thus, France was now in this terrible condition, that it had in it the party of the King's son, the Dauphin Louis; the party of the Duke of Burgundy, who was the father of the Dauphin's ill-used wife; and the party of the Armagnacs; all hating each other; all fighting together; all composed of the most depraved nobles that the earth has ever known; and all tearing unhappy France to pieces.

The late King had watched these dissensions from England, sensible (like the French people) that no enemy of France could injure her more than her own nobility. The present King now advanced a claim to the French throne. His demand being, of course, refused, he reduced his proposal to a certain large amount of French territory, and to demanding the French princess, Catherine, in marriage, with a fortune of two millions of golden crowns. He was offered less territory and fewer crowns, and no princess; but he called his ambassadors home and prepared for war. Then, he proposed to take the princess with one million of crowns. The French Court replied that he should have the princess with two hundred thousand crowns less; he said this would not do (he had never seen the princess in his life), and assembled his army at Southampton. There was a short plot at home just at that time, for deposing him, and making the Earl of March king; but the conspirators were all speedily condemned and executed, and the King embarked for France.

It is dreadful to observe how long a bad example will be followed; but, it is encouraging to know that a good example is never thrown away. The King's first act on disembarking at the mouth of the river Seine, three miles from Harfleur, was to imitate his father, and to proclaim his solemn orders that the lives and property of the peaceable inhabitants should be respected on pain of death. It is agreed by French writers, to his lasting renown, that even while his soldiers were suffering the greatest distress from want of food, these commands were rigidly obeyed.

With an army in all of thirty thousand men, he besieged the town of Harfleur both by sea and land for five weeks; at the end of which time the town surrendered, and the inhabitants were allowed to depart with only fivepence each, and a part of their clothes. All the rest of their possessions was divided amongst the English army. But, that army suffered so much, in spite of its successes, from disease and privation, that it was already reduced one half. Still, the King was determined not to retire until he had stuck a greater blow. Therefore, against the advice of all his counsellors, he moved on with his little force towards Calais. When he came up to the river Somme he was unable to cross, in consequence of the fort being fortified; and, as the English moved up the left bank of the river looking for a crossing, the French, who had broken all the bridges, moved up the right bank, watching them, and waiting to attack them when they should try to pass it. At last the English found a crossing and got safely over. The French held a council of war at Rouen, resolved to give the English battle, and sent heralds to King Henry to know by which road he was going. 'By the road that will take me straight to Calais!' said the King, and sent them away with a present of a hundred crowns.

The English moved on, until they beheld the French, and then the King gave orders to form in line of battle. The French not coming on, the army broke up after remaining in battle array till night, and got good rest and refreshment at a neighbouring village. The French were now all lying in another village, through which they knew the English must pass. They were resolved that the English should begin the battle. The English had no means of retreat, if their King had any such intention; and so the two armies passed the night, close together.

To understand these armies well, you must bear in mind that the immense French army had, among its notable persons, almost the whole of that wicked nobility, whose debauchery had made France a desert; and so besotted were they by pride, and by contempt for the common people, that they had scarcely any bowmen (if indeed they had any at all) in their whole enormous number: which, compared with the English army, was at least as six to one. For these proud fools had said that the bow was not a fit weapon for knightly hands, and that France must be defended by gentlemen only. We shall see, presently, what hand the gentlemen made of it.

Now, on the English side, among the little force, there was a good proportion of men who were not gentlemen by any means, but who were good stout archers for all that. Among them, in the morning – having slept little at night, while the French were carousing and making sure of victory – the King rode, on a grey horse; wearing on his head a helmet of shining steel, surmounted by a crown of gold, sparkling with precious stones; and bearing over his armour, embroidered together, the arms of England and the arms of France. The archers looked at the shining helmet and the crown of gold and the sparkling jewels, and admired them all; but, what they admired most was the King's cheerful face, and his bright blue eye, as he told them that, for himself, he had made up his mind to conquer there or to die there, and that England should never have a ransom to pay for *him*. There was one brave knight who chanced to say that he wished some of the many gallant gentlemen and good soldiers, who were then idle at home in England, were there to increase their numbers. But the King told him that, for his part, he did not wish for one more man. 'The fewer we have,' said he, 'the greater will be the honour we shall win!' His men, being now all in good heart, were refreshed with bread and wine, and heard prayers, and waited quietly for the French. The King waited for the French, because they were drawn up thirty deep (the little English force was only three deep), on very difficult and heavy ground; and he knew that when they moved, there must be confusion among them.

As they did not move, he sent off two parties: – one to lie concealed in a wood on the left of the French: the other to set fire to some houses behind the French after the battle should be begun. This was scarcely done, when three of the proud French gentlemen, who were to defend their country without any help from the base peasants, came riding out, calling upon the English to surrender. The King warned those gentlemen himself to retire with all speed if they cared for their lives, and ordered the English banners to advance. Upon that, Sir Thomas Erpingham, a great English general, who commanded the archers, threw his truncheon into the air, joyfully, and all the English men, kneeling down upon the ground and biting it as if they took possession of the country, rose up with a great shout and fell upon the French.

Every archer was furnished with a great stake tipped with iron; and his orders were, to thrust this stake into the ground, to discharge his arrow, and then to fall back, when the French horsemen came on. As the haughty French gentlemen, who were to break the English archers and utterly destroy them with their knightly lances, came riding up, they were received with such a blinding storm of arrows, that they broke and turned. Horses and men rolled over one another, and the confusion was terrific. Those who rallied and charged the archers got among the stakes on slippery and boggy ground, and were so bewildered that the English archers – who wore no armour, and even took off their leathern coats to be more active – cut them to pieces, root and branch. Only three French horsemen got within the stakes, and these were instantly despatched. All this time the dense French army, being in armour, were sinking knee-deep into the mire; while the light English archers, half-naked, were as fresh and active as if they were fighting on a marble floor.

But now, the second division of the French coming to the relief of the first, closed up in a firm mass; the English, headed by the King, attacked them; and the deadliest part of the battle began. The King's brother, the Duke of Clarence, was struck down, and numbers of the French surrounded him; but, King

Henry, standing over the body, fought like a lion until they were beaten off.

Presently, came up a band of eighteen French knights, bearing the banner of a certain French lord, who had sworn to kill or take the English King. One of them struck him such a blow with a battle-axe that he reeled and fell upon his knees; but, his faithful men, immediately closing round him, killed every one of those eighteen knights, and so that French lord never kept his oath.

The French Duke of Alençon, seeing this, made a desperate charge, and cut his way close up to the Royal Standard of England. He beat down the Duke of York, who was standing near it; and, when the King came to his rescue, struck off a piece of the crown he wore. But, he never struck another blow in this world; for, even as he was in the act of saying who he was, and that he surrendered to the King; and even as the King stretched out his hand to give him a safe and honourable acceptance of the offer; he fell dead, pierced by innumerable wounds.

The death of this nobleman decided the battle. The third division of the French army, which had never struck a blow yet, and which was, in itself, more than double the English power, broke and fled. At this time of the fight, the English, who as yet had made no prisoners, began to take them in immense numbers, and were still occupied in doing so, or in killing those who would not surrender, when a great noise arose in the rear of the French – their flying banners were seen to stop – and King Henry, supposing a great reinforcement to have arrived, gave orders that all the prisoners should be put to death. As soon, however, as it was found that the noise was only occasioned by a body of plundering peasants, the terrible massacre was stopped.

Then King Henry called to him the French herald, and asked him to whom the victory belonged.

The herald replied, 'To the King of England.'

'We have not made this havoc and slaughter,' said the King. 'It is the wrath of Heaven on the sins of France. What is the name of that castle yonder?'

The herald answered him, 'My lord, it is the castle of Azincourt.'

Said the King, 'From henceforth this battle shall be known to posterity by the name of the battle of Azincourt.'

Our English historians have made it Agincourt; but, under that name, it will ever be famous in English annals.

The loss upon the French side was enormous. Three Dukes were killed, two more were taken prisoners, seven Counts were killed, three more were taken prisoners, and ten thousand knights and gentlemen were slain upon the field. The English loss amounted to sixteen hundred men, among whom were the Duke of York and the Earl of Suffolk.

War is a dreadful thing; and it is appalling to know how the English were obliged, next morning, to kill those prisoners mortally wounded, who yet writhed in agony upon the ground; how the dead upon the French side were stripped by their own countrymen and countrywomen, and afterwards buried in great pits; how the dead upon the English side were piled up in a great barn, and how their bodies and the barn were all burned together. It is in such things, and in many more much too horrible to relate, that the real desolation and wickedness of war consist. Nothing can make war otherwise than horrible. But the dark side of it was little thought of and soon forgotten; and it cast no shade of trouble on the English people, except on those who had lost friends or relations in the fight. They welcomed their King home with shouts of rejoicing, and plunged into the water to bear him ashore on their shoulders, and flocked out in crowds to welcome him in every town through which he passed, and hung rich carpets and tapestries out of the windows, and strewed the streets with flowers, and made the fountains run with wine, as the great field of Agincourt had run with blood.

Second Part

That proud and wicked French nobility who dragged their country to destruction, and who were every day and every year regarded with deeper hatred and detestation in the hearts of the French people, learnt nothing, even from the defeat of Agincourt. So far from uniting against the common enemy, they became, among themselves, more violent, more bloody, and more false – if that were possible – than they had been before. The Count of Armagnac persuaded the French King to plunder of her treasures Queen Isabella of Bavaria, and to make her a prisoner. She, who had hitherto been the bitter enemy of the

Duke of Burgundy, proposed to join him, in revenge. He carried her off to Troyes, where she proclaimed herself Regent of France, and made him her lieutenant. The Armagnac party were at that time possessed of Paris; but, one of the gates of the city being secretly opened on a certain night to a party of the duke's men, they got into Paris, threw into the prisons all the Armagnacs upon whom they could lay their hands, and, a few nights afterwards, with the aid of a furious mob of sixty thousand people, broke the prisons open, and killed them all. The former Dauphin was now dead, and the King's third son bore the title. Him, in the height of this murderous scene, a French knight hurried out of bed, wrapped in a sheet, and bore away to Poitiers. So, when the revengeful Isabella and the Duke of Burgundy entered Paris in triumph after the slaughter of their enemies, the Dauphin was proclaimed at Poitiers as the real Regent.

King Henry had not been idle since his victory of Agincourt, but had repulsed a brave attempt of the French to recover Harfleur; had gradually conquered a great part of Normandy; and, at this crisis of affairs, took the important town of Rouen, after a siege of half a year. This great loss so alarmed the French, that the Duke of Burgundy proposed that a meeting to treat of peace should be held between the French and the English kings in a plain by the river Seine. On the appointed day King Henry appeared there, with his two brothers, Clarence and Gloucester, and a thousand men. The unfortunate French King, being more mad than usual that day, could not come; but the Queen came, and with her the Princess Catherine: who was a very lovely creature, and who made a real impression on King Henry, now that he saw her for the first time. This was the most important circumstance that arose out of the meeting.

As if it were impossible for a French nobleman of that time to be true to his word of honour in anything, Henry discovered that the Duke of Burgundy was, at that very moment, in secret treaty with the Dauphin; and he therefore abandoned the negotiation.

The Duke of Burgundy and the Dauphin, each of whom, with the best reason, distrusted the other as a noble ruffian surrounded by a party of noble ruffians, were rather at a loss how to proceed after this; but, at length they agreed to meet, on a bridge over the river Yonne, where it was arranged that there should be two strong gates put up, with an empty space between them; and that the Duke of Burgundy should come into that space by one gate, with ten men only; and that the Dauphin should come into that space by the other gate, also with ten men, and no more.

So far the Dauphin kept his word, but no farther. When the Duke of Burgundy was on his knee before him in the act of speaking, one of the Dauphin's noble ruffians cut the said Duke down with a small axe, and others speedily finished him.

It was in vain for the Dauphin to pretend that this base murder was not done with his consent; it was too bad, even for France, and caused a general horror. The duke's heir hastened to make a treaty with King Henry, and the French Queen engaged that her husband should consent to it, whatever it was. Henry made peace, on condition of receiving the Princess Catherine in marriage, and being made regent of France during the rest of the King's life-time, and succeeding to the French crown at his death. He was soon married to the beautiful Princess, and took her proudly home to England, where she was crowned with great honour and glory.

This peace was called the Perpetual Peace; we shall soon see how long it lasted. It gave great satisfaction to the French people, although they were so poor and miserable, that, at the time of the celebration of the Royal marriage, numbers of them were dying with starvation, on the dung-hills in the streets of Paris. There was some resistance on the part of the Dauphin in some few parts of France, but King Henry beat it all down.

And now, with his great possessions in France secured, and his beautiful wife to cheer him, and a son born to give him greater happiness, all appeared bright before him. But, in the fulness of his triumph and the height of his power, Death came upon him, and his day was done. When he fell ill at Vincennes, and found that he could not recover, he was very calm and quiet, and spoke serenely to those who wept around his bed. His wife and child, he said, he left to the loving care of his brother the Duke of Bedford, and his other faithful nobles. He gave them his advice that England should establish a friendship with the new Duke of Burgundy, and offer him the regency of France; that it should not set free the royal princes who had been taken at Agincourt; and that, whatever quarrel might arise with France, England should never make peace without holding

Normandy. Then, he laid down his head, and asked the attendant priests to chant the penitential psalms. Amid which solemn sounds, on the thirty-first of August, one thousand four hundred and twenty-two, in only the thirty-fourth year of his age and the tenth of his reign, King Henry the Fifth passed away.

Slowly and mournfully they carried his embalmed body in a procession of great state to Paris, and thence to Rouen, where his Queen was: from whom the sad intelligence of his death was concealed until he had been dead some days. Thence, lying on a bed of crimson and gold, with a golden crown upon the head, and a golden ball and sceptre lying in the nerveless hands, they carried it to Calais, with such a great retinue as seemed to dye the road black. The King of Scotland acted as chief mourner, all the Royal Household followed, the knights wore black armour and black plumes of feathers, crowds of men bore torches, making the night as light as day; and the widowed Princess followed last of all. At Calais there was a fleet of ships to bring the funeral host to Dover. And so, by way of London Bridge, where the service for the dead was chanted as it passed along, they brought the body to Westminster Abbey, and there buried it with great respect.

CHAPTER 22

England under Henry the Sixth

First Part

It had been the wish of the late King, that while his infant son KING HENRY THE SIXTH, at this time only nine months old, was under age, the Duke of Gloucester should be appointed Regent. The English Parliament, however, preferred to appoint a Council of Regency, with the Duke of Bedford at its head: to be represented, in his absence only, by the Duke of Gloucester. The Parliament would seem to have been wise in this, for Gloucester soon showed himself to be ambitious and troublesome, and, in the gratification of his own personal schemes, gave dangerous offence to the Duke of Burgundy, which was with difficulty adjusted.

As that duke declined the Regency of France, it was bestowed by the poor French King upon the Duke of Bedford. But, the French King dying within two months, the Dauphin instantly asserted his claim to the French throne, and was actually crowned under the title of CHARLES THE SEVENTH. The Duke of Bedford, to be a match for him, entered into a friendly league with the Dukes of Burgundy and Brittany, and gave them his two sisters in marriage. War with France was immediately renewed, and the Perpetual Peace came to an untimely end.

In the first campaign, the English, aided by this alliance, were speedily successful. As Scotland, however, had sent the French five thousand men, and might send more, or attack the North of England while England was busy with France, it was considered that it would be a good thing to offer the Scottish King, James, who had been so long imprisoned, his liberty, on his paying forty thousand pounds for his board and lodging during nineteen years, and engaging to forbid his subjects from serving under the flag of France. It is pleasant to know, not only that the amiable captive at last regained his freedom upon these terms, but, that he married a noble English lady, with whom he had been long in love, and became an excellent King. I am afraid we have met with some Kings in this history, and shall meet with some more, who would have been very much the better, and would have left the world much happier, if they had been imprisoned nineteen years too.

In the second campaign, the English gained a considerable victory at Verneuil, in a battle which was chiefly remarkable, otherwise, for their resorting to the odd expedient of tying their baggage-horses together by the heads and tails, and jumbling them up with the baggage, so as to convert them into a sort of live fortification – which was found useful to the troops, but which I should think was not agreeable to the horses. For three years afterwards very little was done, owing to both sides being too poor for war, which is a very expensive entertainment; but, a council was then held in Paris, in which it was decided to lay siege to the town of Orleans, which was a place of great importance to the Dauphin's cause. An English army of ten thousand men was despatched on this service, under the command of the Earl of Salisbury, a general of fame. He being unfortunately killed early in the siege, the Earl of Suffolk took his place; under whom (reinforced by SIR JOHN FALSTAFF, who brought up four hundred waggons laden with salt herrings and other provisions for the troops, and, beating off the French who tried to intercept him, came victorious out of a hot skirmish, which was afterwards called in jest the Battle of the Herrings) the town of Orleans was so completely hemmed in, that the besieged proposed to yield it up to their countryman the Duke of Burgundy. The English general, however, replied that his English men had won it, so far, by their blood and valour, and that his English men must have it. There seemed to be no hope for the town, or for the Dauphin, who was so dismayed that he even thought of flying to Scotland or to Spain – when a peasant girl rose up and changed the whole state of affairs.

The story of this peasant girl I have now to tell.

Second Part

THE STORY OF JOAN OF ARC

In a remote village among some wild hills in the province of Lorraine, there lived a countryman whose name was JACQUES D'ARC. He had a daughter, JOAN OF ARC, who was at this time in her twentieth year. She had been a solitary girl from her childhood; she had often tended sheep and cattle for whole days where no human figure was seen or human voice heard; and she had often knelt, for hours together, in the gloomy empty little village chapel, looking up at the altar and at the dim lamp burning before it, until she fancied that she saw shadowy figures standing there, and even that she heard them speak to her. The people in that part of France were very ignorant and superstitious, and they had many ghostly tales to tell about what they had dreamed, and what they saw among the lonely hills when the clouds and the mists were resting on them. So, they easily believed that Joan saw strange sights, and they whispered among themselves that angels and spirits talked to her.

At last, Joan told her father that she had one day been surprised by a great unearthly light, and had afterwards heard a solemn voice, which said it was Saint Michael's voice, telling her that she was to go and help the Dauphin. Soon after this (she said), Saint Catherine and Saint Margaret had appeared to her with sparkling crowns upon their heads, and had encouraged her to be virtuous and resolute. These visions had returned sometimes; but the Voices very often; and the voices always said, 'Joan, thou art appointed by Heaven to go and help the Dauphin!' She almost always heard them while the chapel bells were ringing.

There is no doubt, now, that Joan believed she saw and heard these things. It is very well known that such delusions are a disease which is not by any means uncommon. It is probable enough that there were figures of Saint Michael, and Saint Catherine, and Saint Margaret, in the little chapel (where they would be very likely to have shining crowns upon their heads), and that they first gave Joan the idea of those three personages. She had long been a moping, fanciful girl, and, though she was a very good girl, I dare say she was a little vain, and wishful for notoriety.

Her father, something wiser than his neighbours, said, 'I tell thee, Joan, it is thy fancy. Thou hadst better have a kind husband to take care of thee, girl, and work to employ thy mind!' But Joan told him in reply, that she had taken a vow never to have a husband, and that she must go as Heaven directed her, to help the Dauphin.

It happened, unfortunately for her father's persuasions and most unfortunately for the poor girl, too, that a party of the Dauphin's enemies found their way into the village while Joan's disorder was at this point, and burnt the chapel, and drove out the inhabitants. The cruelties she saw committed, touched Joan's heart and made her worse. She said that the voices and the figures were now continually with her; that they told her she was the girl who, according to an old prophecy, was to deliver France; and she must go and help the Dauphin, and must remain with him until he should be crowned at Rheims: and that she must travel a long way to a certain lord named BAUDRICOURT, who could and would, bring her into the Dauphin's presence.

As her father still said, 'I tell thee, Joan, it is thy fancy,' she set off to find out this lord, accompanied by an uncle, a poor village wheelwright and cart-maker, who believed in the reality of her visions. They travelled a long way and went on and on, over a rough country, full of the Duke of Burgundy's men, and of all kinds of robbers and marauders, until they came to where this lord was.

When his servants told him that there was a poor peasant girl named Joan of Arc, accompanied by nobody but an old village wheelwright and cart-maker, who wished to see him because

Joan of Arc Tending Her Flock

she was commanded to help the Dauphin and save France, Baudricourt burst out a-laughing, and bade them send the girl away. But, he soon heard so much about her, lingering in the town, and praying in the churches, and seeing visions, and doing harm to no one, that he sent for her, and questioned her. As she said the same things after she had been well sprinkled with holy water as she had said before the sprinkling, Baudricourt began to think there might be something in it. At all events, he thought it worth while to send her on to the town of Chinon, where the Dauphin was. So, he bought her a horse, and a sword, and gave her two squires to conduct her. As the Voices had told Joan that she was to wear a man's dress, now, she put one on, and girded her sword to her side, and bound spurs to her heels, and mounted her horse and rode away with her two squires. As to her uncle the wheelwright, he stood staring at his niece in wonder until she was out of sight – as well he might – and then went home again. The best place, too.

Joan and her two squires rode on and on, until they came to Chinon, where she was, after some doubt, admitted into the Dauphin's presence. Picking him out immediately from all his court, she told him that she came commanded by Heaven to subdue his enemies and conduct him to his coronation at Rheims. She also told him (or he pretended so afterwards, to make the greater impression upon his soldiers) a number of his secrets known only to himself, and, furthermore, she said there was an old, old sword in the cathedral of Saint Catherine at Fierbois, marked with five old crosses on the blade, which Saint Catherine had ordered her to wear.

Now, nobody knew anything about this old, old sword, but when the cathedral came to be examined – which was immediately done – there, sure enough, the sword was found! The Dauphin then required a number of grave priests and bishops to give him their opinion whether the girl derived her power from good spirits or from evil spirits, which they held prodigiously long debates about, in the course of which several learned men fell fast asleep and snored loudly. At last, when one gruff old gentleman had said to Joan, 'What language do your Voices speak?' and when Joan had replied to the gruff old gentleman, 'A pleasanter language than yours,' they agreed that it was all correct, and that Joan of Arc was inspired from Heaven. This wonderful circumstance put new heart into the Dauphin's soldiers when they heard of it, and dispirited the English army, who took Joan for a witch.

So Joan mounted horse again, and again rode on and on, until she came to Orleans. But she rode now, as never peasant girl had ridden yet. She rode upon a white war-horse, in a suit of glittering armour; with the old, old sword from the cathedral, newly burnished, in her belt; with a white flag carried before her, upon which were a picture of God, and the words JESUS MARIA. In this splendid state, at the head of a great body of troops escorting provisions of all kinds for the starving inhabitants of Orleans, she appeared before that beleaguered city.

When the people on the walls beheld her, they cried out 'The Maid is come! The Maid of the Prophecy is come to deliver us!' And this, and the sight of the Maid fighting at the head of their men, made the French so bold, and made the English so fearful, that the English line of forts was soon broken, the troops and provisions were got into the town, and Orleans was saved.

Joan, henceforth called THE MAID OF ORLEANS, remained within the walls for a few days, and caused letters to be thrown over, ordering Lord Suffolk and his Englishmen to depart from the town according to the will of Heaven. As the English general very positively declined to believe that Joan knew anything about the will of Heaven (which did not mend the matter with his soldiers, for they stupidly said if she were not inspired she was a witch, and it was of no use to fight against a witch), she mounted her white war-horse again, and ordered her white banner to advance.

The besiegers held the bridge, and some strong towers upon the bridge; and here the Maid of Orleans attacked them. The fight was fourteen hours long. She planted a scaling ladder with her own hands, and mounted a tower wall, but was struck by an English arrow in the neck, and fell into the trench. She was carried away and the arrow was taken out, during which operation she screamed and cried with the pain, as any other girl might have done; but presently she said that the Voices were speaking to her and soothing her to rest. After a while, she got up, and was again foremost in the fight. When the English who had seen her fall and supposed her dead, saw this, they were troubled with the strangest fears, and some of them cried out that they beheld Saint Michael on a white horse (probably Joan herself) fighting for the French. They lost the bridge, and lost the towers, and next day set their chain of forts on fire, and left the place.

But as Lord Suffolk himself retired no farther than the town of Jargeau, which was only a few miles off, the Maid of Orleans besieged him there, and he was taken prisoner. As the white banner scaled the wall, she was struck upon the head with a stone, and was again tumbled down into the ditch; but, she only cried all the more, as she lay there, 'On, on, my countrymen! And fear nothing, for the Lord hath delivered them into our hands!' After this new success of the Maid's, several other fortresses and places which had previously held out against the Dauphin were delivered up without a battle; and at Patay she defeated the remainder of the English army and set up her victorious white banner on a field where twelve hundred Englishmen lay dead.

She now urged the Dauphin (who always kept out of the way when there was any fighting) to proceed to Rheims, as the first part of her mission was accomplished; and to complete the whole by being crowned there. The Dauphin was in no particular hurry to do this, as Rheims was a long way off, and the English and the Duke of Burgundy were still strong in the country through which the road lay. However, they set forth, with ten thousand men, and again the Maid of Orleans rode on and on, upon her white war-horse, and in her shining armour. Whenever they came to a town which yielded readily, the soldiers believed in her; but, whenever they came to a town which gave them any trouble, they began to murmur that she was an impostor. The latter was particularly the case at Troyes, which finally yielded, however, through the persuasion of one Richard, a friar of the place. Friar Richard was in the old doubt about the Maid of Orleans, until he had sprinkled her well with holy water, and had also well sprinkled the threshold of the gate by which she came into the city. Finding that it made no change in her or the gate, he said, as the other grave old gentlemen had said, that it was all right, and became her great ally.

So, at last, by dint of riding on and on, the Maid of Orleans, and the Dauphin, and the ten thousand sometimes believing and sometimes unbelieving men, came to Rheims. And in the great cathedral of Rheims, the Dauphin actually was crowned Charles the Seventh in a great assembly of the people. Then, the Maid, who with her white banner stood beside the King in that hour of his triumph, kneeled down upon the pavement at his feet, and said, with tears, that what she had been inspired to do, was done, and that the only recompense she asked for, was, that she should now have leave to go back to her distant home, and her sturdily incredulous father, and her first simple escort the village wheelwright and cart-maker. But the King said 'No!' and made her and her family as noble as a King could, and settled upon her the income of a Count.

Ah! happy had it been for the Maid of Orleans, if she had resumed her rustic dress that day, and had gone home to the little chapel and the wild hills, and had forgotten all these things, and had been a good man's wife, and had heard no stranger voices than the voices of little children!

It was not to be, and she continued helping the King (she did a world for him, in alliance with Friar Richard), and trying to improve the lives of the coarse soldiers, and leading a religious, an unselfish, and a modest life, herself, beyond any doubt. Still, many times she prayed the King to let her go home; and once she even took off her bright armour and hung it up in a church, meaning never to wear it more. But, the King always won her back again – while she was of any use to him – and so she went on and on and on, to her doom.

When the Duke of Bedford, who was a very able man, began to be active for England, and, by bringing the war back into France and by holding the Duke of Burgundy to his faith, to distress and disturb Charles very much, Charles sometimes asked the Maid of Orleans what the Voices said about it? But, the Voices had become (very like ordinary voices in perplexed times) contradictory and confused, so that now they said one thing, and now said another, and the Maid lost credit every day. Charles marched on Paris, which was opposed to him, and attacked the suburb of Saint Honoré. In this fight, being again struck down into the ditch, she was abandoned by the whole army. She lay unaided among a heap of dead, and crawled out how she could. Then, some of her believers went over to an opposition Maid, Catherine of La Rochelle, who said she was inspired to tell where there were treasures of buried money – though she never did – and then Joan accidentally broke the old, old sword, and others said that her power was broken with it. Finally, at the siege of Compiègne, held by the Duke of Burgundy, where she did valiant service, she was basely left alone in a retreat, though facing about and fighting to the last; and an archer pulled her off her horse.

O the uproar that was made, and the thanksgivings that were sung, about the capture of this one poor country-girl! O the way in which she was demanded to be tried for sorcery and heresy, and anything else you like, by the Inquisitor-General of France, and by this great man, and by that great man, until it is wearisome to think of! She was bought at last by the Bishop of Beauvais for ten thousand francs, and was shut up in her narrow prison: plain Joan of Arc again, and Maid of Orleans no more.

I should never have done if I were to tell you how they had Joan out to examine her, and cross-examine her, and re-examine her, and worry her into saying anything and everything; and how all sorts of scholars and doctors bestowed their utmost tediousness upon her. Sixteen times she was brought out and shut up again, and worried, and entrapped, and argued with, until she was heart-sick of the dreary business. On the last occasion of this kind she was brought into a burial-place at Rouen, dismally decorated with a scaffold, and a stake and faggots, and the executioner, and a pulpit with a friar therein, and an awful sermon ready. It is very affecting to know that even at that pass the poor girl honoured the mean vermin of a King, who had so used her for his purposes and so abandoned her; and, that while she had been regardless of reproaches heaped upon herself, she spoke out courageously for him.

It was natural in one so young to hold to life. To save her life, she signed a declaration prepared for her – signed it with a cross, for she couldn't write – that all her visions and Voices had come from the Devil. Upon her recanting the past, and protesting that she would never wear a man's dress in future, she was condemned to imprisonment for life, 'on the bread of sorrow and the water of affliction.'

But, on the bread of sorrow and the water of affliction, the visions and the Voices soon returned. It was quite natural that they should do so, for that kind of disease is much aggravated by fasting, loneliness, and anxiety of mind. It was not only got out of Joan that she considered herself inspired again, but, she was taken in a man's dress, which had been left – to entrap her – in her prison, and which she put on, in her solitude; perhaps, in remembrance of her past glories, perhaps, because the imaginary Voices told her. For this relapse into the sorcery and heresy and anything else you like, she was sentenced to be burnt to death. And, in the market-place of Rouen, in the hideous dress which the monks had invented for such spectacles; with priests and bishops sitting in a gallery looking on, though some had the Christian grace to go away, unable to endure the infamous scene; this shrieking girl – last seen amidst the smoke and fire, holding a crucifix between her hands; last heard, calling upon Christ – was burnt to ashes. They threw her ashes into the river Seine; but they will rise against her murderers on the last day.

From the moment of her capture, neither the French King nor one single man in all his court raised a finger to save her. It is no defence of them that they may have never really believed in her, or that they may have won her victories by their skill and bravery. The more they pretended to believe in her, the more they had caused her to believe in herself; and she had ever been true to them, ever brave, ever nobly devoted. But, it is no wonder, that they, who were in all things false to themselves, false to one another, false to their country, false to Heaven, false to Earth, should be monsters of ingratitude and treachery to a helpless peasant girl.

In the picturesque old town of Rouen, where weeds and grass grow high on the cathedral towers, and the venerable Norman streets are still warm in the blessed sunlight though the monkish fires that once gleamed horribly upon them have long grown cold, there is a statue of Joan of Arc, in the scene of her last agony, the square to which she has given its present name. I know some statues of modern times – even in the World's metropolis, I think – which commemorate less constancy, less earnestness, smaller claims upon the world's attention, and much greater impostors.

Third Part

Bad deeds seldom prosper, happily for mankind; and the English cause gained no advantage from the cruel death of Joan of Arc. For a long time, the war went heavily on. The Duke of Bedford died; the alliance with the Duke of Burgundy was broken; and Lord Talbot became a great general on the English side in France. But, two of the consequences of wars are, Famine – because the people cannot peacefully cultivate the ground – and Pestilence, which comes of want, misery, and suffering. Both these horrors broke out in both countries, and lasted for two wretched years. Then, the war went on again, and came by slow degrees to be so badly conducted by the English government, that, within twenty years from the execution of the Maid of Orleans, of all the great French conquests, the town of Calais alone remained in English hands.

While these victories and defeats were taking place in the course of time, many strange things happened at home. The young King, as he grew up, proved to be very unlike his great father, and showed himself a miserable puny creature. There was no harm in him – he had a great aversion to shedding blood: which was something – but, he was a weak, silly, helpless young man, and a mere shuttlecock to the great lordly battle-dores about the Court.

Of these battledores, Cardinal Beaufort, a relation of the King, and the Duke of Gloucester, were at first the most powerful. The Duke of Gloucester had a wife, who was non-sensically accused of practising witchcraft to cause the King's death and lead to her husband's coming to the throne, he being the next heir. She was charged with having, by the help of a ridiculous old woman named Margery (who was called a witch), made a little waxen doll in the King's likeness, and put it before a slow fire that it might gradually melt away. It was supposed, in such cases, that the death of the person whom the doll was made to represent, was sure to happen. Whether the duchess was as ignorant as the rest of them, and really did make such a doll with such an intention, I don't know; but, you and I know very well that she might have made a thousand dolls, if she had been stupid enough, and might have melted them all, without hurting the King or anybody else. However, she was tried for it, and so was old Margery, and so was one of the duke's chaplains, who was charged with having assisted them. Both he and Margery were put to death, and the duchess, after being taken on foot and bearing a lighted candle, three times round the City, as a penance, was imprisoned for life. The duke, himself, took all this pretty quietly, and made as little stir about the matter as if he were rather glad to be rid of the duchess.

But, he was not destined to keep himself out of trouble long. The royal shuttlecock being three and twenty, the battledores were very anxious to get him married. The Duke of Gloucester wanted him to marry a daughter of the Count of Armagnac;

but, the Cardinal and the Earl of Suffolk were all for MAR-
GARET, the daughter of the King of Sicily, who they knew was a
resolute ambitious woman and would govern the King as she
chose. To make friends with this lady, the Earl of Suffolk, who
went over to arrange the match, consented to accept her for the
King's wife without any fortune, and even to give up the two
most valuable possessions England then had in France. So, the
marriage was arranged, on terms very advantageous to the lady;
and Lord Suffolk brought her to England, and she was married
at Westminster. On what pretence this queen and her party
charged the Duke of Gloucester with high treason within a
couple of years, it is impossible to make out, the matter is so
confused; but, they pretended that the King's life was in danger,
and they took the duke prisoner. A fortnight afterwards, he was
found dead in bed (they said), and his body was shown to the
people, and Lord Suffolk came in for the best part of his estates.
You know by this time how strangely liable state prisoners were
to sudden death.

If Cardinal Beaufort had any hand in this matter, it did him
no good, for he died within six weeks; thinking it very hard and
curious – at eighty years old! – that he could not live to be Pope.

This was the time when England had completed her loss of all
her great French conquests. The people charged the loss principally upon the Earl of Suffolk, now a duke, who had made those
easy terms about the Royal Marriage, and who, they believed,
had even been bought by France. So he was impeached as a
traitor, on a great number of charges, but chiefly on accusations
of having aided the French King, and of designing to make his
own son King of England. The Commons and the people being
violent against him, the King was made (by his friends) to
interpose to save him, by banishing him for five years, and
proroguing the Parliament. The duke had much ado to escape
from a London mob, two thousand strong, who lay in wait for
him in St Giles's fields; but, he got down to his own estates in
Suffolk, and sailed away from Ipswich. Sailing across the
Channel, he sent into Calais to know if he might land there; but
they kept his boat and men in the harbour, until an English ship,
carrying a hundred and fifty men and called the Nicholas of the
Tower, came alongside his little vessel, and ordered him on
board. 'Welcome, traitor, as men say,' was the captain's grim
and not very respectful salutation. He was kept on board, a

prisoner, for eight-and-forty hours, and then a small boat appeared rowing toward the ship. As this boat came nearer, it was seen to have in it a block, a rusty sword, and an executioner in a black mask. The duke was handed down into it, and there his head was cut off with six strokes of the rusty sword. Then, the little boat rowed away to Dover beach, where the body was cast out, and left until the duchess claimed it. By whom, high in authority, this murder was committed, has never appeared. No one was ever punished for it.

There now arose in Kent an Irishman, who gave himself the name of Mortimer, but whose real name was JACK CADE. Jack, in imitation of Wat Tyler, though he was a very different and inferior sort of man, addressed the Kentish men upon their wrongs, occasioned by the bad government of England, among so many battledores and such a poor shuttlecock; and the Kentish men rose up to the number of twenty thousand. Their place of assembly was Blackheath, where, headed by Jack, they put forth two papers, which they called 'The Complaint of the Commons of Kent,' and 'The Requests of the Captain of the Great Assembly in Kent.' They then retired to Sevenoaks. The royal army coming up with them here, they beat it and killed their general. Then, Jack dressed himself in the dead general's armour, and led his men to London.

Jack passed into the City from Southwark, over the bridge, and entered it in triumph, giving the strictest orders to his men not to plunder. Having made a show of his forces there, while the citizens looked on quietly, he went back into Southwark in good order, and passed the night. Next day, he came back again, having got hold in the meantime of Lord Say, an unpopular nobleman. Says Jack to the Lord Mayor and judges: 'Will you be so good as to make a tribunal in Guildhall, and try me this nobleman?' The court being hastily made, he was found guilty, and Jack and his men cut his head off on Cornhill. They also cut off the head of his son-in-law, and then went back in good order to Southwark again.

But, although the citizens could bear the beheading of an unpopular lord, they could not bear to have their houses pillaged. And it did so happen that Jack, after dinner – perhaps he had drunk a little too much – began to plunder the house where he lodged; upon which, of course, his men began to imitate him. Wherefore, the Londoners took counsel with Lord

Scales, who had a thousand soldiers in the Tower; and defended London Bridge, and kept Jack and his people out. This advantage gained, it was resolved by divers great men to divide Jack's army in the old way, by making a great many promises on behalf of the state, that were never intended to be performed. This *did* divide them; some of Jack's men saying that they ought to take the conditions which were offered, and others saying that they ought not, for they were only a snare; some going home at once; others staying where they were; and all doubting and quarrelling among themselves.

Jack, who was in two minds about fighting or accepting a pardon, and who indeed did both, saw at last that there was nothing to expect from his men, and that it was very likely some of them would deliver him up and get a reward of a thousand marks, which was offered for his apprehension. So, after they had travelled and quarrelled all the way from Southwark to Blackheath, and from Blackheath to Rochester, he mounted a good horse and galloped away into Sussex. But, there galloped after him, on a better horse, one Alexander Iden, who came up with him, had a hard fight with him, and killed him. Jack's head was set aloft on London Bridge, with the face looking towards Blackheath, where he had raised his flag; and Alexander Iden got the thousand marks.

It is supposed by some, that the Duke of York, who had been removed from a high post abroad through the Queen's influence, and sent out of the way, to govern Ireland, was at the bottom of this rising of Jack and his men, because he wanted to trouble the government. He claimed (though not yet publicly) to have a better right to the throne than Henry of Lancaster, as one of the family of the Earl of March, who Henry the Fourth had set aside. Touching this claim, which, being through female relationship, was not according to the usual descent, it is enough to say that Henry the Fourth was the free choice of the people and the Parliament, and that his family had now reigned undisputed for sixty years. The memory of Henry the Fifth was so famous, and the English people loved it so much, that the Duke of York's claim would, perhaps, never have been thought of (it would have been so hopeless) but for the unfortunate circumstance of the present King's being by this time quite an idiot, and the country very ill governed. These two circumstances gave the Duke of York a power he could not otherwise have had.

Whether the Duke knew anything of Jack Cade, or not, he came over from Ireland while Jack's head was on London Bridge; being secretly advised that the Queen was setting up his enemy, the Duke of Somerset, against him. He went to Westminster, at the head of four thousand men, and on his knees before the King, represented to him the bad state of the country, and petitioned him to summon a Parliament to consider it. This the King promised. When the Parliament was summoned, the Duke of York accused the Duke of Somerset, and the Duke of Somerset accused the Duke of York; and, both in and out of Parliament, the followers of each party were full of violence and hatred towards the other. At length the Duke of York put himself at the head of a large force of his tenants, and, in arms, demanded the reformation of the Government. Being shut out of London, he encamped at Dartford, and the royal army encamped at Blackheath. According as either side triumphed, the Duke of York was arrested, or the Duke of Somerset was arrested. The trouble ended, for the moment, in the Duke of York renewing his oath of allegiance, and going in peace to one of his own castles.

Half a year afterwards the Queen gave birth to a son, who was very ill received by the people, and not believed to be the son of the King. It shows the Duke of York to have been a moderate man, unwilling to involve England in new troubles, that he did not take advantage of the general discontent at this time, but really acted for the public good. He was made a member of the cabinet, and the King being now so much worse that he could not be carried about and shown to the people with any decency, the duke was made Lord Protector of the kingdom, until the King should recover, or the Prince should come of age. At the same time the Duke of Somerset was committed to the Tower. So, now the Duke of Somerset was down, and the Duke of York was up. By the end of the year, however, the King recovered his memory and some spark of sense; upon which the Queen used her power – which recovered with him – to get the Protector disgraced, and her favourite released. So now the Duke of York was down, and the Duke of Somerset was up.

These ducal ups and downs gradually separated the whole nation into the two parties of York and Lancaster, and led to those terrible civil wars long known as the Wars of the Red and White Roses, because the red rose was the badge of the House of Lancaster, and the white rose was the badge of the House of York.

The Duke of York, joined by some other powerful noblemen of the White Rose party, and leading a small army, met the King with another small army at St Alban's, and demanded that the Duke of Somerset should be given up. The poor King, being made to say in answer that he would sooner die, was instantly attacked. The Duke of Somerset was killed, and the King himself was wounded in the neck, and took refuge in the house of a poor tanner. Whereupon, the Duke of York went to him, led him with great submission to the Abbey, and said he was very sorry for what had happened. Having now the King in his possession, he got a Parliament summoned and himself once more made Protector, but, only for a few months; for, on the King getting a little better again, the Queen and her party got him into their possession, and disgraced the Duke once more. So, now the Duke of York was down again.

Some of the best men in power, seeing the danger of these constant changes, tried even then to prevent the Red and the White Rose Wars. They brought about a great council in London between the two parties. The White Roses assembled in Blackfriars, the Red Roses in Whitefriars; and some good priests communicated between them, and made the proceedings known at evening to the King and the judges. They ended in a peaceful agreement that there should be no more quarrelling; and there was a great royal procession to St Paul's, in which the Queen walked arm-in-arm with her old enemy, the Duke of York, to show the people how comfortable they all were. This state of peace lasted half a year, when a dispute between the Earl of Warwick (one of the Duke's powerful friends) and some of the King's servants at Court, led to an attack upon that Earl – who was a White Rose – and to a sudden breaking out of all old animosities. So, here were greater ups and downs than ever.

There were even greater ups and downs than these, soon after. After various battles, the Duke of York fled to Ireland, and his son the Earl of March to Calais, with their friends the Earls of Salisbury and Warwick; and a Parliament was held declaring them all traitors. Little the worse for this, the Earl of Warwick presently came back, landed in Kent, was joined by the Archbishop of Canterbury and other powerful noblemen and gentlemen, engaged the King's forces at Northampton, signally defeated them, and took the King himself prisoner, who was found in his tent. Warwick would have been glad, I dare say, to have taken the Queen and Prince too, but they escaped into Wales and thence into Scotland.

The King was carried by the victorious force straight to London, and made to call a new Parliament, which immediately declared that the Duke of York and those other noblemen were not traitors, but excellent subjects. Then, back comes the Duke from Ireland at the head of five hundred horsemen, rides from London to Westminster, and enters the House of Lords. There, he laid his hand upon the cloth of gold which covered the empty throne, as if he had half a mind to sit down in it — but he did not. On the Archbishop of Canterbury asking him if he would visit the King, who was in his palace close by, he replied, 'I know no one in this country, my lord, who ought not to visit *me*.' None of the lords present, spoke a single word; so, the duke went out as he had come in, established himself royally in the King's palace, and, six days afterwards, sent in to the Lords a formal statement of his claim to the throne. The lords went to the King on this momentous subject, and after a great deal of discussion, in which the judges and the other law officers were afraid to give an opinion on either side, the question was compromised. It was agreed that the present King should retain the crown for his life, and that it should then pass to the Duke of York and his heirs.

But, the resolute Queen, determined on asserting her son's right, would hear of no such thing. She came from Scotland to the north of England, where several powerful lords armed in her cause. The Duke of York, for his part, set off with some five thousand men, a little time before Christmas Day, one thousand four hundred and sixty, to give her battle. He lodged at Sandal Castle, near Wakefield, and the Red Roses defied him to come out on Wakefield Green, and fight them then and there. His generals said, he had best wait until his gallant son, the Earl of March, came up with his power; but, he was determined to accept the challenge. He did so, in an evil hour. He was hotly pressed on all sides, two thousand of his men lay dead on Wakefield Green, and he himself was taken prisoner. They set him down in mock state on an ant-hill, and twisted grass about his head, and pretended to pay court to him on their knees, saying, 'O King, without a kingdom, and Prince without a people, we hope your gracious Majesty is very well and happy!' They did worse than this; they cut his head off, and handed it on a pole to the Queen, who laughed with delight when she saw it (you recollect their walking so religiously and comfortably to St Paul's!), and had it fixed, with a paper crown upon its head, on the walls of York. The Earl of Salisbury lost his head, too; and the Duke of York's second son, a handsome boy who was flying with his tutor over Wakefield Bridge, was stabbed in the heart by a murderous lord – Lord Clifford by name – whose father had been killed by the White Roses in the fight at St Alban's. There was awful sacrifice of life in this battle, for no quarter was given, and the Queen was wild for revenge. When men unnaturally fight against their own countrymen, they are always observed to be more unnaturally cruel and filled with rage than they are against any other enemy.

But, Lord Clifford had stabbed the second son of the Duke of York – not the first. The eldest son, Edward Earl of March, was at Gloucester; and, vowing vengeance for the death of his father, his brother, and their faithful friends, he began to march against the Queen. He had to turn and fight a great body of Welsh and Irish first, who worried his advance. These he defeated in a great fight at Mortimer's Cross, near Hereford, where he beheaded a number of the Red Roses taken in battle, in retaliation for the beheading of the White Roses at Wakefield. The Queen had the next turn of beheading. Having moved towards London, and falling in, between St Alban's and Barnet, with the Earl of Warwick and the Duke of Norfolk, White Roses both, who were there with an army to oppose her, and had got the King with them; she defeated them with great loss, and struck off the heads of two prisoners of note, who were in the King's tent with him, and to whom the King had promised his protection. Her triumph, however, was very short. She had no treasure, and her army subsisted by plunder. This caused them to be hated and dreaded by the people, and particularly by the London people, who were wealthy. As soon as the Londoners heard that Edward, Earl of March, united with the Earl of Warwick, was advancing towards the city, they refused to send the Queen supplies, and made a great rejoicing.

The Queen and her men retreated with all speed, and Edward

and Warwick came on, greeted with loud acclamations on every side. The courage, beauty, and virtues of young Edward could not be sufficiently praised by the whole people. He rode into London like a conqueror, and met with an enthusiastic welcome. A few days afterwards, Lord Falconbridge and the Bishop of Exeter assembled the citizens in St John's Field, Clerkenwell, and asked them if they would have Henry of Lancaster for their King? To this they all roared, 'No, no, no!' and 'King Edward! King Edward!' Then, said those noblemen, would they love and serve young Edward? To this they all cried, 'Yes, yes!' and threw up their caps and clapped their hands, and cheered tremendously.

Therefore, it was declared that by joining the Queen and not protecting those two prisoners of note, Henry of Lancaster had forfeited the crown; and Edward of York was proclaimed King. He made a great speech to the applauding people at Westminster, and sat down as sovereign of England on that throne, on the golden covering of which his father – worthy of a better fate than the bloody axe which cut the thread of so many lives in England, through so many years – had laid his hand.

CHAPTER 23

England under Edward the Fourth

KING EDWARD THE FOURTH was not quite twenty-one years of age when he took that unquiet seat upon the throne of England. The Lancaster party, the Red Roses, were then assembling in great numbers near York, and it was necessary to give them battle instantly. But, the stout Earl of Warwick leading for the young King, and the young King himself closely following him, and the English people crowding round the Royal standard, the White and the Red Roses met, on a wild March day when the snow was falling heavily, at Towton; and there such a furious battle raged between them, that the total loss amounted to forty thousand men – all Englishmen, fighting, upon English ground, against one another. The young King gained the day, took down the heads of his father and brother from the walls of York, and put up the heads of some of the most famous noblemen engaged in the battle on the other side. Then, he went to London and was crowned with great splendour.

A new Parliament met. No fewer than one hundred and fifty of the principal noblemen and gentlemen on the Lancaster side were declared traitors, and the King – who had very little humanity, though he was handsome in person and agreeable in manners – resolved to do all he could, to pluck up the Red Rose root and branch.

Queen Margaret, however, was still active for her young son. She obtained help from Scotland and from Normandy, and took several important English castles. But, Warwick soon retook them; the Queen lost all her treasure on board ship in a great storm; and both she and her son suffered great misfortunes. Once, in the winter weather, as they were riding through a forest, they were attacked and plundered by a party of robbers; and, when they had escaped from these men and were passing alone and on foot through a thick dark part of the wood, they came, all at once, upon another robber. So the Queen, with a stout heart, took the little Prince by the hand, and going straight up to that robber, said to him, 'My friend, this is the young son of your lawful King! I confide him to your care.' The robber was surprised, but took the boy in his arms, and faithfully restored him and his mother to their friends. In the end, the Queen's soldiers being beaten and dispersed, she went abroad again, and kept quiet for the present.

Now, all this time, the deposed King Henry was concealed by a Welsh knight, who kept him close in his castle. But, next year, the Lancaster party recovering their spirits, raised a large body of men, and called him out of his retirement, to put him at their head. They were joined by some powerful noblemen who had sworn fidelity to the new King, but who were ready, as usual, to break their oaths, whenever they thought there was anything to be got by it. One of the worst things in the history of the war of the Red and White Roses, is the ease with which these noblemen, who should have set an example of honour to the people, left either side as they took slight offence, or were disappointed in their greedy expectations, and joined the other. Well! Warwick's brother soon beat the Lancastrians, and the false noblemen, being taken, were beheaded without a moment's loss of time. The deposed King had a narrow escape; three of his servants were taken, and one of them bore his cap of estate, which was set with pearls and embroidered with two golden crowns. However, the head to which the cap belonged, got safely into Lancashire, and lay pretty quietly there (the people in the secret being very true) for more than a year. At length, an old monk gave such intelligence as led to Henry's being taken while he was sitting at dinner in a place called Waddington Hall. He was immediately sent to London, and met at Islington by the Earl of Warwick, by whose direction he was put upon a horse, with his legs tied under it, and paraded three times round the pillory. Then, he was carried off to the Tower, where they treated him well enough.

The White Rose being so triumphant, the young King abandoned himself entirely to pleasure, and led a jovial life. But, thorns were springing up under his bed of roses, as he soon found out. For, having been privately married to ELIZABETH WOODVILLE, a young widow lady, very beautiful and very captivating; and at last resolving to make his secret known, and to declare her his Queen; he gave some offence to the Earl of Warwick, who was usually called the King-Maker, because of his power and influence, and because of his having lent such great help to placing Edward on the throne. This offence was not lessened by the jealousy with which the Nevil family (the Earl of Warwick's) regarded the promotion of the Woodville family. For, the young Queen was so bent on providing for her relations, that she made her father an earl and a great officer of state; married her five sisters to young noblemen of the highest rank; and provided for her younger brother, a young man of twenty, by marrying him to an immensely rich old duchess of eighty. The Earl of Warwick took all this pretty graciously for a man of his proud temper, until the question arose to whom the King's sister, MARGARET, should be married. The Earl of Warwick said, 'To one of the French King's sons,' and was allowed to go over to the French King to make some friendly proposals for that purpose, and to hold all manner of friendly interviews with him. But, while he was so engaged, the Woodville party married the young lady to the Duke of Burgundy! Upon this he came back in great rage and scorn, and shut himself up discontented, in his Castle of Middleham.

A reconciliation, though not a very sincere one, was patched up between the Earl of Warwick and the King, and lasted until

Queen Margaret and the Robbers

the Earl married his daughter, against the King's wishes, to the Duke of Clarence. While the marriage was being celebrated at Calais, the people in the north of England, where the influence of the Nevil family was strongest, broke out into rebellion; their complaint was, that England was oppressed and plundered by the Woodville family, whom they demanded to have removed from power. As they were joined by great numbers of people, and as they openly declared that they were supported by the Earl of Warwick, the King did not know what to do. At last, as he wrote to the Earl beseeching his aid, he and his new son-in-law came over to England, and began to arrange the business by shutting the King up in Middleham Castle in the safe keeping of the Archbishop of York; so England was not only in the strange position of having two kings at once, but they were both prisoners at the same time.

Even as yet, however, the King-Maker was so far true to the King, that he dispersed a new rising of the Lancastrians, took their leader prisoner, and brought him to the King, who ordered him to be immediately executed. He presently allowed the King to return to London, and there innumerable pledges of forgiveness and friendship were exchanged between them, and between the Nevils and the Woodvilles; the King's eldest daughter was promised in marriage to the heir of the Nevil family; and more friendly oaths were sworn, and more friendly promises made, than this book would hold.

They lasted about three months. At the end of that time, the Archbishop of York made a feast for the King, the Earl of Warwick, and the Duke of Clarence, at his house, the Moor, in Hertfordshire. The King was washing his hands before supper, when some one whispered him that a body of a hundred men were lying in ambush outside the house. Whether this were true or untrue, the King took fright, mounted his horse, and rode through the dark night to Windsor Castle. Another reconciliation was patched up between him and the King-Maker, but it was a short one, and it was the last. A new rising took place in Lincolnshire, and the King marched to repress it. Having done so, he proclaimed that both the Earl of Warwick and the Duke of Clarence were traitors, who had secretly assisted it, and who had been prepared publicly to join in on the following day. In these dangerous circumstances they both took ship and sailed away to the French court.

And here a meeting took place between the Earl of Warwick and his old enemy, the Dowager Queen Margaret, through whom his father had had his head struck off, and to whom he had been a bitter foe. But, now, when he said that he had done with the ungrateful and perfidious Edward of York, and that henceforth he devoted himself to the restoration of the House of Lancaster, either in the person of her husband or of her little son, she embraced him as if he had ever been her dearest friend. She did more than that; she married her son to his second daughter, the Lady Anne. However agreeable this marriage was to the new friends, it was very disagreeable to the Duke of Clarence, who perceived that his father-in-law, the King-Maker, would never make *him* King, now. So, being but a weak-minded young traitor, possessed of very little worth or sense, he readily listened to an artful court lady sent over for the purpose, and promised to turn traitor once more, and go over to his brother, King Edward, when a fitting opportunity should come.

The Earl of Warwick, knowing nothing of this, soon redeemed his promise to the Dowager Queen Margaret, by invading England and landing at Plymouth, where he instantly proclaimed King Henry, and summoned all Englishmen between the ages of sixteen and sixty, to join his banner. Then, with his army increasing as he marched along, he went northward, and came so near King Edward, who was in that part of the country, that Edward had to ride hard for it to the coast of Norfolk, and thence to get away in such ships as he could find, to Holland. Thereupon, the triumphant King-Maker and his false son-in-law, the Duke of Clarence, went to London, took the old King out of the Tower, and walked him in a great procession to Saint Paul's Cathedral with the crown upon his head. This did not improve the temper of the Duke of Clarence, who saw himself farther off from being King than ever; but he kept his secret, and said nothing. The Nevil family were restored to all their honours and glories, and the Woodvilles and the rest were disgraced. The King-Maker, less sanguinary than the King, shed no blood except that of the Earl of Worcester, who had been so cruel to the people as to have gained the title of the Butcher. Him they caught hidden in a tree, and him they tried and executed. No other death stained the King-Maker's triumph.

To dispute this triumph, back came King Edward again, next year, landing at Ravenspur, coming on to York, causing all his men to cry 'Long live King Henry!' and swearing on the altar, without a blush, that he came to lay no claim to the crown. Now was the time for the Duke of Clarence, who ordered his men to assume the White Rose, and declare for his brother. The Marquis of Montague, though the Earl of Warwick's brother, also declining to fight against King Edward, he went on successfully to London, where the Archbishop of York let him into the City, and where the people made great demonstrations in his favour. For this they had four reasons. Firstly, there were great numbers of the King's adherents hiding in the City and ready to break out; secondly, the King owed them a great deal of money, which they could never hope to get if he were unsuccessful; thirdly, there was a young prince to inherit the crown; and fourthly, the King was gay and handsome, and more popular than a better man might have been with the City ladies. After a stay of only two days with these worthy supporters, the King marched out to Barnet Common, to give the Earl of Warwick battle. And now it was to be seen, for the last time, whether the King or the King-Maker was to carry the day.

While the battle was yet pending, the faint-hearted Duke of Clarence began to repent, and sent over secret messages to his father-in-law, offering his services in mediation with the King. But, the Earl of Warwick disdainfully rejected them, and replied that Clarence was false and perjured, and that he would settle the quarrel by the sword. The battle began at four o'clock in the morning and lasted until ten, and during the greater part of the time it was fought in a thick mist – absurdly supposed to be raised by a magician. The loss of life was very great, for the hatred was strong on both sides. The King-Maker was defeated, and the King triumphed. Both the Earl of Warwick and his brother were slain, and their bodies lay in St Paul's, for some days, as a spectacle to the people.

Margaret's spirit was not broken even by this great blow. Within five days she was in arms again, and raised her standard in Bath, whence she set off with her army, to try and join Lord Pembroke, who had a force in Wales. But, the King, coming up with her outside the town of Tewkesbury, and ordering his brother, the DUKE OF GLOUCESTER, who was a brave soldier, to attack her men, she sustained an entire defeat, and was taken prisoner, together with her son, now only eighteen years of age. The conduct of the King to this poor youth was worthy of his cruel character. He ordered him to be led into his tent. 'And what,' said he, 'brought *you* to England?' 'I came to England,' replied the prisoner, with a spirit which a man of spirit might have admired in a captive, 'to recover my father's kingdom, which descended to him as his right, and from him descends to me, as mine.' The King, drawing off his iron gauntlet, struck him with it in the face; and the Duke of Clarence and some other lords, who were there, drew their noble swords, and killed him.

His mother survived him, a prisoner, for five years; after her ransom by the King of France, she survived for six years more. Within three weeks of this murder, Henry died one of those convenient sudden deaths which were so common in the Tower; in plainer words, he was murdered by the King's order.

Having no particular excitement on his hands after this great defeat of the Lancaster party, and being perhaps desirous to get rid of some of his fat (for he was now getting too corpulent to be handsome), the King thought of making war on France. As he wanted more money for this purpose than the Parliament could give him, though they were usually ready enough for war, he invented a new way of raising it, by sending for the principal citizens of London, and telling them, with a grave face, that he was very much in want of cash, and would take it very kind in them if they would lend him some. It being impossible for them safely to refuse, they complied, and the moneys thus forced from them were called – no doubt to the great amusement of the King and the Court – as if they were free gifts, 'Benevolences.' What with grants from Parliament, and what with Benevolences, the King raised an army and passed over to Calais. As nobody wanted war, however, the French King made proposals of peace, which were accepted, and a truce was concluded for seven long years. The proceedings between the Kings of France and England on this occasion, were very friendly, very splendid, and very distrustful. They finished with a meeting between the two Kings, on a temporary bridge over the river Somme, where they embraced through two holes in a strong wooden grating like a lion's cage, and made several bows and fine speeches to one another.

It was time, now, that the Duke of Clarence should be punished for his treacheries; and Fate had his punishment in store. He was, probably, not trusted by the King – for who could trust him who knew him! – and he had certainly a powerful opponent in his brother Richard, Duke of Gloucester, who, being avaricious and ambitious, wanted to marry that widowed daughter of the Earl of Warwick's who had been espoused to the deceased young Prince, at Calais. Clarence, who wanted all the family wealth for himself, secreted this lady, whom Richard found disguised as a servant in the City of London, and whom he married; arbitrators appointed by the King, then divided the property between the brothers. This led to ill-will and mistrust between them. Clarence's wife dying, and he wishing to make another marriage, which was obnoxious to the King, his ruin was hurried by that means, too. At first, the Court struck at his retainers and dependents, and accused some of them of magic and witchcraft, and similar nonsense. Successful against this small game, it then mounted to the Duke himself, who was impeached by his brother the King, in person, on a variety of such charges. He was found guilty, and sentenced to be publicly executed. He never was publicly executed, but he met his death somehow, in the Tower, and, no doubt, through some agency of the King or his brother Gloucester, or both. It was supposed at the time that he was told to choose the manner of his death, and that he chose to be drowned in a butt of Malmsey wine. I hope the story may be true, for it would have been a becoming death for such a miserable creature.

The King survived him some five years. He died in the forty-second year of his life, and the twenty-third of his reign. He had a very good capacity and some good points, but he was selfish, careless, sensual, and cruel. He was a favourite with the people for his showy manners; and the people were a good example to him in the constancy of their attachment. He was penitent on his death-bed for his 'Benevolences,' and other extortions, and ordered restitution to be made to the people who had suffered from them. He also called about his bed the enriched members of the Woodville family, and the proud lords whose honours were of older date, and endeavoured to reconcile them, for the sake of the peaceful succession of his son and the tranquillity of England.

CHAPTER 24

England under Edward the Fifth

The late King's eldest son, the Prince of Wales, called EDWARD after him, was only thirteen years of age at his father's death. He was at Ludlow Castle with his uncle, the Earl of Rivers. The prince's brother, the Duke of York, only eleven years of age, was in London with his mother. The boldest, most crafty, and most dreaded nobleman in England at that time was their uncle RICHARD, Duke of Gloucester, and everybody wondered how the two poor boys would fare with such an uncle for a friend or a foe.

The Queen, their mother, being exceedingly uneasy about this, was anxious that instructions should be sent to Lord Rivers to raise an army to escort the young King safely to London. But, Lord Hastings, who was of the Court party opposed to the Woodvilles, and who disliked the thought of giving them that power, argued against the proposal, and obliged the Queen to be satisfied with an escort of two thousand horse. The Duke of Gloucester did nothing, at first, to justify suspicion. He came from Scotland (where he was commanding an army) to York, and was there the first to swear allegiance to his nephew. He then wrote a condoling letter to the Queen-Mother, and set off to be present at the coronation in London.

Now, the young King, journeying towards London too, with Lord Rivers and Lord Gray, came to Stony Stratford, as his uncle came to Northampton, about ten miles distant; and when those two lords heard that the Duke of Gloucester was so near, they proposed to the young King that they should go back and greet him in his name. The boy being very willing that they should do so, they rode off and were received with great friendliness, and asked by the Duke of Gloucester to stay and dine with him. In the evening, while they were merry together, up came the Duke of Buckingham with three hundred horsemen; and next morning the two lords and the two dukes, and the three hundred horsemen, rode away together to rejoin the King. Just as they were entering Stony Stratford, the Duke of Glouces-ter, checking his horse, turned suddenly on the two lords, charged them with alienating from him the affections of his sweet nephew, and caused them to be arrested by the three hundred horsemen and taken back. Then, he and the Duke of Buckingham went straight to the King (whom they had now in their power), to whom they made a show of kneeling down, and offering great love and submission; and then they ordered his attendants to disperse, and took him, alone with them, to Northampton.

A few days afterwards they conducted him to London, and lodged him in the Bishop's Palace. But, he did not remain there long; for, the Duke of Buckingham with a tender face made a speech expressing how anxious he was for the Royal boy's safety, and how much safer he would be in the Tower until his coronation, than he could be anywhere else. So, to the Tower he was taken, very carefully, and the Duke of Gloucester was named Protector of the State.

Although Gloucester had proceeded thus far with a very smooth countenance – and although he was a clever man, fair of speech, and not ill-looking, in spite of one of his shoulders being something higher than the other – and although he had come into the City riding bareheaded at the King's side, and looking very fond of him – he had made the King's mother more uneasy yet; and when the Royal boy was taken to the Tower, she became so alarmed that she took sanctuary in Westminster with her five daughters.

Nor did she do this without reason, for, the Duke of Gloucester, finding that the lords who were opposed to the Woodville family were faithful to the young King nevertheless, quickly resolved to strike a blow for himself. Accordingly, while those lords met in council at the Tower, he and those who were in his interest met in separate council at his own residence, Crosby Palace, in Bishopsgate Street. Being at last quite prepared, he one day appeared unexpectedly at the council in the Tower, and appeared to be very jocular and merry. He was particularly gay with the Bishop of Ely: praising the strawberries that grew in his garden on Holborn Hill, and asking him to have some gathered that he might eat them at dinner. The Bishop, quite proud of the honour, sent one of his men to fetch some; and the Duke, still very jocular and gay, went out; and the council all said what a very agreeable duke he was! In a little time, however, he came back quite altered – not at all jocular – frowning and fierce – and suddenly said, –

'What do those persons deserve who have compassed my destruction; I being the King's lawful, as well as natural, protector?'

To this strange question, Lord Hastings replied, that they deserved death, whosoever they were.

'Then,' said the Duke, 'I tell you that they are that sorceress my brother's wife;' meaning the Queen: 'and that other sorceress, Jane Shore. Who, by witchcraft, have withered my body, and caused my arm to shrink as I now show you.'

He then pulled up his sleeve and showed them his arm, which was shrunken, it is true, but which had been so, as they all very well knew, from the hour of his birth.

Jane Shore, being then the lover of Lord Hastings, as she had formerly been of the late King, that lord knew that he himself was attacked. So, he said, in some confusion, 'Certainly, my Lord, if they have done this, they be worthy of punishment.'

'If?' said the Duke of Gloucester; 'do you talk to me of ifs? I tell you that they *have* so done, and I will make it good upon thy body, thou traitor!'

With that, he struck the table a great blow with his fist. This was a signal to some of his people outside to cry 'Treason!' They immediately did so, and there was a rush into the chamber of so many armed men that it was filled in a moment.

'First,' said the Duke of Gloucester to Lord Hastings, 'I arrest thee, traitor! And let him,' he added to the armed men who took him, 'have a priest at once, for by St Paul I will not dine until I have seen his head off!'

Lord Hastings was hurried to the green by the Tower chapel, and there beheaded on a log of wood that happened to be lying on the ground. Then, the Duke dined with a good appetite, and after dinner summoning the principal citizens to attend him, told them that Lord Hastings and the rest had designed to murder both himself and the Duke of Buckingham, who stood by his side, if he had not providentially discovered their design. He requested them to be so obliging as to inform their fellow-citizens of the truth of what he said, and issued a proclamation (prepared and neatly copied out beforehand) to the same effect.

On the same day that the Duke did these things in the Tower, Sir Richard Ratcliffe, the boldest and most undaunted of his men, went down to Pontefract; arrested Lord Rivers, Lord Gray, and two other gentlemen; and publicly executed them on the scaffold, without any trial, for having intended the Duke's death. Three days afterwards the Duke, not to lose time, went down the river to Westminster in his barge, attended by divers bishops, lords, and soldiers, and demanded that the Queen should deliver her second son, the Duke of York, into his safe keeping. The Queen, being obliged to comply, resigned the child after she had wept over him; and Richard of Gloucester placed him with his brother in the Tower. Then, he seized Jane Shore, and, because she had been the lover of the late King, confiscated her property, and got her sentenced to do public penance in the streets by walking in a scanty dress, with bare feet, and carrying a lighted candle, to St Paul's Cathedral, through the most crowded part of the City.

Having now all things ready for his own advancement, he caused a friar to preach a sermon at the cross which stood in front of St Paul's Cathedral, in which he dwelt upon the profligate manners of the late King, and upon the late shame of Jane Shore, and hinted that the princes were not his children. 'Whereas, good people,' said the friar, whose name was SHAW, 'my Lord the Protector, the noble Duke of Gloucester, that sweet prince, the pattern of all the noblest virtues, is the perfect image and express likeness of his father.' There had been a little plot between the Duke and the friar, that the Duke should appear in the crowd at this moment, when it was expected that the people would cry 'Long live King Richard!' But, either through the friar saying the words too soon, or through the Duke's coming too late, the Duke and the words did not come together, and the people only laughed, and the friar sneaked off ashamed.

The Duke of Buckingham was a better hand at such business than the friar, so he went to the Guildhall the next day, and addressed the citizens in the Lord Protector's behalf. A few dirty men, who had been hired and stationed there for the purpose, crying when he had done, 'God save King Richard!' he made them a great bow, and thanked them with all his heart. Next day, to make an end of it, he went with the mayor and some lords and citizens to Bayard Castle, by the river, where Richard then was, and read an address, humbly entreating him to accept the Crown of England. Richard, who looked down upon them out of a window and pretended to be in great uneasiness and alarm, assured them there was nothing he desired less, and that his deep affection for his nephews forbade him to think of it. To this the Duke of Buckingham replied, with pretended warmth, that the free people of England would never submit to his nephew's rule, and that if Richard, who was the lawful heir, refused the Crown, why then they must find some one else to wear it. The Duke of Gloucester returned, that since he used that strong language, it became his painful duty to think no more of himself, and to accept the Crown.

Upon that, the people cheered and dispersed; and the Duke of Gloucester and the Duke of Buckingham passed a pleasant evening, talking over the play they had just acted with so much success, and every word of which they had prepared together.

CHAPTER 25

England under Richard the Third

KING RICHARD THE THIRD was up betimes in the morning, and went to Westminster Hall. In the Hall was a marble seat, upon which he sat himself down between two great noblemen, and told the people that he began the new reign in that place, because the first duty of a sovereign was to administer the laws equally to all, and to maintain justice. He then mounted his horse and rode back to the City, where he was received by the clergy and the crowd as if he really had a right to the throne, and really were a just man. The clergy and the crowd must have been rather ashamed of themselves in secret, I think, for being such poor-spirited knaves.

The new King and his Queen were soon crowned with a great deal of show and noise, which the people liked very much; and then the King set forth on a royal progress through his dominions. He was crowned a second time at York, in order that the people might have show and noise enough; and wherever he went was received with shouts of rejoicing – from a good many people of strong lungs, who were paid to strain their throats in crying, 'God save King Richard!' The plan was so successful that I am told it has been imitated since, by other usurpers, in other progresses through other dominions.

While he was on this journey, King Richard stayed a week at Warwick. And from Warwick he sent instructions home for one of the wickedest murders that ever was done – the murder of the two young princes, his nephews, who were shut up in the Tower of London.

Sir Robert Brackenbury was at that time Governor of the Tower. To him, by the hands of a messenger named JOHN GREEN, did King Richard send a letter, ordering him by some means to put the two young princes to death. But Sir Robert – I hope because he had children of his own, and loved them – sent John Green back again, riding and spurring along the dusty roads, with the answer that he could not do so horrible a piece of work. The King, having frowningly considered a little, called to him SIR JAMES TYRREL, his master of the horse, and to him gave authority to take command of the Tower, whenever he would, for twenty-four hours, and to keep all the keys of the Tower during that space of time. Tyrrel, well knowing what was wanted, looked about him for two hardened ruffians, and chose JOHN DIGHTON, one of his own grooms, and MILES FOREST, who was a murderer by trade. Having secured these two assistants, he went, upon a day in August, to the Tower, showed his authority from the King, took the command for four-and-twenty hours, and obtained possession of the keys. And when the black night came, he went creeping, creeping, like a guilty villain as he was, up the dark stone winding stairs, and along the dark stone passages, until he came to the door of the room where the two young princes, having said their prayers, lay fast asleep, clasped in each other's arms. And while he watched and listened at the door, he sent in those evil demons, John Dighton and Miles Forest, who smothered the two princes with the bed and pillows, and carried their bodies down the stairs, and buried them under a great heap of stones at the staircase foot. And when the day came, he gave up the command of the Tower, and restored the keys, and hurried away without once looking behind him; and Sir Robert Brackenbury went with fear and sadness to the princes' room, and found the princes gone for ever.

You know, through all this history, how true it is that traitors are never true, and you will not be surprised to learn that the

Duke of Buckingham soon turned against King Richard, and joined a great conspiracy that was formed to dethrone him, and to place the crown upon its rightful owner's head. Richard had meant to keep the murder secret; but when he heard through his spies that this conspiracy existed, and that many lords and gentlemen drank in secret to the healths of the two young princes in the Tower, he made it known that they were dead. The conspirators, though thwarted for a moment, soon resolved to set up for the crown against the murderous Richard, HENRY Earl of Richmond, grandson of Catherine: that widow of Henry the Fifth who married Owen Tudor. And as Henry was of the house of Lancaster, they proposed that he should marry the Princess Elizabeth, the eldest daughter of the late King, now the heiress of the house of York, and thus by uniting the rival families put an end to the fatal wars of the Red and White Roses. All being settled, a time was appointed for Henry to come over from Brittany, and for a great rising against Richard to take place in several parts of England at the same hour. On a certain day, therefore, in October, the revolt took place; but unsuccessfully. Richard was prepared, Henry was driven back at sea by a storm, his followers in England were dispersed, and the Duke of Buckingham was taken, and at once beheaded in the market-place at Salisbury.

The time of his success was a good time, Richard thought, for summoning a Parliament and getting some money. So, a Parliament was called, and it flattered and fawned upon him as much as he could possibly desire, and declared him to be the rightful King of England, and his only son Edward, then eleven years of age, the next heir to the throne.

Richard knew full well that, let the Parliament say what it would, the Princess Elizabeth was remembered by people as the heiress of the house of York; and having accurate information besides, of its being designed by the conspirators to marry her to Henry of Richmond, he felt that it would much strengthen him and weaken them, to be beforehand with them, and marry her to his son. With this view he went to the Sanctuary at Westminster, where the late King's widow and her daughter still were, and besought them to come to Court; where (he swore by anything and everything) they should be safely and honourably entertained. They came, accordingly, but had scarcely been at

Court a month when his son died suddenly – or was poisoned – and his plan was crushed to pieces.

In this extremity, King Richard, always active, thought, 'I must make another plan.' And he made the plan of marrying the Princess Elizabeth himself, although she was his niece. There was one difficulty in the way: his wife, the Queen Anne, was alive. But, he knew (remembering his nephews) how to remove that obstacle, and he made love to the Princess Elizabeth, telling her he felt perfectly confident that the Queen would die in February. The Princess was not a very scrupulous young lady, for, instead of rejecting the murderer of her brothers with scorn and hatred, she openly declared she loved him dearly; and, when February came and the Queen did not die, she expressed her impatient opinion that she was too long about it. However, King Richard was not so far out in his prediction, but that she died in March – he took good care of that – and then this precious pair hoped to be married. But they were disappointed, for the idea of such a marriage was so unpopular in the country, that the King's chief counsellors, RATCLIFFE and CATESBY, would by no means undertake to propose it, and the King was even obliged to declare in public that he had never thought of such a thing.

He was, by this time, dreaded and hated by all classes of his subjects. His nobles deserted every day to Henry's side; he dared not call another Parliament, lest his crimes should be denounced there; and for want of money, he was obliged to get Benevolences from the citizens, which exasperated them all against him. It was said too, that, being stricken by his conscience, he dreamed frightful dreams, and started up in the night-time, wild with terror and remorse. Active to the last, through all this, he issued vigorous proclamations against Henry of Richmond and all his followers, when he heard that they were coming against him with a Fleet from France; and took the field as fierce and savage as a wild boar – the animal represented on his shield.

Henry of Richmond landed with six thousand men at Milford Haven, and came on against King Richard, then encamped at Leicester with an army twice as great, through North Wales. On Bosworth Field the two armies met; and Richard, looking along Henry's ranks, and seeing them crowded with the English nobles who had abandoned him, turned pale when he beheld the powerful Lord Stanley and his son (whom he had tried hard to retain) among them. But, he was as brave as he was wicked, and plunged into the thickest of the fight. He was riding hither and thither, laying about him in all directions, when he observed the Earl of Northumberland – one of his few great allies – to stand inactive, and the main body of his troops to hesitate. At the same moment, his desperate glance caught Henry of Richmond among a little group of his knights. Riding hard at him, and crying 'Treason!' he killed his standard-bearer, fiercely unhorsed another gentleman, and aimed a powerful stroke at Henry himself, to cut him down. But, Sir William Stanley parried it as it fell, and before Richard could raise his arm again, he was borne down in a press of numbers, unhorsed, and killed. Lord Stanley picked up the crown, all bruised and trampled, and stained with blood, and put it upon Richmond's head, amid loud and rejoicing cries of 'Long live King Henry!'

That night, a horse was led up to the church of the Grey Friars at Leicester; across whose back was tied, like some worthless sack, a naked body brought there for burial. It was the body of the last of the Plantagenet line, King Richard the Third, usurper and murderer, slain at the battle of Bosworth Field in the thirty-second year of his age, after a reign of two years.

CHAPTER 26

England under Henry the Seventh

KING HENRY THE SEVENTH did not turn out to be as fine a fellow as the nobility and people hoped, in the first joy of their deliverance from Richard the Third. He was very cold, crafty, and calculating, and would do almost anything for money. He possessed considerable ability, but his chief merit appears to have been that he was not cruel when there was nothing to be got by it.

The new King had promised the nobles who had espoused his cause that he would marry the Princess Elizabeth. The first thing he did, was, to direct her to be removed from the castle of Sheriff Hutton in Yorkshire, where Richard had placed her, and restored to the care of her mother in London. The young Earl of Warwick, Edward Plantagenet, son and heir of the late Duke of Clarence, had been kept a prisoner in the same old Yorkshire Castle with her. This boy, who was now fifteen, the new King placed in the Tower for safety. Then he came to London in great state, and gratified the people with a fine procession; on which kind of show he often very much relied for keeping them in good humour. The sports and feasts which took place were followed by a terrible fever, called the Sweating Sickness; of which great numbers of people died. Lord Mayors and Alder-men are thought to have suffered most from it; whether, because they were in the habit of over-eating themselves, or because they were very jealous of preserving filth and nuisances in the City (as they have been since), I don't know.

The King's coronation was postponed on account of the general ill-health, and he afterwards deferred his marriage, as if he were not very anxious that it should take place: and, even after that, deferred the Queen's coronation so long that he gave offence to the York party. However, he set these things right in the end, by hanging some men and seizing on the rich pos-sessions of others; by granting more popular pardons to the followers of the late King than could, at first, be got from him; and, by employing about his Court, some not very scrupulous persons who had been employed in the previous reign.

As this reign was principally remarkable for two very curious impostures which have become famous in history, we will make those two stories its principal feature.

There was a priest at Oxford of the name of Simons, who had for a pupil a handsome boy named Lambert Simnel, the son of a baker. Partly to gratify his own ambitious ends, and partly to carry out the designs of a secret party formed against the King, this priest declared that his pupil, the boy, was no other than the young Earl of Warwick; who (as everybody might have known) was safely locked up in the Tower of London. The priest and the boy went over to Ireland; and, at Dublin, enlisted in their cause all ranks of the people: who seem to have been generous enough, but exceedingly irrational. The Earl of Kil-dare, the governor of Ireland, declared that he believed the boy to be what the priest represented; and the boy, who had been well tutored by the priest, told them such things of his child-hood, and gave them so many descriptions of the Royal Family, that they were perpetually shouting and hurrahing, and drinking his health, and making all kinds of noisy and thirsty demonstrations, to express their belief in him. Nor was this feeling confined to Ireland alone, for the Earl of Lincoln – whom the late usurper had named as his successor – went over to the young Pretender; and, after holding a secret correspondence with the Dowager Duchess of Burgundy – the sister of Edward the Fourth, who detested the present King and all his race – sailed to Dublin with two thousand German soldiers of her providing. In this promising state of the boy's fortunes, he was crowned there, with a crown taken off the head of a statue of the Virgin Mary; and was then, according to the Irish custom of those days, carried home on the shoulders of a big chieftain possessing a great deal more strength than sense. Father Simons, you may be sure, was mighty busy at the coronation.

Ten days afterwards, the Germans, and the Irish, and the priest, and the boy, and the Earl of Lincoln, all landed in Lancashire to invade England. The King, who had good intelligence of their movements, set up his standard at Nottingham, where vast numbers resorted to him every day; while the Earl of Lincoln could gain but very few. With his small force he tried to make for the town of Newark; but the King's army getting between him and that place, he had no choice but to risk a battle at Stoke. It soon ended in the complete destruction of the Pretender's forces, one half of whom were killed; among them, the Earl himself. The priest and the baker's boy were taken prisoners. The priest, after confessing the trick, was shut up in prison, where he afterwards died – suddenly perhaps. The boy was taken into the King's kitchen and made a turnspit. He was afterwards raised to the station of one of the King's falconers; and so ended this strange imposition.

There seems reason to suspect that the Dowager Queen – always a restless and busy woman – had had some share in tutoring the baker's son. The King was very angry with her, whether or no. He seized upon her property, and shut her up in a convent at Bermondsey.

One might suppose that the end of this story would have put the Irish people on their guard; but they were quite ready to receive a second impostor, as they had received the first, and that same troublesome Duchess of Burgundy soon gave them the opportunity. All of a sudden there appeared at Cork, in a vessel arriving from Portugal, a young man of excellent abilities, of very handsome appearance and most winning manners, who declared himself to be Richard, Duke of York, the second son of King Edward the Fourth. 'O,' said some, even of those ready Irish believers, 'but surely that young Prince was murdered by his uncle in the Tower!'— 'It *is* supposed so,' said the engaging young man; 'and my brother *was* killed in that gloomy prison; but I escaped – it don't matter how, at present – and have been wandering about the world for seven long years.' This explanation being quite satisfactory to numbers of the Irish people, they began again to shout and to hurrah, and to drink his health, and to make the noisy and thirsty demonstrations all over again. And the big chieftain in Dublin began to look out for another coronation, and another young King to be carried home on his back.

Now, King Henry being then on bad terms with France, the French King, Charles the Eighth, saw that, by pretending to believe in the handsome young man, he could trouble his enemy sorely. So, he invited him over to the French Court, and appointed him a body-guard, and treated him in all respects as if he really were the Duke of York. Peace, however, being soon concluded between the two Kings, the pretended Duke was turned adrift, and wandered for protection to the Duchess of Burgundy. She, after feigning to inquire into the reality of his claims, declared him to be the very picture of her dear departed brother; gave him a body-guard at her Court, of thirty halberdiers; and called him by the sounding name of the White Rose of England.

The leading members of the White Rose party in England sent over an agent, named Sir Robert Clifford, to ascertain whether the White Rose's claims were good: the King also sent over his agents to inquire into the Rose's history. The White Roses declared the young man to be really the Duke of York; the King declared him to be PERKIN WARBECK, the son of a merchant of the city of Tournay, who had acquired his knowledge of England, its language and manners, from the English merchants who traded in Flanders; it was also stated by the Royal agents that he had been in the service of Lady Brompton, the wife of an exiled English nobleman, and that the Duchess of Burgundy had caused him to be trained and taught, expressly for this deception. The King then required the Archduke Philip – who was the sovereign of Burgundy – to banish this new Pretender, or to deliver him up; but, as the Archduke replied that he could not control the Duchess in her own land, the King, in revenge, took the market of English cloth away from Antwerp, and prevented all commercial intercourse between the two countries.

He also, by arts and bribes, prevailed on Sir Robert Clifford to betray his employers; and he denouncing several famous English noblemen as being secretly the friends of Perkin Warbeck, the King had three of the foremost executed at once. Whether he pardoned the remainder because they were poor, I do not know; but it is only too probable that he refused to pardon one famous nobleman against whom the same Clifford soon afterwards informed separately, because he was rich. This was no other than Sir William Stanley, who had saved the King's life at the battle of Bosworth Field. It is very doubtful whether his treason amounted to much more than his having said, that if he were sure the young man was the Duke of York, he would not take arms against him. Whatever he had done he admitted, like an honourable spirit; and he lost his head for it, and the covetous King gained all his wealth.

Perkin Warbeck kept quiet for three years; but, as the Flemings began to complain heavily of the loss of their trade by the stoppage of the Antwerp market on his account, and as it was not unlikely that they might even go so far as to take his life, or give him up, he found it necessary to do something. Accordingly, he made a desperate sally, and landed, with only a few hundred men, on the coast of Deal. But he was soon glad to get back to the place from whence he came; for the country people rose against his followers, killed a great many, and took a hundred and fifty prisoners: who were all driven to London, tied together with ropes, like a team of cattle. Every one of them was hanged on some part or other of the sea-shore; in order, that if any more men should come over with Perkin Warbeck, they might see the bodies as a warning before they landed.

Then the wary King, by making a treaty of commerce with the Flemings, drove Perkin Warbeck out of that country; and, by completely gaining over the Irish to his side, deprived him of that asylum too. He wandered away to Scotland, and told his story at that Court. King James the Fourth of Scotland, who was no friend to King Henry and had no reason to be (for King Henry had bribed his Scotch lords to betray him more than once; but had never succeeded in his plots), gave him a great reception, called him his cousin, and gave him in marriage the Lady Catherine Gordon, a beautiful and charming creature related to the royal house of Stuart.

Alarmed by this successful reappearance of the Pretender, the King still undermined, and bought, and bribed, and kept his doings and Perkin Warbeck's story in the dark, when he might, one would imagine, have rendered the matter clear to all England. But, for all this bribing of the Scotch lords at the Scotch King's Court, he could not procure the Pretender to be delivered up to him. James, though not very particular in many respects, would not betray him; and the ever-busy Duchess of Burgundy so provided him with arms, and good soldiers, and with money besides, that he had soon a little army of fifteen hundred men of various nations. With these, and aided by the Scottish King in person, he crossed the border into England, and made a proclamation to the people, in which he called the King 'Henry Tudor;' offered large rewards to any who should take or distress him; and announced himself as King Richard the Fourth come to receive the homage of his faithful subjects. His faithful subjects, however, cared nothing for him, and hated his faithful troops: who, being of different nations, quarrelled also among themselves. Worse than this, if worse were possible, they began to plunder the country; upon which the White Rose said, that he would rather lose his rights, than gain them through the miseries of the English people. The Scottish King made a jest of his scruples; but they and their whole force went back again without fighting a battle.

The worst consequence of this attempt was, that a rising took place among the people of Cornwall, who considered themselves too heavily taxed to meet the charges of the expected war. Stimulated by Flammock, a lawyer, and Joseph, a blacksmith, and joined by Lord Audley and some other country gentlemen, they marched on all the way to Deptford Bridge, where they fought a battle with the King's army. They were defeated – though the Cornish men fought with great bravery – and the lord was beheaded, and the lawyer and the blacksmith were hanged, drawn, and quartered. The rest were pardoned. The King, who believed every man to be as avaricious as himself, and thought that money could settle anything, allowed them to make bargains for their liberty with the soldiers who had taken them.

Perkin Warbeck, doomed to wander up and down, and never to find rest anywhere – a sad fate: almost a sufficient punishment for an imposture, which he seems in time to have half believed himself – lost his Scottish refuge through a truce being made between the two Kings; and found himself, once more, without a country before him in which he could lay his head. But James (always honourable and true to him, alike when he melted down his plate, and even the great gold chain he had been used to wear, to pay soldiers in his cause; and now, when that cause was lost and hopeless) did not conclude the treaty, until he had safely departed out of the Scottish dominions. He, and his beautiful wife, who was faithful to him under all reverses, and left her state and home to follow his poor fortunes, were put aboard ship with everything necessary for their comfort and protection, and sailed for Ireland.

But the Irish people had had enough of counterfeit Earls of Warwick and Dukes of York, for one while; and would give the White Rose no aid. So, the White Rose – encircled by thorns indeed – resolved to go with his beautiful wife to Cornwall as a forlorn resource, and see what might be made of the Cornish men, who had risen so valiantly a little while before, and who had fought so bravely at Deptford Bridge.

To Whitsand Bay, in Cornwall, accordingly, came Perkin Warbeck and his wife; and the lovely lady he shut up for safety in the Castle of St Michael's Mount, and then marched into Devonshire at the head of three thousand Cornish men. These were increased to six thousand by the time of his arrival in Exeter; but, there the people made a stout resistance, and he went on to Taunton, where he came in sight of the King's army. The stout Cornish men, although they were few in number, and badly armed, were so bold, that they never thought of retreating; but bravely looked forward to a battle on the morrow. Unhappily for them, the man who was possessed of so many engaging qualities, and who attracted so many people to his side when he had nothing else with which to tempt them, was not as brave as they. In the night, when the two armies lay opposite to each other, he mounted a swift horse and fled. When morning dawned, the poor confiding Cornish men, discovering that they had no leader, surrendered to the King's power. Some of them were hanged, and the rest were pardoned and went miserably home.

Before the King pursued Perkin Warbeck to the sanctuary of Beaulieu, in the New Forest, where it was soon known that he had taken refuge, he sent a body of horsemen to St Michael's Mount, to seize his wife. She was soon taken and brought as a captive before the King. But she was so beautiful, and so good, and so devoted to the man in whom she believed, that the King regarded her with compassion, treated her with great respect, and placed her at Court, near the Queen's person. And many years after Perkin Warbeck was no more, and when his strange story had become like a nursery tale, *she* was called the White Rose, by the people, in remembrance of her beauty.

The sanctuary at Beaulieu was soon surrounded by the King's men; and the King, pursuing his usual dark artful ways, sent pretended friends to Perkin Warbeck to persuade him to come out and surrender himself. This he soon did; the King having taken a good look at the man of whom he had heard so much – from behind a screen – directed him to be well mounted, and to ride behind him at a little distance, guarded, but not bound in any way. So they entered London with the King's favourite show – a procession; and some of the people hooted as the Pretender rode slowly through the streets to the Tower; but the greater part were quiet, and very curious to see him. From the Tower, he was taken to the Palace at Westminster, and there lodged like a gentleman, though closely watched. He was examined every now and then as to his imposture; but the King was so secret in all he did, that even then he gave it a consequence, which it cannot be supposed to have in itself deserved.

At last Perkin Warbeck ran away, and took refuge in another sanctuary near Richmond in Surrey. From this he was again persuaded to deliver himself up; and, being conveyed to London, he stood in the stocks for a whole day, outside Westminster Hall, and there read a paper purporting to be his full confession, and relating his history as the King's agents had originally described it. He was then shut up in the Tower again, in the company of the Earl of Warwick, who had now been there for fourteen years: ever since his removal out of Yorkshire, except when the King had had him at Court, and had shown him to the people, to prove the imposture of the Baker's boy. It is but too probable, when we consider the crafty character of Henry the Seventh that these two were brought together for a cruel purpose. A plot was soon discovered between them and the keepers, to murder the Governor, get possession of the keys, and proclaim Perkin Warbeck as King Richard the Fourth. That there was some such plot, is likely; that they were tempted into it, is at least as likely; that the unfortunate Earl of Warwick – last male of the Plantagenet line – was too unused to the world, and too ignorant and simple to know much about it, whatever it was, is perfectly certain; and that it was the King's interest to get rid of him, is no less so. He was beheaded on Tower Hill, and Perkin Warbeck was hanged at Tyburn.

Such was the end of the pretended Duke of York, whose shadowy history was made more shadowy – and ever will be – by the mystery and craft of the King. If he had turned his great natural advantages to a more honest account, he might have lived a happy and respected life, even in those days. But he died upon a gallows at Tyburn, leaving the Scottish lady, who had loved him so well, kindly protected at the Queen's Court. After some time she forgot her old loves and troubles, as many people do with Time's merciful assistance, and married a Welsh gentleman. Her second husband, SIR MATTHEW CRADOC, more honest and more happy than her first, lies beside her in a tomb in the old church of Swansea.

The ill-blood between France and England in this reign, arose out of the continued plotting of the Duchess of Burgundy, and disputes respecting the affairs of Brittany. The King feigned to be very patriotic, indignant, and war-like; but he always contrived so as never to make war in reality, and always to make money. His taxation of the people, on pretence of war with France, involved, at one time, a very dangerous insurrection, headed by Sir John Egremont, and a common man called John à Chambre. But it was subdued by the royal forces, under the command of the Earl of Surrey. The knighted John escaped to the Duchess of Burgundy, who was ever ready to receive any one who gave the King trouble; and the plain John was hanged at York, in the midst of a number of his men, but on a much higher gibbet, as being a greater traitor. Hung high or hung low, however, hanging is much the same to the person hung.

Within a year after her marriage, the Queen had given birth to a son, who was called Prince Arthur in remembrance of the old British prince of romance and story; and who, when all these events had happened, being then in his fifteenth year, was married to CATHERINE, the daughter of the Spanish monarch, with great rejoicings and bright prospects; but in a very few months he sickened and died. As soon as the King had recovered from his grief, he thought it a pity that the fortune of the Spanish Princess, amounting to two hundred thousand crowns, should go out of the family; and therefore arranged that the young widow should marry his second son HENRY, then twelve years of age, when he too should be fifteen. There were objections to this marriage on the part of the clergy; but, as the infallible Pope was gained over, and, as he *must* be right, that settled the business for the time. The King's eldest daughter was provided for, and a long course of disturbance was considered to be set at rest, by her being married to the Scottish King.

And now the Queen died. When the King had got over that grief too, his mind once more reverted to his darling money for consolation, and he thought of marrying the Dowager Queen of Naples, who was immensely rich: but, as it turned out not to be practicable to gain the money however practicable it might have been to gain the lady, he gave up the idea. He was not so fond of her but that he soon proposed to marry the Dowager Duchess of Savoy; and, soon afterwards, the widow of the King of Castile, who was raving mad. But he made a money-bargain instead, and married neither.

The Duchess of Burgundy, among the other discontented people to whom she had given refuge, had sheltered EDMUND DE LA POLE (younger brother of that Earl of Lincoln who was killed at Stoke), now Earl of Suffolk. The King had prevailed upon him to return to the marriage of Prince Arthur; but, he soon afterwards went away again; and then the King, suspecting a conspiracy, resorted to his favourite plan of sending him some treacherous friends, and buying of those scoundrels the secrets they disclosed or invented. In the end, the King, on a promise of not taking his life, obtained possession of the person of Edmund de la Pole, and shut him up in the Tower.

This was his last enemy. If he had lived much longer he would have made many more among the people, by the grinding exaction to which he constantly exposed them, and by the tyrannical acts of his two prime favourites in all money-raising matters, EDMUND DUDLEY and RICHARD EMPSON. But Death

– the enemy who is not to be bought off or deceived, and on whom no money, and no treachery, has any effect – presented himself at this juncture, and ended the King's reign. He died of the gout, on the twenty-second of April, one thousand five hundred and nine, and in the fifty-third year of his age, after reigning twenty-four years; he was buried in the beautiful Chapel of Westminster Abbey, which he had himself founded, and which still bears his name.

It was in this reign that the great CHRISTOPHER COLUMBUS, on behalf of Spain, discovered what was then called The New World. Great wonder, interest, and hope of wealth being awakened in England thereby, the King and the merchants of London and Bristol fitted out an English expedition for further discoveries in the New World, and entrusted it to SEBASTIAN CABOT, of Bristol, the son of a Venetian pilot there. He was very successful in his voyage, and gained high reputation, both for himself and England.

CHAPTER 27

England under Henry the Eighth, called Bluff King Hal and Burly King Harry

First Part

We now come to King Henry the Eighth, whom it has been too much the fashion to call 'Bluff King Hal,' and 'Burly King Harry,' and other fine names; but whom I shall take the liberty to call, plainly, one of the most detestable villains that ever drew breath. You will be able to judge, long before we come to the end of his life, whether he deserves the character.

He was just eighteen years of age when he came to the throne. People said he was handsome then; but I don't believe it. He was a big, burly, noisy, small-eyed, large-faced, double-chinned, swinish-looking fellow in later life (as we know from the likenesses of him, painted by the famous HANS HOLBEIN), and it is not easy to believe that so bad a character can ever have been veiled under a prepossessing appearance.

He was anxious to make himself popular; and the people, who had long disliked the late King, were very willing to believe that he deserved to be so. He was extremely fond of show and display, and so were they. Therefore there was great rejoicing when he married the Princess Catherine, and when they were both crowned. And the King fought at tournaments and always came off victorious – for the courtiers took care of that – and there was a general outcry that he was a wonderful man. Empson, Dudley, and their supporters were accused of a variety of crimes they had never committed, instead of the offences of which they really had been guilty; and they were pilloried, and set upon horses with their faces to the tails, and knocked about and beheaded, to the satisfaction of the people, and the enrichment of the King.

The Pope, so indefatigable in getting the world into trouble, had mixed himself up in a war on the continent of Europe, occasioned by the reigning Princes of little quarrelling states in Italy having at various times married into other Royal families, and so led to *their* claiming a share in those petty Governments. The King, who discovered that he was very fond of the Pope, sent a herald to the King of France, to say that he must not make war upon that holy personage, because he was the father of all Christians. As the French King did not mind this relationship in the least, and also refused to admit a claim King Henry made to certain lands in France, war was declared between the two countries. Not to perplex this story with an account of the tricks and designs of all the sovereigns who were engaged in it, it is enough to say that England made a blundering alliance with Spain, and got stupidly taken in by that country; which made its own terms with France when it could, and left England in the lurch. SIR EDWARD HOWARD, a bold admiral, son of the Earl of Surrey, distinguished himself by his bravery against the French in this business; but, unfortunately, he was more brave than wise, for, skimming into the French harbour of Brest with only a few row-boats, he attempted (in revenge for the defeat and death of SIR THOMAS KNYVETT, another bold English admiral) to take some strong French ships, well defended with batteries of cannon. The upshot was, that he was left on board of one of them (in consequence of its shooting away from his own boat), with not more than about a dozen men, and was thrown into the sea and drowned: though not until he had taken from his breast his gold chain and gold whistle, which were the signs of his office, and had cast them into the sea to prevent their being made a boast of by the enemy. After this defeat – which was a great one, for Sir Edward Howard was a man of valour and fame – the King took it into his head to invade France in person; first executing that dangerous Earl of Suffolk whom his father had left in the Tower, and appointing Queen Catherine to the charge of his kingdom in his absence. He sailed to Calais, where he was joined by MAXIMILIAN, Emperor of Germany, who pretended to be his soldier, and who took pay in his service: with a good deal of nonsense of that sort, flattering enough to the vanity of a vain blusterer. The King might be successful enough in sham fights; but his idea of real battles chiefly consisted in pitching silken tents of bright colours that were ignominiously blown down by the wind, and in making a vast display of gaudy flags and golden curtains. Fortune, how- ever, favoured him better than he deserved; for, after much waste of time in tent pitching, flag flying, gold curtaining, and other such masquerading, he gave the French battle at a place called Guinegate: where they took such an unaccountable panic, and fled with such swiftness, that it was ever afterwards called by the English the Battle of Spurs. Instead of following up his advantage, the King, finding that he had had enough of real fighting, came home again.

The Scottish King, though nearly related to Henry by mar- riage, had taken part against him in this war. The Earl of Surrey, as the English general, advanced to meet him when he came out of his own dominions and crossed the river Tweed. The two armies came up with one another when the Scottish King had also crossed the river Till, and was encamped upon the last of the Cheviot Hills, called the Hill of Flodden. Along the plain below it, the English, when the hour of battle came, advanced. The Scottish army, which had been drawn up in five great bodies, then came steadily down in perfect silence. So they, in their turn, advanced to meet the English army, which came on in one long line; and they attacked it with a body of spearmen, under LORD HOME. At first they had the best of it; but the English recovered themselves so bravely, and fought with such valour, that, when the Scottish King had almost made his way up to the Royal standard, he was slain, and the whole Scottish power routed. Ten thousand Scottish men lay dead that day on

Flodden Field; and among them, numbers of the nobility and gentry. For a long time afterwards, the Scottish peasantry used to believe that their King had not been really killed in this battle, because no Englishman had found an iron belt he wore about his body as a penance for having been an unnatural and undutiful son. But, whatever became of his belt, the English had his sword and dagger, and the ring from his finger, and his body too, covered with wounds. There is no doubt of it; for it was seen and recognised by English gentlemen who had known the Scottish King well.

When King Henry was making ready to renew the war in France, the French King was contemplating peace. His queen, dying at this time, he proposed, though he was upwards of fifty years old, to marry King Henry's sister, the Princess Mary, who, besides being only sixteen, was betrothed to the Duke of Suffolk. As the inclinations of young Princesses were not much considered in such matters, the marriage was concluded, and the poor girl was escorted to France, where she was immediately left as the French King's bride, with only one of all her English attendants. That one was a pretty young girl named ANNE BOLEYN, niece of the Earl of Surrey, who had been made Duke of Norfolk, after the victory of Flodden Field. Anne Boleyn's is a name to be remembered, as you will presently find.

And now the French King, who was very proud of his young wife, was preparing for many years of happiness, and she was looking forward, I dare say, to many years of misery, when he died within three months, and left her a young widow. The new French monarch, FRANCIS THE FIRST, seeing how important it was to his interests that she should take for her second husband no one but an Englishman, advised her first lover, the Duke of Suffolk, when King Henry sent him over to France to fetch her home, to marry her. The Princess being herself so fond of that Duke, as to tell him that he must either do so then, or for ever lose her, they were wedded; and Henry afterwards forgave them. In making interest with the King, the Duke of Suffolk had addressed his most powerful favourite and adviser, THOMAS WOLSEY – a name very famous in history for its rise and downfall.

Wolsey was the son of a respectable butcher at Ipswich, in Suffolk, and received so excellent an education that he became a tutor to the family of the Marquis of Dorset, who afterwards got him appointed one of the late King's chaplains. On the accession of Henry the Eighth, he was promoted and taken into great favour. He was now Archbishop of York; the Pope had made him a Cardinal besides; and whoever wanted influence in England or favour with the King – whether he were a foreign monarch or an English nobleman – was obliged to make a friend of the great Cardinal Wolsey.

He was a gay man, who could dance and jest, and sing and drink; and those were the roads to so much, or rather so little, of a heart as King Henry had. He was wonderfully fond of pomp and glitter, and so was the King. He knew a good deal of the Church learning of that time; much of which consisted in finding artful excuses and pretences for almost any wrong thing, and in arguing that black was white, or any other colour. This kind of learning pleased the King too. For many such reasons, the Cardinal was high in estimation with the King; and, being a man of far greater ability, knew as well how to manage him, as a clever keeper may know how to manage a wolf or a tiger, or any other cruel and uncertain beast, that may turn upon him and tear him any day. Never had there been seen in England such state as my Lord Cardinal kept. His wealth was enormous; equal, it was reckoned, to the riches of the Crown. His palaces were as splendid as the King's, and his retinue was eight hundred strong. He held his Court, dressed out from top to toe in flaming scarlet; and his very shoes were golden, set with precious stones. His followers rode on blood horses; while he, with a wonderful affectation of humility in the midst of his great splendour, ambled on a mule with a red velvet saddle and bridle and golden stirrups.

Through the influence of this stately priest, a grand meeting was arranged to take place between the French and English Kings in France; but on ground belonging to England. A prodigious show of friendship and rejoicing was to be made on the occasion; and heralds were sent to proclaim with brazen trumpets through all the principal cities of Europe, that, on a certain day, the Kings of France and England, as companions and brothers in arms, each attended by eighteen followers, would hold a tournament against all knights who might choose to come.

CHARLES, the new Emperor of Germany (the old one being dead), wanted to prevent too cordial an alliance between these sovereigns, and came over to England before the King could repair to the place of meeting; and, besides making an agreeable impression upon him, secured Wolsey's interest by promising that his influence should make him Pope when the next vacancy occurred. On the day when the Emperor left England, the King and all the Court went over to Calais, and thence to the place of meeting, between Ardres and Guisnes, commonly called the Field of the Cloth of Gold. Here, all manner of expense and prodigality was lavished on the decorations of the show; many of the knights and gentlemen being so superbly dressed that it was said they carried their whole estates upon their shoulders.

There were sham castles, temporary chapels, fountains running wine, great cellars full of wine free as water to all comers, silk tents, gold lace and foil, gilt lions, and such things without end; and, in the midst of all, the rich Cardinal out-shone and out-glittered all the noblemen and gentlemen assembled. After a treaty made between the two Kings with as much solemnity as if they had intended to keep it, the lists – nine hundred feet long, and three hundred and twenty broad – were opened for the tournament; the Queens of France and England looking on with great array of lords and ladies. Then, for ten days, the two sovereigns fought five combats every day, and always beat their polite adversaries; though they *do* write that the King of England, being thrown in a wrestle one day by the King of France, lost his kingly temper with his brother in arms, and wanted to make a quarrel of it. Then, there is a great story belonging to this Field of the Cloth of Gold, showing how the English were distrustful of the French, and the French of the English, until Francis rode alone one morning to Henry's tent; and, going in before he was out of bed, told him in joke that he was his prisoner; and how Henry jumped out of bed and embraced Francis; and how Francis helped Henry to dress, and warmed his linen for him; and how Henry gave Francis a splendid jewelled collar, and how Francis gave Henry, in return, a costly bracelet. All this and a great deal more was so written about, and sung about, and talked about at that time (and, indeed, since that time too), that the world has had good cause to be sick of it, for ever.

Of course, nothing came of all these fine doings but a speedy renewal of the war between England and France, in which the two Royal companions and brothers in arms longed very earnestly to damage one another. But, before it broke out again, the Duke of Buckingham was shamefully executed on Tower Hill, on the evidence of a discharged servant – really for nothing, except the folly of having believed in a friar of the name of HOPKINS, who had pretended to be a prophet, and who had mumbled and jumbled out some nonsense about the Duke's son being destined to be very great in the land. It was believed that the unfortunate Duke had given offence to the great Cardinal by expressing his mind freely about the expense and absurdity of the whole business of the Field of the Cloth of Gold. At any rate, he was beheaded, as I have said, for nothing. And the people who saw it done were very angry, and cried out that it was the work of 'the butcher's son!'

The new war was a short one, though the Earl of Surrey invaded France again, and did some injury to that country. It ended in another treaty of peace between the two kingdoms, and in the discovery that the Emperor of Germany was not such a good friend to England in reality, as he pretended to be. Neither did he keep his promise to Wolsey to make him Pope, though the King urged him. Two Popes died in pretty quick succession; but the foreign priests were too much for the Cardinal, and kept him out of the post. So the Cardinal and King together found out that the Emperor of Germany was not a man to keep faith with; broke off a projected marriage between the King's daughter MARY, Princess of Wales, and that sovereign, and began to consider whether it might not be well to marry the young lady, either to Francis himself, or to his eldest son.

There now arose at Wittemberg, in Germany, the great leader of the mighty change in England which is called The Reformation, and which set the people free from their slavery to the priests. This was a learned Doctor, named MARTIN LUTHER, who knew all about them, for he had been a priest, and even a monk, himself. The preaching and writing of Wickliffe had set a number of men thinking on this subject; and Luther, finding one day to his great surprise, that there really was a book called the New Testament which the priests did not allow to be read, and which contained truths that they suppressed, began to be very vigorous against the whole body, from the Pope downward. It happened, while he was yet only beginning his vast work of awakening the nation, that an impudent fellow named TETZEL, a friar of very bad character, came into his neighbourhood selling what were called Indulgences, by wholesale, to raise money for beautifying the great Cathedral of St Peter's, at Rome. Whoever bought an Indulgence of the Pope was supposed to buy himself off from the punishment of Heaven for his offences. Luther told the people that these Indulgences were worthless bits of paper, before God, and that Tetzel and his masters were a crew of impostors in selling them.

The King and the Cardinal were mightily indignant at this presumption; and the King (with the help of SIR THOMAS MORE, a wise man, whom he afterwards repaid by striking off his head) even wrote a book about it, with which the Pope was so well pleased that he gave the King the title of Defender of the Faith. The King and the Cardinal also issued flaming warnings to the people not to read Luther's books, on pain of excommunication. But they did read them for all that; and the rumour of what was in them spread far and wide.

When this great change was thus going on, the King began to show himself in his truest and worst colours. Anne Boleyn, the pretty little girl who had gone abroad to France with his sister, was by this time grown up to be very beautiful, and was one of the ladies in attendance on Queen Catherine. Now, Queen Catherine was no longer pretty or handsome, and it is likely that she was not particularly good-tempered; having been always rather melancholy, and having been made more so by the deaths of four of her children when they were very young. So, the King fell in love with the fair Anne Boleyn, and said to himself, 'How can I be best rid of my own troublesome wife whom I am tired of, and marry Anne?'

You recollect that Queen Catherine had been the wife of Henry's brother. What does the King do, after thinking it over, but calls his favourite priests about him, and says, O! his mind is in such a dreadful state, and he is so frightfully uneasy, because he is afraid it was not lawful for him to marry the Queen! Not one of those priests had the courage to hint that it was rather curious he had never thought of that before, and that his mind seemed to have been in a tolerably jolly condition during a great many years, in which he certainly had not fretted himself thin; but, they all said, Ah! that was very true, and it was a serious business; and perhaps the best way to make it right, would be for his Majesty to be divorced! The King replied,

Yes, he thought that would be the best way, certainly; so they all went to work.

If I were to relate to you the intrigues and plots that took place in the endeavour to get this divorce, you would think the History of England the most tiresome book in the world. So I shall say no more, than that after a vast deal of negotiation and evasion, the Pope issued a commission to Cardinal Wolsey and CARDINAL CAMPEGGIO (whom he sent over from Italy for the purpose), to try the whole case in England. It is supposed – and I think with reason – that Wolsey was the Queen's enemy, because she had reproved him for his proud and gorgeous manner of life. But, he did not at first know that the King wanted to marry Anne Boleyn; and when he did know it, he even went down on his knees, in the endeavour to dissuade him.

The Cardinals opened their court in the Convent of the Black Friars, near to where the bridge of that name in London now stands; and the King and Queen, that they might be near it, took up their lodgings at the adjoining palace of Bridewell, of which nothing now remains but a bad prison. On the opening of the court, when the King and Queen were called on to appear, that poor ill-used lady, with a dignity and firmness and yet with a womanly affection worthy to be always admired, went and kneeled at the King's feet, and said that she had come, a stranger, to his dominions; that she had been a good and true wife to him for twenty years; and that she could acknowledge no power in those Cardinals to try whether she should be considered his wife after all that time, or should be put away. With that, she got up and left the court, and would never afterwards come back to it.

The King pretended to be very much overcome, and said, O! my lords and gentlemen, what a good woman she was to be sure, and how delighted he would be to live with her unto death, but for that terrible uneasiness in his mind which was quite wearing him away! So, the case went on, and there was nothing but talk for two months. Then Cardinal Campeggio, who, on behalf of the Pope, wanted nothing so much as delay, adjourned it for two more months; and before that time was elapsed, the Pope himself adjourned it indefinitely, by requiring the King and Queen to come to Rome and have it tried there. But by good luck for the King, word was brought to him by some of his people, that they had happened to meet at supper, THOMAS CRANMER, a learned Doctor of Cambridge, who had proposed to urge the Pope on, by referring the case to all the learned doctors and bishops, here and there and everywhere, and getting their opinions that the King's marriage was unlawful. The King, who was now in a hurry to marry Anne Boleyn, thought this such a good idea, that he sent for Cranmer, post haste, and said to LORD ROCHFORT, Anne Boleyn's father, 'Take this learned Doctor down to your country-house, and there let him have a good room for a study, and no end of books out of which to prove that I may marry your daughter.' Lord Rochfort, not at all reluctant, made the learned Doctor as comfortable as he could; and the learned Doctor went to work to prove his case. All this time, the King and Anne Boleyn were writing letters to one another almost daily, full of impatience to have the case settled; and Anne Boleyn was showing herself (as I think) very worthy of the fate which afterwards befell her.

It was bad for Cardinal Wolsey that he had left Cranmer to render this help. It was worse for him that he had tried to dissuade the King from marrying Anne Boleyn. Such a servant as he, to such a master as Henry, would probably have fallen in any case; but, between the hatred of the party of the Queen that was, and the hatred of the party of the Queen that was to be, he fell suddenly and heavily. Going down one day to the Court of Chancery, where he now presided, he was waited upon by the Dukes of Norfolk and Suffolk, who told him that they brought an order to him to resign that office, and to withdraw quietly to a house he had at Esher, in Surrey. The Cardinal refusing, they rode off to the King; and next day came back with a letter from him, on reading which, the Cardinal submitted. An inventory was made out of all the riches in his palace at York Place (now Whitehall), and he went sorrowfully up the river, in his barge, to Putney. An abject man he was, in spite of his pride; for being overtaken, riding out of that place towards Esher, by one of the King's chamberlains who brought him a kind message and a ring, he alighted from his mule, took off his cap, and kneeled down in the dirt. His poor Fool, whom in his prosperous days he had always kept in his palace to entertain him, cut a far better figure than he; for, when the Cardinal said to the chamberlain that he had nothing to send to his lord the King as a present, but that jester who was a most excellent one, it took six strong yeomen to remove the faithful fool from his master.

The once proud Cardinal was soon further disgraced, and

wrote the most abject letters to his vile sovereign; who humbled him one day and encouraged him the next, according to his humour, until he was at last ordered to go and reside in his diocese of York. He said he was too poor; but I don't know how he made that out, for he took a hundred and sixty servants with him, and seventy-two cartloads of furniture, food, and wine. He remained in that part of the country for the best part of a year, and showed himself so improved by his misfortunes, and was so mild and so conciliating, that he won all hearts. And indeed, even in his proud days, he had done some magnificent things for learning and education. At last, he was arrested for high treason; and, coming slowly on his journey towards London, got as far as Leicester. Arriving at Leicester Abbey after dark, and very ill, he said – when the monks came out at the gate with lighted torches to receive him – that he had come to lay his bones among them. He had indeed; for he was taken to a bed, from which he never rose again. His last words were, 'Had I but served God as diligently as I have served the King, He would not have given me over, in my grey hairs. Howbeit, this is my just reward for my pains and diligence, not regarding my service to God, but only my duty to my prince.' The news of his death was quickly carried to the King, who was amusing himself with archery in the garden of the magnificent Palace at Hampton Court, which that very Wolsey had presented to him. The greatest emotion his royal mind displayed at the loss of a servant so faithful and so ruined, was a particular desire to lay hold of fifteen hundred pounds which the Cardinal was reported to have hidden somewhere.

The opinions concerning the divorce, of the learned doctors and bishops and others, being at last collected, and being generally in the King's favour, were forwarded to the Pope, with an entreaty that he would now grant it. The unfortunate Pope, who was a timid man, was half distracted between his fear of his authority being set aside in England if he did not do as he was asked, and his dread of offending the Emperor of Germany, who was Queen Catherine's nephew. In this state of mind he still evaded and did nothing. Then, THOMAS CROMWELL, who had been one of Wolsey's faithful attendants, and had remained so even in his decline, advised the King to take the matter into his own hands, and make himself the head of the whole Church. This the King, by various artful means, began to do; but he recompensed the clergy by allowing them to burn as many people as they pleased, for holding Luther's opinions. You must understand that Sir Thomas More, the wise man who had helped the King with his book, had been made Chancellor in Wolsey's place. But, as he was truly attached to the Church as it was even in its abuses, he, in this state of things, resigned.

Being now quite resolved to get rid of Queen Catherine, and to marry Anne Boleyn without more ado, the King made Cranmer Archbishop of Canterbury, and directed Queen Catherine to leave the Court. She obeyed; but replied that wherever she went, she was Queen of England still, and would remain so, to the last. The King then married Anne Boleyn privately; and the new Archbishop of Canterbury, within half a year, declared his marriage to Queen Catherine void, and crowned Anne Boleyn Queen.

She might have known that no good could ever come from such wrong, and that the corpulent brute who had been so faithless and so cruel to his first wife, could be more faithless and more cruel to his second. She might have known that, even when he was in love with her, he had been a mean and selfish coward, running away, like a frightened cur, from her society and her house, when a dangerous sickness broke out in it, and when she might easily have taken it and died, as several of the household did. But, Anne Boleyn arrived at all this knowledge too late, and bought it at a dear price. Her bad marriage with a worse man came to its natural end. Its natural end was not, as we shall too soon see, a natural death for her.

CHAPTER 28

England under Henry the Eighth

Second Part

The Pope was thrown into a very angry state of mind when he heard of the King's marriage, and fumed exceedingly. Many of the English monks and friars, seeing that their order was in danger, did the same; some even declaimed against the King in church before his face, and were not to be stopped until he himself roared out 'Silence!' The King, not much the worse for this, took it pretty quietly; and was very glad when his Queen gave birth to a daughter, who was christened ELIZABETH, and declared Princess of Wales as her sister Mary had already been.

One of the most atrocious features of this reign was that Henry the Eighth was always trimming between the reformed religion and the unreformed one; so that the more he quarrelled with the Pope, the more of his own subjects he roasted alive for not holding the Pope's opinions. Thus, an unfortunate student named John Frith, and a poor simple tailor named Andrew Hewet who loved him very much, and said that whatever John Frith believed *he* believed, were burnt in Smithfield – to show what a capital Christian the King was.

But, these were speedily followed by two much greater victims, Sir Thomas More, and John Fisher, the Bishop of Rochester. The latter, who was a good and amiable old man, had committed no greater offence than believing in Elizabeth Barton, called the Maid of Kent – another of those ridiculous women who pretended to be inspired, and to make all sorts of heavenly revelations, though they indeed uttered nothing but evil nonsense. For this offence – as it was pretended, but really for denying the King to be the supreme Head of the Church – he got into trouble, and was put in prison; but, even then, he might have been suffered to die naturally (short work having been made of executing the Kentish Maid and her principal followers), but that the Pope, to spite the King, resolved to make him a cardinal. Upon that the King made a ferocious joke to the effect that the Pope might send Fisher a red hat – which is the way they make a cardinal – but he should have no head on which to wear it; and he was tried with all unfairness and injustice and sentenced to death. He died like a noble and virtuous old man, and left a worthy name behind him. The King supposed, I dare say, that Sir Thomas More would be frightened by this example; but, as he was not to be easily terrified, and, thoroughly believing in the Pope, had made up his mind that the King was not the rightful Head of the Church, he positively refused to say that he was. For this crime he too was tried and sentenced, after having been in prison a whole year. When he was doomed to death, and came away from his trial with the edge of the executioner's axe turned towards him – as was always done in those times when a state prisoner came to that hopeless pass – he bore it quite serenely, and gave his blessing to his son, who pressed through the crowd in Westminster Hall and kneeled down to receive it. But, when he got to the Tower Wharf on his way back to his prison, and his favourite daughter, MARGARET ROPER, a very good woman, rushed through the guards again and again, to kiss him and to weep upon his neck, he was overcome at last. He soon recovered, and never more showed any feeling but cheerfulness and courage. When he was going up the steps of the scaffold to his death, he said jokingly to the Lieutenant of the Tower, observing that they were weak and shook beneath his tread, 'I pray you, master Lieutenant, see me safe up; and, for my coming down, I can shift for myself.' Also he said to the executioner, after he had laid his head upon the block, 'Let me put my beard out of the way; for that, at least, has never committed any treason.' Then his head was struck off at a blow. These two executions were worthy of King Henry the Eighth. Sir Thomas More was one of the most virtuous men in his dominions, and the Bishop was one of his oldest and truest friends. But to be a friend of that fellow was almost as dangerous as to be his wife.

When the news of these two murders got to Rome, the Pope raged against the murderer more than ever Pope raged since the world began, and prepared a Bull, ordering his subjects to take arms against him and dethrone him. The King took all possible precautions to keep that document out of his dominions, and set to work in return to suppress a great number of the English monasteries and abbeys.

This destruction was begun by a body of commissioners, of whom Cromwell (whom the King had taken into great favour) was the head; and was carried on through some few years to its entire completion. There is no doubt that many of these religious establishments were religious in nothing but in name, and were crammed with lazy, indolent, and sensual monks. There is no doubt that they imposed upon the people in every possible way; that they had images moved by wires, which they pretended were miraculously moved by Heaven; that they had among them a whole tun measure full of teeth, all purporting to have come out of the head of one saint, who must indeed have been a very extraordinary person with that enormous allowance of grinders; that they had bits of coal which they said had fried Saint Lawrence, and bits of toe-nails which they said belonged to other famous saints; penknives, and boots, and girdles, which they said belonged to others; and that all these bits of rubbish were called Relics, and adored by the ignorant people. But, on the other hand, there is no doubt either, that the King's officers and men punished the good monks with the bad; did great injustice; demolished many beautiful things and many valuable libraries; destroyed numbers of paintings, stained glass windows, fine pavements, and carvings; and that the whole court were ravenously greedy and rapacious for the division of this great spoil among them. The King seems to have grown almost mad in the ardour of this pursuit; for he declared Thomas à Becket a traitor, though he had been dead so many years, and had his body dug up out of his grave. He must have been as miraculous as the monks pretended, if they had told the truth, for he was found with one head on his shoulders, and they had shown another as his undoubted and genuine head ever since his death; it had brought them vast sums of money, too. The gold and jewels on his shrine filled two great chests, and eight men tottered as they carried them away. How rich the monasteries were you may infer from the fact that, when they were all suppressed, one hundred and thirty thousand pounds a year – in those days an immense sum – came to the Crown.

These things were not done without causing great discontent among the people. The monks had been good landlords and hospitable entertainers of all travellers, and had been accustomed to give away a great deal of corn, and fruit, and meat, and other things. In those days it was difficult to change goods into money, in consequence of the roads being very few and very bad, and the carts and waggons of the worst description; and they must either have given away some of the good things they possessed in enormous quantities, or have suffered them to spoil and moulder. So, many of the people missed what it was more agreeable to get idly than to work for; and the monks who were driven out of their homes and wandered about encouraged their discontent; and there were, consequently, great risings in Lincolnshire and Yorkshire. These were put down by terrible executions, from which the monks themselves did not escape, and the King went on grunting and growling in his own fat way, like a Royal pig.

I have told all this story of the religious houses at one time, to make it plainer, and to get back to the King's domestic affairs.

The unfortunate Queen Catherine was by this time dead; and the King was by this time as tired of his second Queen as he had been of his first. As he had fallen in love with Anne when she was in the service of Catherine, so he now fell in love with another lady in the service of Anne. See how wicked deeds are punished, and how bitterly and self-reproachfully the Queen must now have thought of her own rise to the throne! The new fancy was a LADY JANE SEYMOUR; and the King no sooner set his mind on her, than he resolved to have Anne Boleyn's head. So, he brought a number of charges against Anne, accusing her of dreadful crimes which she had never committed, and implicating in them her own brother and certain gentlemen in her service; among whom one Norris, and Mark Smeaton a musician, are best remembered. As the lords and councillors were as afraid of the King and as subservient to him as the meanest peasant in England was, they brought in Anne Boleyn guilty, and the other unfortunate persons accused with her, guilty too. Those gentlemen died like men, with the exception of Smeaton, who had been tempted by the King into telling lies, which he called confessions, and who had expected to be pardoned; but who, I am very glad to say, was not. There was then only the Queen to dispose of. She had been surrounded in the Tower with women spies; had been monstrously persecuted and foully slandered; and had received no justice. But her spirit rose with her afflictions; and, after having in vain tried to soften the King by writing an affecting letter to him which still exists, 'from her doleful prison in the Tower,' she resigned herself to death. She said to those about her, very cheerfully, that she had heard say the executioner was a good one, and that she had a little neck (she laughed and clasped it with her hands as she said that), and would soon be out of her pain. And she *was* soon out of her pain, poor creature, on the Green inside the Tower, and her body was flung into an old box and put away in the ground under the chapel.

There is a story that the King sat in his palace listening very anxiously for the sound of the cannon which was to announce this new murder; and that, when he heard it come booming on the air, he rose up in great spirits and ordered out his dogs to go a-hunting. He was bad enough to do it; but whether he did it or not, it is certain that he married Jane Seymour the very next day.

I have not much pleasure in recording that she lived just long enough to give birth to a son who was christened EDWARD, and then to die of a fever: for, I cannot but think that any woman who married such a ruffian, and knew what innocent blood was on his hands, deserved the axe that would assuredly have fallen on the neck of Jane Seymour, if she had lived much longer.

Cranmer had done what he could to save some of the Church property for purposes of religion and education; but, the great families had been so hungry to get hold of it, that very little could be rescued for such objects. Even MILES COVERDALE, who did the people the inestimable service of translating the Bible into English (which the unreformed religion never permitted to be done), was left in poverty while the great families clutched the Church lands and money. The people had been told that when the Crown came into possession of these funds, it would not be necessary to tax them; but they were taxed afresh directly afterwards. It was fortunate for them, indeed, that so many nobles were so greedy for this wealth; since, if it had remained with the Crown, there might have been no end to tyranny for hundreds of years. One of the most active writers on the Church's side against the King was a member of his own family – a sort of distant cousin, REGINALD POLE by name – who attacked him in the most violent manner (though he received a pension from him all the time), and fought for the Church with his pen, day and night. As he was beyond the King's reach – being in Italy – the King politely invited him over to discuss the subject; but he, knowing better than to come, and wisely staying where he was, the King's rage fell upon his brother Lord Montague, the Marquis of Exeter, and some other gentlemen: who were tried for high treason in corresponding with him and aiding him – which they probably did – and were all executed. The Pope made Reginald Pole a cardinal; but, so much against his will, that it is thought he even aspired in his own mind to the vacant throne of England, and had hopes of marrying the Princess Mary. His being made a high priest, however, put an end to all that. His mother, the venerable Countess of Salisbury – who was, unfortunately for herself, within the tyrant's reach – was the last of his relatives on whom his wrath fell. When she was told to lay her grey head upon the block, she answered the executioner, 'No! My head never committed treason, and if you want it, you shall seize it.' So, she ran round and round the scaffold with the executioner striking at her, and her grey hair bedabbled with blood; and even when they held her down upon the block she moved her head about to the last, resolved to be no party to her own barbarous murder. All this the people bore, as they had borne everything else.

Indeed they bore much more; for the slow fires of Smithfield were continually burning, and people were constantly being roasted to death – still to show what a good Christian the King was. He defied the Pope and his Bull, which was now issued, and had come into England; but he burned innumerable people whose only offence was that they differed from the Pope's religious opinions. There was a wretched man named LAMBERT, among others, who was tried for this before before the King, and with whom six bishops argued one after another. When he was quite exhausted (as well he might be, after six bishops), he threw himself on the King's mercy; but the King blustered out that he had no mercy for heretics. So, *he* too fed the fire.

All this the people bore, and more than all this yet. The national spirit seems to have been banished from the kingdom at this time. The very people who were executed for treason, the very wives and friends of the 'bluff' King, spoke of him on the scaffold as a good prince, and a gentle prince – just as serfs in similar circumstances have been known to do, under the Sultan and Bashaws of the East, or under the fierce old tyrants of Russia, who poured boiling and freezing water on them alternately, until they died. The Parliament were as bad as the rest, and gave the King whatever he wanted; among other vile accommodations, they gave him new powers of murdering, at his will and pleasure, any one whom he might choose to call a traitor. But the worst measure they passed was an Act of Six Articles, commonly called at the time 'the whip with six strings;' which punished offences against the Pope's opinions, without mercy, and enforced the very worst parts of the monkish religion. Cranmer would have modified it, if he could; but, being overborne by the Romish party, had not the power. As one of the articles declared that priests should not marry, and as he was married himself, he sent his wife and children into Germany, and began to tremble at his danger; none the less because he was, and had long been, the King's friend. This whip of six strings was made under the King's own eye. It should never be forgotten of him how cruelly he supported the worst of the Popish doctrines when there was nothing to be got by opposing them.

This amiable monarch now thought of taking another wife. He proposed to the French King to have some of the ladies of the French Court exhibited before him, that he might make his Royal choice; but the French King answered that he would rather not have his ladies trotted out to be shown like horses at a fair. He proposed to the Dowager Duchess of Milan, who replied that she might have thought of such a match if she had had two heads; but, that only owning one, she must beg to keep it safe. At last Cromwell presented that there was a Protestant Princess in Germany – those who held the reformed religion were called Protestants, because their leaders had Protested against the abuses and impositions of the unreformed Church – named ANNE OF CLEVES, who was beautiful, and would answer the purpose admirably. The King said was she a large woman, because he must have a fat wife? 'O yes,' said Cromwell; 'she was very large, just the thing.' On hearing this the King sent over his famous painter, Hans Holbein, to take her portrait. Hans made her out to be so good-looking that the King was satisfied, and the marriage was arranged. But, whether anybody had paid Hans to touch up the picture; or whether Hans, like one or two other painters, flattered a princess in the ordinary way of business, I cannot say: all I know is, that when Anne came over and the King went to Rochester to meet her, and first saw her without her seeing him, he swore she was 'a great Flanders mare,' and said he would never marry her. Being obliged to do it now matters had gone so far, he would not give her the presents he had prepared, and would never notice her. He never forgave Cromwell his part in the affair. His downfall dates from that time.

It was quickened by his enemies, in the interests of the unreformed religion, putting in the King's way, at a state dinner, a niece of the Duke of Norfolk, CATHERINE HOWARD, a young lady of fascinating manners, though small in stature and not particularly beautiful. Falling in love with her on the spot, the King soon divorced Anne of Cleves after making her the subject of much brutal talk, on pretence that she had been previously betrothed to some one else – which would never do for one of his dignity – and married Catherine. It is probable that on his wedding day, of all days in the year, he sent his faithful Cromwell to the scaffold, and had his head struck off. He further celebrated the occasion by burning at one time, and causing to be drawn to the fire on the same hurdles, some Protestant prisoners for denying the Pope's doctrines, and some Roman Catholic prisoners for denying his own supremacy. Still the people bore it, and not a gentleman in England raised his hand.

But, by a just retribution, it soon came out that Catherine Howard, before her marriage, had been really guilty of such crimes as the King had falsely attributed to his second wife Anne Boleyn; so, again the dreadful axe made the King a widower, and this Queen passed away as so many in that reign had passed away before her. As an appropriate pursuit under the circumstances, Henry then applied himself to superintending the composition of a religious book called 'A necessary doctrine for any Christian Man.' He must have been a little confused in his mind, I think, at about this period; for he was so false to himself as to be true to some one; that some one being Cranmer, whom the Duke of Norfolk and others of his enemies tried to ruin; but to whom the King was steadfast, and to whom he one night gave his ring, charging him when he should find himself, next day, accused of treason, to show it to the council board. This Cranmer did to the confusion of his enemies. I suppose the King thought he might want him a little longer.

He married yet once more. Yes, strange to say, he found in England another woman who would become his wife, and she was CATHERINE PARR, widow of Lord Latimer. She leaned towards the reformed religion; and it is some comfort to know, that she tormented the King considerably by arguing a variety of doctrinal points with him on all possible occasions. She had very nearly done this to her own destruction. After one of these conversations the King in a very black mood actually instructed GARDINER, one of his Bishops who favoured the Popish opinions, to draw a bill of accusation against her, which would have inevitably brought her to the scaffold where her predecessors had died, but that one of her friends picked up the paper of instructions which had been dropped in the palace, and gave her timely notice. She fell ill with terror; but managed the King so well when he came to entrap her into further statements – by saying that she had only spoken on such points to divert his mind and to get some information from his extraordinary wisdom – that he gave her a kiss and called her his sweetheart. And, when the Chancellor came next day actually to take her to the Tower, the King sent him about his business, and honoured him with the epithets of a beast, a knave, and a fool. So near was Catherine Parr to the block, and so narrow was her escape!

There was war with Scotland in this reign, and a short clumsy war with France for favouring Scotland; but, the events at home were so dreadful, and leave such an enduring stain on the country, that I need say no more of what happened abroad.

A few more horrors, and this reign is over. There was a lady, ANNE ASKEW, in Lincolnshire, who inclined to the Protestant opinions, and whose husband, being a fierce Catholic, turned her out of his house. She came to London, and was considered as offending against the six articles, and was taken to the Tower, and put upon the rack – probably because it was hoped that she might, in her agony, criminate some obnoxious persons; if falsely, so much the better. She was tortured without uttering a cry, until the Lieutenant of the Tower would suffer his men to torture her no more; and then two priests who were present actually pulled off their robes, and turned the wheels of the rack with their own hands, so rending and twisting and breaking her that she was afterwards carried to the fire in a chair. She was burned with three others, a gentleman, a clergyman, and a tailor; and so the world went on.

Either the King became afraid of the power of the Duke of Norfolk, and his son the Earl of Surrey, or they gave him some offence, but he resolved to pull *them* down, to follow all the rest who were gone. The son was tried first – of course for nothing – and defended himself bravely; but of course he was found guilty, and of course he was executed. Then his father was laid hold of, and left for death too.

But the King himself was left for death by a Greater King, and the earth was to be rid of him at last. He was now a swollen, hideous spectacle, with a great hole in his leg, and so odious to every sense that it was dreadful to approach him. When he was found to be dying, Cranmer was sent for from his palace at Croydon, and came with all speed, but found him speechless. Happily, in that hour he perished. He was in the fifty-sixth year of his age, and the thirty-eighth of his reign.

Henry the Eighth has been favoured by some Protestant

writers, because the Reformation was achieved in his time. But the mighty merit of it lies with other men and not with him; and it can be rendered none the worse by this monster's crimes, and none the better by any defence of them. The plain truth is, that he was a most intolerable ruffian, a disgrace to human nature, and a blot of blood and grease upon the History of England.

CHAPTER 29

England under Edward the Sixth

Henry the Eighth had made a will, appointing a council of sixteen to govern the kingdom for his son while he was under age (he was now only ten years old), and another council of twelve to help them. The most powerful of the first council was the EARL OF HERTFORD, the young King's uncle, who lost no time in bringing his nephew with great state up to Enfield, and thence to the Tower. It was considered at the time a striking proof of virtue in the young King that he was sorry for his father's death; but, as common subjects have that virtue too, sometimes, we will say no more about it.

There was a curious part of the late King's will, requiring his executors to fulfil whatever promises he had made. Some of the court wondering what these might be, the Earl of Hertford and the other noblemen interested, said that they were promises to advance and enrich *them*. So, the Earl of Hertford made himself DUKE OF SOMERSET, and made his brother EDWARD SEYMOUR a baron; and there were various similar promotions, all very agreeable to the parties concerned, and very dutiful, no doubt, to the late King's memory. To be more dutiful still, they made themselves rich out of the Church lands, and were very comfortable. The new Duke of Somerset caused himself to be declared PROTECTOR of the kingdom, and was, indeed, the King.

As young Edward the Sixth had been brought up in the principles of the Protestant religion, everybody knew that they would be maintained. But Cranmer, to whom they were chiefly entrusted, advanced them steadily and temperately. Many superstitious and ridiculous practices were stopped; but practices which were harmless were not interfered with.

The Duke of Somerset, the Protector, was anxious to have the young King engaged in marriage to the young Queen of Scotland, in order to prevent that princess from making an alliance with any foreign power; but, as a large party in Scotland were unfavourable to this plan, he invaded that country. His excuse for doing so was, that the Border men – that is, the Scotch who lived in that part of the country where England and Scotland joined – troubled the English very much. But there were two sides to this question; for the English Border men troubled the Scotch too; and, through many long years, there were perpetual border quarrels which gave rise to numbers of old tales and songs. However, the Protector invaded Scotland; and ARRAN, the Scottish Regent, with an army twice as large as his, advanced to meet him. They encountered on the banks of the river Esk, within a few miles of Edinburgh; and there, after a little skirmish, the Protector made such moderate proposals, in offering to retire if the Scotch would only engage not to marry their princess to any foreign prince, that the Regent thought the English were afraid. But in this he made a horrible mistake; for the English soldiers on land, and the English sailors on the water, so set upon the Scotch, that they broke and fled, and more than ten thousand of them were killed. It was a dreadful battle, for the fugitives were slain without mercy. The ground for four miles, all the way to Edinburgh, was strewn with dead men, and with arms, and legs, and heads. Some hid themselves in streams and were drowned; some threw away their armour and were killed running, almost naked; but in this battle of Pinkey the English lost only two or three hundred men. They were much better clothed than the Scotch; at the poverty of whose appearance and country they were exceedingly astonished.

A Parliament was called when Somerset came back, and it repealed the whip with six strings, and did one or two other good things; though it unhappily retained the punishment of burning for those people who did not make believe to believe, in all religious matters, what the Government had declared that they must and should believe. It also made a foolish law (meant to put down beggars), that any man who lived idly and loitered about for three days together, should be burned with a hot iron, made a slave, and wear an iron fetter. But this savage absurdity soon came to an end, and went the way of a great many other foolish laws.

The Protector was now so proud that he sat in Parliament before all the nobles, on the right hand of the throne. Many other noblemen, who only wanted to be as proud if they could get a chance, became his enemies of course; and it is supposed that he came back suddenly from Scotland because he had received news that his brother, LORD SEYMOUR, was becoming dangerous to him. This lord was now High Admiral of England; a very handsome man, and a great favourite with the Court ladies – even with the young Princess Elizabeth, who romped with him a little more than young princesses in these times do with any one. He had married Catherine Parr, the late King's widow, who was now dead; and, to strengthen his power, he secretly supplied the young King with money. He may even have engaged with some of his brother's enemies in a plot to carry the boy off. On these and other accusations, at any rate, he was confined in the Tower, impeached, and found guilty; his own brother's name being – unnatural and sad to tell – the first signed to the warrant for his execution. He was executed on Tower Hill, and died denying his treason. One of his last proceedings in this world was to write two letters, one to the Princess Elizabeth, and one to the Princess Mary, which a servant of his took charge of, and concealed in his shoe. These letters are supposed to have urged them against his brother, and to revenge his death. What they truly contained is not known; but there is no doubt that he had, at one time, obtained great influence over the Princess Elizabeth.

All this while, the Protestant religion was making progress. The images which the people had gradually come to worship, were removed from the churches; the people were informed that they need not confess themselves to priests unless they chose; a common prayer-book was drawn up in the English language, which all could understand; and many other improvements were made; still moderately. For Cranmer was a very moderate man, and even restrained the Protestant clergy from violently abusing the unreformed religion – as they very often did, and which was not a good example. But the people were at this time in great distress. The rapacious nobility who had come into possession of the Church lands, were very bad landlords. They enclosed great quantities of ground for the feeding of sheep, which was then more profitable than the growing of crops; and this increased the general distress. So the people, who still understood little of what was going on about them, and still readily believed what the homeless monks told them – many of whom had been their good friends in their better days – took it into their heads that all this was owing to the reformed religion, and therefore rose in many parts of the country.

The most powerful risings were in Devonshire and Norfolk. In Devonshire, the rebellion was so strong that ten thousand men united within a few days, and even laid siege to Exeter. But LORD RUSSELL, coming to the assistance of the citizens who defended that town, defeated the rebels; and, not only hanged the Mayor of one place, but hanged the vicar of another from his own church steeple. What with hanging and killing by the sword, four thousand of the rebels are supposed to have fallen in that one county. In Norfolk (where the rising was more against the enclosure of open lands than against the reformed religion), the popular leader was a man named ROBERT KET, a tanner of Wymondham. The mob were, in the first instance, excited against the tanner by one JOHN FLOWERDEW, a gentleman who owed him a grudge: but the tanner was more than a match for the gentleman, since he soon got the people on his side, and established himself near Norwich with quite an army. There was a large oak-tree in that place, on a spot called Mousehold Hill, which Ket named the Tree of Reformation; and under its green boughs, he and his men sat, in the midsummer weather, holding courts of justice, and debating affairs of state. They were even impartial enough to allow some rather tiresome speakers to get up into this Tree of Reformation, and point out their errors to them, in long discourses, while they lay listening (not always without some grumbling and growling) in the shade below. At last, one sunny July day, a herald appeared below the tree, and proclaimed Ket and all his men traitors, unless from that moment they dispersed and went home; in which case they were to receive a pardon. But, Ket and his men made light of the herald and became stronger than ever, until the Earl of Warwick went after them with a sufficient force, and cut them all to pieces. A few were hanged, drawn, and quartered, as traitors, and their limbs were sent into various country places to be a terror to the people. Nine of them were hanged upon nine green branches of the Oak of Reformation; and so, for the time, that tree may be said to have withered away.

The Protector, though a haughty man, had compassion for the real distresses of the common people, and a sincere desire to help them. But he was too proud and too high in degree to hold even their favour steadily; and many of the nobles always envied and hated him, because they were as proud and not as high as he. He was at this time building a great Palace in the Strand: to get the stone for which he blew up church steeples with gunpowder, and pulled down bishops' houses: thus making himself still more disliked. At length, his principal enemy, the Earl of Warwick – Dudley by name, and the son of that Dudley who had made himself so odious with Empson, in the reign of Henry the Seventh – joined with seven other members of the Council against him, formed a separate Council; and, becoming stronger in a few days, sent him to the Tower under twenty-nine articles of accusation. After being sentenced by the Council to the forfeiture of all his offices and lands, he was liberated and pardoned, on making a very humble submission. He was even taken back into the Council again, after having suffered this fall, and married his daughter, LADY ANNE SEYMOUR, to Warwick's eldest son. But such a reconciliation was little likely to last, and did not outlive a year. Warwick, having got himself made Duke of Northumberland, and having advanced the more important of his friends, then finished the history by causing the Duke of Somerset and his friend LORD GREY, and others, to be arrested for treason, in having conspired to seize and dethrone the King. They were also accused of having intended to seize the new Duke of Northumberland, with his friends LORD NORTHAMP-TON and LORD PEMBROKE; to murder them if they found need; and to raise the City to revolt. All this the fallen Protector positively denied; except that he confessed to having spoken of the murder of those three noblemen, but having never designed it. He was acquitted of the charge of treason, and found guilty of the other charges; so when the people – who remembered his having been their friend, now that he was disgraced and in danger, saw him come out from his trial with the axe turned from him – they thought he was altogether acquitted, and set up a loud shout of joy.

But the Duke of Somerset was ordered to be beheaded on Tower Hill, at eight o'clock in the morning, and proclamations were issued bidding the citizens keep at home until after ten. They filled the streets, however, and crowded the place of execution as soon as it was light; and, with sad faces and sad hearts, saw the once powerful Protector ascend the scaffold to lay his head upon the dreadful block. While he was yet saying his last words to them with manly courage, and telling them, in particular, how it comforted him, at that pass, to have assisted in reforming the national religion, a member of the Council was seen riding up on horseback. They again thought that the Duke was saved by his bringing a reprieve, and again shouted for joy. But the Duke himself told them they were mistaken, and laid down his head and had it struck off at a blow.

Many of the bystanders rushed forward and steeped their handkerchiefs in his blood, as a mark of their affection. He had, indeed, been capable of many good acts, and one of them was discovered after he was no more. The Bishop of Durham, a very good man, had been informed against to the Council, when the Duke was in power, as having answered a treacherous letter proposing a rebellion against the reformed religion. As the answer could not be found, he could not be declared guilty; but it was now discovered, hidden by the Duke himself among some private papers, in his regard for that good man. The Bishop lost his office, and was deprived of his possessions.

It is not very pleasant to know that while his uncle lay in prison under sentence of death, the young King was being vastly entertained by plays, and dances, and sham fights: but there is no doubt of it, for he kept a journal himself. It is pleasanter to know that not a single Roman Catholic was burnt in this reign for holding that religion; though two wretched victims suffered for heresy. One, a woman named JOAN BOCHER, for professing some opinions that even she could only explain in unintelligible jargon. The other, a Dutchman, named VON PARIS, who practised as a surgeon in London. Edward was, to his credit, exceedingly unwilling to sign the warrant for the woman's execution: shedding tears before he did so, and telling Cranmer, who urged him to do it (though Cranmer really would have spared the woman at first, but for her own determined obstinacy), that the guilt was not his, but that of the man who so strongly urged the dreadful act. We shall see, too soon, whether the time ever came when Cranmer is likely to have remembered this with sorrow and remorse.

Cranmer and RIDLEY (at first Bishop of Rochester, and afterwards Bishop of London) were the most powerful of the clergy of this reign. Others were imprisoned and deprived of their property for still adhering to the unreformed religion; the most important among whom were GARDINER Bishop of Winchester, HEATH Bishop of Worcester, DAY Bishop of Chichester, and BONNER that Bishop of London who was superseded by Ridley. The Princess Mary, who inherited her mother's gloomy temper, and hated the reformed religion as connected with her mother's wrongs and sorrows – she knew nothing else about it, always refusing to read a single book in which it was truly described – held by the unreformed religion too, and was the only person in the kingdom for whom the old Mass was allowed to be performed; nor would the young King have made that exception even in her favour, but for the strong persuasions of Cranmer and Ridley. He always viewed it with horror; and when he fell into a sickly condition, after having been very ill, first of the measles and then of the small-pox, he was greatly troubled in mind to think that if he died, and she, the next heir to the throne, succeeded, the Roman Catholic religion would be set up again.

This uneasiness, the Duke of Northumberland was not slow to encourage: for, if the Princess Mary came to the throne, he, who had taken part with the Protestants, was sure to be disgraced. Now, the Duchess of Suffolk was descended from King Henry the Seventh; and, if she resigned what little or no right she had, in favour of her daughter LADY JANE GREY, that would be the succession to promote the Duke's greatness; because LORD GUILFORD DUDLEY, one of his sons, was, at this very time, newly married to her. So, he worked upon the King's fears, and persuaded him to set aside both the Princess Mary and the Princess Elizabeth, and assert his right to appoint his successor. Accordingly the young King handed to the Crown lawyers a writing signed half a dozen times over by himself appointing Lady Jane Grey to succeed to the Crown, and requiring them to have his will made out according to law. They were much against it at first, and told the King so; but the Duke of Northumberland – being so violent about it that the lawyers even expected him to beat them, and hotly declaring that, stripped to his shirt, he would fight any man in such a quarrel – they yielded. Cranmer, also, at first hesitated; pleading that he had sworn to maintain the succession of the Crown to the Princess Mary; but, he was a weak man in his resolutions, and afterwards signed the document with the rest of the council.

It was completed none too soon; for Edward was now sinking in a rapid decline; and, by way of making him better, they handed him over to a woman-doctor who pretended to be able to cure it. He speedily got worse. On the sixth of July, in the year one thousand five hundred and fifty-three, he died, very peaceably and piously, praying God, with his last breath, to protect the reformed religion.

This King died in the sixteenth year of his age, and in the seventh of his reign. It is difficult to judge what the character of one so young might afterwards have become among so many bad, ambitious, quarrelling nobles. But, he was an amiable boy, of very good abilities, and had nothing coarse or cruel or brutal in his disposition – which in the son of such a father is rather surprising.

CHAPTER 30

England under Mary

The Duke of Northumberland was very anxious to keep the young King's death a secret, in order that he might get the two Princesses into his power. But, the Princess Mary, being informed of that event as she was on her way to London to see her sick brother, turned her horse's head, and rode away into Norfolk. The Earl of Arundel was her friend, and it was he who sent her warning of what had happened.

As the secret could not be kept, the Duke of Northumberland and the council sent for the Lord Mayor of London and some of the aldermen, and made a merit of telling it to them. Then, they made it known to the people, and set off to inform Lady Jane Grey that she was to be Queen.

She was a pretty girl of only sixteen, and was amiable, learned, and clever. When the lords who came to her, fell on their knees before her, and told her what tidings they brought, she was so astonished that she fainted. On recovering, she expressed her sorrow for the young King's death, and said that she knew she was unfit to govern the kingdom; but that if she must be Queen, she prayed God to direct her. She was then at Sion House, near Brentford; and the lords took her down the river in state to the Tower, that she might remain there (as the custom was) until she was crowned. But the people were not at all favourable to Lady Jane, considering that the right to be Queen was Mary's, and greatly disliking the Duke of Northumberland. They were not put into a better humour by the Duke's causing a vintner's servant, one Gabriel Pot, to be taken up for expressing his dissatisfaction among the crowd, and to have his ears nailed to the pillory, and cut off. Some powerful men among the nobility declared on Mary's side. They raised troops to support her cause, had her proclaimed Queen at Norwich, and gathered around her at the castle of Framlingham, which belonged to the Duke of Norfolk. For, she was not considered so safe as yet, but that it was best to keep her in a castle on the sea-coast, from whence she might be sent abroad, if necessary.

The Council would have despatched Lady Jane's father, the Duke of Suffolk, as the general of the army against this force; but, as Lady Jane implored that her father might remain with her, and as he was known to be but a weak man, they told the Duke of Northumberland that he must take the command himself. He was not very ready to do so, as he mistrusted the Council much; but there was no help for it, and he set forth with a heavy heart, observing to a lord who rode beside him through Shoreditch at the head of the troops, that, although the people pressed in great numbers to look at them, they were terribly silent.

And his fears for himself turned out to be well founded. While he was waiting at Cambridge for further help from the Council, the Council took it into their heads to turn their backs on Lady Jane's cause, and to take up the Princess Mary's. This was chiefly owing to the before-mentioned Earl of Arundel, who represented to the Lord Mayor and aldermen, in a second interview with those sagacious persons, that, as for himself, he did not perceive the Reformed religion to be in much danger – which Lord Pembroke backed by flourishing his sword as another kind of persuasion. The Lord Mayor and aldermen, thus enlightened, said there could be no doubt that the Princess Mary ought to be Queen. So, she was proclaimed at the Cross by St Paul's, and barrels of wine were given to the people, and they got very drunk, and danced round blazing bonfires – little thinking, poor wretches, what other bonfires would soon be blazing in Queen Mary's name.

After a ten days' dream of royalty, Lady Jane Grey resigned the Crown with great willingness, saying that she had only accepted it in obedience to her father and mother; and went gladly back to her pleasant house by the river, and her books. Mary then came on towards London; and at Wanstead in Essex, was joined by her half-sister, the Princess Elizabeth. They passed through the streets of London to the Tower, and there the new Queen met some eminent prisoners then confined in it, kissed them, and gave them their liberty. Among these was that Gardiner, Bishop of Winchester, who had been imprisoned in the last reign for holding to the unreformed religion. Him she soon made chancellor.

The Duke of Northumberland had been taken prisoner, and, together with his son and five others, was quickly brought before the Council. He, not unnaturally, asked that Council, in his defence, whether it was treason to obey orders that had been issued under the great seal; and, if it were, whether they, who had obeyed them too, ought to be his judges? But they made light of these points; and, being resolved to have him out of the way, soon sentenced him to death. He had risen into power upon the death of another man, and made but a poor show (as might be expected) when he himself lay low. He entreated Gardiner to let him live, if it were only in a mouse's hole; and, when he ascended the scaffold to be beheaded on Tower Hill, addressed the people in a miserable way, saying that he had been incited by others, and exhorting them to return to the unreformed religion, which he told them was his faith. There seems reason to suppose that he expected a pardon even then, in return for this confession; but it matters little whether he did or not. His head was struck off.

Mary was now crowned Queen. She was thirty-seven years of age, short and thin, wrinkled in the face, and very unhealthy. But she had a great liking for show and for bright colours, and all the ladies of her Court were magnificently dressed. She had a great liking too for old customs, without much sense in them; and she was oiled in the oldest way, and blessed in the oldest way, and done all manner of things to in the oldest way, at her coronation. I hope they did her good.

She soon began to show her desire to put down the Reformed religion, and put up the unreformed one: though it was dangerous work as yet, the people being something wiser than they used to be. They even cast a shower of stones – and among them a dagger – at one of the royal chaplains who attacked the Reformed religion in a public sermon. But the Queen and her priests went steadily on. Ridley, the powerful bishop of the last reign, was seized and sent to the Tower. LATIMER, also celebrated among the Clergy of the last reign, was likewise sent to the Tower, and Cranmer speedily followed. Latimer was an aged man; and, as his guards took him through Smithfield, he looked round it, and said, 'This is a place that hath long groaned for me.' For he knew well, what kind of bonfires would soon be burning. Nor was the knowledge confined to him. The prisons were fast filled with the chief Protestants, who were there left rotting in darkness, hunger, dirt, and separation from their friends; many, who had time left them for escape, fled from the kingdom; and the dullest of the people began, now, to see what was coming.

It came on fast. A Parliament was got together; not without strong suspicion of unfairness; and they annulled the divorce, formerly pronounced by Cranmer between the Queen's mother and King Henry the Eighth, and unmade all the laws on the subject of religion that had been made in the last King Edward's reign. They began their proceedings, in violation of the law, by having the old mass said before them in Latin, and by turning out a bishop who would not kneel down. They also declared guilty of treason, Lady Jane Grey for aspiring to the Crown; her husband, for being her husband; and Cranmer, for not believing in the mass aforesaid. They then prayed the Queen graciously to choose a husband for herself, as soon as might be.

Now, the question who should be the Queen's husband had given rise to a great deal of discussion, and to several contending parties. Some said Cardinal Pole was the man – but the Queen was of opinion that he was *not* the man, he being too old and too much of a student. Others said that the gallant young COURTENAY, whom the Queen had made Earl of Devonshire, was the man – and the Queen thought so too, for a while; but she changed her mind. At last it appeared that PHILIP, PRINCE

OF SPAIN, was certainly the man – though certainly not the people's man; for they detested the idea of such a marriage from the beginning to the end, and murmured that the Spaniard would establish in England, by the aid of foreign soldiers, the worst abuses of the Popish religion, and even the terrible Inquisition itself.

These discontents gave rise to a conspiracy for marrying young Courtenay to the Princess Elizabeth, and setting them up, with popular tumults all over the kingdom, against the Queen. This was discovered in time by Gardiner; but in Kent, the old bold county, the people rose in their old bold way. SIR THOMAS WYAT, a man of great daring, was their leader. He raised his standard at Maidstone, marched on to Rochester, established himself in the old castle there, and prepared to hold out against the Duke of Norfolk, who came against him with a party of the Queen's guards, and a body of five hundred London men. The London men, however, were all for Elizabeth, and not at all for Mary. They declared, under the castle walls, for Wyat; the Duke retreated; and Wyat came on to Deptford, at the head of fifteen thousand men.

But these, in their turn, fell away. When he came to Southwark, there were only two thousand left. Not dismayed by finding the London citizens in arms, and the guns at the Tower ready to oppose his crossing the river there, Wyat led them off to Kingston-upon-Thames, intending to cross the bridge that he knew to be in that place, and so to work his way round to Ludgate, one of the old gates of the City. He found the bridge broken down, but mended it, came across, and bravely fought his way up Fleet Street to Ludgate Hill. Finding the gate closed against him, he fought his way back again, sword in hand, to Temple Bar. Here, being overpowered, he surrendered himself, and three or four hundred of his men were taken, besides a hundred killed. Wyat, in a moment of weakness (and perhaps of torture) was afterwards made to accuse the Princess Elizabeth as his accomplice to some very small extent. But his manhood soon returned to him, and he refused to save his life by making any more false confessions. He was quartered and distributed in the usual brutal way, and from fifty to a hundred of his followers were hanged. The rest were led out, with halters round their necks, to be pardoned, and to make a parade of crying out, 'God save Queen Mary!'

In the danger of this rebellion, the Queen showed herself to be a woman of courage and spirit. She disdained to retreat to any place of safety, and went down to the Guildhall, sceptre in hand, and made a gallant speech to the Lord Mayor and citizens. But on the day after Wyat's defeat, she did the most cruel act, even of her cruel reign, in signing the warrant for the execution of Lady Jane Grey.

They tried to persuade Lady Jane to accept the unreformed religion; but she steadily refused. On the morning when she was to die, she saw from her window the bleeding and headless body of her husband brought back in a cart from the scaffold on Tower Hill where he had laid down his life. But, as she had declined to see him before his execution, lest she should be overpowered and not make a good end, so, she even now showed a constancy and calmness that will never be forgotten. She came up to the scaffold with a firm step and a quiet face, and addressed the bystanders in a steady voice. They were not numerous; for she was too young, too innocent and fair, to be murdered before the people on Tower Hill, as her husband had just been; so, the place of her execution was within the Tower itself. She said that she had done an unlawful act in taking what was Queen Mary's right; but that she had done so with no bad intent, and that she died a humble Christian. She begged the executioner to despatch her quickly, and she asked him, 'Will you take my head off before I lay me down?' He answered, 'No, Madam,' and then she was very quiet while they bandaged her eyes. Being blinded, and unable to see the block on which she was to lay her young head, she was seen to feel about for it with her hands, and was heard to say, confused, 'O what shall I do! Where is it?' Then they guided her to the right place, and the executioner struck off her head. You know too well, now, what dreadful deeds the executioner did in England, through many many years, and how his axe descended on the hateful block through the necks of some of the bravest, wisest, and best in the land. But it never struck so cruel and so vile a blow as this.

The father of Lady Jane soon followed, but was little pitied. Queen Mary's next object was to lay hold of Elizabeth, and this was pursued with great eagerness. Five hundred men were sent to her retired house at Ashridge, by Berkhampstead, with orders to bring her up, alive or dead. They got there at ten at night, when she was sick in bed. But, their leaders followed her lady

Lady Jane Grey Watching the Body of Her Husband Being Carried Past Her
Window after Execution

into her bedchamber, whence she was brought out betimes next morning, and put into a litter to be conveyed to London. She was so weak and ill, that she was five days on the road; still, she was so resolved to be seen by the people that she had the curtains of the litter opened; and so, very pale and sickly, passed through the streets. She wrote to her sister, saying she was innocent of any crime, and asking why she was made a prisoner; but she got no answer, and was ordered to the Tower. They took her in by the Traitor's Gate, to which she objected, but in vain. One of the lords who conveyed her offered to cover her with his cloak, as it was raining, but she put it away from her, proudly and scornfully, and passed into the Tower, and sat down in a court-yard on a stone. They besought her to come in out of the wet; but she answered that it was better sitting there, than in a worse place. At length she went to her apartment, where she was kept a prisoner, though not so close a prisoner as at Woodstock, whither she was afterwards removed, and where she is said to have one day envied a milkmaid whom she heard singing in the sunshine as she went through the green fields. Gardiner, than whom there were not many worse men among the fierce and sullen priests, cared little to keep secret his stern desire for her death: being used to say that it was of little service to shake off the leaves, and lop the branches of the tree of heresy, if its root, the hope of heretics, were left. He failed, however, in his benevolent design. Elizabeth was, at length, released; and Hatfield House was assigned to her as a residence, under the care of one SIR THOMAS POPE.

It would seem that Philip, the Prince of Spain, was a main cause of this change in Elizabeth's fortunes. He was not an amiable man, being, on the contrary, proud, overbearing, and gloomy; but he and the Spanish lords who came over with him, assuredly did discountenance the idea of doing any violence to the Princess. It may have been mere prudence, but we will hope it was manhood and honour. The Queen had been expecting her husband with great impatience, and at length he came, to her great joy, though he never cared much for her. They were married by Gardiner, at Winchester, and there was more holi-day-making among the people; but they had their old distrust of this Spanish marriage, in which even the Parliament shared. Though the members of that Parliament were far from honest, and were strongly suspected to have been bought with Spanish money, they would pass no bill to enable the Queen to set aside the Princess Elizabeth and appoint her own successor.

Although Gardiner failed in this object, as well as in the darker one of bringing the Princess to the scaffold, he went on at a great pace in the revival of the unreformed religion. A new Parliament was packed, in which there were no Protestants. Preparations were made to receive Cardinal Pole in England as the Pope's messenger, bringing his holy declaration that all the nobility who had acquired Church property, should keep it – which was done to enlist their selfish interest on the Pope's side. Then a great scene was enacted, which was the triumph of the Queen's plans. Cardinal Pole arrived in great splendour and dignity, and was received with great pomp. The Parliament joined in a petition expressive of their sorrow at the change in the national religion, and praying him to receive the country again into the Popish Church. With the Queen sitting on her throne, and the King on one side of her, and the Cardinal on the other, and the Parliament present, Gardiner read the petition aloud. The Cardinal then made a great speech, and was so obliging as to say that all was forgotten and forgiven, and that the kingdom was solemnly made Roman Catholic again.

Everything was now ready for the lighting of the terrible bonfires. The Queen having declared to the Council, in writing, that she would wish none of her subjects to be burnt without some of the Council being present, and that she would particularly wish there to be good sermons at all burnings, the Council knew pretty well what was to be done next. So, after the Cardinal had blessed all the bishops as a preface to the burnings, the Chancellor Gardiner opened a High Court at Saint Mary Overy, on the Southwark side of London Bridge, for the trial of heretics. Here, two of the late Protestant clergymen, HOOPER, Bishop of Gloucester, and ROGERS, a Prebendary of St Paul's, were brought to be tried. Hooper was tried first for being married, though a priest, and for not believing in the mass. He admitted both of these accusations, and said that the mass was a wicked imposition. Then they tried Rogers, who said the same. Next morning the two were brought up to be sentenced; and then Rogers said that his poor wife, being a German woman and a stranger in the land, he hoped might be allowed to come to speak to him before he died. To this the inhuman Gardiner replied, that she was not his wife. 'Yea, but she is, my lord,' said Rogers, 'and she hath been my wife these eighteen years.' His request was still refused, and they were both sent to Newgate; all those who stood in the streets to sell things, being ordered to put out their lights that the people might not see them. But, the people stood at their doors with candles in their hands, and prayed for them as they went by. Soon afterwards, Rogers was taken out of jail to be burnt in Smithfield; and, in the crowd as he went along, he saw his poor wife and his ten children, of whom the youngest was a little baby. And so he was burnt to death.

The next day, Hooper, who was to be burnt at Gloucester, was brought out to take his last journey, and was made to wear a hood over his face that he might not be known by the people. But, they did know him for all that, down in his own part of the country; and, when he came near Gloucester, they lined the road, making prayers and lamentations. His guards took him to a lodging, where he slept soundly all night. At nine o'clock next morning, he was brought forth leaning on a staff; for he had taken cold in prison, and was infirm. The iron stake, and the iron chain which was to bind him to it, were fixed up near a great elm-tree in a pleasant open place before the cathedral, where, on peaceful Sundays, he had been accustomed to preach and to pray, when he was bishop of Gloucester. This tree, which had no leaves then, it being February, was filled with people; and the priests of Gloucester College were looking complacently on from a window, and there was a great concourse of spectators in every spot from which a glimpse of the dreadful sight could be beheld. When the old man kneeled down on the small platform at the foot of the stake, and prayed aloud, the nearest people were observed to be so attentive to his prayers that they were ordered to stand farther back; for it did not suit the Romish Church to have those Protestant words heard. His prayers concluded, he went up to the stake and was stripped to his shirt, and chained ready for the fire. One of his guards had such compassion on him that, to shorten his agonies, he tied some packets of gunpowder about him. Then they heaped up wood and straw and reeds, and set them all alight. But, unhappily, the wood was green and damp, and there was a wind blowing that blew what flame there was, away. Thus, through three-quarters of an hour, the good old man was scorched and roasted and smoked, as the fire rose and sank; and all that time they saw him, as he burned, moving his lips in prayer, and beating his breast with one hand, even after the other was burnt away and had fallen off.

Cranmer, Ridley, and Latimer, were taken to Oxford to dispute with a commission of priests and doctors about the mass. They were shamefully treated; and it is recorded that the Oxford scholars hissed and howled and groaned, and misconducted themselves in an anything but a scholarly way. The prisoners were taken back to jail, and afterwards tried in St Mary's Church. They were all found guilty. On the sixteenth of the month of October, Ridley and Latimer were brought out, to make another of the dreadful bonfires.

The scene of the suffering of these two good Protestant men was in the City ditch, near Balliol College. On coming to the dreadful spot, they kissed the stakes, and then embraced each other. And then a learned doctor got up into a pulpit which was placed there, and preached a sermon from the text, 'Though I give my body to be burned, and have not charity, it profiteth me nothing.' When you think of the charity of burning men alive, you may imagine that this learned doctor had a rather brazen face. Ridley would have answered his sermon when it came to an end, but was not allowed. When Latimer was stripped, it appeared that he had dressed himself under his other clothes, in a new shroud; and, as he stood in it before all the people, it was noted of him, and long remembered, that, whereas he had been stooping and feeble but a few minutes before, he now stood upright and handsome, in the knowledge that he was dying for a just and a great cause. Ridley's brother-in-law was there with bags of gunpowder; and when they were both chained up, he tied them round their bodies. Then, a light was thrown upon the pile to fire it. 'Be of good comfort, Master Ridley,' said Latimer, at that awful moment, 'and play the man! We shall this day light such a candle, by God's grace, in England, as I trust shall never be put out.' And then he was seen to make motions with his hands as if he were washing them in the flames, and to stroke his aged face with them, and was heard to cry, 'Father of Heaven, receive my soul!' He died quickly, but the fire, after having burned the legs of Ridley, sunk. There he lingered, chained to the iron post, and crying, 'O! I cannot burn! O! for Christ's sake let the fire come unto me!' And still, when his brother-in-law had heaped on more wood, he was heard through the blinding smoke, still dismally crying, 'O! I cannot burn, I cannot burn!' At last, the gunpowder caught fire, and ended his miseries.

Five days after this fearful scene, Gardiner went to his tremendous account before God, for the cruelties he had so much assisted in committing.

Cranmer remained still alive and in prison. He was brought out again in February, for more examining and trying, by Bonner, Bishop of London: another man of blood, who had succeeded to Gardiner's work, even in his lifetime, when Gardiner was tired of it. Cranmer was now degraded as a priest, and left for death; but, if the Queen hated any one on earth, she hated him, and it was resolved that he should be ruined and disgraced to the utmost. There is no doubt that the Queen and her husband personally urged on these deeds, because they wrote to the Council, urging them to be active in the kindling of the fearful fires. As Cranmer was known not to be a firm man, a plan was laid for surrounding him with artful people, and inducing him to recant to the unreformed religion. Deans and friars visited him, played at bowls with him, showed him various attentions, talked persuasively with him, gave him money for his prison comforts, and induced him to sign, I fear, as many as six recantations. But when, after all, he was taken out to be burnt, he was nobly true to his better self, and made a glorious end.

After prayers and a sermon, Dr Cole, the preacher of the day (who had been one of the artful priests about Cranmer in prison), required him to make a public confession of his faith before the people. This, Cole did, expecting that he would declare himself a Roman Catholic. 'I *will* make a profession of my faith,' said Cranmer, 'and with a good will too.'

Then, he arose before them all, and took from the sleeve of his robe a written prayer and read it aloud. That done, he kneeled and said the Lord's Prayer, all the people joining; and then he arose again and told them that he believed in the Bible, and that in what he had lately written, he had written what was not the truth, and that, because his right hand had signed those papers, he would burn his right hand first when he came to the fire. As for the Pope, he did refuse him and denounce him as the enemy of Heaven. Hereupon the pious Dr Cole cried out to the guards to stop that heretic's mouth and take him away.

So they took him away, and chained him to the stake, where he hastily took off his own clothes to make ready for the flames. And he stood before the people with a bald head and a white and flowing beard. He was so firm now when the worst was come, that he again declared against his recantation, and was so impressive and so undismayed, that a certain lord, who was one of the directors of the execution, called out to the men to make haste! When the fire was lighted, Cranmer, true to his latest word, stretched out his right hand, and crying out, 'This hand hath offended!' held it among the flames, until it blazed and burned away. His heart was found entire among his ashes, and he left at last a memorable name in English history. Cardinal Pole celebrated the day by saying his first mass, and next day he was made Archbishop of Canterbury in Cranmer's place.

The Queen's husband, who was now mostly abroad in his own dominions, and generally made a coarse jest of her to his more familiar courtiers, was at war with France, and came over to seek the assistance of England. England was very unwilling to engage in a French war for his sake; but it happened that the King of France, at this very time, aided a descent upon the English coast. Hence, war was declared, greatly to Philip's satisfaction; and the Queen raised a sum of money with which to carry it on, by every unjustifiable means in her power. It met with no profitable return, for the French Duke of Guise surprised Calais, and the English sustained a complete defeat. The losses they met with in France greatly mortified the national pride, and the Queen never recovered the blow.

There was a bad fever raging in England at this time, and I am glad to write that the Queen took it, and the hour of her death came. 'When I am dead and my body is opened,' she said to those around her, 'ye shall find CALAIS written on my heart.' I should have thought, if anything were written on it, they would have found the words – JANE GREY, HOOPER, ROGERS, RIDLEY, LATIMER, CRANMER, AND THREE HUNDRED PEOPLE BURNT ALIVE WITHIN FOUR YEARS OF MY WICKED REIGN, INCLUDING SIXTY WOMEN AND FORTY LITTLE CHILDREN. But it is enough that their deaths were written in Heaven.

The Queen died on the seventeenth of November, fifteen hundred and fifty-eight, after reigning not quite five years and a half, and in the forty-fourth year of her age. Cardinal Pole died of the same fever next day.

As BLOODY QUEEN MARY, this woman has become famous, and as BLOODY QUEEN MARY, she will ever be justly remembered with horror and detestation in Great Britain. Her memory has been held in such abhorrence that some writers have arisen in later years to take her part, and to show that she was, upon the whole, quite an amiable and cheerful sovereign! 'By their fruits ye shall know them,' said OUR SAVIOUR. The stake and the fire were the fruits of this reign, and you will judge this Queen by nothing else.

CHAPTER 31

England under Elizabeth

First Part

There was great rejoicing all over the land when the Lords of the Council went down to Hatfield, to hail the Princess Elizabeth as the new Queen of England. Weary of the barbarities of Mary's reign, the people looked with hope and gladness to the new Sovereign. The nation seemed to wake from a horrible dream; and Heaven, so long hidden by the smoke of the fires that roasted men and women to death, appeared to brighten once more.

Queen Elizabeth was five-and-twenty years of age when she rode through the streets of London, from the Tower to Westminster Abbey, to be crowned. Her countenance was strongly marked, but on the whole, commanding and dignified; her hair was red, and her nose something too long and sharp for a woman's. She was not the beautiful creature her courtiers made out; but she was well enough, and no doubt looked all the better for coming after the dark and gloomy Mary. She was well educated, but a roundabout writer, and rather a hard swearer and coarse talker. She was clever, but cunning and deceitful, and inherited much of her father's violent temper. I mention this now, because she has been so over-praised by one party, and so over-abused by another, that it is hardly possible to understand the greater part of her reign without first understanding what kind of woman she really was.

She began her reign with the great advantage of having a very wise and careful Minister, SIR WILLIAM CECIL, whom she afterwards made LORD BURLEIGH. Altogether, the people had greater reason for rejoicing than they usually had, when there were processions in the streets; and they were happy with some reason. All kinds of shows and images were set up; GOG and MAGOG were hoisted to the top of Temple Bar; and (which was more to the purpose) the Corporation dutifully presented the young Queen with the sum of a thousand marks in gold – so heavy a present, that she was obliged to take it into her carriage with both hands. The coronation was a great success; and, on the next day, one of the courtiers presented a petition to the new Queen, praying that as it was the custom to release some prisoners on such occasions, she would have the goodness to release the four Evangelists, Matthew, Mark, Luke, and John, and also the Apostle Saint Paul, who had been for some time shut up in a strange language so that the people could not get at them.

To this, the Queen replied that it would be better first to inquire of themselves whether they desired to be released or not; and, as a means of finding out, a great public discussion – a sort of religious tournament – was appointed to take place between certain champions of the two religions, in Westminster Abbey. You may suppose that it was soon made pretty clear to common sense, that for people to benefit by what they repeat or read, it is rather necessary they should understand something about it. Accordingly, a Church Service in plain English was settled, and other laws and regulations were made, completely establishing the great work of the Reformation. The Romish bishops and champions were not harshly dealt with, all things considered; and the Queen's ministers were both prudent and merciful.

The one great trouble of this reign, and the unfortunate cause of the greater part of such turmoil and bloodshed as occurred in it, was MARY STUART, QUEEN OF SCOTS. We will try to understand, in as few words as possible, who Mary was, what she was, and how she came to be a thorn in the royal pillow of Elizabeth.

She was the daughter of the Queen Regent of Scotland, MARY OF GUISE. She had been married, when a mere child, to the Dauphin, the son and heir of the King of France. The Pope, who pretended that no one could rightfully wear the crown of

England without his gracious permission, was strongly opposed to Elizabeth, who had not asked for the said gracious permission. And as Mary Queen of Scots would have inherited the English crown in right of her birth, supposing the English Parliament not to have altered the succession, the Pope himself, and most of the discontented who were followers of his, maintained that Mary was the rightful Queen of England, and Elizabeth the wrongful Queen. Mary being so closely connected with France, and France being jealous of England, there was far greater danger in this than there would have been if she had had no alliance with that great power. And when her young husband, on the death of his father, became FRANCIS THE SECOND, King of France, the matter grew very serious. For, the young couple styled themselves King and Queen of England, and the Pope was disposed to help them by doing all the mischief he could.

Now, the reformed religion, under the guidance of a stern and powerful preacher named JOHN KNOX, and other such men, had been making fierce progress in Scotland. It was still a half savage country, where there was a great deal of murdering and rioting continually going on; and the Reformers, instead of reforming those evils as they should have done, went to work in the ferocious old Scottish spirit, laying churches and chapels waste, pulling down pictures and altars, and knocking about the Grey Friars, and the Black Friars, and the White Friars, and the friars of all sorts of colours, in all directions. This obdurate and harsh spirit of the Scottish reformers (the Scotch have always been rather a sullen and frowning people in religious matters) put up the blood of the Romish French court, and caused France to send troops over to Scotland, with the hope of setting the friars of all sorts of colours on their legs again; of conquering that country first, and England afterwards; and so crushing the Reformation all to pieces. The Scottish Reformers, who had formed a great league which they called The Congregation of the Lord, secretly represented to Elizabeth that, if the reformed religion got the worst of it with them, it would be likely to get the worst of it in England too; and thus, Elizabeth, though she had a high notion of the rights of Kings and Queens to do anything they liked, sent an army to Scotland to support the Reformers, who were in arms against their sovereign. All these proceedings led to a treaty of peace at Edinburgh, under which the French consented to depart from the kingdom. By a separate treaty, Mary and her young husband engaged to renounce their assumed title of King and Queen of England. But this treaty they never fulfilled.

It happened, soon after matters had got to this state, that the young French King died, leaving Mary a young widow. She was then invited by her Scottish subjects to return home and reign over them; and as she was not now happy where she was, she, after a little time, complied.

Elizabeth had been Queen three years, when Mary Queen of Scots embarked at Calais for her own rough quarrelling country. As she came out of the harbour, a vessel was lost before her eyes, and she said, 'O! good God! what an omen this is for such a voyage!' She was very fond of France, and sat on the deck, looking back at it and weeping, until it was quite dark. When she went to bed, she directed to be called at daybreak, if the French coast were still visible, that she might behold it for the last time. As it proved to be a clear morning, this was done, and she again wept for the country she was leaving, and said many times, 'Farewell, France! Farewell, France! I shall never see thee again!' All this was long remembered afterwards, as sorrowful and interesting in a fair young princess of nineteen. Indeed, I am afraid it gradually came, together with her other distresses, to surround her with greater sympathy than she deserved.

When she came to Scotland, and took up her abode at the palace of Holyrood in Edinburgh, she found herself among uncouth strangers and wild uncomfortable customs very different from her experiences in the court of France. The very people who were disposed to love her, made her head ache when she was tired out by her voyage, with a serenade of discordant music – a fearful concert of bagpipes, I suppose – and brought her and her train home to her palace on miserable little Scotch horses that appeared to be half starved. Among the people who were not disposed to love her, she found the powerful leaders of the Reformed Church, who were bitter upon her amusements, however innocent, and denounced music and dancing as works of the devil. John Knox himself often lectured her, violently and angrily, and did much to make her life unhappy. All these reasons confirmed her old attachment to the Romish religion, and caused her, there is no doubt, most imprudently and dangerously both for herself and for England too, to give a solemn pledge to the heads of the Romish Church that if she ever succeeded to the English crown, she would set up that religion again. In reading her unhappy history, you must always remember this; and also that during her whole life she was constantly put forward against the Queen, in some form or other, by the Romish party.

That Elizabeth, on the other hand, was not inclined to like her, is pretty certain. Elizabeth was very vain and jealous, and had an extraordinary dislike to people being married. She treated Lady Catherine Grey, sister of the beheaded Lady Jane, with such shameful severity, for no other reason than her being secretly married, that she died and her husband was ruined; so, when a second marriage for Mary began to be talked about, probably Elizabeth disliked her more. Not that Elizabeth wanted suitors of her own, for they started up from Spain, Austria, Sweden, and England. Her English lover at this time, and one whom she much favoured too, was LORD ROBERT DUDLEY, Earl of Leicester – himself secretly married to AMY ROBSART, the daughter of an English gentleman, whom he was strongly suspected of causing to be murdered, down at his country seat, Cumnor Hall in Berkshire, that he might be free to marry the Queen. Upon this story, the great writer, SIR WALTER SCOTT, has founded one of his best romances. But if Elizabeth knew how to lead her handsome favourite on, for her own vanity and pleasure, she knew how to stop him for her own pride; and his love, and all the other proposals, came to nothing. The Queen always declared in good set speeches, that she would never be married at all, but would live and die a Maiden Queen. It was a very pleasant and meritorious declaration, I suppose; but it has been puffed and trumpeted so much, that I am rather tired of it myself.

Divers princes proposed to marry Mary, but the English court had reasons for being jealous of them all, and even proposed as a matter of policy that she should marry that very Earl of Leicester who had aspired to be the husband of Elizabeth. At last, LORD DARNLEY, son of the Earl of Lennox, and himself descended from the Royal Family of Scotland, went over with Elizabeth's consent to try his fortune at Holyrood. He was a tall simpleton; and could dance and play the guitar; but I know of nothing else he could do, unless it was to get very drunk, and eat gluttonously, and make a contemptible spectacle of himself in many mean and vain ways. However, he gained Mary's heart, not disdaining in the pursuit of his object to ally himself with one of her secretaries, DAVID RIZZIO, who had great influence with her. He soon married the Queen. This marriage does not say much for her, but what followed will presently say less.

Mary's brother, the EARL OF MURRAY, and head of the Protestant party in Scotland, had opposed this marriage, partly on religious grounds, and partly perhaps from personal dislike of the very contemptible bridegroom. When it had taken place, through Mary's gaining over to it the more powerful of the lords about her, she banished Murray for his pains; and, when he and some other nobles rose in arms to support the reformed religion, she herself, within a month of her wedding day, rode against them in armour with loaded pistols in her saddle. Driven out of Scotland, they presented themselves before Elizabeth – who called them traitors in public, and assisted them in private, according to her crafty nature.

Mary had been married but a little while, when she began to hate her husband, who, in his turn, began to hate that David Rizzio, with whom he had leagued to gain her favour, and whom he now believed to be her lover. He hated Rizzio to that extent, that he made a compact with LORD RUTHVEN and three other lords to get rid of him by murder. This wicked agreement they made in solemn secrecy upon the first of March, fifteen hundred and sixty-six, and on the night of Saturday the ninth, the conspirators were brought by Darnley up a private staircase, dark and steep, into a range of rooms where they knew that Mary was sitting at supper with her sister, Lady Argyle, and this doomed man. When they went into the room, Darnley took the Queen round the waist, and Lord Ruthven, who had risen from a bed of sickness to do this murder, came in, gaunt and ghastly, leaning on two men. Rizzio ran behind the Queen for shelter and protection. 'Let him come out of the room,' said Ruthven. 'He shall not leave the room,' replied the Queen; 'I read his danger in your face, and it is my will that he remain here.' They then set upon him, struggled with him, overturned the table, dragged him out, and killed him with fifty-six stabs. When the Queen heard that he was dead, she said, 'No more tears. I will think now of revenge!'

Within a day or two, she gained her husband over, and prevailed on the tall idiot to abandon the conspirators and fly with her to Dunbar. There, he issued a proclamation, audaciously and falsely denying that he had any knowledge of the late bloody business; and there they were joined by the EARL BOTHWELL and some other nobles. With their help, they raised eight thousand men, returned to Edinburgh, and drove the assassins into England. Mary soon afterwards gave birth to a son – still thinking of revenge.

That she should have had a greater scorn for her husband after his late cowardice and treachery than she had had before, was natural enough. There is little doubt that she now began to love Bothwell instead, and to plan with him means of getting rid of Darnley. Bothwell had such power over her that he induced her even to pardon the assassins of Rizzio. The arrangements for the christening of the young Prince were entrusted to him, and he was one of the most important people at the ceremony, where the child was named JAMES: Elizabeth being his godmother, though not present on the occasion. A week afterwards, Darnley, who had left Mary and gone to his father's house at Glasgow, being taken ill with the small-pox, she sent her own physician to attend him. But there is reason to apprehend that this was merely a show and a pretence, and that she knew what was doing, when Bothwell within another month proposed to one of the late conspirators against Rizzio, to murder Darnley, 'for that it was the Queen's mind that he should be taken away.' It is certain that on that very day she wrote to her ambassador in France, complaining of him, and yet went immediately to Glasgow, feigning to be very anxious about him, and to love him very much. If she wanted to get him in her power, she succeeded to her heart's content; for she induced him to go back with her to Edinburgh, and to occupy, instead of the palace, a lone house outside the city called the Kirk of Field. Here, he lived for about a week. One Sunday night, she remained with him until ten o'clock, and then left him, to go to Holyrood to be present at an entertainment given in celebration of the marriage of one of her favourite servants. At two o'clock in the morning the city was shaken by a great explosion, and the Kirk of Field was blown to atoms.

Darnley's body was found next day lying under a tree at some distance. How it came there, undisfigured and unscorched by gunpowder, and how this crime came to be so clumsily and strangely committed, it is impossible to discover. The deceitful character of Mary, and the deceitful character of Elizabeth, have rendered almost every part of their joint history uncertain and obscure. But, I fear that Mary was unquestionably a party to her husband's murder, and that this was the revenge she had threatened. The Scotch people universally believed it. Voices cried out in the streets of Edinburgh in the dead of the night, for justice on the murderess. Placards were posted by unknown hands in the public places denouncing Bothwell as the murderer, and the Queen as his accomplice; and, when he afterwards married her (though himself already married), previously making a show of taking her prisoner by force, the indignation of the people knew no bounds. The women particularly are described as having been quite frantic against the Queen, and to have hooted and cried after her in the streets with terrific vehemence.

Such guilty unions seldom prosper. This husband and wife had lived together but a month, when they were separated for ever by the successes of a band of Scotch nobles who associated against them for the protection of the young Prince: whom Bothwell had vainly endeavoured to lay hold of, and whom he would certainly have murdered, if the EARL OF MAR, in whose hands the boy was, had not been firmly and honourably faithful to his trust. Before this angry power, Bothwell fled abroad, where he died, a prisoner and mad, nine miserable years afterwards. Mary being found by the associated lords to deceive them at every turn, was sent a prisoner to Lochleven Castle; which, as it stood in the midst of a lake, could only be approached by boat. Here, one LORD LINDSAY, who was so much of a brute that the nobles would have done better if they had chosen a mere gentleman for their messenger, made her sign her abdication, and appoint Murray, Regent of Scotland. Here, too, Murray saw her in a sorrowing and humbled state.

She had better have remained in the castle of Lochleven, dull prison as it was, with the rippling of the lake against it, and the moving shadows of the water on the room-walls; but she could not rest there, and more than once tried to escape. The first time she had nearly succeeded, dressed in the clothes of her own washerwoman, but putting up her hand to prevent one of the boatmen from lifting her veil, the men suspected her, seeing how white it was, and rowed her back again. A short time afterwards, her fascinating manners enlisted in her cause a boy in the Castle, called the little DOUGLAS, who, while the family were at supper, stole the keys of the great gate, went softly out with the Queen, locked the gate on the outside, and rowed her away across the lake, sinking the keys as they went along. On the opposite shore she was met by another Douglas, and some few lords; and, so accompanied, rode away on horseback to Hamilton, where they raised three thousand men. Here, she issued a proclamation declaring that the abdication she had signed in her prison was illegal, and requiring the Regent to yield to his lawful Queen. Being a steady soldier, and in no way discomposed although he was without an army, Murray pretended to treat with her, until he had collected a force about half equal to her own, and then he gave her battle. In one quarter of an hour he cut down all her hopes. She had another weary ride on horseback of sixty long Scotch miles, and took shelter at Dundrennan Abbey, whence she fled for safety to Elizabeth's dominions.

Mary Queen of Scots came to England – to her own ruin, the trouble of the kingdom, and the misery and death of many – in the year one thousand five hundred and sixty-eight. How she left it and the world, nineteen years afterwards, we have now to see.

Second Part

When Mary Queen of Scots arrived in England, without money and even without any other clothes than those she wore, she wrote to Elizabeth, representing herself as an innocent and injured piece of Royalty, and entreating her assistance to oblige her Scottish subjects to take her back again and obey her. But, as her character was already known in England to be a very different one from what she made herself out to be, she was told in answer that she must first clear herself. Made uneasy by this condition, Mary, rather than stay in England, would have gone to Spain, or to France, or would even have gone back to Scotland. But, as her doing either would have been likely to trouble England afresh, it was decided that she should be detained here. She first came to Carlisle, and, after that, was moved about from castle to castle, as was considered necessary; but England she never left again.

After trying very hard to get rid of the necessity of clearing herself, Mary, advised by LORD HERRIES, her best friend in

England, agreed to answer the charges against her, if the Scottish noblemen who made them would attend to maintain them before such English noblemen as Elizabeth might appoint for that purpose. Accordingly, such an assembly, under the name of a conference, met, first at York, and afterwards at Hampton Court. In its presence Lord Lennox, Darnley's father, openly charged Mary with the murder of his son; and whatever Mary's friends may now say or write in her behalf, there is no doubt that, when her brother Murray produced against her a casket containing certain guilty letters and verses which he stated to have passed between her and Bothwell, she withdrew from the inquiry. Consequently, it is to be supposed that she was then considered guilty by those who had the best opportunities of judging of the truth, and that the feeling which afterwards arose in her behalf was a very generous but not a very reasonable one.

However, the DUKE OF NORFOLK, an honourable but rather weak nobleman, partly because Mary was captivating, partly because he was ambitious, partly because he was over-persuaded by artful plotters against Elizabeth, conceived a strong idea that he would like to marry the Queen of Scots – though he was a little frightened, too, by the letters in the casket. This idea being secretly encouraged by some of the noblemen of Elizabeth's court, and even by the favourite Earl of Leicester (because it was objected to by other favourites who were his rivals), Mary expressed her approval of it, and the King of France and the King of Spain are supposed to have done the same. It was not so quietly planned, though, but that it came to Elizabeth's ears, who warned the Duke 'to be careful what sort of pillow he was going to lay his head upon.' He made a humble reply at the time; but turned sulky soon afterwards, and, being considered dangerous, was sent to the Tower.

Thus, from the moment of Mary's coming to England she began to be the centre of plots and miseries.

A rise of the Catholics in the north was the next of these, and it was only checked by many executions and much bloodshed. It was followed by a great conspiracy of the Pope and some of the Catholic sovereigns of Europe to depose Elizabeth, place Mary on the throne, and restore the unreformed religion. It is almost impossible to doubt that Mary knew and approved of this; and the Pope himself was so hot in the matter that he issued a bull, in which he openly called Elizabeth the 'pretended

Queen' of England, excommunicated her, and excommunicated all her subjects who should continue to obey her. A copy of this miserable paper got into London, and was found one morning publicly posted on the Bishop of London's gate. A great hue and cry being raised, another copy was found in the chamber of a student of Lincoln's Inn, who confessed, being put upon the rack, that he had received it from one JOHN FELTON, a rich gentleman who lived across the Thames, near Southwark. This John Felton, being put upon the rack too, confessed that he had posted the placard on the Bishop's gate. For this offence he was, within four days, taken to St Paul's Churchyard, and there hanged and quartered. As to the Pope's bull, the people by the reformation having thrown off the Pope, did not care much, you may suppose, for the Pope's throwing off them. It was a mere dirty piece of paper, and not half so powerful as a street ballad.

On the very day when Felton was brought to his trial, the poor Duke of Norfolk was released. It would have been well for him if he had kept away from the Tower evermore, and from the snares that had taken him there. But, even while he was in that dismal place he corresponded with Mary, and as soon as he was out of it, he began to plot again. Being discovered in correspondence with the Pope, with a view to a rising in England which should force Elizabeth to consent to his marriage with Mary and to repeal the laws against the Catholics, he was re-committed to the Tower and brought to trial. He was found guilty by the unanimous verdict of the Lords who tried him, and was sentenced to the block.

It is very difficult to make out, at this distance of time, and between opposite accounts, whether Elizabeth really was a humane woman, or desired to appear so, or was fearful of shedding the blood of people of great name who were popular in the country. Twice she commanded, and countermanded the execution of this Duke, and it did not take place until five months after his trial. The scaffold was erected on Tower Hill, and there he died like a brave man. He refused to have his eyes bandaged, saying that he was not at all afraid of death; and he admitted the justice of his sentence, and was much regretted by the people.

Although Mary had shrunk at the most important time from disproving her guilt, she was very careful never to do anything that would admit it. All such proposals as were made to her by

Elizabeth for her release, required that admission in some form or other, and therefore came to nothing. Moreover, both women being artful and treacherous, and neither ever trusting the other, it was not likely that they could ever make an agreement. So, the Parliament, aggravated by what the Pope had done, made new and strong laws against the spreading of the Catholic religion in England, and declared it treason in any one to say that the Queen and her successors were not the lawful sovereigns of England. It would have done more than this, but for Elizabeth's moderation.

Since the Reformation, there had come to be three great sects of religious people – or people who called themselves so – in England; that is to say, those who belonged to the Reformed Church, those who belonged to the Unreformed Church, and those who were called the Puritans, because they said that they wanted to have everything very pure and plain in all the Church service. These last were for the most part an uncomfortable people, who thought it highly meritorious to dress in a hideous manner, talk through their noses, and oppose all harmless enjoyments. But they were powerful too, and very much in earnest, and they were one and all the determined enemies of the Queen of Scots. The Protestant feeling in England was further strengthened by the tremendous cruelties to which Protestants were exposed in France and in the Netherlands. Scores of thousands of them were put to death in those countries with every cruelty that can be imagined, and at last, in the autumn of the year one thousand five hundred and seventy-two, one of the greatest barbarities ever committed in the world took place at Paris.

It is called in history, THE MASSACRE OF SAINT BARTHOLO-MEW, because it took place on Saint Bartholomew's Eve. The day fell on Saturday the twenty-third of August. On that day all the great leaders of the Protestants (who were there called HUGUENOTS) were assembled together, for the purpose, as was represented to them, of doing honour to the marriage of their chief, the young King of Navarre, with the sister of CHARLES THE NINTH; a miserable young King who then occupied the French throne. This dull creature was made to believe by his mother and other fierce Catholics about him that the Huguenots meant to take his life; and he was persuaded to give secret orders that, on the tolling of a great bell, they should be fallen upon by an overpowering force of armed men, and slaughtered wherever they could be found. When the appointed hour was close at hand, the stupid wretch, trembling from head to foot, was taken into a balcony by his mother to see the atrocious work begun. The moment the bell tolled, the murderers broke forth. During all that night and the two next days, they broke into the houses, fired the houses, shot and stabbed the Protestants, men, women, and children, and flung their bodies into the streets. They were shot at in the streets as they passed along, and their blood ran down the gutters. Upwards of ten thousand Protestants were killed in Paris alone; in all France four or five times that number. To return thanks to Heaven for these diabolical murders, the Pope and his train actually went in public procession at Rome, and as if this were not shame enough for them, they had a medal struck to commemorate the event. But, however comfortable the wholesale murders were to these high authorities, they had not that soothing effect upon the doll-King. I am happy to state that he never knew a moment's peace afterwards; that he was continually crying out that he saw the Huguenots covered with blood and wounds falling dead before him; and that he died within a year, shrieking and yelling and raving to that degree, that if all the Popes who had ever lived had been rolled into one, they would not have afforded His guilty Majesty the slightest consolation.

When the terrible news of the massacre arrived in England, it made a powerful impression indeed upon the people. If they began to run a little wild against the Catholics at about this time, this fearful reason for it, coming so soon after the days of bloody Queen Mary, must be remembered in their excuse. The Court was not quite so honest as the people – but perhaps it sometimes is not. It received the French ambassador, with all the lords and ladies dressed in deep mourning, and keeping a profound silence. Nevertheless, a proposal of marriage which he had made to Elizabeth only two days before the eve of Saint Bartholomew, on behalf of the Duke of Alençon, the French King's brother, a boy of seventeen, still went on; while on the other hand, in her usual crafty way, the Queen secretly supplied the Huguenots with money and weapons.

I must say that for a Queen who made all those fine speeches, of which I have confessed myself to be rather tired, about living and dying a Maiden Queen, Elizabeth was 'going' to be married pretty often. Besides always having some English favourite or other whom she by turns encouraged and swore at and knocked about – for the Maiden Queen was very free with her fists – she held this French Duke off and on through several years. When he at last came over to England, the marriage articles were actually drawn up, and it was settled that the wedding should take place in six weeks. The Queen was then so bent upon it, that she prosecuted a poor Puritan named STUBBS, and a poor bookseller named PAGE, for writing and publishing a pamphlet against it. Their right hands were chopped off for this crime; and poor Stubbs – more loyal than I should have been myself under the circumstances – immediately pulled off his hat with his left hand, and cried, 'God save the Queen!' Stubbs was cruelly treated; for the marriage never took place after all, though the Queen pledged herself to the Duke with a ring from her own finger. He went away, no better than he came, when the courtship had lasted some ten years altogether; and he died a couple of years afterwards, mourned by Elizabeth, who appears to have been really fond of him. It is not much to her credit, for he was a bad enough member of a bad family.

To return to the Catholics. There arose two orders of priests, who were very busy in England, and who were much dreaded. These were the JESUITS (who were everywhere in all sorts of disguises), and the SEMINARY PRIESTS. The people had a great horror of the first, because they were known to have taught that murder was lawful if it were done with an object of which they approved; and they had a great horror of the second, because they came to teach the old religion, and to be the successors of 'Queen Mary's priests,' as those yet lingering in England were called, when they should die out. The severest laws were made against them, and were most unmercifully executed. Those who sheltered them in their houses often suffered heavily for what was an act of humanity; and the rack, that cruel torture which tore men's limbs asunder, was constantly kept going. What these unhappy men confessed, or what was ever confessed by any one under that agony, must always be received with great doubt, as it is certain that people have frequently owned to the most absurd and impossible crimes to escape such dreadful suffering. But I cannot doubt it to have been proved by papers, that there were many plots, both among the Jesuits, and with France, and with Scotland, and with Spain, for the destruction of Queen

Elizabeth, for the placing of Mary on the throne, and for the revival of the old religion.

If the English people were too ready to believe in plots, there were, as I have said, good reasons for it. When the massacre of Saint Bartholomew was yet fresh in their recollection, a great Protestant Dutch hero, the PRINCE OF ORANGE, was shot by an assassin, who confessed that he had been kept and trained for the purpose in a college of Jesuits. The Dutch, in this surprise and distress, offered to make Elizabeth their sovereign, but she declined the honour, and sent them a small army instead, under the command of the Earl of Leicester, who, although a capital Court favourite, was not much of a general. He did so little in Holland, that his campaign there would probably have been forgotten, but for its occasioning the death of one of the best writers, the best knights, and the best gentlemen, of that or any age. This was SIR PHILIP SIDNEY, who was wounded by a musket ball in the thigh as he mounted a fresh horse, after having had his own killed under him. He had to ride back wounded, a long distance, and was very faint with fatigue and loss of blood, when some water, for which he had eagerly asked, was handed to him. But he was so good and gentle even then, that seeing a poor badly wounded common soldier lying on the ground, looking at the water with longing eyes, he said, 'Thy necessity is greater than mine,' and gave it up to him. This touching action of a noble heart is perhaps as well known as any incident in history – is as famous far and wide as the blood-stained tower of London, with its axe, and block, and murders out of number. So delightful is an act of true humanity, and so glad are mankind to remember it.

At home, intelligence of plots began to thicken every day. I suppose the people never did live under such continual terrors as those by which they were possessed now, of Catholic risings, and burnings, and poisonings, and I don't know what. Still, we must always remember that they lived near and close to awful realities of that kind, and that with their experience it was not difficult to believe in any enormity. The government had the same fear, and did not take the best means of discovering the truth – for, besides torturing the suspected, it employed paid spies, who will always lie for their own profit. It even made some of the conspiracies it brought to light, by sending false letters to disaffected people, inviting them to join in pretended plots, which they too readily did.

But, one great real plot was at length discovered, and it ended the career of Mary, Queen of Scots. A seminary priest named BALLARD, and a Spanish soldier named SAVAGE, set on and encouraged by certain French priests, imparted a design to one ANTONY BABINGTON – a gentleman of fortune in Derbyshire, who had been for some time a secret agent of Mary's – for murdering the Queen. Babington then confided the scheme to some other Catholic gentlemen who were his friends, and they joined in it heartily. They were vain weak-headed young men, ridiculously confident, and preposterously proud of their plan; for they got a gimcrack painting made, of the six choice spirits who were to murder Elizabeth, with Babington in an attitude for the centre figure. Two of their number, however, one of whom was a priest, kept Elizabeth's wisest minister, SIR FRANCIS WALSINGHAM, acquainted with the whole project from the first. The conspirators were completely deceived to the final point, when Babington gave Savage, because he was shabby, a ring from his finger, and some money from his purse, wherewith to buy himself new clothes in which to kill the Queen. Walsingham, having then full evidence against the whole band, and two letters of Mary's besides, resolved to seize them. Suspecting something wrong, they stole out of the city, one by one, and hid themselves in St John's Wood, and other places which really were hiding places then; but they were all taken, and all executed. When they were seized, a gentleman was sent from Court to inform Mary of the fact, and of her being involved in the discovery. Her friends have complained that she was kept in very hard and severe custody. It does not appear very likely, for she was going out a hunting that very morning.

Queen Elizabeth had been warned long ago, by one in France who had good information of what was secretly doing, that in holding Mary alive, she held 'the wolf who would devour her.' The Bishop of London had, more lately, given the Queen's favourite minister the advice in writing, 'forthwith to cut off the Scottish Queen's head.' The question now was, what to do with her? The Earl of Leicester wrote a little note home from Holland, recommending that she should be quietly poisoned; that noble favourite having accustomed his mind, it is possible, to remedies of that nature. His black advice, however, was disregarded, and she was brought to trial at Fotheringay Castle in Northampton-shire, before a tribunal of forty, composed of both religions. There, and in the Star Chamber at Westminster, the trial lasted a fortnight. She defended herself with great ability, but could only deny the confessions that had been made by Babington and others; could only call her own letters, produced against her by her own secretaries, forgeries; and, in short, could only deny everything. She was found guilty, and declared to have incurred the penalty of death. The Parliament met, approved the sentence, and prayed the Queen to have it executed. The Queen replied that she requested them to consider whether no means could be found of saving Mary's life without endangering her own. The Parliament rejoined, No; and the citizens illuminated their houses and lighted bonfires, in token of their joy that all these plots and troubles were to be ended by the death of the Queen of Scots.

She, feeling sure that her time was now come, wrote a letter to the Queen of England, making three entreaties; first, that she might be buried in France; secondly, that she might not be executed in secret, but before her servants and some others; thirdly, that after her death, her servants should not be molested, but should be suffered to go home with the legacies she left them. It was an affecting letter, and Elizabeth shed tears over it, but sent no answer. Then came a special ambassador from France, and another from Scotland, to intercede for Mary's life; and then the nation began to clamour, more and more, for her death.

What the real feelings or intentions of Elizabeth were, can never be known now; but I strongly suspect her of only wishing one thing more than Mary's death, and that was to keep free of the blame of it. On the first of February, one thousand five hundred and eighty-seven, Lord Burleigh having drawn out the warrant for the execution, the Queen sent to the secretary DAVISON to bring it to her, that she might sign it: which she did. Next day, when Davison told her it was sealed, she angrily asked him why such haste was necessary? Next day but one, she joked about it, and swore a little. Again, next day but one, she seemed to complain that it was not yet done, but still she would not be plain with those about her. So, on the seventh, the Earls of Kent and Shrewsbury, with the Sheriff of Northamptonshire, came with the warrant to Fotheringay, to tell the Queen of Scots to prepare for death.

When those messengers of ill omen were gone, Mary made a frugal supper, drank to her servants, read over her will, went to bed, slept for some hours, and then arose and passed the remainder of the night saying prayers. In the morning she dressed herself in her best clothes; and, at eight o'clock when the sheriff came for her to her chapel, took leave of her servants who were there assembled praying with her, and went down-stairs, carrying a Bible in one hand and a crucifix in the other. Two of her women and four of her men were allowed to be present in the hall; where a low scaffold, only two feet from the ground, was erected and covered with black; and where the executioner from the Tower, and his assistant, stood, dressed in black velvet. The hall was full of people. While the sentence was being read she sat upon a stool; and, when it was finished, she again denied her guilt, as she had done before. The Earl of Kent and the Dean of Peterborough, in their Protestant zeal, made some very unnecessary speeches to her; to which she replied that she died in the Catholic religion, and they need not trouble themselves about that matter. When her head and neck were uncovered by the executioners, she said that she had not been used to be undressed by such hands, or before so much company. Finally, one of her women fastened a cloth over her face, and she laid her neck upon the block, and repeated more than once in Latin, 'Into thy hands, O Lord, I commend my spirit!' Some say her head was struck off in two blows, some say in three. However that be, when it was held up streaming with blood, the real hair beneath the false hair she had long worn was seen to be as grey as that of a woman of seventy though she was at that time only in her forty-sixth year. All her beauty was gone.

But she was beautiful enough to her little dog, who cowered under her dress, frightened, when she went upon the scaffold, and who lay down beside her headless body when all her earthly sorrows were over.

Third Part

On its being formally made known to Elizabeth that the sentence had been executed on the Queen of Scots, she showed the utmost grief and rage, drove her favourites from her with violent indignation, and sent Davison to the Tower; from which place he was only released in the end by paying an immense fine which completely ruined him. Elizabeth not only over-acted her part in making these pretences, but most basely reduced to poverty one of her faithful servants for no other fault than obeying her commands.

James, King of Scotland, Mary's son, made a show likewise of being very angry on the occasion; but he was a pensioner of England to the amount of five thousand pounds a year, and he had known very little of his mother, and he possibly regarded her as the murderer of his father, and he soon took it quietly.

Philip, King of Spain, however, threatened to do greater things than ever had been done yet, to set up the Catholic religion and punish Protestant England. Elizabeth, hearing that he and the Prince of Parma were making great preparations for this purpose, in order to be beforehand with them sent out ADMIRAL DRAKE (a famous navigator, who had sailed about the world, and had already brought great plunder from Spain) to the port of Cadiz, where he burnt a hundred vessels full of stores. This great loss obliged the Spaniards to put off the invasion for a year; but it was none the less formidable for that, amounting to one hundred and thirty ships, nineteen thousand soldiers, eight thousand sailors, two thousand slaves, and between two and three thousand great guns. England was not idle in making ready to resist this great force. All the men between sixteen years old and sixty, were trained and drilled; the national fleet of ships (in number only thirty-four at first) was enlarged by public contributions and by private ships, fitted out by noblemen; the city of London, of its own accord, furnished double the number of ships and men that it was required to provide; and, if ever the national spirit was up in England, it was up all through the country to resist the Spaniards. Some of the Queen's advisers were for seizing the principal English Catholics, and putting them to death; but the Queen – who, to her honour, used to say, that she would never believe any ill of her subjects, which a parent would not believe of her own children – rejected the advice, and only confined a few of those who were the most suspected, in the fens in Lincolnshire. The great body of Catholics deserved this confidence; for they behaved most loyally, nobly, and bravely.

So, with all England firing up like one strong angry man, and with both sides of the Thames fortified, and with the soldiers under arms, and with the sailors in their ships, the country waited for the coming of the proud Spanish fleet, which was called THE INVINCIBLE ARMADA. The Queen herself, riding in armour on a white horse, and the Earl of Essex and the Earl of Leicester holding her bridle rein, made a brave speech to the troops at Tilbury Fort opposite Gravesend, which was received with such enthusiasm as is seldom known. Then came the Spanish Armada into the English Channel, sailing along in the form of a half moon, of such great size that it was seven miles broad. But the English were quickly upon it, and woe then to all the Spanish ships that dropped a little out of the half moon, for the English took them instantly! And it soon appeared that the great Armada was anything but invincible, for on a summer night, bold Drake sent eight blazing fire-ships right into the midst of it. In terrible consternation the Spaniards tried to get out to sea, and so became dispersed; the English pursued them at a great advantage; a storm came on, and drove the Spaniards among rocks and shoals; and the swift end of the Invincible fleet was, that it lost thirty great ships and ten thousand men, and, defeated and disgraced, sailed home again. Being afraid to go by the English Channel, it sailed all round Scotland and Ireland; some of the ships getting cast away on the latter coast in bad weather, the Irish, who were a kind of savages, plundered those vessels and killed their crews. So ended this great attempt to invade and conquer England. And I think it will be a long time before any other invincible fleet coming to England with the same object, will fare much better than the Spanish Armada.

Though the Spanish king had had this bitter taste of English bravery, he was so little the wiser for it, as still to entertain his old designs, and even to conceive the absurd idea of placing his daughter on the English throne. But the Earl of Essex, SIR WALTER RALEIGH, SIR THOMAS HOWARD, and some other distinguished leaders, put to sea from Plymouth, entered the port of Cadiz once more, obtained a complete victory over the shipping assembled there, and got possession of the town. In obedience to the Queen's express instructions, they behaved with great humanity; and the principal loss of the Spaniards was a vast sum of money which they had to pay for ransom. This was one of many gallant achievements on the sea effected in this reign. Sir Walter Raleigh himself, after marrying a maid of honour and giving offence to the Maiden Queen thereby, had already sailed to South America in search of gold.

The Earl of Leicester was now dead, and so was Sir Thomas Walsingham, whom Lord Burleigh was soon to follow. The principal favourite was the EARL OF ESSEX, a spirited and handsome man, a favourite with the people too as well as with the Queen, and possessed of many admirable qualities. It was much debated at Court whether there should be peace with Spain or no, and he was very urgent for war. He also tried hard to have his own way in the appointment of a deputy to govern in Ireland. One day, while this question was in dispute, he hastily took offence, and turned his back upon the Queen; as a gentle reminder of which impropriety, the Queen gave him a tremendous box on the ear, and told him to go to the devil. He went home instead, and did not reappear at Court for half a year or so, when he and the Queen were reconciled, though never (as some suppose) thoroughly.

From this time the fate of the Earl of Essex and that of the Queen seemed to be blended together. The Irish were still perpetually quarrelling and fighting among themselves, and he went over to Ireland as Lord Lieutenant, to the great joy of his enemies (Sir Walter Raleigh among the rest), who were glad to have so dangerous a rival far off. Not being by any means successful there, and knowing that his enemies would take advantage of that circumstance to injure him with the Queen, he came home again, though against her orders. The Queen being taken by surprise when he appeared before her, gave him her hand to kiss, and he was overjoyed – though it was not a very lovely hand by this time – but in the course of the same day she ordered him to confine himself to his room, and two or three days afterwards had him taken into custody. With the same sort of caprice – and as capricious an old woman she now was, as ever wore a crown or a head either – she sent him broth from her own table on his falling ill from anxiety, and cried about him.

He was a man who could find comfort and occupation in his books, and he did so for a time; not the least happy time, I dare say, of his life. But it happened unfortunately for him, that he held a monopoly in sweet wines; which means that nobody could sell them without purchasing his permission. This right, which was only for a term, expiring, he applied to have it renewed. The Queen refused, with the rather strong observation – but she *did* make strong observations – that an unruly beast must be stinted in his food. Upon this, the angry Earl, who had been already deprived of many offices, thought himself in danger of complete ruin, and turned against the Queen, whom he called a vain old woman who had grown as crooked in her mind as she had in her figure. These uncomplimentary expressions the ladies of the Court immediately snapped up and carried to the Queen, whom they did not put in a better temper, you may believe. The same Court ladies, when they had beautiful dark hair of their own, used to wear false red hair, to be like the Queen. So they were not very high-spirited ladies, however high in rank.

The worst object of the Earl of Essex, and some friends of his who used to meet at LORD SOUTHAMPTON's house, was to obtain possession of the Queen, and oblige her by force to dismiss her ministers and change her favourites. On Saturday the seventh of February, one thousand six hundred and one, the council suspecting this, summoned the Earl to come before them. He, pretending to be ill, declined; it was then settled among his friends, that as the next day would be Sunday, when many of the citizens usually assembled at the Cross by St Paul's Cathedral, he should make one bold effort to induce them to rise and follow him to the Palace.

So, on the Sunday morning, he and a small body of adherents started out of his house – Essex House by the Strand, with steps to the river – having first shut up in it, as prisoners, some members of the council who came to examine him – and hurried into the City with the Earl at their head, crying out 'For the Queen! For the Queen! A plot is laid for my life!' No one heeded them, however, and when they came to St Paul's there were no citizens there. In the meantime the prisoners at Essex House had been released by one of the Earl's own friends; he had been promptly proclaimed a traitor in the City itself; and the streets were barricaded with carts and guarded by soldiers. The Earl got back to his house by water, with difficulty, and after an attempt to defend his house against the troops and cannon by which it was soon surrounded, gave himself up that night. He was brought to trial on the nineteenth, and found guilty; on the twenty-fifth, he was executed on Tower Hill, where he died, at thirty-four years old, both courageously and penitently. His step-father suffered with him. His enemy, Sir Walter Raleigh, stood near the scaffold all the time – but not so near it as we shall see him stand, before we finish his history.

In this case, as in the cases of the Duke of Norfolk and Mary Queen of Scots, the Queen had commanded, and counter-manded, and again commanded, the execution. It is probable that the death of her young and gallant favourite in the prime of his good qualities, was never off her mind afterwards, but she held out, the same vain obstinate and capricious woman, for another year. Then she danced before her Court on a state occasion – and cut, I should think, a mighty ridiculous figure, doing so in an immense ruff, stomacher and wig, at seventy years old. For another year still, she held out, but, without any more dancing, and as a moody sorrowful broken creature. At last, on the tenth of March, one thousand six hundred and three, having been ill of a very bad cold, and made worse by the death of the Countess of Nottingham who was her intimate friend, she fell into a stupor and was supposed to be dead. She recovered her consciousness, however, and then nothing would induce her to go to bed; for she said that she knew that if she did, she should never get up again. There she lay for ten days, on cushions on the floor, without any food, until the Lord Admiral got her into bed at last, partly by persuasions and partly by main force. When they asked her who should succeed her, she replied that her seat had been the seat of Kings, and that she would have for her successor, 'No rascal's son, but a King's.' Upon this, the lords present stared at one another, and took the liberty of asking whom she meant; to which she replied, 'Whom should I mean, but our cousin of Scotland!' This was on the twenty-third of March. They asked her once again that day, after she was speechless, whether she was still in the same mind? She struggled up in bed, and joined her hands over her head in the form of a crown, as the only reply she could make. At three o'clock next morning, she very quietly died, in the forty-fifth year of her reign.

That reign had been a glorious one, and is made for ever memorable by the distinguished men who flourished in it. Apart from the great voyagers, statesmen, and scholars, whom it produced, the names of BACON, SPENSER, and SHAKESPEARE, will always be remembered with pride and veneration by the civilised world, and will always impart (though with no great reason, perhaps) some portion of their lustre to the name of Elizabeth herself. It was a great reign for discovery, for commerce, and for English enterprise and spirit in general. It was a great reign for the Protestant religion and for the Reformation which made England free. The Queen was very popular, and in her progresses, or journeys about her dominions, was everywhere received with the liveliest joy. I think the truth is, that she was not half so good as she has been made out, and not half so bad as she has been made out. She had her fine qualities, but she was coarse, capricious, and treacherous, and had all the faults of an excessively vain young woman long after she was an old one. On the whole, she had a great deal too much of her father in her, to please me.

Many improvements and luxuries were introduced in the course of these five-and-forty years in the general manner of living; but cock-fighting, bull-baiting, and bear-baiting, were still the national amusements; and a coach was so rarely seen, and was such an ugly and cumbersome affair when it was seen, that even the Queen herself, on many high occasions, rode on horseback on a pillion behind the Lord Chancellor.

CHAPTER 32

England under James the First

First Part

'Our cousin of Scotland' was ugly, awkward, and shuffling both in mind and person. His tongue was much too large for his mouth, his legs were much too weak for his body, and his dull goggle-eyes stared and rolled like an idiot's. He was cunning, covetous, wasteful, idle, drunken, greedy, dirty, cowardly, a great swearer, and the most conceited man on earth. His figure – what is commonly called rickety from his birth – presented a most ridiculous appearance, dressed in thick padded clothes, as a safeguard against being stabbed (of which he lived in continual fear), of a grass-green colour from head to foot, with a hunting-horn dangling at his side instead of a sword, and his hat and feather sticking over one eye, or hanging on the back of his head, as he happened to toss it on. He used to loll on the necks of his favourite courtiers, and slobber their faces, and kiss and pinch their cheeks; and the greatest favourite he ever had, used to sign himself in his letters to his royal master, His Majesty's 'dog and slave,' and used to address his majesty as 'his Sowship.' His majesty was the worst rider ever seen, and thought himself the best. He was one of the most impertinent talkers (in the broadest Scotch) ever heard, and boasted of being unanswerable in all manner of argument. He wrote some of the most wearisome treatises ever read – among others, a book upon witchcraft, in which he was a devout believer – and thought himself a prodigy of authorship. He thought, and wrote, and said, that a king had a right to make and unmake what laws he pleased, and ought to be accountable to nobody on earth. This is the plain true character of the personage whom the greatest men about the court praised and flattered to that degree, that I doubt if there be anything much more shameful in the annals of human nature.

He came to the English throne with great ease. The miseries of a disputed succession had been felt so long, and so dreadfully, that he was proclaimed within a few hours of Elizabeth's death, and was accepted by the nation, even without being asked to give any pledge that he would govern well, or that he would redress crying grievances. He took a month to come from Edinburgh to London; and, by way of exercising his new power, hanged a pickpocket on the journey without any trial, and knighted everybody he could lay hold of. He made two hundred knights before he got to his palace in London, and seven hundred before he had been in it three months. He also shovelled sixty-two new peers into the House of Lords – and there was a pretty large sprinkling of Scotchmen among them, you may believe.

His Sowship's prime Minister, CECIL (for I cannot do better than call his majesty what his favourite called him), was the enemy of Sir Walter Raleigh, and also of Sir Walter's political friend, LORD COBHAM; and his Sowship's first trouble was a plot originated by these two, and entered into by some others, with the old object of seizing the King and keeping him in imprisonment until he should change his ministers. There were Catholic priests in the plot, and there were Puritan noblemen too; for, although the Catholics and Puritans were strongly opposed to each other, they united at this time against his Sowship, because they knew that he had a design against both, after pretending to be friendly to each; this design being to have only one high and convenient form of the Protestant religion, which everybody should be bound to belong to, whether they liked it or not. This plot was mixed up with another, which may or may not have had some reference to placing on the throne, at some time, the LADY ARABELLA STUART; whose misfortune it was, to be the daughter of the younger brother of his Sowship's father, but who was quite innocent of any part in the scheme. Sir Walter Raleigh was accused on the confession of Lord Cobham – a miserable creature, who said one thing at one time, and another thing at another time, and could be relied upon in nothing. The trial of Sir Walter Raleigh lasted from eight in the morning until nearly midnight; he defended himself with such eloquence, genius, and spirit against all accusations, and against the insults of COKE, the Attorney General – who, according to the custom of the time, foully abused him – that those who went there detesting the prisoner, came away admiring him, and declaring that anything so wonderful and so captivating was never heard. He was found guilty, nevertheless, and sentenced to death. Execution was deferred, and he was taken to the Tower. The two Catholic priests, less fortunate, were executed with the usual atrocity; and Lord Cobham and two others were pardoned on the scaffold. His Sowship thought it wonderfully knowing in him to surprise the people by pardoning these three at the very block; but, blundering and bungling, as usual, he had very nearly overreached himself. For, the messenger on horseback who brought the pardon, came so late, that he was pushed to the outside of the crowd, and was obliged to shout and roar out what he came for. The miserable Cobham did not gain much by being spared that day. He lived, both as a prisoner and a beggar, utterly despised, and miserably poor, for thirteen years, and then died in an old outhouse belonging to one of his former servants.

This plot got rid of, and Sir Walter Raleigh safely shut up in the Tower, his Sowship held a great dispute with the Puritans on their presenting a petition to him, and had it all his own way – not so very wonderful, as he would talk continually, and would not hear anybody else – and filled the Bishops with admiration. It was comfortably settled that there was to be only one form of religion, and that all men were to think exactly alike. But, although this was arranged two centuries and a half ago, and although the arrangement was supported by much fining and imprisonment, I do not find that it is quite successful, even yet.

His Sowship, having that uncommonly high opinion of himself as a king, had a very low opinion of Parliament as a power that audaciously wanted to control him. When he called his first Parliament after he had been king a year, he accordingly thought he would take pretty high ground with them, and told them that he commanded them 'as an absolute king.' The Parliament thought those strong words, and saw the necessity of upholding their authority. His Sowship had three children: Prince Henry, Prince Charles, and the Princess Elizabeth. It would have been well for one of these, and we shall too soon see which, if he had learnt a little wisdom concerning Parliaments from his father's obstinacy.

Now, the people still labouring under their old dread of the Catholic religion, this Parliament revived and strengthened the severe laws against it. And this so angered ROBERT CATESBY, a restless Catholic gentleman of an old family, that he formed one of the most desperate and terrible designs ever conceived in the mind of man, no less a scheme than the Gunpowder Plot.

His object was, when the King, lords, and commons, should be assembled at the next opening of Parliament, to blow them up, one and all, with a great mine of gunpowder. The first person to whom he confided this horrible idea was THOMAS WINTER, a Worcestershire gentleman who had served in the army abroad, and had been secretly employed in Catholic projects. While Winter was yet undecided, and when he had gone over to the Netherlands, to learn from the Spanish Ambassador there whether there was any hope of Catholics being relieved through the intercession of the King of Spain with his Sowship, he found at Ostend a tall dark daring man, whom he had known when they were both soldiers abroad, and whose name was GUIDO – or GUY – FAWKES. Resolved to join the plot, he proposed it to this man, knowing him to be the man for any desperate deed, and they two came back to England together. Here, they admitted two other conspirators: THOMAS PERCY, related to the Earl of Northumberland, and JOHN WRIGHT, his brother-in-law. All these met together in a solitary house in the open fields which were then near Clement's Inn, now a closely blocked-up part of London; and when they had all taken a great oath of secrecy, Catesby told the rest what his plan was. They then went up-stairs into a garret, and received the Sacrament from FATHER GERARD, a Jesuit, who is said not to have known actually of the Gunpowder Plot, but who, I think, must have had his suspicions that there was something desperate afoot.

Percy was a Gentleman Pensioner, and as he had occasional duties to perform about the Court, then kept at Whitehall, there would be nothing suspicious in his living at Westminster. So, having looked well about him, and having found a house to let, the back of which joined the Parliament House, he hired it of a person named FERRIS, for the purpose of undermining the wall. Having got possession of this house, the conspirators hired another on the Lambeth side of the Thames, which they used as a storehouse for wood, gunpowder, and other combustible matters. These were to be removed at night (and afterwards were removed), bit by bit, to the house at Westminster; and, that there might be some trusty person to keep watch over the Lambeth stores, they admitted another conspirator, by name ROBERT KAY, a very poor Catholic gentleman.

All these arrangements had been made some months, and it was a dark wintry December night, when the conspirators, who had been in the meantime dispersed to avoid observation, met in the house at Westminster, and began to dig. They had laid in a good stock of eatables, to avoid going in and out, and they dug and dug with great ardour. But, the wall being tremendously thick, and the work very severe, they took into their plot CHRISTOPHER WRIGHT, a younger brother of John Wright, that they might have a new pair of hands to help. And Christopher Wright fell to like a fresh man, and they dug and dug by night and by day, and Fawkes stood sentinel all the time. And if any man's heart seemed to fail him at all, Fawkes said, 'Gentlemen, we have abundance of powder and shot here, and there is no fear of our being taken alive, even if discovered.' The same Fawkes, who, in the capacity of sentinel, was always prowling about, soon picked up the intelligence that the King had prorogued the Parliament again, from the seventh of February, the day first fixed upon, until the third of October. When the conspirators knew this, they agreed to separate until after the Christmas holidays, and to take no notice of each other in the meanwhile, and never to write letters to one another on any account. So, the house in Westminster was shut up again, and I suppose the neighbours thought that those strange-looking men who lived there so gloomily, and went out so seldom, were gone away to have a merry Christmas somewhere.

It was the beginning of February sixteen hundred and five, when Catesby met his fellow-conspirators again at this West-minster house. He had now admitted three more: JOHN GRANT, a Warwickshire gentleman of a melancholy temper, who lived in a doleful house near Stratford-upon-Avon, with a frowning wall all round it, and a deep moat; ROBERT WINTER, eldest brother of Thomas; and Catesby's own servant, THOMAS BATES, who, Catesby thought, had had some suspicion of what his master was about. These three had all suffered more or less for their religion in Elizabeth's time. And now, they all began to dig again, and they dug and dug by night and by day.

They found it dismal work alone there, underground, with such a fearful secret on their minds, and so many murders before them. They were filled with wild fancies. Sometimes, they thought they heard a great bell tolling, deep down in the earth under the Parliament House; sometimes, they thought they heard low voices muttering about the Gunpowder Plot; once in the morning, they really did hear a great rumbling noise over their heads, as they dug and sweated in their mine. Every man stopped and looked aghast at his neighbour, wondering what had happened, when that bold prowler, Fawkes, who had been out to look, came in and told them that it was only a dealer in coals who had occupied a cellar under the Parliament House, removing his stock in trade to some other place. Upon this, the conspirators, who with all their digging and digging had not yet dug through the tremendously thick wall, changed their plan; hired that cellar, which was directly under the House of Lords; put six-and-thirty barrels of gunpowder in it, and covered them over with fagots and coals. Then they all dispersed again till September, when the following new conspirators were admitted: SIR EDWARD BAYNHAM, of Gloucestershire; SIR EVERARD DIGBY, of Rutlandshire; AMBROSE ROOKWOOD, of Suffolk; FRANCIS TRESHAM, of Northamptonshire. Most of those were rich and were to assist the plot, some with money and some with horses on which the conspirators were to ride through the country and rouse the Catholics after the Parliament should be blown into air.

Parliament being again prorogued from the third of October to the fifth of November, and the conspirators being uneasy lest their design should have been found out, Thomas Winter said he would go up into the House of Lords on the day of the prorogation, and see how matters looked. Nothing could be better. The unconscious Commissioners were walking about and talking to one another, just over the six-and-thirty barrels of gunpowder. He came back and told the rest so, and they went on with their preparations. They hired a ship, and kept it ready in the Thames, in which Fawkes was to sail for Flanders after firing with a slow match the train that was to explode the powder. A number of Catholic gentlemen not in the secret, were invited, on pretence of a hunting party, to meet Sir Everard Digby at Dunchurch on the fatal day, that they might be ready to act together. And now all was ready.

But, now, the great wickedness and danger which had been all along at the bottom of this wicked plot, began to show itself. As the fifth of November drew near, most of the conspirators, remembering that they had friends and relations who would be in the House of Lords that day, felt some natural relenting, and a wish to warn them to keep away. They were not much comforted by Catesby's declaring that in such a cause he would blow up his own son. LORD MOUNTEAGLE, Tresham's brother-in-law, was certain to be in the House; and when Tresham found that he could not prevail upon the rest to devise any means of sparing their friends, he wrote a mysterious letter to this lord and left it at his lodging in the dusk, urging him to keep away from the opening of Parliament, 'since God and man had concurred to punish the wickedness of the times.' It contained the words 'that the Parliament should receive a terrible blow, and yet should not see who hurt them.' And it added, 'the danger is past, as soon as you have burnt the letter.'

The ministers and courtiers made out that his Sowship, by a direct miracle from Heaven, found out what this letter meant. The truth is, that they were not long (as few men would be) in finding it out for themselves; and it was decided to let the conspirators alone, until the very day before the opening of Parliament. That the conspirators had their fears, is certain; for, Tresham himself said before them all, that they were every one dead men; and, although even he did not take flight, there is reason to suppose that he had warned other persons besides Lord Mounteagle. However, they were all firm; and Fawkes, who was a man of iron, went down every day and night to keep watch in the cellar as usual. He was there about two in the afternoon of the fourth, when the Lord Chamberlain and Lord Mounteagle threw open the door and looked in. 'Who are you, friend?' said they. 'Why,' said Fawkes, 'I am Mr Percy's servant, and am looking after his store of fuel here.' 'Your master has laid in a pretty good store,' they returned, and shut the door, and went away. Fawkes, upon this, posted off to the other conspirators to tell them all was quiet, and went back and shut himself up in the dark black cellar again, where he heard the bell go twelve o'clock and usher in the fifth of November. About two hours afterwards, he slowly opened the door, and came out to look about him, in his old prowling way. He was instantly seized and bound, by a party of soldiers under SIR THOMAS KNEVETT. He had a watch upon him, some touchwood, some tinder, some slow matches; and there was a dark lantern with a candle in it, lighted, behind the door. He had his boots and spurs on – to ride to the ship, I suppose – and it was well for the soldiers that they took him so suddenly. If they had left him but a moment's time to light a match, he certainly would have tossed it in among the powder, and blown up himself and them.

They took him to the King's bed-chamber first of all, and there the King (causing him to be held very tight, and keeping a good way off), asked him how he could have the heart to intend to destroy so many innocent people? 'Because,' said Guy Fawkes, 'desperate diseases need desperate remedies.' To a little Scotch favourite, with a face like a terrier, who asked him (with no particular wisdom) why he had collected so much gunpowder, he replied, because he had meant to blow Scotchmen back to Scotland, and it would take a deal of powder to do that. Next day he was carried to the Tower, but would make no confession. Even after being horribly tortured, he confessed nothing that the Government did not already know; though he must have been in a fearful state – as his signature, still preserved, in contrast with his natural handwriting before he was put upon the dreadful rack, most frightfully shows. Bates, a very different man, soon said the Jesuits had had to do with the plot, and probably, under the torture, would as readily have said anything. Tresham, taken and put in the Tower too, made confessions and unmade them, and died of an illness that was heavy upon him. Rookwood, who had stationed relays of his own horses all the way to Dunchurch, did not mount to escape until the middle of the day, when the news of the plot was all over London. On the road, he came up with the two Wrights, Catesby, and Percy; and they all galloped together into Northamptonshire. Thence to Dunchurch, where they found the proposed party assembled. Finding, however, that there had been a plot, and that it had been discovered, the party disappeared in the course of the night and left them alone with Sir Everard Digby. Away they all rode again, through Warwickshire and Worcestershire, to a house called Holbeach, on the borders of Staffordshire. They tried to raise the Catholics on their way, but were indignantly driven off by them. All this time they were hotly pursued by the sheriff of Worcester, and a fast increasing concourse of riders. At last, resolving to defend themselves at Holbeach, they shut themselves up in the house, and put some wet powder before the fire to dry. But it blew up, and Catesby was singed and blackened, and almost killed, and some of the others were sadly hurt. Still, knowing that they must die, they resolved to die there, and with only their swords in their hands appeared at the windows to be shot at by the sheriff and his assistants. Catesby said to Thomas Winter, after Thomas had been hit in the right arm which dropped powerless by his side, 'Stand by me, Tom, and we will die together!' – which they did, being shot through the body by two bullets from one gun. John Wright, and Christopher Wright, and Percy, were also shot. Rookwood and Digby were taken: the former with a broken arm and a wound in his body too.

It was the fifteenth of January, before the trial of Guy Fawkes, and such of the other conspirators as were left alive, came on. They were all found guilty, all hanged, drawn, and quartered: some, in St Paul's Churchyard, on the top of Ludgate-hill; some, before the Parliament House. A Jesuit priest, named HENRY GARNET, to whom the dreadful design was said to have been communicated, was taken and tried; and two of his servants, as well as a poor priest who was taken with him, were tortured without mercy. He himself was not tortured, but was surrounded in the Tower by tamperers and traitors, and so was made unfairly to convict himself out of his own mouth. He said, upon his trial, that he had done all he could to prevent the deed, and that he could not make public what had been told him in confession – though I am afraid he knew of the plot in other ways. He was found guilty and executed, after a manful defence, and the Catholic Church made a saint of him; some rich and powerful persons, who had had nothing to do with the project, were fined and imprisoned for it by the Star Chamber; the Catholics, in general, who had recoiled with horror from the idea of the infernal contrivance, were unjustly put under more severe laws than before; and this was the end of the Gunpowder Plot.

Second Part

His Sowship would pretty willingly, I think, have blown the House of Commons into the air himself; for, his dread and jealousy of it knew no bounds all through his reign. When he was hard pressed for money he was obliged to order it to meet, as he could get no money without it; and when it asked him first to abolish some of the monopolies in necessaries of life which were a great grievance to the people, and to redress other public wrongs, he flew into a rage and got rid of it again. At one time he wanted it to consent to the Union of England with Scotland, and quarrelled about that. At another time it wanted him to put down a most infamous Church abuse, called the High Commission Court, and he quarrelled with it about that. At another time it entreated him not to be quite so fond of his archbishops and bishops who made speeches in his praise too awful to be related, but to have some little consideration for the poor Puritan clergy who were persecuted for preaching in their own way, and not according to the archbishops and bishops; and they quarrelled about that. In short, what with hating the House of Commons, and pretending not to hate it; and what with now sending some of its members who opposed him, to Newgate or to the Tower, and now telling the rest that they must not presume to make speeches about the public affairs which could not possibly concern them; and what with cajoling, and bullying, and fighting, and being frightened; the House of Commons was the plague of his Sowship's existence. It was pretty firm, however, in maintaining its rights, and insisting that the Parliament should make the laws, and not the King by his own single proclamations (which he tried hard to do); and his Sowship was so often distressed for money, in consequence, that he sold every sort of title and public office as if they were merchandise, and even invented a new dignity called a Baronetcy, which anybody could buy for a thousand pounds.

These disputes with his Parliaments, and his hunting, and his drinking, and his lying in bed – for he was a great sluggard – occupied his Sowship pretty well. The rest of his time he chiefly passed in hugging and slobbering his favourites. The first of these was SIR PHILIP HERBERT, who had no knowledge whatever, except of dogs, and horses, and hunting, but whom he soon made EARL OF MONTGOMERY. The next, and a much more famous one, was ROBERT CARR, or KER (for it is not certain which was his right name), who came from the Border country, and whom he soon made VISCOUNT ROCHESTER, and afterwards, EARL OF SOMERSET. The way in which his Sowship doted on this handsome young man, is even more odious to think of, than the way in which the really great men of England condescended to bow down before him. The favourite's great friend was a certain SIR THOMAS OVERBURY, who wrote his love-letters for him, and assisted him in the duties of his many high places, which his own ignorance prevented him from discharging. But this same Sir Thomas having just manhood enough to dissuade the favourite from a wicked marriage with the beautiful Countess of Essex, who was to get a divorce from her husband for the purpose, the said Countess, in her rage, got Sir Thomas put into the Tower, and there poisoned him. Then the favourite and this bad woman were publicly married by the King's pet bishop, with as much to-do and rejoicing, as if he had been the best man, and she the best woman, upon the face of the earth.

But, after a longer sunshine than might have been expected – of seven years or so, that is to say – another handsome young man started up and eclipsed the EARL OF SOMERSET. This was GEORGE VILLIERS, the youngest son of a Leicestershire gentleman: who came to Court with all the Paris fashions on him, and could dance as well as the best mountebank that ever was seen. He soon danced himself into the good graces of his Sowship, and danced the other favourite out of favour. Then, it was all at once discovered that the Earl and Countess of Somerset had not deserved all those great promotions and mighty rejoicings, and they were separately tried for the murder of Sir Thomas Over-bury, and for other crimes. But, the King was so afraid of his late favourite's publicly telling some disgraceful things he knew of him – which he darkly threatened to do – that he was even examined with two men standing, one on either side of him, each with a cloak in his hand, ready to throw it over his head and stop his mouth if he should break out with what he had it in his power to tell. So, a very lame affair was purposely made of the trial, and his punishment was an allowance of four thousand pounds a year in retirement, while the Countess was pardoned, and allowed to pass into retirement too. They hated one another by this time, and lived to revile and torment each other some years.

While these events were in progress, and while his Sowship was making such an exhibition of himself, from day to day and from year to year, as is not often seen in any sty, three remarkable deaths took place in England. The first was that of the Minister, Robert Cecil, Earl of Salisbury, who was past sixty, and had never been strong, being deformed from his birth. He said at last that he had no wish to live; and no Minister need have had, with his experience of the meanness and wickedness of those disgraceful times. The second was that of the Lady Arabella Stuart, who alarmed his Sowship mightily, by privately marrying WILLIAM SEYMOUR, son of LORD BEAUCHAMP, who was a descendant of King Henry the Seventh, and who, his Sowship thought, might consequently increase and strengthen any claim she might one day set up to the throne. She was separated from her husband (who was put in the Tower) and thrust into a boat to be confined at Durham. She escaped in a man's dress to get away in a French ship from Gravesend to France, but unhappily missed her husband, who had escaped too, and was soon taken. She went raving mad in the miserable Tower, and died there after four years. The last, and the most important of these three deaths, was that of Prince Henry, the heir to the throne, in the nineteenth year of his age. He was a promising young prince, and greatly liked; a quiet well-conducted youth, of whom two very good things are known: first, that his father was jealous of him; secondly, that he was the friend of Sir Walter Raleigh, languishing through all those years in the Tower, and often said that no man but his father would keep such a bird in such a cage. On the occasion of the preparations for the marriage of his sister the Princess Elizabeth with a foreign prince (and an unhappy marriage it turned out), he came from Richmond, where he had been very ill, to greet his new brother-in-law, at the palace at Whitehall. There he played a great game at tennis, in his shirt, though it was very cold weather, and was seized with an alarming illness, and died within a fortnight of a putrid fever. For this young prince Sir Walter Raleigh wrote, in his prison in the Tower, the beginning of a History of the World: a wonderful instance how little his Sowship could do to confine a great man's mind, however long he might imprison his body.

And this mention of Sir Walter Raleigh, who had many faults, but who never showed so many merits as in trouble and adversity, may bring me at once to the end of his sad story. After an imprisonment in the Tower of twelve long years, he proposed to resume those old sea voyages of his, and to go to South America in search of gold. His Sowship, divided between his wish to be on good terms with the Spaniards through whose territory Sir Walter must pass (he had long had an idea of marrying Prince Henry to a Spanish Princess), and his avaricious eagerness to get hold of the gold, did not know what to do. But, in the end, he set Sir Walter free, taking securities for his return; and Sir Walter fitted out an expedition at his own cost, and, on the twenty-eighth of March, one thousand six hundred and seventeen, sailed away in command of one of its ships, which he ominously called the Destiny. The expedition failed; the common men, not finding the gold they had expected, mutinied; a quarrel broke out between Sir Walter and the Spaniards, who hated him for old successes of his against them; and he took and burnt a little town called SAINT THOMAS. For this he was denounced to his Sowship by the Spanish Ambassador as a pirate; and returning almost broken-hearted, with his hopes and fortunes shattered, his company of friends dispersed, and his brave son (who had been one of them) killed, he was taken – through the treachery of SIR LEWIS STUKELY, his near relation, a scoundrel and a Vice-Admiral – and was once again immured in his prison-home of so many years.

His Sowship being mightily disappointed in not getting any gold, Sir Walter Raleigh was tried as unfairly, and with as many lies and evasions as the judges and law officers and every other authority in Church and State habitually practised under such a

King. After a great deal of prevarication on all parts but his own, it was declared that he must die under his former sentence, now fifteen years old. So, on the twenty-eighth of October, one thousand six hundred and eighteen, he was shut up in the Gate House at Westminster to pass his last night on earth, and there he took leave of his good and faithful lady, who was worthy to have lived in better days. At eight o'clock next morning, after a cheerful breakfast, and a pipe, and a cup of good wine, he was taken to Old Palace Yard in Westminster, where the scaffold was set up, and where so many people of high degree were assembled to see him die, that it was a matter of some difficulty to get him through the crowd. He behaved most nobly, but if anything lay heavy on his mind, it was that Earl of Essex, whose head he had seen roll off; and he solemnly said that he had had no hand in bringing him to the block, and that he had shed tears for him when he died. As the morning was very cold, the Sheriff said, would he come down to a fire for a little space, and warm himself? But Sir Walter thanked him, and said no, he would rather it were done at once, for he was ill of fever and ague, and in another quarter of an hour his shaking fit would come upon him if he were still alive, and his enemies might then suppose that he trembled for fear. With that, he kneeled and made a very beautiful and Christian prayer. Before he laid his head upon the block he felt the edge of the axe, and said, with a smile upon his face, that it was a sharp medicine, but would cure the worst disease. When he was bent down ready for death, he said to the executioner, finding that he hesitated, 'What dost thou fear? Strike, man!' So, the axe came down and struck his head off, in the sixty-sixth year of his age.

The new favourite got on fast. He was made a viscount, he was made Duke of Buckingham, he was made a marquis, he was made Master of the Horse, he was made Lord High Admiral – and the Chief Commander of the gallant English forces that had dispersed the Spanish Armada, was displaced to make room for him. He had the whole kingdom at his disposal, and his mother sold all the profits and honours of the State, as if she had kept a shop. He blazed all over with diamonds and other precious stones, from his hatband and his earrings to his shoes. Yet he was an ignorant presumptuous swaggering compound of knave and fool, with nothing but his beauty and his dancing to recommend him. This is the gentleman who called himself his

Majesty's dog and slave, and called his Majesty Your Sowship. His Sowship called him STEENIE; it is supposed, because that was a nickname for Stephen, and because St Stephen was generally represented in pictures as a handsome saint.

His Sowship was driven sometimes to his wits'-end by his trimming between the general dislike of the Catholic religion at home, and his desire to wheedle and flatter it abroad, as his only means of getting a rich princess for his son's wife: a part of whose fortune he might cram into his greasy pockets. Prince Charles – or as his Sowship called him, Baby Charles – being now PRINCE OF WALES, the old project of a marriage with the Spanish King's daughter had been revived for him; and as she could not marry a Protestant without leave from the Pope, his Sowship himself secretly and meanly wrote to his Infallibility, asking for it. The negotiation for this Spanish marriage takes up a larger space in great books, than you can imagine, but the upshot of it all is, that when it had been held off by the Spanish Court for a long time, Baby Charles and Steenie set off in disguise as Mr Thomas Smith and Mr John Smith, to see the Spanish Princess, that Baby Charles pretended to be desperately in love with her, and jumped off walls to look at her, and made a considerable fool of himself in a good many ways; that she was called Princess of Wales, and that the whole Spanish Court believed Baby Charles to be all but dying for her sake, as he expressly told them he was; that Baby Charles and Steenie came back to England, and were received with as much rapture as if they had been a blessing to it; that Baby Charles had actually fallen in love with HENRIETTA MARIA, the French King's sister, whom he had seen in Paris; that he thought it a wonderfully fine and princely thing to have deceived the Spaniards, all through; and that he openly said, with a chuckle, as soon as he was safe and sound at home again, that the Spaniards were great fools to have believed him.

Like most dishonest men, the Prince and the favourite complained that the people whom they had deluded were dishonest. They made such misrepresentations of the treachery of the Spaniards in this business of the Spanish match, that the English nation became eager for a war with them. Although the gravest Spaniards laughed at the idea of his Sowship in a warlike attitude, the Parliament granted money for the beginning of hostilities, and the treaties with Spain were publicly declared to be at an end. The Spanish ambassador in London – probably with the help of the fallen favourite, the Earl of Somerset – being unable to obtain speech with his Sowship, slipped a paper into his hand, declaring that he was a prisoner in his own house, and was entirely governed by Buckingham and his creatures. The first effect of this letter was that his Sowship began to cry and whine, and took Baby Charles away from Steenie, and went down to Windsor, gabbling all sorts of nonsense. The end of it was that his Sowship hugged his dog and slave, and said he was quite satisfied.

He had given the Prince and the favourite almost unlimited power to settle anything with the Pope as to the Spanish marriage; and he now, with a view to the French one, signed a treaty that all Roman Catholics in England should exercise their religion freely, and should never be required to take any oath contrary thereto. In return for this, and for other concessions much less to be defended, Henrietta Maria was to become the Prince's wife, and was to bring him a fortune of eight hundred thousand crowns.

His Sowship's eyes were getting red with eagerly looking for the money, when the end of a gluttonous life came upon him; and, after a fortnight's illness, on Sunday the twenty-seventh of March, one thousand six hundred and twenty-five, he died. He had reigned twenty-two years, and was fifty-nine years old. I know of nothing more abominable in history than the adulation that was lavished on this King, and the vice and corruption that such a barefaced habit of lying produced in his court. It is much to be doubted whether one man of honour, and not utterly self-disgraced, kept his place near James the First. Lord Bacon, that able and wise philosopher, as the First Judge in the Kingdom in this reign, became a public spectacle of dishonesty and corruption; and in his base flattery of his Sowship, and in his crawling servility to his dog and slave, disgraced himself even more. But, a creature like his Sowship set upon a throne is like the Plague, and everybody receives infection from him.

CHAPTER 33

England under Charles the First

First Part

Baby Charles became KING CHARLES THE FIRST, in the twenty-fifth year of his age. Unlike his father he was usually amiable in his private character, and grave and dignified in his bearing; but, like his father, he had monstrously exaggerated notions of the rights of a king, and was evasive, and not to be trusted. If his word could have been relied upon, his history might have had a different end.

His first care was to send over that insolent upstart, Buckingham, to bring Henrietta Maria from Paris to be his Queen; upon which occasion Buckingham — with his usual audacity — made love to the young Queen of Austria, and was very indignant indeed with CARDINAL RICHELIEU, the French Minister, for thwarting his intentions. The English people were very well disposed to like their new Queen, and to receive her with great favour when she came among them as a stranger. But, she held the Protestant religion in great dislike, and brought over a crowd of unpleasant priests, who made her do some very ridiculous things, and forced themselves upon the public notice in many disagreeable ways. Hence, the people soon came to dislike her, and she soon came to dislike them; and she did so much all through this reign in setting the King (who was dotingly fond of her) against his subjects, that it would have been better for him if she had never been born.

Now, you are to understand that King Charles the First — of his own determination to be a high and mighty King not to be called to account by anybody, and urged on by his Queen besides — deliberately set himself to put his Parliament down and to put himself up. You are also to understand, that even in pursuit of this wrong idea (enough in itself to have ruined any king) he never took a straight course, but always took a crooked one.

He was bent upon war with Spain, though neither the House of Commons nor the people were quite clear as to the justice of that war, now that they began to think a little more about the story of the Spanish match. But the King rushed into it hotly, raised money by illegal means to meet its expenses, and encountered a miserable failure at Cadiz, in the very first year of his reign. An expedition to Cadiz had been made in the hope of plunder, but as it was not successful, it was necessary to get a grant of money from the Parliament; and when they met, in no very complying humour, the King told them, 'to make haste to let him have it, or it would be the worse for themselves.' Not put in a more complying humour by this, they impeached the King's favourite, the Duke of Buckingham, as the cause (which he undoubtedly was) of many great public grievances and wrongs. The King, to save him, dissolved the Parliament without getting the money he wanted; and when the Lords implored him to consider and grant a little delay, he replied, 'No, not one minute.' He then began to raise money for himself by the following means among others.

He levied certain duties called tonnage and poundage which had not been granted by the Parliament, and could lawfully be levied by no other power; he called upon the seaport towns to furnish, and to pay all the cost for three months of, a fleet of armed ships; and he required the people to unite in lending him large sums of money, the repayment of which was very doubtful. If the poor people refused, they were pressed as soldiers or sailors; if the gentry refused, they were sent to prison. Five gentlemen, named SIR THOMAS DARNEL, JOHN CORBET, WALTER EARL, JOHN HEVENINGHAM, and EVERARD HAMP-DEN, for refusing were taken up by a warrant of the King's privy council, and were sent to prison without any cause but the King's pleasure being stated for their imprisonment. Then the question came to be solemnly tried, whether this was not a violation of Magna Charta, and an encroachment by the King on the highest rights of the English people. His lawyers contended No, because to encroach upon the rights of the English people would be to do wrong, and the King could do no wrong. The accommodating judges decided in favour of this wicked nonsense; and here was a fatal division between the King and the people.

For all this, it became necessary to call another Parliament. The people, sensible of the danger in which their liberties were, chose for it those who were best known for their determined opposition to the King; but still the King, quite blinded by his determination to carry everything before him, addressed them when they met, in a contemptuous manner, and just told them in so many words that he had only called them together because he wanted money. The Parliament, strong enough and resolute enough to know that they would lower his tone, cared little for what he said, and laid before him one of the great documents of history, which is called the PETITION OF RIGHT, requiring that the free men of England should no longer be called upon to lend the King money, and should no longer be pressed or imprisoned for refusing to do so; further, that the free men of England should no longer be seized by the King's special mandate or warrant, it being contrary to their rights and liberties and the laws of their country. At first the King returned an answer to this petition, in which he tried to shirk it altogether; but, the House of Commons then showing their determination to go on with the impeachment of Buckingham, the King in alarm returned an answer, giving his consent to all that was required of him. He not only afterwards departed from his word and honour on these points, over and over again, but, at this very time, he did the mean and dissembling act of publishing his first answer and not his second – merely that the people might suppose that the Parliament had not got the better of him.

That pestilent Buckingham, to gratify his own wounded vanity, had by this time involved the country in war with France, as well as with Spain. For such miserable causes and such miserable creatures are wars sometimes made! But he was destined to do little more mischief in this world. One morning, as he was going out of his house to his carriage, he turned to speak to a certain Colonel FRYER who was with him; and he was violently stabbed with a knife, which the murderer left sticking in his heart. This happened in his hall. He had had angry words up-stairs, just before, with some French gentlemen, who were immediately suspected by his servants, and had a close escape from being set upon and killed. In the midst of the noise, the real murderer, who had gone to the kitchen and might easily have got away, drew his sword and cried out, 'I am the man!' His name was JOHN FELTON, a Protestant and a retired officer in the army. He said he had had no personal ill-will to the Duke, but had killed him as a curse to the country. He had aimed his blow well, for Buckingham had only had time to cry out, 'Villain!' and then he drew out the knife, fell against a table, and died.

The council made a mighty business of examining John Felton about this murder, though it was a plain case enough, one would think. He had come seventy miles to do it, he told them, and he did it for the reason he had declared; if they put him upon the rack, as that noble MARQUIS OF DORSET whom he saw before him, had the goodness to threaten, he gave that marquis warning, that he would accuse *him* as his accomplice! The King was unpleasantly anxious to have him racked, nevertheless; but as the judges now found out that torture was contrary to the law of England – it is a pity they did not make the discovery a little sooner – John Felton was simply executed for the murder he had done. A murder it undoubtedly was, and not in the least to be defended: though he had freed England from one of the most profligate, contemptible, and base court favourites to whom it has ever yielded.

A very different man now arose. This was SIR THOMAS WENTWORTH, a Yorkshire gentleman, who had sat in Parliament for a long time, and who had favoured arbitrary and haughty principles, but who had gone over to the people's side on receiving offence from Buckingham. The King, much wanting such a man – for, besides being naturally favourable to the King's cause, he had great abilities – made him first a Baron, and then a Viscount, and gave him high employment, and won him most completely.

A Parliament, however, was still in existence, and was *not* to be won. On the twentieth of January, one thousand six hundred and twenty-nine, SIR JOHN ELIOT, a great man who had been active in the Petition of Right, brought forward other strong resolutions against the King's chief instruments, and called upon the Speaker to put them to the vote. To this the Speaker answered, 'he was commanded otherwise by the King,' and he got up to leave the chair – which, according to the rules of the House of Commons would have obliged it to adjourn without doing anything more – when two members, named Mr HOLLIS and Mr VALENTINE, held him down. A scene of great confusion arose among the members; and while many swords were drawn and flashing about, the King, who was kept informed of all that was going on, told the captain of his guard to go down to the House and force the doors. The resolutions were by that time, however, voted, and the House adjourned. Sir John Eliot and those two members who had held the Speaker down, were quickly summoned before the council. As they claimed it to be their privilege not to answer out of Parliament for anything they had said in it, they were committed to the Tower. The King then went down and dissolved the Parliament, in a speech wherein he made mention of these gentlemen as 'Vipers'—which did not do him much good that ever I have heard of.

As they refused to gain their liberty by saying they were sorry for what they had done, the King, always remarkably unforgiving, never overlooked their offence. When they demanded to be brought up before the court of King's Bench, he even resorted to the meanness of having them moved about from prison to prison, so that the writs issued for that purpose should not legally find them. At last they came before the court and were sentenced to heavy fines, and to be imprisoned during the King's pleasure. When Sir John Eliot's health had quite given way, and he so longed for change of air and scene as to petition for his release, the King sent back the answer (worthy of his Sowship himself) that the petition was not humble enough. When he sent another petition by his young son, in which he pathetically offered to go back to prison when his health was restored, if he might be released for its recovery, the King still disregarded it. When he died in the Tower, and his children petitioned to be allowed to take his body down to Cornwall, there to lay it among the ashes of his forefathers, the King returned for answer, 'Let Sir John Eliot's body be buried in the church of that parish where he died.' All this was like a very little King indeed, I think.

And now, for twelve long years, steadily pursuing his design of setting himself up and putting the people down, the King called no Parliament; but ruled without one. If twelve thousand volumes were written in his praise (as a good many have been) it would still remain a fact, impossible to be denied, that for twelve years King Charles the First reigned in England unlawfully and despotically, seized upon his subjects' goods and money at his pleasure, and punished according to his unbridled will all who ventured to oppose him. It is a fashion with some people to think that this King's career was cut short; but I must say myself that I think he ran a pretty long one.

WILLIAM LAUD, Archbishop of Canterbury, was the King's right-hand man in the religious part of the putting down of the people's liberties. Laud, who was a sincere man, of large learning but small sense – for the two things sometimes go together in very different quantities – though a Protestant, held opinions so near those of the Catholics, that the Pope wanted to make a Cardinal of him, if he would have accepted that favour. He looked upon vows, robes, lighted candles, images, and so forth, as amazingly important in religious ceremonies; and he brought in an immensity of bowing and candle-snuffing. He also regarded archbishops and bishops as a sort of miraculous persons, and was inveterate in the last degree against any who thought otherwise. Accordingly, he offered up thanks to Heaven, and was in a state of much pious pleasure, when a Scotch clergyman, named LEIGHTON, was pilloried, whipped, branded in the cheek, and had one of his ears cut off and one of his nostrils slit, for calling bishops trumpery and the inventions of men. He originated on a Sunday morning the prosecution of WILLIAM PRYNNE, a barrister who was of similar opinions, and who was fined a thousand pounds; who was pilloried; who had his ears cut off on two occasions – one ear at a time – and who was imprisoned for life. He highly approved of the punishment of DOCTOR BASTWICK, a physician; who was also fined a thousand pounds; and who afterwards had *his* ears cut off, and was imprisoned for life. These were gentle methods of persuasion, some will tell you: I think, they were rather calculated to be alarming to the people.

In the money part of the putting down of the people's liberties, the King was equally gentle, as some will tell you: as I think, equally alarming. He levied those duties of tonnage and pound-age, and increased them as he thought fit. He granted monopolies to companies of merchants on their paying him for them, notwithstanding the great complaints that had, for years and years, been made on the subject of monopolies. He fined the people for disobeying proclamations issued by his Sowship in direct violation of law. He revived the detested Forest laws, and took private property to himself as his forest right. Above all, he determined to have what was called Ship Money; that is to say, money for the support of the fleet – not only from the seaports, but from all the counties of England: having found out that, in some ancient time or other, all the counties paid it. The grievance of this ship money being somewhat too strong, JOHN CHAMBERS, a citizen of London, refused to pay his part of it.

For this the Lord Mayor ordered John Chambers to prison, and for that John Chambers brought a suit against the Lord Mayor. LORD SAY, also, behaved like a real nobleman, and declared he would not pay. But, the sturdiest and best opponent of the ship money was JOHN HAMPDEN, a gentleman of Buckinghamshire, who had sat among the 'vipers' in the House of Commons when there was such a thing, and who had been the bosom friend of Sir John Eliot. This case was tried before the twelve judges in the Court of Exchequer, and again the King's lawyers said it was impossible that ship money could be wrong, because the King could do no wrong, however hard he tried – and he really did try very hard during these twelve years. Seven of the judges said that was quite true, and Mr Hampden was bound to pay: five of the judges said that was quite false, and Mr Hampden was not bound to pay. So, the King triumphed (as he thought), by making Hampden the most popular man in England; where matters were getting to that height now, that many honest Englishmen could not endure their country, and sailed away across the seas to found a colony in Massachusetts Bay in America. It is said that Hampden himself and his relation OLIVER CROMWELL were going with a company of such voyagers, and were actually on board ship, when they were stopped by a proclamation, prohibiting sea captains to carry out such passengers without the royal license. But O! it would have been well for the King if he had let them go!

This was the state of England. If Laud had been a madman just broke loose, he could not have done more mischief than he did in Scotland. In his endeavours (in which he was seconded by the King, then in person in that part of his dominions) to force his own ideas of bishops, and his own religious forms and ceremonies upon the Scotch, he roused that nation to a perfect frenzy. They formed a solemn league, which they called The Covenant, for the preservation of their own religious forms; they rose in arms throughout the whole country; they summoned all their men to prayers and sermons twice a day by beat of drum; they sang psalms, in which they compared their enemies to all the evil spirits that ever were heard of; and they solemnly vowed to smite them with the sword. At first the King tried force, then treaty, then a Scottish Parliament which did not answer at all. Then he tried the EARL OF STRAFFORD, formerly Sir Thomas Wentworth; who, as LORD WENTWORTH, had been governing Ireland. He, too, had carried it with a very high hand there, though to the benefit and prosperity of that country.

Strafford and Laud were for conquering the Scottish people by force of arms. Other lords who were taken into council, recommended that a Parliament should at last be called; to which the King unwillingly consented. So, on the thirteenth of April, one thousand six hundred and forty, that then strange sight, a Parliament, was seen at Westminster. It is called the Short Parliament, for it lasted a very little while. While the members were all looking at one another, doubtful who would dare to speak, Mr PYM arose and set forth all that the King had done unlawfully during the past twelve years, and what was the position to which England was reduced. This great example set, other members took courage and spoke the truth freely, though with great patience and moderation. The King, a little frightened, sent to say that if they would grant him a certain sum on certain terms, no more ship money should be raised. They debated the matter for two days; and then, as they would not give him all he asked without promise or inquiry, he dissolved them.

But they knew very well that he must have a Parliament now; and he began to make that discovery too, though rather late in the day. Wherefore, on the twenty-fourth of September, being then at York with an army collected against the Scottish people, but his own men sullen and discontented like the rest of the nation, the King told the great council of the Lords, whom he had called to meet him there, that he would summon another Parliament to assemble on the third of November. The soldiers of the Covenant had now forced their way into England and had taken possession of the northern counties, where the coals are got. As it would never do to be without coals, and as the King's troops could make no head against the Covenanters so full of gloomy zeal, a truce was made, and a treaty with Scotland was taken into consideration. Meanwhile the northern counties paid the Covenanters to leave the coals alone, and keep quiet.

We have now disposed of the Short Parliament. We have next to see what memorable things were done by the Long one.

Second Part

The Long Parliament assembled on the third of November, one thousand six hundred and forty-one. That day week the Earl of

Strafford arrived from York, very sensible that the spirited and determined men who formed that Parliament were no friends towards him, who had not only deserted the cause of the people, but who had on all occasions opposed himself to their liberties. The King told him, for his comfort, that the Parliament 'should not hurt one hair of his head.' But, on the very next day Mr Pym, in the House of Commons, and with great solemnity, impeached the Earl of Strafford as a traitor. He was immediately taken into custody and fell from his proud height.

It was the twenty-second of March before he was brought to trial in Westminster Hall; where, although he was very ill and suffered great pain, he defended himself with such ability and majesty, that it was doubtful whether he would not get the best of it. But on the thirteenth day of the trial, Pym produced in the House of Commons a copy of some notes of a council, found by young SIR HARRY VANE in a red velvet cabinet belonging to his father (Secretary Vane, who sat at the council-table with the Earl), in which Strafford had distinctly told the King that he was free from all rules and obligations of government, and might do with his people whatever he liked; and in which he had added – 'You have an army in Ireland that you may employ to reduce this kingdom to obedience.' It was not clear whether by the words 'this kingdom' he had really meant England or Scotland; but the Parliament contended that he meant England, and this was treason. At the same sitting of the House of Commons it was resolved to bring in a bill of attainder declaring the treason to have been committed: in preference to proceeding with the trial by impeachment, which would have required the treason to be proved.

So, a bill was brought in at once, was carried through the House of Commons by a large majority, and was sent up to the House of Lords. While it was still uncertain whether the House of Lords would pass it and the King consent to it, Pym disclosed to the House of Commons that the King and Queen had both been plotting with the officers of the army to bring up the soldiers and control the Parliament, and also to introduce two hundred soldiers into the Tower of London to effect the Earl's escape. The plotting with the army was revealed by one GEORGE GORING, the son of a lord of that name: a bad fellow who was one of the original plotters, and turned traitor. The King had actually given his warrant for the admission of the two hundred men into the Tower, and they would have got in too, but for the refusal of the governor – a sturdy Scotchman of the name of BALFOUR – to admit them. These matters being made public, great numbers of people began to riot outside the Houses of Parliament, and to cry out for the execution of the Earl of Strafford, as one of the King's chief instruments against them. The bill passed the House of Lords while the people were in this state of agitation, and was laid before the King for his assent, together with another bill declaring that the Parliament then assembled should not be dissolved or adjourned without their own consent. The King – not unwilling to save a faithful servant, though he had no great attachment for him – was in some doubt what to do; but he gave his consent to both bills, although he in his heart believed that the bill against the Earl of Strafford was unlawful and unjust. The Earl had written to him, telling him that he was willing to die for his sake. But he had not expected that his royal master would take him at his word quite so readily; for, when he heard his doom, he laid his hand upon his heart, and said, 'Put not your trust in Princes!'

The King, who never could be straightforward and plain, through one single day or through one single sheet of paper, wrote a letter to the Lords, and sent it by the young Prince of Wales, entreating them to prevail with the Commons that 'that unfortunate man should fulfil the natural course of his life in a close imprisonment.' In a postscript to the very same letter, he added, 'If he must die, it were charity to reprieve him till Saturday.' If there had been any doubt of his fate, this weakness and meanness would have settled it. The very next day, which was the twelfth of May, he was brought out to be beheaded on Tower Hill.

Archbishop Laud, who had been so fond of having people's ears cropped off and their noses slit, was now confined in the Tower too; and when the Earl went by his window to his death, he was there, at his request, to give him his blessing. They had been great friends in the King's cause, and the Earl had written to him in the days of their power that he thought it would be an admirable thing to have Mr Hampden publicly whipped for refusing to pay the ship money. However, those high and mighty doings were over now, and the Earl went his way to death with dignity and heroism. The governor wished him to get into a coach at the Tower gate, for fear the people should tear him to pieces; but he said it was all one to him whether he died by the axe or by the people's hands. So, he walked, with a firm tread and a stately look, and sometimes pulled off his hat to them as he passed along. They were profoundly quiet. He made a speech on the scaffold from some notes he had prepared (the paper was found lying there after his head was struck off), and one blow of the axe killed him, in the forty-ninth year of his age.

This bold and daring act, the Parliament accompanied by other famous measures, all originating (as even this did) in the King's having so grossly and so long abused his power. The name of DELINQUENTS was applied to all sheriffs and other officers who had been concerned in raising the ship money, or any other money, from the people, in an unlawful manner; the Hampden judgment was reversed; the judges who had decided against Hampden were called upon to give large securities that they would take such consequences as Parliament might impose upon them; and one was arrested as he sat in High Court, and carried off to prison. Laud was impeached; the unfortunate victims whose ears had been cropped and whose noses had been slit, were brought out of prison in triumph; and a bill was passed declaring that a Parliament should be called every third year, and that if the King and the King's officers did not call it, the people should assemble of themselves and summon it, as of their own right and power. Great illuminations and rejoicings took place over all these things, and the country was wildly excited. That the Parliament took advantage of this excitement and stirred them up by every means, there is no doubt; but you are always to remember those twelve long years, during which the King had tried so hard whether he really could do any wrong or not.

All this time there was a great religious outcry against the right of the Bishops to sit in Parliament; to which the Scottish people particularly objected. The English were divided on this subject, and, partly on this account and partly because they had had foolish expectations that the Parliament would be able to take off nearly all the taxes, numbers of them sometimes wavered and inclined towards the King.

I believe myself, that if, at this or almost any other period of his life, the King could have been trusted by any man not out of his senses, he might have saved himself and kept his throne. But, on the English army being disbanded, he plotted with the officers again, as he had done before, and established the fact beyond all doubt by putting his signature of approval to a petition against the Parliamentary leaders, which was drawn up by certain officers. When the Scottish army was disbanded, he went to Edinburgh in four days – which was going very fast at that time – to plot again, and so darkly too, that it is difficult to decide what his whole object was. Some suppose that he wanted to gain over the Scottish Parliament, as he did in fact gain over, by presents and favours, many Scottish lords and men of power. Some think that he went to get proofs against the Parliamentary leaders in England of their having treasonably invited the Scottish people to come and help them. With whatever object he went to Scotland, he did little good by going. At the instigation of the EARL OF MONTROSE, a desperate man who was then in prison for plotting, he tried to kidnap three Scottish lords who escaped. A committee of the Parliament at home, who had followed to watch him, writing an account of this INCIDENT, as it was called, to the Parliament, the Parliament made a fresh stir about it; were, or feigned to be, much alarmed for themselves; and wrote to the EARL OF ESSEX, the commander-in-chief, for a guard to protect them.

It is not absolutely proved that the King plotted in Ireland besides, but it is very probable that he did, and that the Queen did, and that he had some wild hope of gaining the Irish people over to his side by favouring a rise among them. Whether or no, they did rise in a most brutal and savage rebellion; in which, encouraged by their priests, they committed such atrocities upon numbers of the English, of both sexes and of all ages, as nobody could believe, but for their being related on oath by eyewitnesses. Whether one hundred thousand or two hundred thousand Protestants were murdered in this outbreak, is uncertain; but, that it was as ruthless and barbarous an outbreak as ever was known among any savage people, is certain.

The King came home from Scotland, determined to make a great struggle for his lost power. He believed that, through his presents and favours, Scotland would take no part against him; and the Lord Mayor of London received him with such a magnificent dinner that he thought he must have become popular again in England. It would take a good many Lord Mayors, however, to make a people, and the King soon found himself mistaken.

Not so soon, though, but that there was a great opposition in the Parliament to a celebrated paper put forth by Pym and Hampden and the rest, called 'THE REMONSTRANCE,' which set forth all the illegal acts that the King had ever done, but politely laid the blame of them on his bad advisers. Even when it was passed and presented to him, the King still thought himself strong enough to discharge Balfour from his command in the Tower, and to put in his place a man of bad character; to whom the Commons instantly objected, and whom he was obliged to abandon. At this time, the old outcry about the Bishops became louder than ever, and the old Archbishop of York was so near being murdered as he went down to the House of Lords – being laid hold of by the mob and violently knocked about, in return for very foolishly scolding a shrill boy who was yelping out 'No Bishops!' – that he sent for all the Bishops who were in town, and proposed to them to sign a declaration that, as they could no longer without danger to their lives attend their duty in Parliament, they protested against the lawfulness of everything done in their absence. This they asked the King to send to the House of Lords, which he did. Then the House of Commons impeached the whole party of Bishops and sent them off to the Tower.

Taking no warning from this, but encouraged by there being a moderate party in the Parliament who objected to these strong measures, the King, on the third of January, one thousand six hundred and forty-two, took the rashest step that ever was taken by mortal man.

Of his own accord and without advice, he sent the Attorney-General to the House of Lords, to accuse of treason certain members of Parliament who as popular leaders were the most obnoxious to him; LORD KIMBOLTON, SIR ARTHUR HASEL-RIG, DENZIL HOLLIS, JOHN PYM (they used to call him King Pym, he possessed such power and looked so big), JOHN HAMPDEN, and WILLIAM STRODE. The houses of those members he caused to be entered, and their papers to be sealed up. At the same time, he sent a messenger to the House of Commons demanding to have the five gentlemen who were members of that House immediately produced. To this the House replied that they should appear as soon as there was any legal charge against them, and immediately adjourned.

Next day, the House of Commons sent into the City to let the

Lord Mayor know that their privileges are invaded by the King, and that there is no safety for anybody or anything. Then, when the five members are gone out of the way, down comes the King himself, with all his guard and from two to three hundred gentlemen and soldiers, of whom the greater part were armed. These he leaves in the hall; and then, with his nephew at his side, goes into the House, takes off his hat, and walks up to the Speaker's chair. The Speaker leaves it, the King stands in front of it, looks about him steadily for a little while, and says he has come for those five members. No one speaks, and then he calls John Pym by name. No one speaks, and then he calls Denzil Hollis by name. No one speaks, and then he asks the Speaker of the House where those five members are? The Speaker, answering on his knee, nobly replies that he is the servant of that House, and that he has neither eyes to see, nor tongue to speak, anything but what the House commands him. Upon this, the King, beaten from that time evermore, replies that he will seek them himself, for they have committed treason; and goes out, with his hat in his hand, amid some audible murmurs from the members.

No words can describe the hurry that arose out of doors when all this was known. The five members had gone for safety to a house in Coleman-street, in the City, where they were guarded all night; and indeed the whole city watched in arms like an army. At ten o'clock in the morning, the King, already frightened at what he had done, came to the Guildhall, with only half a dozen lords, and made a speech to the people, hoping they would not shelter those whom he accused of treason. Next day, he issued a proclamation for the apprehension of the five members; but the Parliament minded it so little that they made great arrangements for having them brought down to Westminster in great state, five days afterwards. The King was so alarmed now at his own imprudence, if not for his own safety, that he left his palace at Whitehall, and went away with his Queen and children to Hampton Court.

It was the eleventh of May, when the five members were carried in state and triumph to Westminster. They were taken by water. The river could not be seen for the boats on it; and the five members were hemmed in by barges full of men and great guns, ready to protect them, at any cost. Along the Strand a large body of the train-bands of London, under their commander, SKIPPON, marched to be ready to assist the little fleet. Beyond them, came a crowd who choked the streets, roaring incessantly about the Bishops and the Papists, and crying out contemptuously as they passed Whitehall, 'What has become of the King?' With this great noise outside the House of Commons, and with great silence within, Mr Pym rose and informed the House of the great kindness with which they had been received in the City. Upon that, the House called the sheriffs in and thanked them, and requested the train-bands, under their commander Skippon, to guard the House of Commons every day. Then, came four thousand men on horseback out of Buckinghamshire, offering their services as a guard too, and bearing a petition to the King, complaining of the injury that had been done to Mr Hampden, who was their county man and much beloved and honoured.

When the King set off for Hampton Court, the gentlemen and soldiers who had been with him followed him out of town as far as Kingston-upon-Thames; next day, Lord Digby came to them from the King at Hampton Court, in his coach and six, to inform them that the King accepted their protection. This, the Parliament said, was making war against the kingdom, and Lord Digby fled abroad. The Parliament then immediately applied themselves to getting hold of the military power of the country, well knowing that the King was already trying hard to use it against them, and that he had secretly sent the Earl of Newcastle to Hull, to secure a valuable magazine of arms and gunpowder that was there. In those times, every county had its own magazines of arms and powder, for its own train-bands or militia; so, the Parliament brought in a bill claiming the right (which up to this time had belonged to the King) of appointing the Lord Lieutenants of counties, who commanded these train-bands; also, of having all the forts, castles, and garrisons in the kingdom, put into the hands of such governors as they, the Parliament, could confide in. It also passed a law depriving the Bishops of their votes. The King gave his assent to that bill, but would not abandon the right of appointing the Lord Lieutenants, though he said he was willing to appoint such as might be suggested to him by the Parliament. When the Earl of Pembroke asked him whether he would not give way on that question for a time, he said, 'By God! not for one hour!' and upon this he and the Parliament went to war.

His young daughter was betrothed to the Prince of Orange. On pretence of taking her to the country of her future husband, the Queen was already got safely away to Holland, there to pawn the Crown jewels for money to raise an army on the King's side. The Lord Admiral being sick, the House of Commons now named the Earl of Warwick to hold his place for a year. The King named another gentleman; the House of Commons took its own way, and the Earl of Warwick became Lord Admiral without the King's consent. The Parliament sent orders down to Hull to have that magazine removed to London; the King went down to Hull to take it himself. The citizens would not admit him into the town, and the governor would not admit him into the castle. The Parliament resolved that whatever the two Houses passed, and the King would not consent to, should be called an ORDINANCE, and should be as much a law as if he did consent to it. The King protested against this, and gave notice that these ordinances were not to be obeyed. The King, attended by the majority of the House of Peers, and by many members of the House of Commons, established himself at York. The Chancellor went to him with the Great Seal, and the Parliament made a new Great Seal. The Queen sent over a ship full of arms and ammunition, and the King issued letters to borrow money at high interest. The Parliament raised twenty regiments of foot and seventy-five troops of horse; and the people willingly aided them with their money, plate, jewellery, and trinkets – the married women even with their wedding-rings. Every member of Parliament who could raise a troop or a regiment in his own part of the country, dressed it according to his taste and in his own colours, and commanded it. Foremost among them all, OLIVER CROMWELL raised a troop of horse – thoroughly in earnest and thoroughly well armed – who were, perhaps, the best soldiers that ever were seen.

In some of their proceedings, this famous Parliament passed the bounds of previous law and custom, yielded to and favoured riotous assemblages of the people, and acted tyrannically in imprisoning some who differed from the popular leaders. But again, you are always to remember that the twelve years during which the King had had his own wilful way, had gone before; and that nothing could make the times what they might, could, would, or should have been, if those twelve years had never rolled away.

Third Part

I shall not try to relate the particulars of the great civil war between King Charles the First and the Long Parliament, which lasted nearly four years, and a full account of which would fill many large books. It was a sad thing that Englishmen should once more be fighting against Englishmen on English ground; but, it is some consolation to know that on both sides there was great humanity, forbearance, and honour. The soldiers of the Parliament were far more remarkable for these good qualities than the soldiers of the King (many of whom fought for mere pay without much caring for the cause); but those of the nobility and gentry who were on the King's side were so brave, and so faithful to him, that their conduct cannot but command our highest admiration. Among them were great numbers of Catholics, who took the royal side because the Queen was so strongly of their persuasion.

The King might have distinguished some of these gallant spirits, if he had been as generous a spirit himself, by giving them the command of his army. Instead of that, however, true to his old high notions of royalty, he entrusted it to his two nephews, PRINCE RUPERT and PRINCE MAURICE, who were of royal blood and came over from abroad to help him. It might have been better for him if they had stayed away; since Prince Rupert was an impetuous hot-headed fellow, whose only idea was to dash into battle at all times and seasons, and lay about him.

The general-in-chief of the Parliamentary army was the Earl of Essex, a gentleman of honour and an excellent soldier. A little while before the war broke out, there had been some rioting at Westminster between certain officious law students and noisy soldiers, and the shopkeepers and their apprentices, and the general people in the streets. At that time the King's friends called the crowd, Roundheads, because the apprentices wore short hair; the crowd, in return, called their opponents Cavaliers, meaning that they were a blustering set, who pretended to be very military. These two words now began to be used to distinguish the two sides in the civil war. The Royalists also called the Parliamentary men Rebels and Rogues, while the Parliamentary men called *them* Malignants, and spoke of themselves as the Godly, the Honest, and so forth.

The war broke out at Portsmouth, where that double traitor

Goring had again gone over to the King and was besieged by the Parliamentary troops. Upon this, the King proclaimed the Earl of Essex and the officers serving under him, traitors, and called upon his loyal subjects to meet him in arms at Nottingham on the twenty-fifth of August. But his loyal subjects came about him in scanty numbers, and it was a windy gloomy day, and the Royal Standard got blown down, and the whole affair was very melancholy. The chief engagements after this, took place in the vale of the Red Horse near Banbury, at Brentford, at Devizes, at Chalgrove Field (where Mr Hampden was so sorely wounded while fighting at the head of his men, that he died within a week), at Newbury (in which battle LORD FALKLAND, one of the best noblemen on the King's side, was killed), at Leicester, at Naseby, at Winchester, at Marston Moor near York, at Newcastle, and in many other parts of England and Scotland. These battles were attended with various successes. At one time, the King was victorious; at another time, the Parliament. But almost all the great and busy towns were against the King; and when it was considered necessary to fortify London, all ranks of people, from labouring men and women, up to lords and ladies, worked hard together with heartiness and good will. The most distinguished leaders on the Parliamentary side were HAMPDEN, SIR THOMAS FAIRFAX, and, above all, OLIVER CROMWELL, and his son-in-law IRETON.

During the whole of this war, the people, to whom it was very expensive and irksome, and to whom it was made the more distressing by almost every family being divided – some of its members attaching themselves to one side and some to the other – were over and over again most anxious for peace. So were some of the best men in each cause. Accordingly, treaties of peace were discussed between commissioners from the Parliament and the King; at York, at Oxford (where the King held a little Parliament of his own), and at Uxbridge. But they came to nothing. In all these negotiations, and in all his difficulties, the King showed himself at his best. He was courageous, cool, self-possessed, and clever; but, the old taint of his character was always in him, and he was never for one single moment to be trusted. Lord Clarendon, the historian, one of his highest admirers, supposes that he had unhappily promised the Queen never to make peace without her consent, and that this must often be taken as his excuse. He never kept his word from night to morning. He signed a cessation of hostilities with the blood-stained Irish rebels for a sum of money, and invited the Irish regiments over, to help him against the Parliament. In the battle of Naseby, his cabinet was seized and was found to contain a correspondence with the Queen, in which he expressly told her that he had deceived the Parliament – a mongrel Parliament, he called it now, as an improvement on his old term of vipers – in pretending to recognise it and to treat with it; and from which it further appeared that he had long been in secret treaty with the Duke of Lorraine for a foreign army of ten thousand men. Disappointed in this, he sent a most devoted friend of his, the EARL OF GLAMORGAN, to Ireland, to conclude a secret treaty with the Catholic powers, to send him an Irish army of ten thousand men; in return for which he was to bestow great favours on the Catholic religion. And, when this treaty was discovered in the carriage of a fighting Irish Archbishop who was killed in one of the many skirmishes of those days, he basely denied and deserted his attached friend, the Earl, on his being charged with high treason; and – even worse than this – had left blanks in the secret instructions he gave him with his own kingly hand, expressly that he might thus save himself.

At last, on the twenty-seventh day of April, one thousand six hundred and forty-six, the King found himself in the city of Oxford, so surrounded by the Parliamentary army who were closing in upon him on all sides that he felt that if he would escape he must delay no longer. So, that night, having altered the cut of his hair and beard, he was dressed up as a servant and put upon a horse with a cloak strapped behind him, and rode out of the town behind one of his own faithful followers, with a clergyman of that country who knew the road well, for a guide. He rode towards London as far as Harrow, and then altered his plans and resolved, it would seem, to go to the Scottish camp. The Scottish men had been invited over to help the Parliamentary army, and had a large force then in England. The King was so desperately intriguing in everything he did, that it is doubtful what he exactly meant by this step. He took it, anyhow, and delivered himself up to the EARL OF LEVEN, the Scottish general-in-chief, who treated him as an honourable prisoner. Negotiations between the Parliament on the one hand and the Scottish authorities on the other, as to what should be done with him, lasted until the following February. Then, when the King had refused to the Parliament the concession of that old militia point for twenty years, and had refused to Scotland the recognition of its Solemn League and Covenant, Scotland got a handsome sum for its army and its help, and the King into the bargain. He was taken, by certain Parliamentary commissioners appointed to receive him, to one of his own houses, called Holmby House, near Althorpe, in Northamptonshire.

While the Civil War was still in progress, John Pym died, and was buried with great honour in Westminster Abbey – not with greater honour than he deserved, for the liberties of Englishmen owe a mighty debt to Pym and Hampden. The war was but newly over when the Earl of Essex died, of an illness brought on by his having over-heated himself in a stag hunt in Windsor Forest. He, too, was buried in Westminster Abbey, with great state. I wish it were not necessary to add that Archbishop Laud died upon the scaffold when the war was not yet done. His trial lasted in all nearly a year, and, it being doubtful even then whether the charges brought against him amounted to treason, the odious old contrivance of the worst kings was resorted to, and a bill of attainder was brought in against him. He was a violently prejudiced and mischievous person; had had strong ear-cropping and nose-splitting propensities, as you know; and had done a world of harm. But he died peaceably, and like a brave old man.

Fourth Part

When the Parliament had got the King into their hands, they became very anxious to get rid of their army, in which Oliver Cromwell had begun to acquire great power; not only because of his courage and high abilities, but because he professed to be very sincere in the Scottish sort of Puritan religion that was then exceedingly popular among the soldiers. They were as much opposed to the Bishops as to the Pope himself; and the very privates, drummers, and trumpeters, had such an inconvenient habit of starting up and preaching long-winded discourses, that I would not have belonged to that army on any account.

So, the Parliament, being far from sure but that the army might begin to preach and fight against them now it had nothing else to do, proposed to disband the greater part of it, to send another part to serve in Ireland against the rebels, and to keep only a small force in England. But, the army would not consent to be broken up, except upon its own conditions; and, when the Parliament showed an intention of compelling it, it acted for itself in an unexpected manner. A certain cornet, of the name of JOICE, arrived at Holmby House one night, attended by four hundred horsemen, went into the King's room with his hat in one hand and a pistol in the other, and told the King that he had come to take him away. The King was willing enough to go, and only stipulated that he should be publicly required to do so next morning. Next morning, accordingly, he appeared on the top of the steps of the house, and asked Cornet Joice before his men and the guard set there by the Parliament, what authority he had for taking him away? To this Cornet Joice replied, 'The authority of the army.' 'Have you a written commission?' said the King. Joice, pointing to his four hundred men on horseback, replied, 'That is my commission.' 'Well,' said the King, smiling, as if he were pleased, 'I never before read such a commission; but it is written in fair and legible characters. This is a company of as handsome proper gentlemen as I have seen a long while.' He was asked where he would like to live, and he said at Newmarket. So, to Newmarket he and Cornet Joice and the four hundred horsemen rode; the King remarking, in the same smiling way, that he could ride as far at a spell as Cornet Joice, or any man there.

The King quite believed, I think, that the army were his friends. He said as much to Fairfax when that general, Oliver Cromwell, and Ireton, went to persuade him to return to the custody of the Parliament. He preferred to remain as he was, and resolved to remain as he was. And when the army moved nearer and nearer London to frighten the Parliament into yielding to their demands, they took the King with them. It was a deplorable thing that England should be at the mercy of a great body of soldiers with arms in their hands; but the King certainly favoured them at this important time of his life, as compared with the more lawful power that tried to control him. It must be added, however, that they treated him, as yet, more respectfully and kindly than the Parliament had done. They allowed him to be attended by his own servants, to be splendidly entertained at various houses, and to see his children — at Caversham House, near Reading — for two days. Whereas, the Parliament had been rather hard with him, and had only allowed him to ride out and play at bowls.

It is much to be believed that if the King could have been trusted, even at this time, he might have been saved. Even Oliver Cromwell expressly said that he did believe that no man could enjoy his possessions in peace, unless the King had his rights. He was not unfriendly towards the King; he had been present when he received his children, and had been much affected by the pitiable nature of the scene; he saw the King often; he frequently walked and talked with him in the long galleries and pleasant gardens of the Palace at Hampton Court, whither he was now removed; and in all this risked something of his influence with the army. But, the King was in secret hopes of help from the Scottish people; and the moment he was encouraged to join them he began to be cool to his new friends, the army, and to tell the officers that they could not possibly do without him. At the very time, too, when he was promising to make Cromwell and Ireton noblemen, if they would help him up to his old height, he was writing to the Queen that he meant to hang them. They both afterwards declared that they had been privately informed that such a letter would be found, on a certain evening, sewed up in a saddle which would be taken to the Blue Boar in Holborn to be sent to Dover; and that they went there, disguised as common soldiers, and sat drinking in the inn-yard until a man came with the saddle, which they ripped up with their knives, and therein found the letter. I see little reason to doubt the story. It is certain that Oliver Cromwell told one of the King's most faithful followers that the King could not be trusted, and that he would not be answerable if anything amiss were to happen to him. Still, even after that, he kept a promise he had made to the King, by letting him know that there was a plot with a certain portion of the army to seize him. I believe that, in fact, he sincerely wanted the King to escape abroad, and so to be got rid of without more trouble or danger. That Oliver himself had work enough with the army is pretty plain; for some of the troops were so mutinous against him, and against those who acted with him at this time, that he found it necessary to have one man shot at the head of his regiment to overawe the rest.

The King, when he received Oliver's warning, made his escape from Hampton Court; after some indecision and uncertainty, he went to Carisbrooke Castle in the Isle of Wight. At first, he was pretty free there; but, even there, he carried on a pretended treaty with the Parliament, while he was really treating with commissioners from Scotland to send an army into England to take his part. When he broke off this treaty with the Parliament (having settled with Scotland) and was treated as a prisoner, his treatment was not changed too soon, for he had plotted to escape that very night to a ship sent by the Queen, which was lying off the island.

He was doomed to be disappointed in his hopes from Scotland. The agreement he had made with the Scottish Commissioners was not favourable enough to the religion of that country to please the Scottish clergy; and they preached against it. The consequence was, that the army raised in Scotland and sent over, was too small to do much; and that, although it was helped by a rising of the Royalists in England and by good soldiers from Ireland, it could make no head against the Parliamentary army under such men as Cromwell and Fairfax. The King's eldest son, the Prince of Wales, came over from Holland with nineteen ships (a part of the English fleet having gone over to him) to help his father; but nothing came of his voyage, and he was fain to return. The most remarkable event of this second civil war was the cruel execution by the Parliamentary General, of SIR CHARLES LUCAS and SIR GEORGE LISLE, two grand Royalist generals, who had bravely defended Colchester under every disadvantage of famine and distress for nearly three months. When Sir Charles Lucas was shot, Sir George Lisle kissed his body, and said to the soldiers who were to shoot him, 'Come nearer, and make sure of me.' 'I warrant you, Sir George,' said one of the soldiers, 'we shall hit you.' 'Ay?' he returned with a smile, 'but I have been nearer to you, my friends, many a time, and you have missed me.'

The Parliament, after being fearfully bullied by the army – who demanded to have seven members whom they disliked given up to them – had voted that they would have nothing more to do with the King. On the conclusion, however, of this second civil war (which did not last more than six months), they appointed commissioners to treat with him. The King, then so far released again as to be allowed to live in a private house at Newport, in the Isle of Wight, managed his own part of the negotiation with a sense that was admired by all who saw him, and gave up, in the end, all that was asked of him – even yielding (which he had steadily refused, so far) to the temporary abolition of the bishops, and the transfer of their church land to the Crown. Still, with his old fatal vice upon him, when his best friends joined the commissioners in beseeching him to yield all those points as the only means of saving himself from the army, he was plotting to escape from the island; he was holding correspondence with his friends and the Catholics in Ireland, though declaring that he was not; and he was writing, with his own hand, that in what he yielded he meant nothing but to get time to escape.

Matters were at this pass when the army, resolved to defy the Parliament, marched up to London. The Parliament, not afraid of them now, and boldly led by Hollis, voted that the King's concessions were sufficient ground for settling the peace of the kingdom. Upon that, COLONEL RICH and COLONEL PRIDE went down to the House of Commons with a regiment of horse soldiers and a regiment of foot; and Colonel Pride, standing in the lobby with a list of the members who were obnoxious to the army in his hand, had them pointed out to him as they came through, and took them all into custody. This proceeding was afterwards called by the people, for a joke, PRIDE'S PURGE. Cromwell was in the North, at the head of his men, at the time, but when he came home, approved of what had been done.

What with imprisoning some members and causing others to stay away, the army had now reduced the House of Commons to some fifty or so. These soon voted that it was treason in a king to make war against his parliament and his people, and sent an ordinance up to the House of Lords for the King's being tried as a traitor. The House of Lords, then sixteen in number, to a man rejected it. Thereupon, the Commons made an ordinance of their own, that they were the supreme government of the country, and would bring the King to trial.

The King had been taken for security to a place called Hurst Castle; a lonely house on a rock in the sea, connected with the coast of Hampshire by a rough road two miles long at low water. Thence, he was ordered to be removed to Windsor; thence, after being but rudely used there, and having none but soldiers to wait upon him at table, he was brought up to St James's Palace, in London, and told that his trial was appointed for next day.

On Saturday, the twentieth of January, one thousand six hundred and forty-nine, this memorable trial began. The House of Commons had settled that one hundred and thirty-five persons should form the Court, and these were taken from the House itself, from among the officers of the army, and from among the lawyers and citizens. JOHN BRADSHAW, serjeant-at-law, was appointed president. The place was Westminster Hall. At the upper end, in a red velvet chair, sat the president, with his hat (lined with plates of iron for his protection) on his head. The rest of the Court sat on side benches, also wearing their hats. The King's seat was covered with velvet, like that of the president, and was opposite to it. He was brought from St James's to Whitehall, and from Whitehall he came by water to his trial.

When he came in, he looked round very steadily on the Court, and on the great number of spectators, and then sat down: presently he got up and looked round again. On the indictment, 'against Charles Stuart, for high treason,' being read, he smiled several times, and he denied the authority of the Court, saying that there could be no parliament without a House of Lords, and that he saw no House of Lords there. Also, that the King ought to be there, and that he saw no King in the King's right place. Bradshaw replied, that the Court was satisfied with its authority, and that its authority was God's authority and the kingdom's. He then adjourned the Court to the following Monday. On that day, the trial was resumed, and went on all the week. When the Saturday came, as the King passed forward to his place in the Hall, some soldiers and others cried for 'justice!' and execution on him. That day, too, Bradshaw, like an angry Sultan, wore a red robe, instead of the black robe he had worn before. The King was sentenced to death that day. As he went out, one solitary soldier said, 'God bless you, Sir!' For this, his officer struck him. The King said he thought the punishment exceeded the offence. The silver head of his walking-stick had fallen off while he leaned upon it, at one time of the trial. The accident seemed to disturb him, as if he thought it ominous of the falling of his own head; and he admitted as much, now it was all over.

Being taken back to Whitehall, he sent to the House of Commons, saying that as the time of his execution might be nigh, he wished he might be allowed to see his darling children. It was granted. On the Monday he was taken back to St James's; and his two children then in England, the PRINCESS ELIZABETH thirteen years old, and the DUKE OF GLOUCESTER nine years

Charles the First Taking Leave of His Children

old, were brought to take leave of him, from Sion House, near Brentford. It was a sad and touching scene, when he kissed and fondled those poor children, and made a little present of two diamond seals to the Princess, and gave them tender messages to their mother (who little deserved them, for she had a lover of her own whom she married soon afterwards), and told them that he died 'for the laws and liberties of the land.' I am bound to say that I don't think he did, but I dare say he believed so.

There were ambassadors from Holland that day, to intercede for the unhappy King, whom you and I both wish the Parliament had spared; but they got no answer. The Scottish Commissioners interceded too; so did the Prince of Wales, by a letter in which he offered as the next heir to the throne, to accept any conditions from the Parliament; so did the Queen, by letter likewise. Notwithstanding all, the warrant for the execution was this day signed. There is a story that as Oliver Cromwell went to the table with the pen in his hand to put his signature to it, he drew his pen across the face of one of the commissioners, who was standing near, and marked it with ink. That commissioner had not signed his own name yet, and the story adds that when he came to do it he marked Cromwell's face with ink in the same way.

The King slept well, untroubled by the knowledge that it was his last night on earth, and rose on the thirtieth of January, two hours before day, and dressed himself carefully. He put on two shirts lest he should tremble with the cold, and had his hair very carefully combed. The warrant had been directed to three officers of the army, COLONEL HACKER, COLONEL HUNKS, and COLONEL PHAYER. At ten o'clock, the first of these came to the door and said it was time to go to Whitehall. The King, who had always been a quick walker, walked at his usual speed through the Park, and called out to the guard, with his accustomed voice of command, 'March on apace!' When he came to Whitehall, he was taken to his own bedroom, where a breakfast was set forth. As he had taken the Sacrament, he would eat nothing more; but, at about the time when the church bells struck twelve at noon (for he had to wait, through the scaffold not being ready), he took the advice of the good BISHOP JUXON who was with him, and ate a little bread and drank a glass of claret. Soon after he had taken this refreshment, Colonel Hacker came to the chamber with the warrant in his hand, and called for Charles Stuart.

And then, through the long gallery of Whitehall Palace, which he had often seen light and gay and merry and crowded, in very different times, the fallen King passed along, until he came to the centre window of the Banqueting House, through which he emerged upon the scaffold, which was hung with black. He looked at the two executioners, who were dressed in black and masked; he looked at the troops of soldiers on horseback and on foot, and all looked up at him in silence; he looked at the vast array of spectators, filling up the view beyond, and turning all their faces upon him; he looked at his old Palace of St James's; and he looked at the block. He seemed a little troubled to find that it was so low, and asked, 'if there were no place higher?' Then, to those upon the scaffold, he said 'that it was the Parliament who had begun the war, and not he; but he hoped they might be guiltless too, as ill instruments had gone between them. In one respect,' he said, 'he suffered justly; and that was because he had permitted an unjust sentence to be executed on another.' In this he referred to the Earl of Strafford.

He was not at all afraid to die; but he was anxious to die easily. When some one touched the axe while he was speaking, he broke off and called out, 'Take heed of the axe! take heed of the axe!' He also said to Colonel Hacker, 'Take care that they do not put me to pain.' He told the executioner, 'I shall say but very short prayers, and then thrust out my hands' – as the sign to strike.

He put his hair up, under a white satin cap which the bishop had carried, and said, 'I have a good cause and a gracious God on my side.' The bishop told him that he had but one stage more to travel in this weary world, and that, though it was a turbulent and troublesome stage, it was a short one, and would carry him a great way – all the way from earth to Heaven. The King's last word, as he gave his cloak and the George – the decoration from his breast – to the bishop, was, 'Remember!' He then kneeled down, laid his head on the block, spread out his hands, and was instantly killed. One universal groan broke from the crowd; and the soldiers, who had sat on their horses and stood in their ranks immovable as statues, were of a sudden all in motion, clearing the streets.

Thus, in the forty-ninth year of his age, falling at the same time of his career as Strafford had fallen in his, perished Charles the First. With all my sorrow for him, I cannot agree with him that he died 'the martyr of the people;' for the people had been martyrs to him, and to his ideas of a King's rights, long before. Indeed, I am afraid that he was but a bad judge of martyrs; for he had called that infamous Duke of Buckingham 'the Martyr of his Sovereign.'

CHAPTER 34

England under Oliver Cromwell

First Part

Before sunset on the memorable day on which King Charles the First was executed, the House of Commons passed an act declaring it treason in any one to proclaim the Prince of Wales – or anybody else – King of England. Soon afterwards, it declared that the House of Lords was useless and dangerous, and ought to be abolished; and directed that the late King's statue should be taken down from the Royal Exchange in the City and other public places. Having laid hold of some famous Royalists who had escaped from prison, and having beheaded the DUKE OF HAMILTON, LORD HOLLAND, and LORD CAPEL, in Palace Yard (all of whom died very courageously), they then appointed a Council of State to govern the country. It consisted of forty-one members, of whom five were peers. Bradshaw was made president. The House of Commons also re-admitted members who had opposed the King's death, and made up its numbers to about a hundred and fifty.

But, it still had an army of more than forty thousand men to deal with, and a very hard task it was to manage them. Before the King's execution, the army had appointed some of its officers to remonstrate between them and the Parliament; and now the common soldiers began to take that office upon themselves. The regiments under orders for Ireland mutinied; one troop of horse in the city of London seized their own flag, and refused to obey orders. For this, the ringleader was shot: which did not mend the matter, for, both his comrades and the people made a public funeral for him, and accompanied the body to the grave with sound of trumpets and with a gloomy procession of persons carrying bundles of rosemary steeped in blood. Oliver was the only man to deal with such difficulties as these, and he soon cut them short by bursting at midnight into the town of Burford, near Salisbury, where the mutineers were sheltered, taking four hundred of them prisoners, and shooting a number of them by sentence of court-martial. The soldiers soon found, as all men did, that Oliver was not a man to be trifled with. And there was an end of the mutiny.

The Scottish Parliament did not know Oliver yet; so, on hearing of the King's execution, it proclaimed the Prince of Wales King Charles the Second, on condition of his respecting the Solemn League and Covenant. Charles was abroad at that time, and so was Montrose, from whose help he had hopes enough to keep him holding on and off with commissioners from Scotland, just as his father might have done. These hopes were soon at an end; for, Montrose, having raised a few hundred exiles in Germany, and landed with them in Scotland, found that the people there, instead of joining him, deserted the country at his approach. He was soon taken prisoner and carried to Edinburgh. There he was received with every possible insult, and carried to prison in a cart, his officers going two and two before him. He was sentenced by the Parliament to be hanged on a gallows thirty feet high, to have his head set on a spike in Edinburgh, and his limbs distributed in other places, according to the old barbarous manner. He said he had always acted under the Royal orders, and only wished he had limbs enough to be distributed through Christendom, that it might be the more widely known how loyal he had been. He went to the scaffold in a bright and brilliant dress, and made a bold end at thirty-eight years of age. The breath was scarcely out of his body when Charles abandoned his memory, and denied that he had ever given him orders to rise in his behalf. O the family failing was strong in that Charles then!

Oliver had been appointed by the Parliament to command the army in Ireland, where he took a terrible vengeance for the sanguinary rebellion, and made tremendous havoc, particularly in the siege of Drogheda, where no quarter was given, and where he found at least a thousand of the inhabitants shut up together in the great church: every one of whom was killed by his soldiers, usually known as OLIVER'S IRONSIDES. There were numbers of friars and priests among them, and Oliver gruffly wrote home in his despatch that these were 'knocked on the head' like the rest.

But, Charles having got over to Scotland where the men of the Solemn League and Covenant led him a prodigiously dull life and made him very weary with long sermons and grim Sundays, the Parliament called the redoubtable Oliver home to knock the Scottish men on the head for setting up that Prince. Oliver left his son-in-law, Ireton, as general in Ireland in his stead (he died there afterwards), and he imitated the example of his father-in-law with such good will that he brought the country to subjection, and laid it at the feet of the Parliament. In the end, they passed an act for the settlement of Ireland, generally pardoning all the common people, but exempting from this grace such of the wealthier sort as had been concerned in the rebellion, or in any killing of Protestants, or who refused to lay down their arms. Great numbers of Irish were got out of the country to serve under Catholic powers abroad, and a quantity of land was declared to have been forfeited by past offences, and was given to people who had lent money to the Parliament early in the war. These were sweeping measures; but, if Oliver Cromwell had had his own way fully, and had stayed in Ireland, he would have done more yet.

However, as I have said, the Parliament wanted Oliver for Scotland; so, home Oliver came, and was made Commander of all the Forces of the Commonwealth of England, and in three days away he went with sixteen thousand soldiers to fight the Scottish men. Now, the Scottish men, being then – as you will generally find them now – mighty cautious, reflected that the troops they had, were not used to war like the Ironsides, and would be beaten in an open fight. Therefore they said, 'If we live quiet in our trenches in Edinburgh here, and if all the farmers come into the town and desert the country, the Ironsides will be driven out by iron hunger and be forced to go away.' This was, no doubt, the wisest plan; but as the Scottish clergy *would* interfere with what they knew nothing about, and would perpetually preach long sermons exhorting the soldiers to come out and fight, the soldiers got it in their heads that they absolutely must come out and fight. Accordingly, in an evil hour for themselves, they came out of their safe position. Oliver fell upon them instantly, and killed three thousand, and took ten thousand prisoners.

To gratify the Scottish Parliament, and preserve their favour, Charles had signed a declaration they laid before him, reproaching the memory of his father and mother, and representing himself as a most religious Prince, to whom the Solemn League and Covenant was as dear as life. He meant no sort of truth in this, and soon afterwards galloped away on horseback to join some tiresome Highland friends, who were always flourishing dirks and broadswords. He was overtaken and induced to return; but this attempt, which was called 'The Start,' did him just so much service, that they did not preach quite such long sermons at him afterwards as they had done before.

On the first of January, one thousand six hundred and fifty-one, the Scottish people crowned him at Scone. He immediately took the chief command of an army of twenty thousand men, and marched to Stirling. His hopes were heightened, I dare say, by the redoubtable Oliver being ill of an ague; but Oliver scrambled out of bed in no time, and went to work with such energy that he got behind the Royalist army and cut it off from all communication with Scotland. There was nothing for it then, but to go on to England; so it went on as far as Worcester, where the mayor and some of the gentry proclaimed King Charles the Second straightway. His proclamation, however, was of little use to him, for very few Royalists appeared; and, on the very same day, two people were publicly beheaded on Tower Hill for espousing his cause. Up came Oliver to Worcester too, at double quick speed, and he and his Ironsides so laid about them in the great battle which was fought there, that they completely beat the Scottish men, and destroyed the Royalist army; though the Scottish men fought so gallantly that it took five hours to do.

The escape of Charles after this battle of Worcester did him good service long afterwards, for it induced many of the generous English people to take a romantic interest in him, and to think much better of him than he ever deserved. He fled in the night, with not more than sixty followers, to the house of a Catholic lady in Staffordshire. There, for his greater safety, the whole sixty left him. He cropped his hair, stained his face and hands brown as if they were sunburnt, put on the clothes of a labouring countryman, and went out in the morning with his axe in his hand, accompanied by four wood-cutters who were brothers, and another man who was their brother-in-law. These good fellows made a bed for him under a tree, as the weather was very bad; and the wife of one of them brought him food to eat; and the old mother of the four brothers came and fell down on her knees before him in the wood, and thanked God that her sons were engaged in saving his life. At night, he came out of the forest and went on to another house which was near the river Severn, with the intention of passing into Wales; but the place swarmed with soldiers, and the bridges were guarded, and all the boats were made fast. So, after lying in a hayloft covered over with hay, for some time, he came out of his place, attended by COLONEL CARELESS, a Catholic gentleman who had met him there, and with whom he lay hid, all next day, up in the shady branches of a fine old oak. It was lucky for the King that it was September time, and that the leaves had not begun to fall, since he and the Colonel, perched up in this tree, could catch glimpses of the soldiers riding about below, and could hear the crash in the wood as they went about beating the boughs.

After this, he walked and walked until his feet were all blistered; and, having been concealed all one day in a house which was searched by the troopers while he was there, went with LORD WILMOT, another of his good friends, to a place called Bentley, where one MISS LANE, a Protestant lady, had obtained a pass to be allowed to ride through the guards to see a relation of hers near Bristol. Disguised as a servant, he rode in the saddle before this young lady to the house of SIR JOHN WINTER, while Lord Wilmot rode there boldly, like a plain country gentleman, with dogs at his heels. It happened that Sir John Winter's butler had been servant in Richmond Palace, and knew Charles the moment he set eyes upon him; but, the butler was faithful and kept the secret. As no ship could be found to carry him abroad, it was planned that he should go – still travelling with Miss Lane as her servant – to another house, at Trent near Sherborne in Dorsetshire; and then Miss Lane and her cousin, MR LASCELLES, who had gone on horseback beside her all the way, went home. I hope Miss Lane was going to marry that cousin, for I am sure she must have been a brave kind girl. If I had been that cousin, I should certainly have loved Miss Lane.

When Charles, lonely for the loss of Miss Lane, was safe at

Trent, a ship was hired at Lyme, the master of which engaged to take two gentlemen to France. In the evening of the same day, the King – now riding as servant before another young lady – set off for a public-house at a place called Charmouth, where the captain of the vessel was to take him on board. But, the captain's wife, being afraid of her husband getting into trouble, locked him up and would not let him sail. Then they went away to Bridport; and, coming to the inn there, found the stable-yard full of soldiers who were on the look-out for Charles, and who talked about him while they drank. He had such presence of mind, that he led the horses of his party through the yard as any other servant might have done, and said, 'Come out of the way, you soldiers; let us have room to pass here!' As he went along, he met a half-tipsy ostler, who rubbed his eyes and said to him, 'Why, I was formerly servant to Mr Potter at Exeter, and surely I have sometimes seen you there, young man?' He certainly had, for Charles had lodged there. His ready answer was, 'Ah, I did live with him once; but I have no time to talk now. We'll have a pot of beer together when I come back.'

From this dangerous place he returned to Trent, and lay there concealed several days. Then he escaped to Heale, near Salisbury; where, in the house of a widow lady, he was hidden five days, until the master of a collier lying off Shoreham in Sussex, undertook to convey a 'gentleman' to France. On the night of the fifteenth of October, accompanied by two colonels and a merchant, the King rode to Brighton, then a little fishing village, to give the captain of the ship a supper before going on board; but, so many people knew him, that this captain knew him too, and not only he, but the landlord and landlady also. Before he went away, the landlord came behind his chair, kissed his hand, and said he hoped to live to be a lord and to see his wife a lady; at which Charles laughed. They had had a good supper by this time, and plenty of smoking and drinking, at which the King was a first-rate hand; so, the captain assured him that he would stand by him, and he did. It was agreed that the captain should pretend to sail to Deal, and that Charles should address the sailors and say he was a gentleman in debt who was running away from his creditors, and that he hoped they would join him in persuading the captain to put him ashore in France. As the King acted his part very well indeed, and gave the sailors twenty shillings to drink, they begged the captain to do what such a worthy gentleman asked. He pretended to yield to their entreaties, and the King got safe to Normandy.

Ireland being now subdued, and Scotland kept quiet by plenty of forts and soldiers put there by Oliver, the Parliament would have gone on quietly enough, as far as fighting with any foreign enemy went, but for getting into trouble with the Dutch, who in the spring of the year one thousand six hundred and fifty-one sent a fleet into the Downs under their ADMIRAL VAN TROMP, to call upon the bold English ADMIRAL BLAKE (who was there with half as many ships as the Dutch) to strike his flag. Blake fired a raging broadside instead, and beat off Van Tromp; who, in the autumn, came back again with seventy ships, and challenged the bold Blake – who still was only half as strong – to fight him. Blake fought him all day; but, finding that the Dutch were too many for him, got quietly off at night. What does Van Tromp upon this, but goes cruising and boasting about the Channel, between the North Foreland and the Isle of Wight, with a great Dutch broom tied to his masthead, as a sign that he could and would sweep the English off the sea! Within three months, Blake lowered his tone though, and his broom too; for, he and two other bold commanders, DEAN and MONK, fought him three whole days, took twenty-three of his ships, shivered his broom to pieces, and settled his business.

Things were no sooner quiet again, than the army began to complain to the Parliament that they were not governing the nation properly, and to hint that they thought they could do it better themselves. Oliver, who had now made up his mind to be the head of the state, or nothing at all, supported them in this, and called a meeting of officers and his own Parliamentary friends, at his lodgings in Whitehall, to consider the best way of getting rid of the Parliament. It had now lasted just as many years as the King's unbridled power had lasted, before it came into existence. The end of the deliberation was, that Oliver went down to the House in his usual plain black dress, with his usual grey worsted stockings, but with an unusual party of soldiers behind him. These last he left in the lobby, and then went in and sat down. Presently he got up, made the Parliament a speech, told them that the Lord had done with them, stamped his foot and said, 'You are no Parliament. Bring them in! Bring them in!' At this signal the door flew open, and the soldiers appeared. 'This is not honest,' said Sir Harry Vane, one of the members.

'Sir Harry Vane!' cried Cromwell; 'O, Sir Harry Vane! The Lord deliver me from Sir Harry Vane!' Then he pointed out members one by one, and said this man was a drunkard, and that man a dissipated fellow, and that man a liar, and so on. Then he caused the Speaker to be walked out of his chair, told the guard to clear the House, called the mace upon the table – which is a sign that the House is sitting – 'a fool's bauble,' and said, 'here, carry it away!' Being obeyed in all these orders, he quietly locked the door, put the key in his pocket, walked back to Whitehall again, and told his friends, who were still assembled there, what he had done.

They formed a new Council of State after this extraordinary proceeding, and got a new Parliament together in their own way: which Oliver himself opened in a sort of sermon, and which he said was the beginning of a perfect heaven upon earth. In this Parliament there sat a well-known leather-seller, who had taken the singular name of Praise God Barebones, and from whom it was called, for a joke, Barebones's Parliament, though its general name was the Little Parliament. As it soon appeared that it was not going to put Oliver in the first place, it turned out to be not at all like the beginning of heaven upon earth, and Oliver said it really was not to be borne with. So he cleared off that Parliament in much the same way as he had disposed of the other; and then the council of officers decided that he must be made the supreme authority of the kingdom, under the title of the Lord Protector of the Commonwealth.

So, on the sixteenth of December, one thousand six hundred and fifty-three, a great procession was formed at Oliver's door, and he came out in a black velvet suit and a big pair of boots, and got into his coach and went down to Westminster, attended by the judges, and the lord mayor, and the aldermen, and all the other great and wonderful personages of the country. There, in the Court of Chancery, he publicly accepted the office of Lord Protector. Then he was sworn, and the City sword was handed to him, and the seal was handed to him, and all the other things were handed to him which are usually handed to Kings and Queens on state occasions. When Oliver had handed them all back, he was quite made and completely finished off as Lord Protector; and several of the Ironsides preached about it at great length, all the evening.

Second Part

Oliver Cromwell – whom the people long called OLD NOLL – in accepting the office of Protector, had bound himself by a certain paper which was handed to him, called 'the Instrument,' to summon a Parliament, consisting of between four and five hundred members, in the election of which neither the Royalists nor the Catholics were to have any share. He had also pledged himself that this Parliament should not be dissolved without its own consent until it had sat five months.

When this Parliament met, Oliver made a speech to them of three hours long, very wisely advising them what to do for the credit and happiness of the country. To keep down the more violent members, he required them to sign a recognition of what they were forbidden by 'the Instrument' to do; which was, chiefly, to take the power from one single person at the head of the state or to command the army. Then he dismissed them to go to work. With his usual vigour and resolution he went to work himself with some frantic preachers – who were rather overdoing their sermons in calling him a villain and a tyrant – by shutting up their chapels, and sending a few of them off to prison.

There was not at that time, in England or anywhere else, a man so able to govern the country as Oliver Cromwell. Although he ruled with a strong hand, and levied a very heavy tax on the Royalists (but not until they had plotted against his life), he ruled wisely, and as the times required. He caused England to be so respected abroad, that I wish some lords and gentlemen who have governed it under kings and queens in later days would have taken a leaf out of Oliver Cromwell's book. He sent bold Admiral Blake to the Mediterranean Sea, to make the Duke of Tuscany pay sixty thousand pounds for injuries he had done to British subjects, and spoliation he had committed on English merchants. He further despatched him and his fleet to Algiers, Tunis, and Tripoli, to have every English ship and every English man delivered up to him that had been taken by pirates in those parts. All this was gloriously done; and it began to be thoroughly well known, all over the world, that England was governed by a man in earnest, who would not allow the English name to be insulted or slighted anywhere.

These were not all his foreign triumphs. He sent a fleet to sea against the Dutch; and the two powers, each with one hundred ships upon its side, met in the English Channel off the North Foreland, where the fight lasted all day long. Dean was killed in this fight; but Monk, who commanded in the same ship with him, threw his cloak over his body, that the sailors might not know of his death, and be disheartened. Nor were they. The English broadsides so exceedingly astonished the Dutch that they sheered off at last, though the redoubtable Van Tromp fired upon them with his own guns for deserting their flag. Soon afterwards, the two fleets engaged again, off the coast of Holland. There, the valiant Van Tromp was shot through the heart, and the Dutch gave in, and peace was made.

Further than this, Oliver resolved not to bear the domineering and bigoted conduct of Spain, which country not only claimed a right to all the gold and silver that could be found in South America, and treated the ships of all other countries who visited those regions, as pirates, but put English subjects into the horrible Spanish prisons of the Inquisition. So Oliver told the Spanish ambassador that English ships must be free to go wherever they would, and that English merchants must not be thrown into those same dungeons, no, not for the pleasure of all the priests in Spain. To this the Spanish ambassador replied that the gold and silver country, and the Holy Inquisition, were his King's two eyes, neither of which he could submit to have put out. Very well, said Oliver, then he was afraid he (Oliver) must damage those two eyes directly.

So, another fleet was despatched under two commanders, PENN and VENABLES, for Hispaniola; where, however, the Spaniards got the better of the fight. Consequently, the fleet came home again, after taking Jamaica on the way. Oliver, indignant with the two commanders who had not done what bold Admiral Blake would have done, clapped them both into prison, declared war against Spain, and made a treaty with France, in virtue of which it was to shelter the King and his brother the Duke of York no longer. Then, he sent a fleet abroad under bold Admiral Blake, which brought the King of Portugal to his senses − just to keep its hand in − and then engaged a Spanish fleet, sunk four great ships, and took two more, laden with silver to the value of two millions of pounds: which dazzling prize was brought from Portsmouth to London in waggons, with the populace of all the towns and villages through which the waggons passed, shouting with all their might. After this victory, bold Admiral Blake sailed away to the port of Santa Cruz to cut off the Spanish treasure-ships coming from Mexico. There, he found them, ten in number, with seven others to take care of them, and a big castle, and seven batteries, all roaring and blazing away at him with great guns. Blake cared no more for great guns than for pop-guns – no more for their hot iron balls than for snow-balls. He dashed into the harbour, captured and burnt every one of the ships, and came sailing out again triumphantly, with the victorious English flag flying at his masthead. This was the last triumph of this great commander, who had sailed and fought until he was quite worn out. He died, as his successful ship was coming into Plymouth Harbour amidst the joyful acclamations of the people, and was buried in state in Westminster Abbey. Not to lie there, long.

Over and above all this, Oliver found that the VAUDOIS, or Protestant people of the valleys of Lucerne, were insolently treated by the Catholic powers, and were even put to death for their religion, in an audacious and bloody manner. Instantly, he informed those powers that this was a thing which Protestant England would not allow; and he speedily carried his point, through the might of his great name, and established their right to worship God in peace after their own harmless manner.

Lastly, his English army won such admiration in fighting with the French against the Spaniards, that, after they had assaulted the town of Dunkirk together, the French King in person gave it up to the English, that it might be a token to them of their might and valour.

There were plots enough against Oliver among the frantic religionists (who called themselves Fifth Monarchy Men), and among the disappointed Republicans. He had a difficult game to play, for the Royalists were always ready to side with either party against him. The 'King over the water,' too, as Charles was called, had no scruples about plotting with any one against his life; although there is reason to suppose that he would willingly have married one of his daughters, if Oliver would have had such a son-in-law. There was a certain COLONEL SAXBY of the army, once a great supporter of Oliver's but now turned against him, who was a grievous trouble to him through all this part of his career; and who came and went between the discontented in England and Spain, and Charles who put himself in alliance with Spain on being thrown off by France. This man died in prison at last; but not until there had been very serious plots between the Royalists and Republicans, and an actual rising of them in England, when they burst into the city of Salisbury, on a Sunday night, seized the judges who were going to hold the assizes there next day, and would have hanged them but for the merciful objections of the more temperate of their number. Oliver was so vigorous and shrewd that he soon put this revolt down, as he did most other conspiracies; and it was well for one of its chief managers – that same Lord Wilmot who had assisted in Charles's flight, and was now EARL OF ROCH-ESTER – that he made his escape. Oliver seemed to have eyes and ears everywhere, and secured such sources of information as his enemies little dreamed of. There was a chosen body of six persons, called the Sealed Knot, who were in the closest and most secret confidence of Charles. One of the foremost of these very men, a SIR RICHARD WILLIS, reported to Oliver every-thing that passed among them, and had two hundred a year for it.

MILES SYNDARCOMB, also of the old army, was another conspirator against the Protector. He and a man named CECIL, bribed one of his Life Guards to let them have good notice when he was going out – intending to shoot him from a window. But, owing either to his caution or his good fortune, they could never get an aim at him. Disappointed in this design, they got into the chapel in Whitehall, with a basketful of combustibles, which were to explode by means of a slow match in six hours; then, in the noise and confusion of the fire, they hoped to kill Oliver. But, the Life Guardsman himself disclosed this plot; and they were seized, and Miles died (or killed himself in prison) a little while before he was ordered for execution. A few such plotters Oliver caused to be beheaded, a few more to be hanged, and many more, including those who rose in arms against him, to be sent as slaves to the West Indies. If he were rigid, he was impartial too, in asserting the laws of England. When a Portu-guese nobleman, the brother of the Portuguese ambassador, killed a London citizen in mistake for another man with whom he had had a quarrel, Oliver caused him to be tried before a jury of Englishmen and foreigners, and had him executed in spite of the entreaties of all the ambassadors in London.

One of Oliver's own friends, the DUKE OF OLDENBURGH, in

sending him a present of six fine coach-horses, was very near doing more to please the Royalists than all the plotters put together. One day, Oliver went with his coach, drawn by these six horses, into Hyde Park, to dine with his secretary and some of his other gentlemen under the trees there. After dinner, being merry, he took it into his head to put his friends inside and to drive them home: a postillion riding one of the foremost horses, as the custom was. On account of Oliver's being too free with the whip, the six fine horses went off at a gallop, the postillion got thrown, and Oliver fell upon the coach-pole and narrowly escaped being shot by his own pistol, which got entangled with his clothes in the harness, and went off. He was dragged some distance by the foot, until his foot came out of the shoe, and then he came safely to the ground under the broad body of the coach, and was very little the worse. The gentlemen inside were only bruised, and the discontented people of all parties were much disappointed.

The rest of the history of the Protectorate of Oliver Cromwell is a history of his Parliaments. His first one not pleasing him at all, he waited until the five months were out, and then dissolved it. The next was better suited to his views; and from that he desired to get – if he could with safety to himself – the title of King. He had had this in his mind some time: whether because he thought that the English people, being more used to the title, were more likely to obey it; or whether because he really wished to be a king himself, and to leave the succession to that title in his family, is far from clear. He was already as high, in England and in all the world, as he would ever be, and I doubt if he cared for the mere name. However, a paper, called the 'Humble Petition and Advice,' was presented to him by the House of Commons, praying him to take a high title and to appoint his successor. That he would have taken the title of King there is no doubt, but for the strong opposition of the army. This induced him to forbear, and to assent only to the other points of the petition. Upon which occasion there was another grand show in Westminster Hall, when the Speaker of the House of Commons formally invested him with a purple robe lined with ermine, and presented him with a splendidly-bound Bible, and put a golden sceptre in his hand. The next time the Parliament met, he called a House of Lords of sixty members, as the petition gave him power to do; but as that Parliament did not please him either, and would not proceed to the business of the country, he jumped into a coach one morning, took six Guards with him, and sent them to the right-about. I wish this had been a warning to Parliaments to avoid long speeches, and do more work.

It was the month of August, one thousand six hundred and fifty-eight, when Oliver Cromwell's favourite daughter, ELIZA-BETH CLAYPOLE (who had lately lost her youngest son), lay very ill, and his mind was greatly troubled, because he loved her dearly. Another of his daughters was married to LORD FALCON-BERG, another to the grandson of the Earl of Warwick, and he had made his son RICHARD one of the Members of the Upper House. He was very kind and loving to them all, being a good father and a good husband; but he loved his daughter the best of the family, and went down to Hampton Court to see her, and could hardly be induced to stir from her sick room until she died. Although his religion had been of a gloomy kind, his disposition had been always cheerful. He had been fond of music in his home, and had kept open table once a week for all officers of the army not below the rank of captain, and had always preserved in his house a quiet sensible dignity. He encouraged men of genius and learning, and loved to have them about him. MILTON was one of his great friends. He was good humoured too, with the nobility, whose dresses and manners were very different from his; and to show them what good information he had, he would sometimes jokingly tell them when they were his guests, where they had last drunk the health of the 'King over the water,' and would recommend them to be more private (if they could) another time. But he had lived in busy times, had borne the weight of heavy State affairs, and had often gone in fear of his life. He was ill of the gout and ague; and when the death of his beloved child came upon him in addition, he sank, never to raise his head again. He told his physicians on the twenty-fourth of August that the Lord had assured him that he was not to die in that illness, and that he would certainly get better. This was only his sick fancy, for on the third of September, which was the anniversary of the great battle of Worcester, and the day of the year which he called his fortunate day, he died, in the sixtieth year of his age. He had been delirious, and had lain insensible some hours, but he had been overheard to murmur a very good prayer the day before. The whole country lamented his death. If you want to know the real worth of Oliver Cromwell, and his real services to his country, you can hardly do better than compare England under him, with England under CHARLES THE SECOND.

He had appointed his son Richard to succeed him, and after there had been, at Somerset House in the Strand, a lying in state more splendid than sensible – as all such vanities after death are, I think – Richard became Lord Protector. He was an amiable country gentleman, but had none of his father's great genius, and was quite unfit for such a post in such a storm of parties. Richard's Protectorate, which only lasted a year and a half, is a history of quarrels between the officers of the army and the Parliament, and between the officers among themselves; and of a growing discontent among the people, who had far too many long sermons and far too few amusements, and wanted a change. At last, General Monk got the army well into his own hands, and then in pursuance of a secret plan he seems to have entertained from the time of Oliver's death, declared for the King's cause. He did not do this openly; but, in his place in the House of Commons, as one of the members for Devonshire, strongly advocated the proposals of one SIR JOHN GREENVILLE, who came to the House with a letter from Charles, dated from Breda, and with whom he had previously been in secret communication. There had been plots and counterplots, and a recall of the last members of the Long Parliament, and an end of the Long Parliament, and risings of the Royalists that were made too soon; and most men being tired out, and there being no one to head the country now great Oliver was dead, it was readily agreed to welcome Charles Stuart. Some of the wiser and better members said – what was most true – that in the letter from Breda, he gave no real promise to govern well, and that it would be best to make him pledge himself beforehand as to what he should be bound to do for the benefit of the kingdom. Monk said, however, it would be all right when he came, and he could not come too soon.

So, everybody found out all in a moment that the country *must* be prosperous and happy, having another Stuart to conde-scend to reign over it; and there was a prodigious firing off of guns, lighting of bonfires, ringing of bells, and throwing up of caps. The people drank the King's health by thousands in the open streets, and everybody rejoiced. Down came the Arms of the Commonwealth, up went the Royal Arms instead, and out came the public money. Fifty thousand pounds for the King, ten thousand pounds for his brother the Duke of York, five thousand pounds for his brother the Duke of Gloucester. Prayers for these gracious Stuarts were put up in all the churches; commissioners were sent to Holland (which suddenly found out that Charles was a great man, and that it loved him) to invite the King home; Monk and the Kentish grandees went to Dover, to kneel down before him as he landed. He kissed and embraced Monk, made him ride in the coach with himself and his brothers, came on to London amid wonderful shoutings, and passed through the army at Blackheath on the twenty-ninth of May (his birthday), in the year one thousand six hundred and sixty. Greeted by splendid dinners under tents, by flags and tapestry streaming from all the houses, by delighted crowds in all the streets, by troops of noblemen and gentlemen in rich dresses, by City companies, train-bands, drummers, trumpeters, the great Lord Mayor, and the majestic Aldermen, the King went on to Whitehall. On entering it, he commemorated his Restoration with the joke that it really would seem to have been his own fault that he had not come long ago, since everybody told him that he had always wished for him with all his heart.

CHAPTER 35

England under Charles the Second, called the Merry Monarch

First Part

There never were such profligate times in England as under CHARLES THE SECOND. Whenever you see his portrait, with his swarthy ill-looking face and great nose, you may fancy him in his Court at Whitehall, surrounded by some of the very worst vagabonds in the kingdom (though they were lords and ladies), drinking, gambling, indulging in vicious conversation, and committing every kind of profligate excess. It has been a fashion to call Charles the Second 'The Merry Monarch.' Let me try to give you a general idea of some of the merry things that were done, in the merry days when this merry gentleman sat upon his merry throne, in merry England.

The first merry proceeding was – of course – to declare that he was one of the greatest, the wisest, and the noblest kings that ever shone, like the blessed sun itself, on this benighted earth. The next merry and pleasant piece of business was, for the Parliament, in the humblest manner, to give him one million two hundred thousand pounds a year, and to settle upon him for life that old disputed tonnage and poundage which had been so bravely fought for. Then, General Monk being made EARL OF ALBEMARLE, and a few other Royalists similarly rewarded, the law went to work to see what was to be done to those persons (they were called Regicides) who had been concerned in making a martyr of the late King. Ten of these were merrily executed; that is to say, six of the judges, one of the council, Colonel Hacker and another officer who had commanded the Guards, and HUGH PETERS, a preacher who had preached against the martyr with all his heart. These executions were so extremely merry, that every horrible circumstance which Cromwell had abandoned was revived with appalling cruelty. The hearts of the sufferers were torn out of their living bodies; their bowels were burned before their faces; the executioner cut jokes to the next victim, as he rubbed his filthy hands together, that were reeking with the blood of the last; and the heads of the dead were drawn on sledges with the living to the place of suffering. Still, even so merry a monarch could not force one of these dying men to say that he was sorry for what he had done. Nay, the most memorable thing said among them was, that if the thing were to do again they would do it.

Sir Harry Vane, who had furnished the evidence against Strafford, and was one of the most staunch of the Republicans, was also tried, found guilty, and ordered for execution. When he came upon the scaffold on Tower Hill, after conducting his own defence with great power, his notes of what he had meant to say to the people were torn away from him, and the drums and trumpets were ordered to sound lustily and drown his voice; for, the people had been so much impressed by what the Regicides had calmly said with their last breath, that it was the custom now, to have the drums and trumpets always under the scaffold, ready to strike up. Vane said no more than this: 'It is a bad cause which cannot bear the words of a dying man:' and bravely died.

These merry scenes were succeeded by another, perhaps even merrier. On the anniversary of the late King's death, the bodies of Oliver Cromwell, Ireton, and Bradshaw, were torn out of their graves in Westminster Abbey, dragged to Tyburn, hanged there on a gallows all day long, and then beheaded. Imagine the head of Oliver Cromwell set upon a pole to be stared at by a brutal crowd, not one of whom would have dared to look the living Oliver in the face for half a moment! Think, after you have read this reign, what England was under Oliver Cromwell who was torn out of his grave, and what it was under this merry monarch who sold it, like a merry Judas, over and over again.

Of course, the remains of Oliver's wife and daughter were not to be spared either, though they had been most excellent women. The base clergy of that time gave up their bodies, which had been buried in the Abbey, and – to the eternal disgrace of England – they were thrown into a pit, together with the mouldering bones of Pym and of the brave and bold old Admiral Blake.

The clergy acted this disgraceful part because they hoped to get the nonconformists, or dissenters, thoroughly put down in this reign, and to have but one prayer-book and one service for all kinds of people, no matter what their private opinions were. This was pretty well, I think, for a Protestant Church, which had displaced the Romish Church because people had a right to their own opinions in religious matters. However, they carried it with a high hand, and a prayer-book was agreed upon, in which the extremest opinions of Archbishop Laud were not forgotten. An Act was passed, too, preventing any dissenter from holding any office under any corporation. So, the regular clergy in their triumph were soon as merry as the King. The army being by this time disbanded, and the King crowned, everything was to go on easily for evermore.

I must say a word here about the King's family. He had not been long upon the throne when his brother the Duke of Gloucester, and his sister the PRINCESS OF ORANGE, died within a few months of each other, of small-pox. His remaining sister, the PRINCESS HENRIETTA, married the DUKE OF ORLEANS, the brother of LOUIS THE FOURTEENTH, King of France. His brother JAMES, DUKE OF YORK, was made High Admiral, and by-and-by became a Catholic. He was a gloomy, sullen, bilious sort of man, with a remarkable partiality for the ugliest women in the country. He married, under very discreditable circumstances, ANNE HYDE, the daughter of LORD CLARENDON, then the King's principal Minister – not at all a delicate minister either, but doing much of the dirty work of a very dirty palace. It became important now that the King himself should be married; and divers foreign Monarchs, not very particular about the character of their son-in-law, proposed their daughters to him. The KING OF PORTUGAL offered his daughter, CATHERINE OF BRAGANZA, and fifty thousand pounds: in addition to which, the French King, who was favourable to that match, offered a loan of another fifty thousand. The King of Spain, on the other hand, offered any one out of a dozen of Princesses, and other hopes of gain. But the ready money carried the day, and Catherine came over in state to her merry marriage.

The whole Court was a great flaunting crowd of debauched men and shameless women; and Catherine's merry husband insulted and outraged her in every possible way, until she consented to receive those worthless creatures as her very good friends, and to degrade herself by their companionship. A MRS PALMER, whom the King made LADY CASTLEMAINE, and afterwards DUCHESS OF CLEVELAND, was one of the most powerful of the bad women about the Court, and had great influence with the King nearly all through his reign. Another merry lady named MOLL DAVIES, a dancer at the theatre, was afterwards her rival. So was NELL GWYN, first an orange girl and then an actress, who really had good in her, and of whom one of the worst things I know is, that actually she does seem to have been fond of the King. The first DUKE OF ST ALBANS was this orange girl's child. In like manner the son of a merry waiting-lady, whom the King created DUCHESS OF PORTS-MOUTH, became the DUKE OF RICHMOND. Upon the whole it is not so bad a thing to be a commoner.

The Merry Monarch was so exceedingly merry among these merry ladies, and some equally merry (and equally infamous) lords and gentlemen, that he soon got through his hundred thousand pounds, and then, by way of raising a little pocket-money, made a merry bargain. He sold Dunkirk to the French King for five millions of livres. When I think of the dignity to which Oliver Cromwell raised England in the eyes of foreign powers, and when I think of the manner in which he gained for England this very Dunkirk, I am much inclined to consider that if the Merry Monarch had been made to follow his father for this action, he would have received his just deserts.

Though he was like his father in none of that father's greater qualities, he was like him in being worthy of no trust. When he sent that letter to the Parliament, from Breda, he did expressly promise that all sincere religious opinions should be respected. Yet he was no sooner firm in his power than he consented to one of the worst Acts of Parliament ever passed. Under this law, every minister who should not give his solemn assent to the Prayer-Book by a certain day, was declared to be a minister no longer, and to be deprived of his church. The consequence of this was that some two thousand honest men were taken from their congregations, and reduced to dire poverty and distress. It was followed by another outrageous law, called the Conventicle Act, by which any person above the age of sixteen who was present at any religious service not according to the Prayer-Book, was to be imprisoned three months for the first offence, six for the second, and to be transported for the third. This Act alone filled the prisons, which were then most dreadful dungeons, to overflowing.

The Covenanters in Scotland had already fared no better. A base Parliament, usually known as the Drunken Parliament, in consequence of its principal members being seldom sober, had been got together to make laws against the Covenanters, and to force all men to be of one mind in religious matters. The MARQUIS OF ARGYLE, relying on the King's honour, had given himself up to him; but, he was wealthy, and his enemies wanted his wealth. He was tried for treason, on the evidence of some private letters in which he had expressed opinions – as well he might – more favourable to the government of the late Lord Protector than of the present merry and religious King. He was executed, as were two men of mark among the Covenanters; and SHARP, a traitor who had once been the friend of the Presbyterians and betrayed them, was made Archbishop of St Andrew's, to teach the Scotch how to like bishops.

Things being in this merry state at home, the Merry Monarch undertook a war with the Dutch; principally because they interfered with an African company, established with the two objects of buying gold-dust and slaves, of which the Duke of

York was a leading member. After some preliminary hostilities, the said Duke sailed to the coast of Holland with a fleet of ninety-eight vessels of war, and four fire-ships. This engaged with the Dutch fleet, of no fewer than one hundred and thirteen ships. In the great battle between the two forces, the Dutch lost eighteen ships, four admirals, and seven thousand men. But, the English on shore were in no mood of exultation when they heard the news.

For, this was the year and the time of the Great Plague in London. During the winter of one thousand six hundred and sixty-four it had been whispered about, that some few people had died here and there of the disease called the Plague, in some of the unwholesome suburbs around London. News was not published at that time as it is now, and some people believed these rumours, and some disbelieved them, and they were soon forgotten. But, in the month of May, one thousand six hundred and sixty-five, it began to be said all over the town that the disease had burst out with great violence in St Giles's, and that the people were dying in great numbers. This soon turned out to be awfully true. The roads out of London were choked up by people endeavouring to escape from the infected city, and large sums were paid for any kind of conveyance. The disease soon spread so fast, that it was necessary to shut up the houses in which sick people were, and to cut them off from communication with the living. Every one of these houses was marked on the outside of the door with a red cross, and the words, Lord, have mercy upon us! The streets were all deserted, grass grew in the public ways, and there was a dreadful silence in the air. When night came on, dismal rumblings used to be heard, and these were the wheels of the death-carts, attended by men with veiled faces and holding cloths to their mouths, who rang doleful bells and cried in a loud and solemn voice, 'Bring out your dead!' The corpses put into these carts were buried by torchlight in great pits; no service being performed over them; all men being afraid to stay for a moment on the brink of the ghastly graves. In the general fear, children ran away from their parents, and parents from their children. Some who were taken ill, died alone, and without any help. Some were stabbed or strangled by hired nurses who robbed them of all their money, and stole the very beds on which they lay. Some went mad, dropped from the windows, ran through the streets, and in their pain and frenzy flung themselves into the river.

These were not all the horrors of the time. The wicked and dissolute, in wild desperation, sat in the taverns singing roaring songs, and were stricken as they drank, and went out and died. The fearful and superstitious persuaded themselves that they saw supernatural sights – burning swords in the sky, gigantic arms and darts. Others pretended that at nights vast crowds of ghosts walked round and round the dismal pits. One madman, naked, and carrying a brazier full of burning coals upon his head, stalked through the streets, crying out that he was a Prophet, commissioned to denounce the vengeance of the Lord on wicked London. Another always went to and fro, exclaiming, 'Yet forty days, and London shall be destroyed!' A third awoke the echoes in the dismal streets, by night and by day, and made the blood of the sick run cold, by calling out incessantly, in a deep hoarse voice, 'O, the great and dreadful God!'

Through the months of July and August and September, the Great Plague raged more and more. Great fires were lighted in the streets, in the hope of stopping the infection; but there was a plague of rain too, and it beat the fires out. At last, the winds which usually arise at that time of the year which is called the equinox, when day and night are of equal length all over the world, began to blow, and to purify the wretched town. The deaths began to decrease, the red crosses slowly to disappear, the fugitives to return, the shops to open, pale frightened faces to be seen in the streets. The Plague had been in every part of England, but in close and unwholesome London it had killed one hundred thousand people.

All this time, the Merry Monarch was as merry as ever, and as worthless as ever. All this time, the debauched lords and gentlemen and the shameless ladies danced and gamed and drank, and loved and hated one another, according to their merry ways. So little humanity did the government learn from the late affliction, that one of the first things the Parliament did when it met at Oxford (being as yet afraid to come to London), was to make a law, called the Five Mile Act, expressly directed against those poor ministers who, in the time of the Plague, had manfully come back to comfort the unhappy people. This infamous law, by forbidding them to teach in any school, or to come within five miles of any city, town, or village, doomed them to starvation and death.

The fleet had been at sea, and healthy. The King of France was now in alliance with the Dutch, though his navy was chiefly employed in looking on while the English and Dutch fought. The Dutch gained one victory; and the English gained another and a greater; and Prince Rupert, one of the English admirals, was out in the Channel one windy night, looking for the French Admiral, with the intention of giving him something more to do than he had had yet, when the gale increased to a storm, and blew him into Saint Helen's. That night was the third of September, one thousand and six hundred and sixty-six, and that wind fanned the Great Fire of London.

It broke out at a baker's shop near London Bridge, on the spot on which the Monument now stands as a remembrance of those raging flames. It spread and spread, and burned and burned, for three days. The nights were lighter than the days; in the day-time there was an immense cloud of smoke, and in the night-time there was a great tower of fire mounting up into the sky, which lighted the whole country landscape for ten miles round. Showers of hot ashes rose into the air and fell on distant places; flying sparks carried the conflagration to great distances, and kindled it in twenty new spots at a time; church steeples fell down with tremendous crashes; houses crumbled into cinders by the hundred and the thousand. The summer had been intensely hot and dry, the streets were very narrow, and the houses mostly built of wood and plaster. Nothing could stop the tremendous fire, but the want of more houses to burn; nor did it stop until the whole way from the Tower to Temple Bar was a desert, composed of the ashes of thirteen thousand houses and eighty-nine churches.

This was a terrible visitation at the time, and occasioned great loss and suffering to the two hundred thousand burnt-out people, who were obliged to lie in the fields under the open night sky, or in hastily-made huts of mud and straw, while the lanes and roads were rendered impassable by carts which had broken down as they tried to save their goods. But the Fire was a great blessing to the City afterwards, for it arose from its ruins very much improved – built more regularly, more widely, more cleanly and carefully, and therefore much more healthily. It might be far more healthy than it is, but there are some people in it still – even now, at this time, nearly two hundred years later – so selfish, so pig-headed, and so ignorant, that I doubt if even another Great Fire would warm them up to do their duty.

The Catholics were accused of having wilfully set London in flames; one poor Frenchman, who had been mad for years, even accused himself of having with his own hand fired the first house. There is no reasonable doubt, however, that the fire was accidental. An inscription on the Monument long attributed it to the Catholics; but it is removed now, and was always a malicious and stupid untruth.

Second Part

That the Merry Monarch might be very merry indeed, in the merry times when his people were suffering under pestilence and fire, he drank and gambled and flung away among his favourites the money which the Parliament had voted for the war. The consequence of this was that the stout-hearted English sailors were merrily starving of want, and dying in the streets; while the Dutch, under their admirals DE WITT and DE RUYTER, came into the River Thames, and up the River Medway as far as Upnor, burned the guard-ships, silenced the weak batteries, and did what they would to the English coast for six whole weeks. Most of the English ships that could have prevented them had neither powder nor shot on board; in this merry reign, public officers made themselves as merry as the King did with the public money; and when it was entrusted to them to spend in national defences or preparations, they put it into their own pockets with the merriest grace in the world.

Lord Clarendon had, by this time, run as long a course as is usually allotted to the unscrupulous ministers of bad kings. He was impeached by his political opponents, but unsuccessfully. The King then commanded him to withdraw from England and retire to France, which he did, after defending himself in writing. He was no great loss at home, and died abroad some seven years afterwards.

There then came into power a ministry called the Cabal Ministry, because it was composed of LORD CLIFFORD, the EARL OF ARLINGTON, the DUKE OF BUCKINGHAM (a great rascal, and the King's most powerful favourite), LORD ASHLEY, and the DUKE OF LAUDERDALE, C. A. B. A. L. As the French were making conquests in Flanders, the first Cabal proceeding was to make a treaty with the Dutch, for uniting with Spain to oppose the French. It was no sooner made than the Merry Monarch, who always wanted to get money without being accountable to a Parliament for his expenditure, apologised to the King of France for having had anything to do with it, and concluded a secret treaty with him, making himself his infamous pensioner to the amount of two millions of livres down, and three millions more a year; and engaging to desert that very Spain, to make war against those very Dutch, and to declare himself a Catholic when a convenient time should arrive. This religious king had lately been crying to his Catholic brother on the subject of his strong desire to be a Catholic; and now he merrily concluded this treasonable conspiracy against the country he governed, by undertaking to become one as soon as he safely could. For all of which, though he had had ten merry heads instead of one, he richly deserved to lose them by the headsman's axe.

As his one merry head might have been far from safe, if these things had been known, they were kept very quiet, and war was declared by France and England against the Dutch. But, a very uncommon man, afterwards most important to English history and to the religion and liberty of this land, arose among them, and for many long years defeated the whole projects of France. This was WILLIAM OF NASSAU, PRINCE OF ORANGE, son of the last Prince of Orange of the same name, who married the daughter of Charles the First of England. He was a young man at this time, only just of age; but he was brave, cool, intrepid, and wise. His father had been so detested that, upon his death, the Dutch had abolished the authority to which this son would have otherwise succeeded (Stadtholder it was called), and placed the chief power in the hands of JOHN DE WITT, who educated this young prince. Now, the Prince became very popular, and John de Witt's brother CORNELIUS was sentenced to banishment on a false accusation of conspiring to kill him. John went to the prison where he was, to take him away to exile, in his coach; and a great mob who collected on the occasion, then and there cruelly murdered both the brothers. This left the government in the hands of the Prince, who was really the choice of the nation; and from this time he exercised it with the greatest vigour, against the whole power of France, under its famous generals CONDÉ and TURENNE, and in support of the Protestant religion. It was full seven years before this war ended in a treaty of peace made at Nimeguen, and its details would occupy a very considerable space. It is enough to say that William of Orange established a famous character with the whole world; and that the Merry Monarch, adding to and improving on his former baseness, bound himself to do everything the King of France liked, and nothing the King of France did not like, for a pension of one hundred thousand pounds a year, which was afterwards doubled. Besides this, the King of France, by means of his corrupt ambassador – who wrote accounts of his proceedings in England, which are not always to be believed, I think – bought our English members of Parliament, as he wanted them. So, in point of fact, during a considerable portion of this merry reign, the King of France was the real King of this country.

But there was a better time to come, and it was to come (though his royal uncle little thought so) through that very William, Prince of Orange. He came over to England, saw Mary, the elder daughter of the Duke of York, and married her. We shall see by-and-by what came of that marriage, and why it is never to be forgotten.

This daughter was a Protestant, but her mother died a Catholic. She and her sister ANNE, also a Protestant, were the only survivors of eight children. Anne afterwards married GEORGE, PRINCE OF DENMARK, brother to the King of that country.

Lest you should do the Merry Monarch the injustice of supposing that he was even good humoured (except when he had everything his own way), or that he was high spirited and honourable, I will mention here what was done to a member of the House of Commons, SIR JOHN COVENTRY. He made a remark in a debate about taxing the theatres, which gave the King offence. The King agreed with his illegitimate son, who had been born abroad, and whom he had made DUKE OF MONMOUTH, to take the following merry vengeance. To waylay him at night, fifteen armed men to one, and to slit his nose with a penknife. Like master, like man. The King's favourite, the Duke of Buckingham, was strongly suspected of setting on an assassin to murder the DUKE OF ORMOND as he was returning home from a dinner; and that Duke's spirited son, LORD OSSORY, was so persuaded of his guilt, that he said to him at

Court, even as he stood beside the King, 'My lord, I know very well that you are at the bottom of this late attempt upon my father. But I give you warning, if he ever come to a violent end, his blood shall be upon you, and wherever I meet you I will pistol you! I will do so, though I find you standing behind the King's chair; and I tell you this in his Majesty's presence, that you may be quite sure of my doing what I threaten.' Those were merry times indeed.

There was a fellow named BLOOD, who was seized for making, with two companions, an audacious attempt to steal the crown, the globe, and sceptre, from the place where the jewels were kept in the Tower. This robber, who was a swaggering ruffian, being taken, declared that he was the man who had endeavoured to kill the Duke of Ormond, and that he had meant to kill the King too, but was overawed by the majesty of his appearance, when he might otherwise have done it, as he was bathing at Battersea. The King being but an ill-looking fellow, I don't believe a word of this. Whether he was flattered, or whether he knew that Buckingham had really set Blood on to murder the Duke, is uncertain. But it is quite certain that he pardoned this thief, gave him an estate of five hundred a year in Ireland (which had had the honour of giving him birth), and presented him at Court to the debauched lords and the shameless ladies, who made a great deal of him – as I have no doubt they would have made of the Devil himself, if the King had introduced him.

Infamously pensioned as he was, the King still wanted money, and consequently was obliged to call Parliaments. In these, the great object of the Protestants was to thwart the Catholic Duke of York, who married a second time; his new wife being a young lady only fifteen years old, the Catholic sister of the DUKE OF MODENA. In this they were seconded by the Protestant Dissenters, though to their own disadvantage: since, to exclude Catholics from power, they were even willing to exclude themselves. The King's object was to pretend to be a Protestant, while he was really a Catholic; to swear to the bishops that he was devoutly attached to the English Church, while he knew he had bargained it away to the King of France; and by cheating and deceiving them, and all who were attached to royalty, to become despotic and be powerful enough to confess what a rascal he was. Meantime, the King of France, knowing his merry pensioner well, intrigued with the King's opponents in Parliament, as well as with the King and his friends.

The fears that the country had of the Catholic religion being restored, if the Duke of York should come to the throne, and the low cunning of the King in pretending to share their alarms, led to some very terrible results. A certain DR TONGE, a dull clergyman in the City, fell into the hands of a certain TITUS OATES, a most infamous character, who pretended to have acquired among the Jesuits abroad a knowledge of a great plot for the murder of the King, and the re-establishment of the Catholic religion. Titus Oates, being produced by this unlucky Dr Tonge and solemnly examined before the council, contradicted himself in a thousand ways, told the most ridiculous and improbable stories, and implicated COLEMAN, the Secretary of the Duchess of York. Now, although what he charged against Coleman was not true, and although you and I know very well that the real dangerous Catholic plot was that one with the King of France of which the Merry Monarch was himself the head, there happened to be found among Coleman's papers, some letters, in which he did praise the days of Bloody Queen Mary, and abuse the Protestant religion. This was great good fortune for Titus, as it seemed to confirm him; but better still was in store. SIR EDMUNDBURY GODFREY, the magistrate who had first examined him, being unexpectedly found dead near Primrose Hill, was confidently believed to have been killed by the Catholics. I think there is no doubt that he had been melancholy mad, and that he killed himself; but he had a great Protestant funeral, and Titus was called the Saver of the Nation, and received a pension of twelve hundred pounds a year.

As soon as Oates's wickedness had met with this success, up started another villain, named WILLIAM BEDLOE, who, attracted by a reward of five hundred pounds offered for the apprehension of the murderers of Godfrey, came forward and charged two Jesuits and some other persons with having committed it at the Queen's desire. Oates, going into partnership with this new informer, had the audacity to accuse the poor Queen herself of high treason. Then appeared a third informer, as bad as either of the two, and accused a Catholic banker named STAYLEY of having said that the King was the greatest rogue in the world (which would not have been far from the truth), and that he would kill him with his own hand. This banker, being at once tried and executed, Coleman and two others were tried and executed. Then a miserable wretch named PRANCE, a Catholic silversmith, being accused by Bedloe, was tortured into confessing that he had taken part in Godfrey's murder, and into accusing three other men of having committed it. Then, five Jesuits were accused by Oates, Bedloe, and Prance together, and were all found guilty, and executed on the same kind of contradictory and absurd evidence. The Queen's physician and three monks were next put on their trial; but Oates and Bedloe had for the time gone far enough, and these four were acquitted. The public mind, however, was so full of a Catholic plot, and so strong against the Duke of York, that James consented to obey a written order from his brother, and to go with his family to Brussels, provided that his rights should never be sacrificed in his absence to the Duke of Monmouth. The House of Commons, not satisfied with this as the King hoped, passed a bill to exclude the Duke from ever succeeding to the throne. In return, the King dissolved the Parliament. He had deserted his old favourite, the Duke of Buckingham, who was now in the opposition.

To give any sufficient idea of the miseries of Scotland in this merry reign, would occupy a hundred pages. Because the people would not have bishops, and were resolved to stand by their Solemn League and Covenant, such cruelties were inflicted upon them as make the blood run cold. Ferocious dragoons galloped through the country to punish the peasants for deserting the churches; sons were hanged up at their fathers' doors for refusing to disclose where their fathers were concealed; wives were tortured to death for not betraying their husbands; people were taken out of their fields and gardens, and shot on the public roads without trial; lighted matches were tied to the fingers of prisoners, and a most horrible torment called the Boot was invented, and constantly applied, which ground and mashed the victims' legs with iron wedges. Witnesses were tortured as well as prisoners. All the prisons were full; all the gibbets were heavy with bodies; murder and plunder devastated the whole country. In spite of all, the Covenanters were by no means to be dragged into the churches, and persisted in worshipping God as they thought right. A body of ferocious Highlanders, turned upon them from the mountains of their own country, had no greater effect than the English dragoons under GRAHAME OF

CLAVERHOUSE, the most cruel and rapacious of all their enemies, whose name will ever be cursed through the length and breadth of Scotland. Archbishop Sharp had ever aided and abetted all these outrages. But he fell at last; for, when the injuries of the Scottish people were at their height, he was seen, in his coach-and-six coming across a moor, by a body of men, headed by one JOHN BALFOUR, who were waiting for another of their oppressors. Upon this they cried out that Heaven had delivered him into their hands, and killed him with many wounds. If ever a man deserved such a death, I think Archbishop Sharp did.

It made a great noise directly, and the Merry Monarch – strongly suspected of having goaded the Scottish people on, that he might have an excuse for a greater army than the Parliament were willing to give him – sent down his son, the Duke of Monmouth, as commander-in-chief, with instructions to attack the Scottish rebels, or Whigs as they were called, whenever he came up with them. Marching with ten thousand men from Edinburgh, he found them, in number four or five thousand, drawn up at Bothwell Bridge, by the Clyde. They were soon dispersed; and Monmouth showed a more humane character towards them, than he had shown towards that Member of Parliament whose nose he had caused to be slit with a penknife. But the Duke of Lauderdale was their bitter foe, and sent Claverhouse to finish them.

As the Duke of York became more and more unpopular the Duke of Monmouth became more and more popular. It would have been decent in the latter not to have voted in favour of the renewed bill for the exclusion of James from the throne; but he did so, much to the King's amusement, who used to sit in the House of Lords by the fire, hearing the debates, which he said were as good as a play. The House of Commons passed the bill by a large majority, and it was carried up to the House of Lords by LORD RUSSELL, one of the best of the leaders on the Protestant side. It was rejected there, chiefly because the bishops helped the King to get rid of it; and the fear of Catholic plots revived again. There had been another got up, by a fellow out of Newgate, named DANGERFIELD, which is more famous than it deserves to be, under the name of the MEAL-TUB PLOT. This jail-bird having been got out of Newgate by a MRS CELLIER, a Catholic nurse, had turned Catholic himself, and pretended that he knew of a plot among the Presbyterians against the King's life. This was very pleasant to the Duke of York, who hated the Presbyterians, who returned the compliment. He gave Dangerfield twenty guineas, and sent him to the King his brother. But Dangerfield, breaking down altogether in his charge, and being sent back to Newgate, almost astonished the Duke out of his five senses by suddenly swearing that the Catholic nurse had put that false design into his head, and that what he really knew about, was, a Catholic plot against the King; the evidence of which would be found in some papers, concealed in a meal-tub in Mrs Cellier's house. There they were, of course – for he had put them there himself – and so the tub gave the name to the plot. But, the nurse was acquitted on her trial, and it came to nothing.

Lord Ashley, of the Cabal, was now Lord Shaftesbury, and was strong against the succession of the Duke of York. The House of Commons, aggravated to the utmost extent, as we may well suppose, by suspicions of the King's conspiracy with the King of France, made a desperate point of the exclusion still, and were bitter against the Catholics generally. So unjustly bitter were they, I grieve to say, that they impeached the venerable Lord Stafford, a Catholic nobleman seventy years old, of a design to kill the King. The witnesses were that atrocious Oates and two other birds of the same feather. He was found guilty, on evidence quite as foolish as it was false, and was beheaded on Tower Hill. The people were opposed to him when he first appeared upon the scaffold; but, when he had addressed them and shown them how innocent he was and how wickedly he was sent there, their better nature was aroused, and they said, 'We believe you, my Lord. God bless you, my Lord!'

The House of Commons refused to let the King have any money until he should consent to the Exclusion Bill; but, as he could get it and did get it from his master the King of France, he could afford to hold them very cheap. He called a Parliament at Oxford, to which he went down with a great show of being armed and protected as if he were in danger of his life, and to which the opposition members also went armed and protected, alleging that they were in fear of the Papists, who were numerous among the King's guards. However, they went on with the Exclusion Bill, and were so earnest upon it that they would have carried it again, if the King had not popped his crown and state robes into a sedan-chair, bundled himself into it along with them, hurried down to the chamber where the House of Lords met, and dissolved the Parliament. After which he scampered home, and the members of Parliament scampered home too, as fast as their legs could carry them.

The Duke of York, then residing in Scotland, had, under the law which excluded Catholics from public trusts, no right whatever to public employment. Nevertheless, he was openly employed as the King's representative in Scotland, and there gratified his sullen and cruel nature to his heart's content by directing the dreadful cruelties against the Covenanters. There were two ministers named CARGILL and CAMERON who had escaped from the battle of Bothwell Bridge, and who returned to Scotland, and raised the miserable but still brave and unsubdued Covenanters afresh, under the name of Cameronians. As Cameron publicly posted a declaration that the King was a forsworn tyrant, no mercy was shown to his unhappy followers after he was slain in battle. The Duke of York, who was particularly fond of the Boot and derived great pleasure from having it applied, offered their lives to some of these people, if they would cry on the scaffold 'God save the King.' But their relations, friends, and countrymen, had been so barbarously tortured and murdered in this merry reign, that they preferred to die, and did die. The Duke then obtained his merry brother's permission to hold a Parliament in Scotland, which first, with most shameless deceit, confirmed the laws for securing the Protestant religion against Popery, and then declared that nothing must or should prevent the succession of the Popish Duke. After this double-faced beginning, it established an oath which no human being could understand, but which everybody was to take, as a proof that his religion was the lawful religion. The Earl of Argyle, taking it with the explanation that he did not consider it to prevent him from favouring any alteration either in the Church or State which was not inconsistent with the Protestant religion or with his loyalty, was tried for high treason before a Scottish jury of which the MARQUIS OF MONTROSE was foreman, and was found guilty. He escaped the scaffold, for that time, by getting away, in the disguise of a page in the train of his daughter, LADY SOPHIA LINDSAY. It was absolutely proposed, by certain members of the Scottish Council, that this lady should be whipped through the streets of Edinburgh. But this was too much even for the Duke, who had the manliness then (he had very little at most times) to remark that Englishmen were not accustomed to treat ladies in that manner. In those merry times nothing could equal the brutal servility of the Scottish fawners, but the conduct of similar degraded beings in England.

After the settlement of these little affairs, the Duke returned to England, and soon resumed his place at the Council, and his office of High Admiral – all this by his brother's favour, and in open defiance of the law. It would have been no loss to the country, if he had been drowned when his ship, in going to Scotland to fetch his family, struck on a sand-bank, and was lost with two hundred souls on board. But he escaped in a boat with some friends; and the sailors were so brave and unselfish, that, when they saw him rowing away, they gave three cheers, while they themselves were going down for ever.

The Merry Monarch, having got rid of his Parliament, went to work to make himself despotic, with all speed. Having had the villainy to order the execution of OLIVER PLUNKET, BISHOP OF ARMAGH, falsely accused of a plot to establish Popery in that country by means of a French army – the very thing this royal traitor was himself trying to do at home – and having tried to ruin Lord Shaftesbury, and failed – he turned his hand to controlling the corporations all over the country; because, if he could only do that, he could get what juries he chose, to bring in perjured verdicts, and could get what members he chose, returned to Parliament. These merry times produced, and made Chief Justice of the Court of King's Bench, a drunken ruffian of the name of JEFFREYS; a red-faced swollen bloated horrible creature, with a bullying roaring voice, and a more savage nature perhaps than was ever lodged in any human breast. This monster was the Merry Monarch's especial favourite, and he testified his admiration of him by giving him a ring from his own finger, which the people used to call Judge Jeffreys's Bloodstone. Him the King employed to go about and bully the corporations, beginning with London; or, as Jeffreys himself elegantly called it, 'to give them a lick with the rough side of his tongue.' And he did it so thoroughly, that they soon became the basest and most sycophantic bodies in the kingdom – except the University of Oxford, which, in that respect, was quite pre-eminent and unapproachable.

Lord Shaftesbury (who died soon after the King's failure

against him), LORD WILLIAM RUSSELL, the Duke of Monmouth, LORD HOWARD, LORD JERSEY, ALGERNON SIDNEY,
JOHN HAMPDEN (grandson of the great Hampden), and some
others, used to hold a council together after the dissolution of
the Parliament, arranging what it might be necessary to do, if
the King carried his Popish plot to the utmost height. Lord
Shaftesbury having been much the most violent of this party,
brought two violent men into their secrets – RUMSEY, who had
been a soldier in the Republican army; and WEST, a lawyer.
These two knew an old officer of Cromwell's, called RUMBOLD,
who had married a maltster's widow, and so had come into
possession of a solitary dwelling called the Rye House, near
Hoddesdon, in Hertfordshire. Rumbold said to them what a
capital place this house of his would be from which to shoot at
the King, who often passed there going to and fro from
Newmarket. They liked the idea, and entertained it. But, one of
their body gave information; and they, together with SHEP-
HERD, a wine merchant, Lord Russell, Algernon Sidney, LORD
ESSEX, LORD HOWARD, and Hampden, were all arrested.

Lord Russell might have easily escaped, but scorned to do so,
being innocent of any wrong; Lord Essex might have easily
escaped, but scorned to do so, lest his flight should prejudice
Lord Russell. But it weighed upon his mind that he had brought
into their council, Lord Howard – who now turned a miserable
traitor – against a great dislike Lord Russell had always had of
him. He could not bear the reflection, and destroyed himself
before Lord Russell was brought to trial at the Old Bailey.

He knew very well that he had nothing to hope, having always
been manful in the Protestant cause against the two false
brothers, the one on the throne, and the other standing next to
it. He had a wife, one of the noblest and best of women, who
acted as his secretary on his trial, who comforted him in his
prison, who supped with him on the night before he died, and
whose love and virtue and devotion have made her name
imperishable. Of course, he was found guilty, and was sentenced
to be beheaded in Lincoln's Inn-Fields, not many yards from his
own house. When he had parted from his children on the
evening before his death, his wife still stayed with him until ten
o'clock at night; and when their final separation in this world
was over, and he had kissed her many times, he still sat for a
long while in his prison, talking of her goodness. Hearing the

rain fall fast at that time, he calmly said, 'Such a rain to-morrow will spoil a great show, which is a dull thing on a rainy day.' At midnight he went to bed, and slept till four; even when his servant called him, he fell asleep again while his clothes were being made ready. He rode to the scaffold in his own carriage, attended by two famous clergymen, TILLOTSON and BURNET, and sang a psalm to himself very softly, as he went along. He was as quiet and as steady as if he had been going out for an ordinary ride. After saying that he was surprised to see so great a crowd, he laid down his head upon the block, as if upon the pillow of his bed, and had it struck off at the second blow. His noble wife was busy for him even then; for that true-hearted lady printed and widely circulated his last words, of which he had given her a copy. They made the blood of all the honest men in England boil.

The University of Oxford distinguished itself on the very same day by pretending to believe that the accusation against Lord Russell was true, and by calling the King, in a written paper, the Breath of their Nostrils and the Anointed of the Lord. This paper the Parliament afterwards caused to be burned by the common hangman; which I am sorry for, as I wish it had been framed and glazed and hung up in some public place, as a monument of baseness for the scorn of mankind.

Next, came the trial of Algernon Sidney, at which Jeffreys presided, like a great crimson toad, sweltering and swelling with rage. 'I pray God, Mr Sidney,' said this Chief Justice of a merry reign, after passing sentence, 'to work in you a temper fit to go to the other world, for I see you are not fit for this.' 'My lord,' said the prisoner, composedly holding out his arm, 'feel my pulse, and see if I be disordered. I thank Heaven I never was in better temper than I am now.' Algernon Sidney was executed on Tower Hill, on the seventh of December, one thousand six hundred and eighty-three. He died a hero, and died, in his own words, 'For that good old cause in which he had been engaged from his youth, and for which God had so often and so wonderfully declared himself.'

The Duke of Monmouth had been making his uncle, the Duke of York, very jealous, by going about the country in a royal sort of way, playing at the people's games, becoming godfather to their children, and even touching for the King's evil, or stroking the faces of the sick to cure them – though, for the matter of that, I should say he did them about as much good as any crowned king could have done. His father had got him to write a letter, confessing his having had a part in the conspiracy, for which Lord Russell had been beheaded; but he was ever a weak man, and as soon as he had written it, he was ashamed of it and got it back again. For this, he was banished to the Netherlands; but he soon returned and had an interview with his father, unknown to his uncle. It would seem that he was coming into the Merry Monarch's favour again, and that the Duke of York was sliding out of it, when Death appeared to the merry galleries at Whitehall, and astonished the debauched lords and gentlemen, and the shameless ladies, very considerably.

On Monday, the second of February, one thousand six hundred and eight-five, the merry pensioner and servant of the King of France fell down in a fit of apoplexy. By the Wednesday his case was hopeless, and on the Thursday he was told so. As he made a difficulty about taking the sacrament from the Protestant Bishop of Bath, the Duke of York got all who were present away from the bed, and asked his brother, in a whisper, if he should send for a Catholic priest? The King replied, 'For God's sake, brother, do!' The Duke smuggled in, up the back stairs, disguised in a wig and gown, a priest named HUDDLE-STON, who had saved the King's life after the battle of Worcester: telling him that this worthy man in the wig had once saved his body, and was now come to save his soul.

The Merry Monarch lived through that night, and died before noon on the next day, which was Friday, the sixth. Two of the last things he said were of a human sort, and your remembrance will give him the full benefit of them. When the Queen sent to say she was too unwell to attend him and to ask his pardon, he said, 'Alas! poor woman, *she* beg *my* pardon! I beg hers with all my heart. Take back that answer to her.' And he also said, in reference to Nell Gwyn, 'Do not let poor Nelly starve.'

He died in the fifty-fifth year of his age, and the twenty-fifth of his reign.

CHAPTER 36

England under James the Second

KING JAMES THE SECOND was a man so very disagreeable, that even the best of historians has favoured his brother Charles, as becoming, by comparison, quite a pleasant character. The one object of his short reign was to re-establish the Catholic religion in England; and this he doggedly pursued with such a stupid obstinacy, that his career very soon came to a close.

The first thing he did, was, to assure his council that he would make it his endeavour to preserve the Government, both in Church and State, as it was by law established; and that he would always take care to defend and support the Church. Great public acclamations were raised over this fair speech, and a great deal was said, from the pulpits and elsewhere, about the word of a King which was never broken, by credulous people who little supposed that he had formed a secret council for Catholic affairs, of which a mischievous Jesuit, called FATHER PETRE, was one of the chief members. With tears of joy in his eyes, he received, as the beginning of *his* pension from the King of France, five hundred thousand livres; yet, with a mixture of meanness and arrogance that belonged to his contemptible character, he was always jealous of making some show of being independent of the King of France, while he pocketed his money. As – notwithstanding his publishing two papers in favour of Popery (and not likely to do it much service, I should think) written by the King, his brother, and found in his strong-box; and his open display of himself attending mass – the Parliament was very obsequious, and granted him a large sum of money, he began his reign with a belief that he could do what he pleased, and with a determination to do it.

Before we proceed to its principal events, let us dispose of Titus Oates. He was tried for perjury, a fortnight after the coronation, and besides being very heavily fined, was sentenced to stand twice in the pillory, to be whipped from Aldgate to Newgate one day, and from Newgate to Tyburn two days afterwards, and to stand in the pillory five times a year as long as he lived. This fearful sentence was actually inflicted on the rascal. Being unable to stand after his first flogging, he was dragged on a sledge from Newgate to Tyburn, and flogged as he was drawn along. He was so strong a villain that he did not die under the torture, but lived to be afterwards pardoned and rewarded, though not to be ever believed in any more. Dangerfield, the only other one of that crew left alive, was not so fortunate. He was almost killed by a whipping from Newgate to Tyburn, and, as if that were not punishment enough, a ferocious barrister of Gray's Inn gave him a poke in the eye with his cane, which caused his death; for which the ferocious barrister was deservedly tried and executed.

As soon as James was on the throne, Argyle and Monmouth went from Brussels to Rotterdam, and attended a meeting of Scottish exiles held there, to concert measures for a rising in England. It was agreed that Argyle should effect a landing in Scotland, and Monmouth in England; and that two Englishmen should be sent with Argyle to be in his confidence, and two Scotchmen with the Duke of Monmouth.

Argyle was the first to act upon this contract. But, two of his men being taken prisoners at the Orkney Islands, the Government became aware of his intention, and was able to act against him with such vigour as to prevent his raising more than two or three thousand Highlanders, although he sent a fiery cross, by trusty messengers, from clan to clan and from glen to glen, as the custom then was when those wild people were to be excited by their chiefs. As he was moving towards Glasgow with his small force, he was betrayed by some of his followers, taken, and carried, with his hands tied behind his back, to his old prison in Edinburgh Castle. James ordered him to be executed, on his old shamefully unjust sentence, within three days; and he appears to have been anxious that his legs should have been pounded with his old favourite the boot. However, the boot was not applied; he was simply beheaded, and his head was set upon the top of Edinburgh Jail. One of those Englishmen who had been assigned to him was that old soldier Rumbold, the master of the Rye House. He was sorely wounded, and within a week after Argyle had suffered with great courage, was brought up for trial, lest he should die and disappoint the King. He, too, was executed, after defending himself with great spirit, and saying that he did not believe that God had made the greater part of mankind to carry saddles on their backs and bridles in their mouths, and to be ridden by a few, booted and spurred for the purpose – in which I thoroughly agree with Rumbold.

The Duke of Monmouth, partly through being detained and partly through idling his time away, was five or six weeks behind his friend when he landed at Lyme, in Dorset: having at his right hand an unlucky nobleman called LORD GREY OF WERK, who of himself would have ruined a far more promising expedition. He immediately set up his standard in the market-place, and proclaimed the King a tyrant, and a Popish usurper, and I know not what else; charging him, not only with what he had done, which was bad enough, but with what neither he nor anybody else had done, such as setting fire to London, and poisoning the late King. Raising some four thousand men by these means, he marched on to Taunton, where there were many Protestant dissenters who were strongly opposed to the Catholics. Here, both the rich and poor turned out to receive him, ladies waved a welcome to him from all the windows as he passed along the streets, flowers were strewn in his way, and every compliment and honour that could be devised was showered upon him. Among the rest, twenty young ladies came forward, in their best clothes, and in their brightest beauty, and gave him a Bible ornamented with their own fair hands, together with other presents.

Encouraged by this homage, he proclaimed himself King, and went on to Bridgewater. But, here the Government troops, under the EARL OF FEVERSHAM, were close at hand; and he was so dispirited at finding that he made but few powerful friends after all, that it was a question whether he should disband his army and endeavour to escape. It was resolved, at the instance of that unlucky Lord Grey, to make a night attack on the King's army, as it lay encamped on the edge of a morass called Sedgemoor. The horsemen were commanded by the same unlucky lord, who was not a brave man. He gave up the battle almost at the first obstacle – which was a deep drain; and although the poor countrymen, who had turned out for Monmouth, fought bravely with scythes, poles, pitchforks, and such poor weapons as they had, they were soon dispersed by the trained soldiers, and fled in all directions. When the Duke of Monmouth himself fled, was not known in the confusion; but the unlucky Lord Grey was taken early next day, and then another of the party was taken, who had confessed that he had parted from the Duke only four hours before. Strict search being made, he was found disguised as a peasant, hidden in a ditch under fern and nettles, with a few peas in his pocket which he had gathered in the fields to eat. The only other articles he had upon him were a few papers and little books: one of the latter being a strange jumble, in his own writing, of charms, songs, recipes, and prayers. He was completely broken. He wrote a miserable letter to the King, beseeching and entreating to be allowed to see him. When he was taken to London, and conveyed bound into the King's presence, he crawled to him on his knees, and made a most degrading exhibition. As James never forgave or relented towards anybody, he was not likely to soften towards the issuer of the Lyme proclamation, so he told the suppliant to prepare for death.

On the fifteenth of July, one thousand six hundred and eighty-five, this unfortunate favourite of the people was brought out to die on Tower Hill. The crowd was immense, and the tops of all the houses were covered with gazers. He had seen his wife, the daughter of the Duke of Buccleuch, in the Tower, and had talked much of a lady whom he loved far better – the LADY HARRIET WENTWORTH – who was one of the last persons he remembered in this life. Before laying down his head upon the block he felt the edge of the axe, and told the executioner that he feared it was not sharp enough, and that the axe was not heavy enough. On the executioner replying that it was of the proper kind, the Duke said, 'I pray you have a care, and do not use me so awkwardly as you used my Lord Russell.' The executioner, made nervous by this, and trembling, struck once and merely gashed him in the neck. Upon this, the Duke of Monmouth raised his head and looked the man reproachfully in the face. Then he struck twice, and then thrice, and then threw down the axe, and cried out in a voice of horror that he could not finish that work. The sheriffs, however, threatening him with what should be done to himself if he did not, he took it up again and struck a fourth time and a fifth time. Then the wretched head at last fell off, and, James, Duke of Monmouth, was dead, in the thirty-sixth year of his age. He was a showy graceful man, with many popular qualities, and had found much favour in the open hearts of the English.

The atrocities, committed by the Government, which followed this Monmouth rebellion, form the blackest and most lamentable page in English history. The poor peasants, having been dispersed with great loss, and their leaders having been taken, one would think that the implacable King might have been satisfied. But no; he let loose upon them, among other intolerable monsters, a COLONEL KIRK, who had served against the Moors, and whose soldiers – called by the people Kirk's lambs, because they bore a lamb upon their flag, as the emblem of Christianity – were worthy of their leader. The atrocities committed by these demons in human shape are far too horrible to be related here. It is enough to say, that besides most ruthlessly murdering and robbing them, and ruining them by making them buy their pardons at the price of all they possessed, it was one of Kirk's favourite amusements, as he and his officers sat drinking after dinner, and toasting the King, to have batches of prisoners hanged outside the windows for the company's diversion; and that when their feet quivered in the convulsions of death, he used to swear that they should have music to their dancing, and would order the drums to beat and the trumpets to play. The detestable King informed him as an acknowledgment of these services, that he was 'very well satisfied with his proceedings.' But the King's great delight was in the proceedings of Jeffreys, now a peer, who went down into the west, with four other judges, to try persons accused of having had any share in the rebellion. The King pleasantly called this 'Jeffreys's campaign.' The people down in that part of the country remember it to this day as The Bloody Assize.

It began at Winchester, where a poor deaf old lady, MRS ALICIA LISLE, the widow of one of the judges of Charles the First (who had been murdered abroad by some Royalist assassins), was charged with having given shelter in her house to two fugitives from Sedgemoor. Three times the jury refused to find her guilty, until Jeffreys bullied and frightened them into that false verdict. When he had extorted it from them, he said, 'Gentlemen, if I had been one of you, and she had been my own mother, I would have found her guilty;' – as I dare say he would. He sentenced her to be burned alive, that very afternoon. The clergy of the cathedral and some others interfered in her favour, and she was beheaded within a week. As a high mark of his approbation, the King made Jeffreys Lord Chancellor; and he then went on to Dorchester, to Exeter, to Taunton, and to Wells. It is astonishing, when we read of the enormous injustice and barbarity of this beast, to know that no one struck him dead on the judgment-seat. It was enough for any man or woman to be accused by an enemy, before Jeffreys, to be found guilty of high treason. One man who pleaded not guilty, he ordered to be taken out of court upon the instant, and hanged; and this so terrified the prisoners in general that they mostly pleaded guilty at once. At Dorchester alone, in the course of a few days, Jeffreys hanged eighty people; besides whipping, transporting, imprisoning, and selling as slaves, great numbers. He executed, in all, two hundred and fifty, or three hundred.

These executions took place, among the neighbours and friends of the sentenced, in thirty-six towns and villages. Their bodies were mangled, steeped in caldrons of boiling pitch and tar, and hung up by the roadsides, in the streets, over the very churches. The sight and smell of heads and limbs, the hissing and bubbling of the infernal caldrons, and the tears and terrors of the people, were dreadful beyond all description. One rustic, who was forced to steep the remains in the black pot, was ever afterwards called 'Tom Boilman.' The hangman has ever since been called Jack Ketch, because a man of that name went hanging and hanging, all day long, in the train of Jeffreys. You will hear much of the horrors of the great French Revolution. Many and terrible they were, there is no doubt; but I know of nothing worse, done by the maddened people of France in that awful time, than was done by the highest judge in England, with the express approval of the King of England, in The Bloody Assize.

Nor was even this all. Jeffreys was as fond of money for himself as of misery for others, and he sold pardons wholesale to fill his pockets. The King ordered, at one time, a thousand prisoners to be given to certain of his favourites, in order that they might bargain with them for their pardons. The young ladies of Taunton who had presented the Bible, were bestowed upon the maids of honour at court; and those precious ladies made very hard bargains with them indeed. When The Bloody Assize was at its most dismal height, the King was diverting himself with horse-races in the very place where Mrs Lisle had been executed. When Jeffreys had done his worst, and came home again, he was particularly complimented in the Royal Gazette; and when the King heard that through drunkenness and raging he was very ill, his odious Majesty remarked that such another man could not easily be found in England. Besides all this, a former sheriff of London, named CORNISH, was hanged within sight of his own house, after an abominably conducted trial, for having had a share in the Rye House Plot, on evidence given by Rumsey, which that villain was obliged to confess was directly opposed to the evidence he had given on the trial of Lord Russell. And on the very same day, a worthy widow, named ELIZABETH GAUNT, was burned alive at Tyburn, for having sheltered a wretch who himself gave evidence against her. She settled the fuel about herself with her own hands, so that the flames should reach her quickly: and nobly said, with her last breath, that she had obeyed the sacred command of God, to give refuge to the outcast, and not to betray the wanderer.

After all this hanging, beheading, burning, boiling, mutilating, exposing, robbing, transporting, and selling into slavery, of his unhappy subjects, the King not unnaturally thought that he could do whatever he would. So he went to work to change the religion of the country with all possible speed; and what he did was this.

He first of all tried to get rid of what was called the Test Act – which prevented the Catholics from holding public employments – by his own power of dispensing with the penalties. He tried it in one case, and, eleven of the twelve judges deciding in his favour, he exercised it in three others, being those of three dignitaries of University College, Oxford, who had become Papists, and whom he kept in their places and sanctioned. He revived the hated Ecclesiastical Commission, to get rid of COMPTON, Bishop of London, who manfully opposed him. He solicited the Pope to favour England with an ambassador, which the Pope (who was a sensible man then) rather unwillingly did. He flourished Father Petre before the eyes of the people on all possible occasions. He favoured the establishment of convents in several parts of London. He was delighted to have the streets, and even the court itself, filled with Monks and Friars in the habits of their orders. He constantly endeavoured to make Catholics of the Protestants about him. He held private interviews, which he called 'closetings,' with those Members of Parliament who held offices, to persuade them to consent to the design he had in view. When they did not consent, they were removed, or resigned of themselves, and their places were given to Catholics. He displaced Protestant officers from the army, by every means in his power, and got Catholics into their places too. He tried the same thing with the corporations, and also (though not so successfully) with the Lord Lieutenants of counties. To terrify the people into the endurance of all these measures, he kept an army of fifteen thousand men encamped on Hounslow Heath, where mass was openly performed in the General's tent, and where priests went among the soldiers endeavouring to persuade them to become Catholics. For circulating a paper among those men advising them to be true to their religion, a Protestant clergyman, named JOHNSON, the chaplain of the late Lord Russell, was actually sentenced to stand three times in the pillory, and was actually whipped from Newgate to Tyburn. He dismissed his own brother-in-law from his Council because he was a Protestant, and made a Privy Councillor of the before-mentioned Father Petre. He handed Ireland over to RICHARD TALBOT, EARL OF TYRCONNELL, a worthless, dissolute knave, who played the same game there for his master, and who played the deeper game for himself of one day putting it under the protection of the French King. In going to these extremities, every man of sense and judgment among the Catholics, from the Pope to a porter, knew that the King was a mere bigoted fool, who would undo himself and the cause he sought to advance; but he was deaf to all reason, and, happily for England ever afterwards, went tumbling off his throne in his own blind way.

A spirit began to arise in the country, which the besotted blunderer little expected. He first found it out in the University of Cambridge. Having made a Catholic, a dean, at Oxford, without any opposition, he tried to make a monk a master of arts at Cambridge: which attempt the University resisted, and defeated him. He then went back to his favourite Oxford. On the death of the President of Magdalen College, he commanded that there should be elected to succeed him, one MR ANTHONY FARMER, whose only recommendation was, that he was of the King's religion. The University plucked up courage at last, and refused. The King substituted another man, and it still refused, resolving to stand by its own election of a MR HOUGH. The dull tyrant, upon this, punished Mr Hough, and five-and-twenty more, by causing them to be expelled and declared incapable of holding any church preferment; then he proceeded to what he supposed to be his highest step, but to what was, in fact, his last plunge head-foremost in his tumble off his throne.

He had issued a declaration that there should be no religious tests or penal laws, in order to let in the Catholics more easily; but the Protestant dissenters, unmindful of themselves, had gallantly joined the regular church in opposing it tooth and nail. The King and Father Petre now resolved to have this read, on a certain Sunday, in all the churches, and to order it to be circulated for that purpose by the bishops. The latter took counsel with the Archbishop of Canterbury, who was in disgrace; and they resolved that the declaration should not be read, and that they would petition the King against it. The Archbishop himself wrote out the petition, and six bishops went into the King's bedchamber the same night to present it, to his infinite astonishment. Next day was the Sunday fixed for the reading, and it was only read by two hundred clergymen out of ten thousand. The King resolved against all advice to prosecute the bishops in the Court of King's Bench, and within three weeks they were summoned before the Privy Council, and committed to the Tower. As the six bishops were taken to that dismal place, by water, the people who were assembled in immense numbers fell upon their knees, and wept for them, and prayed for them. When they got to the Tower, the officers and soldiers on guard besought them for their blessing. While they were confined there, the soldiers every day drank to their release with loud shouts. When they were brought up to the Court of King's Bench for their trial, which the Attorney-General said was for the high offence of censuring the Government, and giving their opinion about affairs of state, they were attended by similar multitudes, and surrounded by a throng of noblemen and gentlemen. When the jury went out at seven o'clock at night to consider of their verdict, everybody (except the King) knew that they would rather starve than yield to the King's brewer, who was one of them, and wanted a verdict for his customer. When they came into court next morning, after resisting the brewer all night, and gave a verdict of not guilty, such a shout rose up in Westminster Hall as it had never heard before; and it was passed on among the people away to Temple Bar, and away again to the Tower. It did not pass only to the east, but passed to the west too, until it reached the camp at Hounslow, where the fifteen thousand soldiers took it up and echoed it. And still, when the dull King, who was then with Lord Feversham, heard the mighty roar, asked in alarm what it was, and was told that it was 'nothing but the acquittal of the bishops,' he said, in his dogged way, 'Call you that nothing? It is so much the worse for them.'

Between the petition and the trial, the Queen had given birth to a son, which Father Petre rather thought was owing to Saint Winifred. But I doubt if Saint Winifred had much to do with it as the King's friend, inasmuch as the entirely new prospect of a Catholic successor (for both the King's daughters were Protestants) determined the EARLS OF SHREWSBURY, DANBY, and DEVONSHIRE, LORD LUMLEY, the BISHOP OF LONDON, ADMIRAL RUSSELL, and COLONEL SIDNEY, to invite the Prince of Orange over to England. The Royal Mole, seeing his danger at last, made, in his fright, many great concessions, besides raising an army of forty thousand men; but the Prince of Orange was not a man for James the Second to cope with. His preparations were extraordinarily vigorous, and his mind was resolved.

For a fortnight after·the Prince was ready to sail for England, a great wind from the west prevented the departure of his fleet. Even when the wind lulled, and it did sail, it was dispersed by a storm, and was obliged to put back to refit. At last, on the first of November, one thousand six hundred and eighty-eight, the Protestant east wind, as it was long called, began to blow; and on the third, the people of Dover and the people of Calais saw a fleet twenty miles long sailing gallantly by, between the two places. On Monday, the fifth, it anchored at Torbay in Devonshire, and the Prince, with a splendid retinue of officers and men, marched into Exeter. But the people in that western part of the country had suffered so much in The Bloody Assize, that they had lost heart. Few people joined him; and he began to think of returning, and publishing the invitation he had received from those lords, as his justification for having come at all. At this crisis, some of the gentry joined him; the Royal army began to falter; an engagement was signed, by which all who set their hand to it declared that they would support one another in defence of the laws and liberties of the three Kingdoms, of the Protestant religion, and of the Prince of Orange. From that time, the cause received no check; the greatest towns in England began, one after another, to declare for the Prince; and he knew that it was all safe with him when the University of Oxford offered to melt down its plate, if he wanted any money.

By this time the King was running about in a pitiable way, touching people for the King's evil in one place, reviewing his troops in another, and bleeding from the nose in a third. The young Prince was sent to Portsmouth, Father Petre went off like a shot to France, and there was a general and swift dispersal of all the priests and friars. One after another, the King's most important officers and friends deserted him and went over to the Prince. In the night, his daughter Anne fled from Whitehall Palace; and the Bishop of London, who had once been a soldier, rode before her with a drawn sword in his hand, and pistols at his saddle. 'God help me,' cried the miserable King: 'my very children have forsaken me!' In his wildness, after debating with such lords as were in London, whether he should or should not call a Parliament, and after naming three of them to negotiate with the Prince, he resolved to fly to France. He had the little Prince of Wales brought back from Portsmouth; and the child and the Queen crossed the river to Lambeth in an open boat, on a miserable wet night, and got safely away. This was on the night of the ninth of December.

At one o'clock on the morning of the eleventh, the King, who had, in the meantime, received a letter from the Prince of Orange, stating his objects, got out of bed, told LORD NORTH-UMBERLAND who lay in his room not to open the door until the usual hour in the morning, and went down the back stairs (the same, I suppose, by which the priest in the wig and gown had come up to his brother) and crossed the river in a small boat: sinking the great seal of England by the way. Horses having been provided, he rode, accompanied by SIR EDWARD HALES, to Feversham, where he embarked in a Custom House Hoy. The master of this Hoy, wanting more ballast, ran into the Isle of Sheppy to get it, where the fishermen and smugglers crowded about the boat, and informed the King of their suspicions that he was a 'hatchet-faced Jesuit.' As they took his money and would not let him go, he told them who he was, and that the Prince of Orange wanted to take his life; and he began to scream for a boat – and then to cry, because he had lost a piece of wood on his ride which he called a fragment of Our Saviour's cross. He put himself into the hands of the Lord Lieutenant of the county, and his detention was made known to the Prince of

Orange at Windsor – who, only wanting to get rid of him, and not caring where he went, so that he went away, was very much disconcerted that they did not let him go. However, there was nothing for it but to have him brought back, with some state in the way of Life Guards, to Whitehall. And as soon as he got there, in his infatuation, he heard mass, and set a Jesuit to say grace at his public dinner.

The people had been thrown into the strangest state of confusion by his flight, and had taken it into their heads that the Irish part of the army were going to murder the Protestants. Therefore, they set the bells a ringing, and lighted watch-fires, and burned Catholic Chapels, and looked about in all directions for Father Petre and the Jesuits, while the Pope's ambassador was running away in the dress of a footman. They found no Jesuits; but a man, who had once been a frightened witness before Jeffreys in court, saw a swollen drunken face looking through a window down at Wapping, which he well remembered. The face was in a sailor's dress, but he knew it to be the face of that accursed Judge, and he seized him. The people, to their lasting honour, did not tear him to pieces. After knocking him about a little, they took him, in the basest agonies of terror, to the Lord Mayor, who sent him, at his own shrieking petition, to the Tower for safety. There, he died.

Their bewilderment continuing, the people now lighted bonfires and made rejoicings, as if they had any reason to be glad to have the King back again. But, his stay was very short, for the English guards were removed from Whitehall, Dutch guards were marched up to it, and he was told by one of his late ministers that the Prince would enter London, next day, and he had better go to Ham. He said, Ham was a cold damp place, and he would rather go to Rochester. He thought himself very cunning in this, as he meant to escape from Rochester to France. The Prince of Orange and his friends knew that, perfectly well, and desired nothing more. So, he went to Gravesend, in his royal barge, attended by certain lords, and watched by Dutch troops, and pitied by the generous people, who were far more forgiving than he had ever been, when they saw him in his humiliation. On the night of the twenty-third of December, not even then understanding that everybody wanted to get rid of him, he went out, absurdly, through his Rochester garden, down to the Medway, and got away to France, where he rejoined the Queen.

There had been a council in his absence, of the lords, and the authorities of London. When the Prince came, on the day after the King's departure, he summoned the Lords to meet him, and soon afterwards, all those who had served in any of the Parliaments of King Charles the Second. It was finally resolved by these authorities that the throne was vacant by the conduct of King James the Second; that it was inconsistent with the safety and welfare of this Protestant kingdom, to be governed by a Popish prince; that the Prince and Princess of Orange should be King and Queen during their lives and the life of the survivor of them; and that their children should succeed them, if they had any. That if they had none, the Princess Anne and her children should succeed; that if she had none, the heirs of the Prince of Orange should succeed.

On the thirteenth of January, one thousand six hundred and eighty-nine, the Prince and Princess, sitting on a throne in Whitehall, bound themselves to these conditions. The Protestant religion was established in England, and England's great and glorious Revolution was complete.

CHAPTER 37

Conclusion

I have now arrived at the close of my little history. The events which succeeded the famous Revolution of one thousand six hundred and eighty-eight, would neither be easily related nor easily understood in such a book as this.

William and Mary reigned together, five years. After the death of his good wife, William occupied the throne, alone, for seven years longer. During his reign, on the sixteenth of September, one thousand seven hundred and one, the poor weak creature who had once been James the Second of England, died in France. In the meantime he had done his utmost (which was not much) to cause William to be assassinated, and to regain his lost dominions. James's son was declared, by the French King, the rightful King of England; and was called in France THE CHEVALIER SAINT GEORGE, and in England THE PRETENDER. Some infatuated people in England, and particularly in Scotland, took up the Pretender's cause from time to time – as if the country had not had Stuarts enough! – and many lives were sacrificed, and much misery was occasioned. King William died on Sunday, the seventh of March, one thousand seven hundred and two, of the consequences of an accident occasioned by his horse stumbling with him. He was always a brave patriotic Prince, and a man of remarkable abilities. His manner was cold, and he made but few friends; but he had truly loved his queen. When he was dead, a lock of her hair, in a ring, was found tied with a black ribbon round his left arm.

He was succeeded by the PRINCESS ANNE, a popular Queen, who reigned twelve years. In her reign, in the month of May, one thousand seven hundred and seven, the Union between England and Scotland was effected, and the two countries were incorporated under the name of GREAT BRITAIN. Then, from the year one thousand seven hundred and fourteen to the year one thousand eight hundred and thirty, reigned the four GEORGES.

It was in the reign of George the Second, one thousand seven hundred and forty-five, that the Pretender did his last mischief, and made his last appearance. Being an old man by that time, he and the Jacobites – as his friends were called – put forward his son CHARLES EDWARD, known as the Young Chevalier. The Highlanders of Scotland, an extremely troublesome and wrong-headed race on the subject of the Stuarts, espoused his cause, and he joined them, and there was a Scottish rebellion to make him king, in which many gallant and devoted gentlemen lost their lives. It was a hard matter for Charles Edward to escape abroad again, with a high price on his head; but the Scottish people were extraordinarily faithful to him, and, after undergoing many romantic adventures, not unlike those of Charles the Second, he escaped to France. A number of charming stories and delightful songs arose out of the Jacobite feelings, and belong to the Jacobite times. Otherwise I think the Stuarts were a public nuisance altogether.

It was in the reign of George the Third that England lost North America, by persisting in taxing her without her own consent. That immense country, made independent under

WASHINGTON, and left to itself, became the United States; one of the greatest nations of the earth. In these times in which I write, it is honourably remarkable for protecting its subjects, wherever they may travel, with a dignity and a determination which is a model for England. Between you and me, England has rather lost ground in this respect since the days of Oliver Cromwell.

The Union of Great Britain with Ireland – which had been getting on very ill by itself – took place in the reign of George the Third, on the second of July, one thousand seven hundred and ninety-eight.

WILLIAM THE FOURTH succeeded George the Fourth, in the year one thousand eight hundred and thirty, and reigned seven years. QUEEN VICTORIA, his niece, the only child of the Duke of Kent, the fourth son of George the Third, came to the throne on the twentieth of June, one thousand eight hundred and thirty-seven. She was married to PRINCE ALBERT of Saxe Gotha on the tenth of February, one thousand eight hundred and forty. She is very good, and much beloved. So I end, like the crier, with

GOD SAVE THE QUEEN!

THE END

HOLIDAY ROMANCE

Initial Illustrations for Parts 1–4

PART I

Introductory Romance. From the Pen of William Tinkling Esquire*

This beginning-part is not made out of anybody's head you know. It's real. You must believe this beginning-part more than what comes after, else you won't understand how what comes after came to be written. You 'must believe it all, but you must believe this most, please. I am the Editor of it. Bob Redforth (he's my cousin, and shaking the table on purpose) wanted to be the Editor of it, but I said he shouldn't because he couldn't. *He* has no idea of being an Editor.

Nettie Ashford is my Bride. We were married in the right-hand closet in the corner of the dancing-school where first we met, with a ring (a green one) from Wilkingwater's toy-shop. *I* owed for it out of my pocket-money. When the rapturous ceremony was over, we all four went up the lane and let off a cannon (brought loaded in Bob Redforth's waistcoat-pocket) to announce our Nuptials. It flew right up when it went off, and turned over. Next day, Lieutenant-Colonel Robin Redforth was united, with similar ceremonies, to Alice Rainbird. This time, the cannon bust with a most terrific explosion, and made a puppy bark.

My peerless Bride was, at the period of which we now treat, in captivity at Miss Grimmer's. Drowvey and Grimmer is the partnership, and opinion is divided which the greatest Beast. The lovely Bride of the Colonel was also immured in the Dungeons of the same establishment. A vow was entered into between the Colonel and myself that we would cut them out on the following Wednesday, when walking two and two.

Under the desperate circumstances of the case, the active brain of the Colonel, combining with his lawless pursuit (he is a Pirate), suggested an attack with fireworks. This however, from motives of humanity, was abandoned as too expensive.

* Aged Eight.

Lightly armed with a paper-knife buttoned up under his jacket, and waving the dreaded black flag at the end of a cane, the Colonel took command of me at 2 P.M. on the eventful and appointed day. He had drawn out the plan of attack on a piece of paper which was rolled up round a hoop-stick. He showed it to me. My position and my full-length portrait (but my real ears don't stick out horizontal) was behind a corner-lamp-post, with written orders to remain there till I should see Miss Drowvey fall. The Drowvey who was to fall was the one in spectacles, not the one with the large lavender bonnet. At that signal I was to rush forth, seize my Bride, and fight my way to the lane. There, a junction would be effected between myself and the Colonel, and putting our Brides behind us, between ourselves and the palings, we were to conquer or die.

The enemy appeared – approached. Waving his black flag, the Colonel attacked. Confusion ensued. Anxiously I awaited my signal, but my signal came not. So far from falling, the hated Drowvey in spectacles appeared to me to have muffled the Colonel's head in his outlawed banner, and to be pitching into him with a parasol. The one in the lavender bonnet also performed prodigies of valour with her fists on his back. Seeing that all was for the moment lost, I fought my desperate way hand to hand to the lane. Through taking the back road, I was so fortunate as to meet nobody, and arrived there uninterrupted.

It seemed an age 'ere the Colonel joined me. He had been to the jobbing-tailor's to be sewn up in several places, and attributed our defeat to the refusal of the detested Drowvey to fall. Finding her so obstinate he had said to her in a loud voice, 'Die recreant!' but had found her no more open to reason on that point than the other.

My blooming Bride appeared accompanied by the Colonel's Bride, at the Dancing School next day. What? Was her face averted from me? Hah! Even so. With a look of scorn she put into my hand a bit of paper, and took another partner. On the paper was pencilled, 'Heavens! Can I write the word! Is my husband a Cow?'

In the first bewilderment of my heated brain I tried to think what slanderer could have traced my family to the ignoble animal mentioned above. Vain were my endeavours. At the end of that dance I whispered the Colonel to come into the cloak-room, and I showed him the note.

Redforth and the Pirate-Colonel

'There is a syllable wanting,' said he, with a gloomy brow.

'Hah! What syllable?' was my inquiry.

'She asks, Can she write the word? And no; you see she couldn't,' said the Colonel, pointing out the passage.

'And the word was?' said I.

'Cow – cow – coward,' hissed the Pirate-Colonel in my ear, and gave me back the note.

Feeling that I must for ever tread the earth a branded boy – person I mean – or that I must clear up my honour, I demanded to be tried by a Court-Martial. The Colonel admitted my right to be tried. Some difficulty was found in composing the court, on account of the Emperor of France's aunt refusing to let him come out. He was to be the President. 'Ere yet we had appointed a substitute, he made his escape over the back wall, and stood among us, a free monarch.

The court was held on the grass by the pond. I recognised in a certain Admiral among my judges my deadliest foe. A cocoa-nut had given rise to language that I could not brook. But confiding in my innocence, and also in the knowledge that the President of the United States (who sat next him) owed me a knife, I braced myself for the ordeal.

It was a solemn spectacle, that court. Two executioners with pinafores reversed, led me in. Under the shade of an umbrella, I perceived my Bride, supported by the Bride of the Pirate-Colonel. The President (having reproved a little female ensign for tittering, on a matter of Life and Death) called upon me to plead, 'Coward or no Coward, Guilty or not Guilty?' I pleaded in a firm tone, 'No Coward and Not Guilty.' (The little female ensign being again reproved by the President for misconduct, mutinied, left the court, and threw stones.)

My implacable enemy, the Admiral, conducted the case against me. The Colonel's Bride was called to prove that I had remained behind the corner-lamp-post during the engagement. I might have been spared the anguish of my own Bride's being also made a witness to the same point, but the Admiral knew where to wound me. Be still my soul, no matter. The Colonel was then brought forward with his evidence.

It was for this point that I had saved myself up, as the turning-point of my case. Shaking myself free of my guards – who had no business to hold me, the stupids! unless I was found Guilty – I asked the Colonel what he considered the first duty of a soldier? 'Ere he could reply, the President of the United States rose and informed the court that my foe the Admiral had suggested 'Bravery,' and that prompting a witness wasn't fair. The President of the Court immediately ordered the Admiral's mouth to be filled with leaves, and tied up with string. I had the satisfaction of seeing the sentence carried into effect, before the proceedings went further.

I then took a paper from my trousers-pocket, and asked: 'What do you consider, Colonel Redforth, the first duty of a soldier? Is it obedience?'

'It is,' said the Colonel.

'Is that paper – please to look at it – in your hand?'

'It is,' said the Colonel.

'Is it a military sketch?'

'It is,' said the Colonel.

'Of an engagement?'

'Quite so,' said the Colonel.

'Of the late engagement?'

'Of the late engagement.'

'Please to describe it, and then hand it to the President of the Court.'

From that triumphant moment my sufferings and my dangers were at an end. The court rose up and jumped, on discovering that I had strictly obeyed orders. My foe, the Admiral, who though muzzled was malignant yet, contrived to suggest that I was dishonoured by having quitted the field. But the Colonel himself had done as much, and gave his opinion, upon his word and honour as a Pirate, that when all was lost the field might be quitted without disgrace. I was going to be found 'No Coward and Not Guilty,' and my blooming Bride was going to be publicly restored to my arms in a procession, when an unlooked-for event disturbed the general rejoicing. This was no other than the Emperor of France's aunt catching hold of his hair. The proceedings abruptly terminated, and the court tumultuously dissolved.

It was when the shades of the next evening but one were beginning to fall, 'ere yet the silver beams of Luna touched the earth, that four forms might have been descried slowly advancing towards the weeping willow on the borders of the pond, the now deserted scene of the day before yesterday's agonies and triumphs. On a nearer approach, and by a practised eye, these might have been identified as the forms of the Pirate-Colonel with his Bride, and of the day before yesterday's gallant prisoner with *his* Bride.

On the beauteous faces of the Nymphs, dejection sat enthroned. All four reclined under the willow for some minutes without speaking, till at length the Bride of the Colonel poutingly observed, 'It's of no use pretending any more, and we had better give it up.'

'Hah!' exclaimed the Pirate. 'Pretending?'

'Don't go on like that; you worry me,' returned his Bride.

The lovely Bride of Tinkling echoed the incredible declaration. The two warriors exchanged stoney glances.

'If,' said the Bride of the Pirate-Colonel, 'grown-up people WON'T do what they ought to do, and WILL put us out, what comes of our pretending?'

'We only get into scrapes,' said the Bride of Tinkling.

'You know very well,' pursued the Colonel's Bride, 'that Miss Drowvey wouldn't fall. You complained of it yourself. And you know how disgracefully the court-martial ended. As to our marriage; would my people acknowledge it at home?'

'Or would my people acknowledge ours?' said the Bride of Tinkling.

Again the two warriors exchanged stoney glances.

'If you knocked at the door and claimed me, after you were told to go away,' said the Colonel's Bride, 'you would only have your hair pulled, or your ears, or your nose.'

'If you persisted in ringing at the bell and claiming Me,' said the Bride of Tinkling to that gentleman, 'you would have things dropped on your head from the window over the handle, or you would be played upon by the garden-engine.'

'And at your own homes,' resumed the Bride of the Colonel, 'it would be just as bad. You would be sent to bed, or something equally undignified. Again: how would you support us?'

The Pirate-Colonel replied, in a courageous voice, 'By rapine!' But his Bride retorted, suppose the grown-up people wouldn't be rapined? Then, said the Colonel, they should pay the penalty in Blood. But suppose they should object, retorted his Bride, and wouldn't pay the penalty in Blood or anything else?

A mournful silence ensued.

'Then do you no longer love me, Alice?' asked the Colonel.

'Redforth! I am ever thine,' returned his Bride.

'Then do you no longer love me, Nettie?' asked the present writer.

'Tinkling! I am ever thine,' returned my Bride.

We all four embraced. Let me not be misunderstood by the giddy. The Colonel embraced his own Bride and I embraced mine. But two times two make four.

'Nettie and I,' said Alice, mournfully, 'have been considering our position. The grown-up people are too strong for us. They make us ridiculous. Besides, they have changed the times. William Tinkling's baby-brother was christened yesterday. What took place? Was any king present? Answer, William.'

I said No, unless disguised as great-uncle Chopper.

'Any queen?'

There had been no queen that I knew of at our house. There might have been one in the kitchen; but I didn't think so, or the servants would have mentioned it.

'Any fairies?'

None that were visible.

'We had an idea among us, I think,' said Alice, with a melancholy smile, 'we four, that Miss Grimmer would prove to be the wicked fairy, and would come in at the christening with her crutch-stick, and give the child a bad gift? Was there anything of that sort? Answer, William.'

I said, that Ma had said afterwards (and so she had), that great-uncle Chopper's gift was a shabby one; but she hadn't said a bad one. She had called it shabby, electrotyped, second-hand, and below his income.

'It must be the grown-up people who have changed all this,' said Alice. '*We* couldn't have changed it, if we had been so inclined, and we never should have been. Or perhaps Miss Grimmer *is* a wicked fairy, after all, and won't act up to it, because the grown-up people have persuaded her not to. Either way, they would make us ridiculous if we told them what we expected.'

'Tyrants!' muttered the Pirate-Colonel.

'Nay, my Redforth,' said Alice, 'say not so. Call not names, my Redforth, or they will apply to Pa.'

'Let 'em!' said the Colonel. 'I don't care! Who's he?'

Tinkling here undertook the perilous task of remonstrating with his lawless friend, who consented to withdraw the moody expressions above quoted.

'What remains for us to do?' Alice went on in her mild wise way. 'We must educate, we must pretend in a new manner, we must wait.'

The Colonel clenched his teeth – four out in front, and a piece off another, and he had been twice dragged to the door of a dentist-despot, but had escaped from his guards. 'How educate? How pretend in a new manner? How wait?'

'Educate the grown-up people,' replied Alice. 'We part to-night. – Yes, Redforth!' – for the Colonel tucked up his cuffs, 'part tonight! Let us, in these next Holidays now going to begin, throw our thoughts into something educational for the grown-up people, hinting to them how things ought to be. Let us veil our meaning under a mask of romance; you, I, and Nettie. William Tinkling being the plainest and quickest writer shall copy out. Is it agreed?'

The Colonel answered, sulkily, 'I don't mind!' He then asked, 'How about pretending?'

'We will pretend,' said Alice, 'that we are children; not that we are those grown-up people who won't help us out as they ought, and who understand us so badly.'

The Colonel, still much dissatisfied, growled, 'How about waiting?'

'We will wait,' answered little Alice, taking Nettie's hand in hers, and looking up at the sky, 'we will wait – ever constant and true – till the times have got so changed as that everything helps us out, and nothing makes us ridiculous, and the fairies have come back. We will wait – ever constant and true – till we are eighty, ninety, or one hundred. And then the fairies will send *us* children, and we will help them out, poor pretty little creatures, if they pretend ever so much.'

'So we will, dear,' said Nettie Ashford, taking her round the waist with both arms and kissing her. 'And now if my Husband will go and buy some cherries for us, I have got some money.'

In the friendliest manner I invited the Colonel to go with me; but he so far forgot himself as to acknowledge the invitation by kicking out behind, and then lying down on his stomach on the grass, pulling it up and chewing it. When I came back, however, Alice had nearly brought him out of his vexation, and was soothing him by telling him how soon we should all be ninety.

As we sat under the willow-tree and ate the cherries (fair, for Alice shared them out), we played at being ninety. Nettie complained that she had a bone in her old back and it made her hobble, and Alice sang a song in an old woman's way, but it was very pretty, and we were all merry. At least I don't know about merry exactly, but all comfortable.

There was a most tremendous lot of cherries and Alice always had with her some neat little bag or box or case, to hold things. In it, that night, was a tiny wine-glass. So Alice and Nettie said they would make some cherry wine to drink our love at parting.

Each of us had a glassful and it was delicious, and each of us drank the toast 'Our love at parting.' The Colonel drank his wine last, and it got into my head directly that it got in his directly. Anyhow his eyes rolled immediately after he had turned the glass upside down, and he took me on one side and proposed in a hoarse whisper that we should 'Cut 'em out still.'

'How did he mean?' I asked my lawless friend.

'Cut our Brides out,' said the Colonel, 'and then cut our way, without going down a single turning, Bang to the Spanish Main!'

We might have tried it, though I didn't think it would answer; only we looked round and saw that there was nothing but moonlight under the willow-tree, and that our pretty pretty wives were gone. We burst out crying. The Colonel gave in second, and came to first; but he gave in strong.

We were ashamed of our red eyes, and hung about for half an hour to whiten them. Likewise a piece of chalk round the rims, I doing the Colonel's, and he mine, but afterwards found in the bedroom looking-glass not natural, besides inflammation. Our conversation turned on being ninety. The Colonel told me he had a pair of boots that wanted soleing and heeling, but he thought it hardly worth while to mention it to his father, as he himself should so soon be ninety, when he thought shoes would be more convenient. The Colonel also told me with his hand upon his hip that he felt himself already getting on in life, and turning rheumatic. And I told him the same. And when they said at our house at supper (they are always bothering about something) that I stooped, I felt so glad!

This is the end of the beginning-part that you were to believe most.

PART 2

Romance. From the Pen of Miss Alice Rainbird*

There was once a King, and he had a Queen; and he was the manliest of his sex, and she was the loveliest of hers. The King was, in his private profession, Under Government. The Queen's father had been a medical man out of town.

They had nineteen children, and were always having more. Seventeen of these children took care of the baby, and Alicia, the eldest, took care of them all. Their ages varied from seven years to seven months.

Let us now resume our story.

One day the King was going to the Office, when he stopped at the fishmonger's to buy a pound and a half of salmon not too near the tail, which the Queen (who was a careful housekeeper) had requested him to send home. Mr Pickles, the fishmonger, said, 'Certainly, sir, is there any other article, good morning.'

The King went on towards the Office in a melancholy mood, for Quarter Day was such a long way off, and several of the dear children were growing out of their clothes. He had not proceeded far, when Mr Pickles's errand boy came running after him, and said, 'Sir, you didn't notice the old lady in our shop.'

'What old lady?' inquired the King. 'I saw none.'

Now, the King had not seen any old lady, because this old lady had been invisible to him, though visible to Mr Pickles's boy. Probably because he messed and splashed the water about to that degree, and flopped the pairs of soles down in that violent manner, that, if she had not been visible to him, he would have spoilt her clothes.

Just then the old lady came trotting up. She was dressed in shot-silk of the richest quality, smelling of dried lavender.

'King Watkins the First, I believe?' said the old lady.

'Watkins,' replied the King, 'is my name.'

'Papa, if I am not mistaken, of the beautiful Princess Alicia?' said the old lady.

'And of eighteen other darlings,' replied the King.

---

* Aged Seven.

'Listen. You are going to the Office,' said the old lady.

It instantly flashed upon the King that she must be a Fairy, or how could she know that?

'You are right,' said the old lady, answering his thoughts, 'I am the Good Fairy Grandmarina. Attend! When you return home to dinner, politely invite the Princess Alicia to have some of the salmon you bought just now.'

'It may disagree with her,' said the King.

The old lady became so very angry at this absurd idea, that the King was quite alarmed, and humbly begged her pardon.

'We hear a great deal too much about this thing disagreeing and that thing disagreeing,' said the old lady, with the greatest contempt it was possible to express. 'Don't be greedy. I think you want it all yourself.'

The King hung his head under this reproof, and said he wouldn't talk about things disagreeing, any more.

'Be good then,' said the Fairy Grandmarina, 'and don't! When the beautiful Princess Alicia consents to partake of the salmon – as I think she will – you will find she will leave a fish-bone on her plate. Tell her to dry it, and to rub it, and to polish it till it shines like mother-of-pearl, and to take care of it as a present from me.'

'Is that all?' asked the King.

'Don't be impatient, sir,' returned the Fairy Grandmarina, scolding him severely. 'Don't catch people short, before they have done speaking. Just the way with you grown-up persons. You are always doing it.'

The King again hung his head, and said he wouldn't do so any more.

'Be good then,' said the Fairy Grandmarina, 'and don't! Tell the Princess Alicia, with my love, that the fish-bone is a magic present which can only be used once; but that it will bring her, that once, whatever she wishes for, PROVIDED SHE WISHES FOR IT AT THE RIGHT TIME. That is the message. Take care of it.'

The King was beginning, 'Might I ask the reason – ?' when the Fairy became absolutely furious.

'*Will* you be good, sir?' she exclaimed, stamping her foot on the ground. 'The reason for this, and the reason for that, indeed! You are always wanting the reason. No reason. There! Hoity toity me! I am sick of your grown-up reasons.'

The King was extremely frightened by the old lady's flying

into such a passion, and said he was very sorry to have offended her, and he wouldn't ask for reasons any more.

'Be good then,' said the old lady, 'and don't!'

With those words, Grandmarina vanished, and the King went on and on and on, till he came to the Office. There he wrote and wrote and wrote, till it was time to go home again. Then he politely invited the Princess Alicia, as the Fairy had directed him, to partake of the salmon. And when she had enjoyed it very much, he saw the fish-bone on her plate, as the Fairy had told him he would, and he delivered the Fairy's message, and the Princess Alicia took care to dry the bone, and to rub it, and to polish it till it shone like mother-of-pearl.

And so when the Queen was going to get up in the morning, she said, 'O dear me, dear me; my head, my head!' and then she fainted away.

The Princess Alicia, who happened to be looking in at the chamber door, asking about breakfast, was very much alarmed when she saw her Royal Mamma in this state, and she rang the bell for Peggy – which was the name of the Lord Chamberlain. But remembering where the smelling-bottle was, she climbed on a chair and got it, and after that she climbed on another chair by the bedside and held the smelling-bottle to the Queen's nose, and after that she jumped down and got some water, and after that she jumped up again and wetted the Queen's forehead, and, in short, when the Lord Chamberlain came in, that dear old woman said to the little Princess, 'What a Trot you are! I couldn't have done it better myself!'

But that was not the worst of the good Queen's illness. O no! She was very ill indeed, for a long time. The Princess Alicia kept the seventeen young Princes and Princesses quiet, and dressed and undressed and danced the baby, and made the kettle boil, and heated the soup, and swept the hearth, and poured out the medicine, and nursed the Queen, and did all that ever she could, and was as busy busy busy, as busy could be. For there were not many servants at that Palace, for three reasons; because the King was short of money, because a rise in his office never seemed to come, and because quarter-day was so far off that it looked almost as far off and as little as one of the stars.

But on the morning when the Queen fainted away, where was the magic fish-bone? Why, there it was in the Princess Alicia's pocket. She had almost taken it out to bring the Queen to life again, when she put it back, and looked for the smelling-bottle.

After the Queen had come out of her swoon that morning, and was dozing, the Princess Alicia hurried up-stairs to tell a most particular secret to a most particularly confidential friend of hers, who was a Duchess. People did suppose her to be a Doll, but she was really a Duchess, though nobody knew it except the Princess.

This most particular secret was a secret about the magic fish-bone, the history of which was well known to the Duchess, because the Princess told her everything. The Princess kneeled down by the bed on which the Duchess was lying, full dressed and wide-awake, and whispered the secret to her. The Duchess smiled and nodded. People might have supposed that she never smiled and nodded, but she often did, though nobody knew it except the Princess.

Then the Princess Alicia hurried down-stairs again, to keep watch in the Queen's room. She often kept watch by herself in the Queen's room; but every evening, while the illness lasted, she sat there watching with the King. And every evening the King sat looking at her with a cross look, wondering why she never brought out the magic fish-bone. As often as she noticed this, she ran up-stairs, whispered the secret to the Duchess over again, and said to the Duchess besides, 'They think we children never have a reason or a meaning!' And the Duchess, though the most fashionable Duchess that ever was heard of, winked her eye.

'Alicia,' said the King, one evening when she wished him Good Night.

'Yes, Papa.'

'What is become of the magic fish-bone?'

'In my pocket, Papa.'

'I thought you had lost it?'

'O no, Papa!'

'Or forgotten it?'

'No, indeed, Papa!'

And so another time the dreadful little snapping pug-dog next door made a rush at one of the young Princes as he stood on the steps coming home from school, and terrified him out of his wits, and he put his hand through a pane of glass, and bled bled bled. When the seventeen other young Princes and Princesses saw him bleed bleed bleed, they were terrified out of their wits too, and screamed themselves black in their seventeen faces all at once. But the Princess Alicia put her hands over all their seventeen mouths, one after another, and persuaded them to be quiet because of the sick Queen. And then she put the wounded Prince's hand in a basin of fresh cold water, while they stared with their twice seventeen are thirty-four put down four and carry three eyes, and then she looked in the hand for bits of glass, and there were fortunately no bits of glass there. And then she said to two chubby-legged Princes who were sturdy though small, 'Bring me in the Royal rag-bag; I must snip and stitch and cut and contrive.' So those two young Princes tugged at the Royal rag-bag and lugged it in, and the Princess Alicia sat down on the floor with a large pair of scissors and a needle and thread, and snipped and stitched and cut and contrived, and made a bandage and put it on, and it fitted beautifully, and so when it was all done she saw the King her Papa looking on by the door.

'Alicia.'

'Yes, Papa.'

'What have you been doing?'

'Snipping stitching cutting and contriving, Papa.'

'Where is the magic fish-bone?'

'In my pocket, Papa.'

'I thought you had lost it?'

'O no, Papa.'

'Or forgotten it?'

'No, indeed, Papa!'

'After that, she ran up-stairs to the Duchess and told her what had passed, and told her the secret over again, and the Duchess shook her flaxen curls and laughed with her rosy lips.

Well! and so another time the baby fell under the grate. The seventeen young Princes and Princesses were used to it, for they were almost always falling under the grate or down the stairs, but the baby was not used to it yet, and it gave him a swelled face and a black eye. The way the poor little darling came to tumble was, that he slid out of the Princess Alicia's lap just as she was sitting in a great coarse apron that quite smothered her, in front of the kitchen-fire, beginning to peel the turnips for the broth for dinner; and the way she came to be doing that was, that the King's cook had run away that morning with her own true love who was a very tall but very tipsy soldier. Then, the seventeen young Princes and Princesses, who cried at everything that happened, cried and roared. But the Princess Alicia (who couldn't help crying a little herself) quietly called to them to be still, on account of not throwing back the Queen up-stairs, who was fast getting well, and said, 'Hold your tongues you wicked little monkeys, every one of you, while I examine baby!' Then she examined baby, and found that he hadn't broken anything, and she held cold iron to his poor dear eye, and smoothed his poor dear face, and he presently fell asleep in her arms. Then, she said to the seventeen Princes and Princesses, 'I am afraid to lay him down yet, lest he should wake and feel pain, be good and you shall all be cooks.' They jumped for joy when they heard that, and began making themselves cooks' caps out of old newspapers. So to one she gave the salt box, and to one she gave the barley, and to one she gave the herbs, and to one she gave the turnips, and to one she gave the carrots, and to one she gave the onions, and to one she gave the spice-box, till they were all cooks, and all running about at work, she sitting in the middle smothered in the great coarse apron, nursing baby. By-and-by the broth was done, and the baby woke up smiling like an angel, and was trusted to the sedatest Princess to hold, while the other Princes and Princesses were squeezed into a far-off corner to look at the Princess Alicia turning out the saucepan-full of broth, for fear (as they were always getting into trouble) they should get splashed and scalded. When the broth came tumbling out, steaming beautifully, and smelling like a nosegay good to eat, they clapped their hands. That made the baby clap his hands; and that, and his looking as if he had a comic toothache, made all the Princes and Princesses laugh. So the Princess Alicia said, 'Laugh and be good, and after dinner we will make him a nest on the floor in a corner, and he shall sit in his nest and see a dance of eighteen cooks.' That delighted the young Princes and Princesses, and they ate up all the broth, and washed up all the plates and dishes, and cleared away, and pushed the table into a corner, and then they in their cooks' caps, and the Princess Alicia in the smothering coarse apron that belonged to the cook that had run away with her own true love that was the very tall but very tipsy soldier, danced a dance of eighteen cooks before the angelic baby, who forgot his swelled face and his black eye, and crowed with joy.

And so then, once more the Princess Alicia saw King Watkins the First, her father, standing in the doorway looking on, and he said:

'What have you been doing, Alicia?'

The Princess Alicia

'Cooking and contriving, Papa.'

'What else have you been doing, Alicia?'

'Keeping the children light-hearted, papa.'

'Where is the magic fish-bone, Alicia?'

'In my pocket, Papa.'

'I thought you had lost it?'

'O no, Papa.'

'Or forgotten it?'

'No, indeed, Papa.'

The King then sighed so heavily, and seemed so low-spirited, and sat down so miserably, leaning his head upon his hand, and his elbow upon the kitchen table pushed away in the corner, that the seventeen Princes and Princesses crept softly out of the kitchen, and left him alone with the Princess Alicia and the angelic baby.

'What is the matter, Papa?'

'I am dreadfully poor, my child.'

'Have you no money at all, Papa?'

'None my child.'

'Is there no way left of getting any, Papa?'

'No way,' said the King. 'I have tried very hard, and I have tried all ways.'

When she heard those last words, the Princess Alicia began to put her hand into the pocket where she kept the magic fish-bone.

'Papa,' said she, 'when we have tried very hard, and tried all ways, we must have done our very very best?'

'No doubt, Alicia.'

'When we have done our very very best, Papa, and that is not enough, then I think the right time must have come for asking help of others.' This was the very secret connected with the magic fish-bone, which she had found out for herself from the good fairy Grandmarina's words, and which she had so often whispered to her beautiful and fashionable friend the Duchess.

So she took out of her pocket the magic fish-bone that had been dried and rubbed and polished till it shone like mother-of-pearl, and she gave it one little kiss and wished it was quarter day. And immediately it *was* Quarter Day, and the King's quarter's salary came rattling down the chimney, and bounced into the middle of the floor.

But this was not half of what happened, no not a quarter, for immediately afterwards the good fairy Grandmarina came riding in, in a carriage and four (Peacocks), with Mr Pickles's boy up behind, dressed in silver and gold, with a cocked hat, powdered hair, pink silk stockings, a jewelled cane, and a nosegay. Down jumped Mr Pickles's boy with his cocked hat in his hand and wonderfully polite (being entirely changed by enchantment), and handed Grandmarina out, and there she stood in her rich shot silk smelling of dried lavender, fanning herself with a sparkling fan.

'Alicia, my dear,' said this charming old Fairy, 'how do you do, I hope I see you pretty well, give me a kiss.'

The Princess Alicia embraced her, and then Grandmarina turned to the King, and said rather sharply: – 'Are you good?'

The King said he hoped so.

'I suppose you know the reason, *now*, why my god-Daughter here,' kissing the Princess again, 'did not apply to the fish-bone sooner?' said the Fairy.

The King made a shy bow.

'Ah! But you didn't *then*!' said the Fairy.

The King made her a shyer bow.

'Any more reasons to ask for?' said the Fairy.

The King said no, and he was very sorry.

'Be good then,' said the Fairy, 'and live happy ever afterwards.'

Then, Grandmarina waved her fan, and the Queen came in most splendidly dressed, and the seventeen young Princes and Princesses, no longer grown out of their clothes, came in newly fitted out from top to toe, with tucks in everything to admit of its being let out. After that, the Fairy tapped the Princess Alicia with her fan, and the smothering coarse apron flew away, and she appeared exquisitely dressed, like a little Bride, with a wreath of orange-flowers and a silver veil. After that, the kitchen dresser changed of itself into a wardrobe, made of beautiful woods and gold and looking-glass, which was full of dresses of all sorts, all for her and all exactly fitting her. After that, the angelic baby came in, running alone, with his face and eye not a bit the worse but much the better. Then, Grandmarina begged to be introduced to the Duchess, and when the Duchess was brought down many compliments passed between them.

A little whispering took place between the Fairy and the Duchess, and then the Fairy said out loud, 'Yes. I thought she would have told you.' Grandmarina then turned to the King and Queen, and said, 'We are going in search of Prince Certainper-sonio. The pleasure of your company is requested at church in half an hour precisely.' So she and the Princess Alicia got into the carriage, and Mr Pickles's boy handed in the Duchess who sat by herself on the opposite seat, and then Mr Pickles's boy put up the steps and got up behind, and the Peacocks flew away with their tails spread.

Prince Certainpersonio was sitting by himself, eating barley-sugar and waiting to be ninety. When he saw the Peacocks followed by the carriage, coming in at the window, it immediately occurred to him that something uncommon was going to happen.

'Prince,' said Grandmarina, 'I bring you your Bride.'

The moment the Fairy said those words, Prince Certainpersonio's face left off being stickey, and his jacket and corduroys changed to peach-bloom velvet, and his hair curled, and a cap and feather flew in like a bird and settled on his head. He got into the carriage by the Fairy's invitation, and there he renewed his acquaintance with the Duchess whom he had seen before.

In the church were the Prince's relations and friends, and the Princess Alicia's relations and friends, and the seventeen Princes and Princesses, and the baby, and a crowd of the neighbours. The marriage was beautiful beyond expression. The Duchess was bridesmaid, and beheld the ceremony from the pulpit where she was supported by the cushion of the desk.

Grandmarina gave a magnificent wedding-feast afterwards, in which there was everything and more to eat, and everything and more to drink. The wedding cake was delicately ornamented with white satin ribbons, frosted silver and white lilies, and was forty-two yards round.

When Grandmarina had drunk her love to the young couple, and Prince Certainpersonio had made a speech, and everybody had cried Hip Hip Hip Hurrah! Grandmarina announced to the King and Queen that in future there would be eight Quarter Days in every year, except in leap year, when there would be ten. She then turned to Certainpersonio and Alicia, and said, 'My dears, you will have thirty-five children, and they will all be good and beautiful. Seventeen of your children will be boys, and eighteen will be girls. The hair of the whole of your children will curl naturally. They will never have the measles, and will have recovered from the whooping-cough before being born.'

On hearing such good news, everybody cried out 'Hip Hip Hip Hurrah!' again.

'It only remains,' said Grandmarina in conclusion, 'to make an end of the fish-bone.'

So she took it from the hand of the Princess Alicia, and it intantly flew down the throat of the dreadful little snapping pug-dog next door and choked him, and he expired in convulsions.

PART 3

Romance. From the Pen of Lieutenant-Colonel Robin Redforth*

The subject of our present narrative would appear to have devoted himself to the Pirate profession at a comparatively early age. We find him in command of a splendid schooner of one hundred guns, loaded to the muzzle, 'ere yet he had had a party in honour of his tenth birthday.

It seems that our hero, considering himself spited by a Latin-Grammar-Master, demanded the satisfaction due from one man of honour to another. Not getting it, he privately withdrew his haughty spirit from such low company, bought a second-hand pocket-pistol, folded up some sandwiches in a paper bag, made a bottle of Spanish liquorice-water, and entered on a career of valour.

It were tedious to follow Boldheart (for such was his name) through the commencing stages of his history. Suffice it that we find him bearing the rank of Captain Boldheart, reclining in full uniform on a crimson hearth-rug spread out upon the quarter deck of his schooner the Beauty, in the China Seas. It was a lovely evening, and as his crew lay grouped about him, he favoured them with the following melody:

O landsmen are folly,
O Pirates are jolly,
O Diddleum Dolly
Di!
(<i>Chorus</i>) Heave yo.

The soothing effect of these animated sounds floating over the waters, as the common sailors united their rough voices to take

* Aged Nine.

up the rich tones of Boldheart, may be more easily conceived than described.

It was under these circumstances that the look-out at the mast-head gave the word, 'Whales!'

All was now activity.

'Where away?' cried Captain Boldheart, starting up.

'On the larboard bow, sir,' replied the fellow at the mast-head, touching his hat. For such was the height of discipline on board the Beauty, that even at that height he was obliged to mind it or be shot through the head.

'This adventure belongs to me,' said Boldheart. 'Boy, my harpoon. Let no man follow;' and leaping alone into his boat, the captain rowed with admirable dexterity in the direction of the monster.

All was now excitement.

'He nears him!' said an elderly seaman, following the captain through his spy-glass.

'He strikes him!' said another seaman, a mere stripling, but also with a spy-glass.

'He tows him towards us!' said another seaman, a man in the full vigour of life, but also with a spy-glass.

In fact the captain was seen approaching, with the huge bulk following. We will not dwell on the deafening cries of 'Boldheart! Boldheart!' with which he was received, when, carelessly leaping on the quarter-deck, he presented his prize to his men. They afterwards made two thousand four hundred and seventeen pound ten and sixpence by it.

Ordering the sails to be braced up, the captain now stood W.N.W. The Beauty flew rather than floated over the dark blue waters. Nothing particular occurred for a fortnight, except taking, with considerable slaughter, four Spanish galleons and a Snow from South America, all richly laden. Inaction began to tell upon the spirits of the men. Captain Boldheart called all hands aft, and said:

'My lads, I hear there are discontented ones among ye. Let any such stand forth.'

After some murmuring, in which the expressions, 'Aye, aye, sir,' 'Union Jack,' 'Avast,' 'Starboard,' 'Port,' 'Bowsprit,' and similar indications of a mutinous undercurrent, though subdued, were audible, Bill Boozey, captain of the foretop, came out from the rest. His form was that of a giant, but he quailed under the captain's eye.

'What are your wrongs?' said the captain.

'Why, d'ye see, Captain Boldheart,' returned the towering mariner, 'I've sailed man and boy for many a year, but I never yet know'd the milk served out for the ship's company's teas to be so sour as 'tis aboard this craft.'

At this moment the thrilling cry, 'Man overboard!' announced to the astonished crew that Boozey, in stepping back as the captain (in mere thoughtfulness) laid his hand upon the faithful pocket-pistol which he wore in his belt, had lost his balance, and was struggling with the foaming tide.

All was now stupefaction.

But, with Captain Boldheart, to throw off his uniform coat regardless of the various rich orders with which it was decorated, and to plunge into the sea after the drowning giant, was the work of a moment. Maddening was the excitement when boats were lowered; intense the joy when the captain was seen holding up the drowning man with his teeth; deafening the cheering when both were restored to the main deck of the Beauty. And from the instant of his changing his wet clothes for dry ones, Captain Boldheart had no such devoted though humble friend as William Boozey.

Boldheart now pointed to the horizon, and called the attention of his crew to the taper spars of a ship lying snug in harbour under the guns of a fort.

'She shall be ours at sunrise,' said he. 'Serve out a double allowance of grog, and prepare for action.'

All was now preparation.

When morning dawned after a sleepless night, it was seen that the stranger was crowding on all sail to come out of the harbour and offer battle. As the two ships came nearer to each other, the stranger fired a gun and hoisted Roman colours. Boldheart then perceived her to be the Latin-Grammar-Master's bark. Such indeed she was, and had been tacking about the world in unavailing pursuit, from the time of his first taking to a roving life.

Boldheart now addressed his men, promising to blow them up, if he should feel convinced that their reputation required it, and giving orders that the Latin-Grammar-Master should be taken alive. He then dismissed them to their quarters, and the

The Pirate-Colonel and His Captive

fight began with a broadside from the Beauty. She then veered round and poured in another. The Scorpion (so was the bark of the Latin-Grammar-Master appropriately called) was not slow to return her fire, and a terrific cannonading ensued, in which the guns of the Beauty did tremendous execution.

The Latin-Grammar-Master was seen upon the poop, in the midst of the smoke and fire, encouraging his men. To do him justice, he was no Craven, though his white hat, his short grey trousers, and his long snuff-coloured surtout reaching to his heels – the self-same coat in which he had spited Boldheart – contrasted most unfavourably with the brilliant uniform of the latter. At this moment Boldheart, seizing a pike and putting himself at the head of his men, gave the word to board.

A desperate conflict ensued in the hammock nettings – or somewhere in about that direction – until the Latin-Grammar-Master, having all his masts gone, his hull and rigging shot through and through, and seeing Boldheart slashing a path towards him, hauled down his flag himself, gave up his sword to Boldheart, and asked for quarter. Scarce had he been put into the captain's boat, 'ere the Scorpion went down with all on board.

On Captain Boldheart's now assembling his men, a circumstance occurred. He found it necessary with one blow of his cutlass to kill the Cook, who, having lost his brother in the late action, was making at the Latin-Grammar-Master in an infuriated state, intent on his destruction with a carving-knife.

Captain Boldheart then turned to the Latin-Grammar-Master, severely reproaching him with his perfidy, and put it to his crew what they considered that a master who spited a boy deserved?

They answered with one voice, 'Death.'

'It may be so,' said the Captain, 'but it shall never be said that Boldheart stained his hour of triumph with the blood of his enemy. Prepare the cutter.'

The cutter was immediately prepared.

'Without taking your life,' said the Captain, 'I must yet for ever deprive you of the power of spiting other boys. I shall turn you adrift in this boat. You will find in her, two oars, a compass, a bottle of rum, a small cask of water, a piece of pork, a bag of biscuit, and my Latin grammar. Go! And spite the Natives, if you can find any.'

Deeply conscious of this bitter sarcasm, the unhappy wretch

was put into the cutter, and was soon left far behind. He made no effort to row, but was seen lying on his back with his legs up, when last made out by the ship's telescopes.

A stiff breeze now beginning to blow, Captain Boldheart gave orders to keep her S.S.W., easing her a little during the night by falling off a point or two W. by W., or even by W.S., if she complained much. He then retired for the night, having in truth much need of repose. In addition to the fatigues he had undergone, this brave officer had received sixteen wounds in the engagement, but had not mentioned it.

In the morning a white squall came on, and was succeeded by other squalls of various colours. It thundered and lightened heavily for six weeks. Hurricanes then set in for two months. Waterspouts and tornadoes followed. The oldest sailor on board – and he was a very old one – had never seen such weather. The Beauty lost all idea where she was, and the carpenter reported six feet two of water in the hold. Everybody fell senseless at the pumps every day.

Provisions now ran very low. Our hero put the crew on short allowance, and put himself on shorter allowance than any man in the ship. But his spirit kept him fat. In this extremity, the gratitude of Boozey, the captain of the fore-top whom our readers may remember, was truly affecting. The loving though lowly William repeatedly requested to be killed, and preserved for the captain's table.

We now approach a change in affairs.

One day during a gleam of sunshine and when the weather had moderated, the man at the masthead – too weak now to touch his hat, besides its having been blown away – called out,

'Savages!'

All was now expectation.

Presently fifteen hundred canoes, each paddled by twenty savages, were seen advancing in excellent order. They were of a light green colour (the Savages were), and sang, with great energy, the following strain:

> Choo a choo a choo tooth.
>   Muntch, muntch. Nycey!
> Choo a choo a choo tooth.
>   Muntch, muntch. Nyce!

As the shades of night were by this time closing in, these expressions were supposed to embody this simple people's views of the Evening Hymn. But it too soon appeared that the song was a translation of 'For what we are going to receive, &c.'

The chief, imposingly decorated with feathers of lively colours, and having the majestic appearance of a fighting Parrot, no sooner understood (he understood English perfectly) that the ship was the Beauty, under Captain Boldheart, than he fell upon his face on the deck, and could not be persuaded to rise until the captain had lifted him up, and told him he wouldn't hurt him. All the rest of the savages also fell on their faces with marks of terror, and had also to be lifted up one by one. Thus the fame of the great Boldheart had gone before him, even among these children of nature.

Turtles and oysters were now produced in astonishing numbers, and on these and yams the people made a hearty meal. After dinner the Chief told Captain Boldheart that there was better feeding up at the village, and that he would be glad to take him and his officers there. Apprehensive of treachery, Boldheart ordered his boat's crew to attend him completely armed. And well were it for other commanders if their precautions – but let us not anticipate.

When the canoes arrived at the beach, the darkness of the night was illumined by the light of an immense fire. Ordering his boat's crew (with the intrepid though illiterate William at their head) to keep close and be upon their guard, Boldheart bravely went on, arm-in-arm with the Chief.

But how to depict the captain's surprise when he found a ring of Savages singing in chorus that barbarous translation of 'For what we are going to receive, &c.,' which has been given above, and dancing hand-in-hand round the Latin-Grammar-Master, in a hamper with his head shaved, while two savages floured him, before putting him to the fire to be cooked!

Boldheart now took counsel with his officers on the course to be adopted. In the mean time the miserable captive never ceased begging pardon and imploring to be delivered. On the generous Boldheart's proposal, it was at length resolved that he should not be cooked, but should be allowed to remain raw, on two conditions. Namely,

1. That he should never under any circumstances presume to teach any boy anything any more.

2. That, if taken back to England, he should pass his life in travelling to find out boys who wanted their exercises done, and should do their exercises for those boys for nothing, and never say a word about it.

Drawing his sword from its sheath, Boldheart swore him to these conditions on its shining blade. The prisoner wept bitterly, and appeared acutely to feel the errors of his past career.

The captain then ordered his boat's crew to make ready for a volley, and after firing to re-load quickly. 'And expect a score or two on ye to go head over heels,' murmured William Boozey, 'for I'm a looking at ye.' With those words the derisive though deadly William took a good aim.

'Fire!'

The ringing voice of Boldheart was lost in the report of the guns and the screeching of the savages. Volley after volley awakened the numerous echoes. Hundreds of savages were killed, hundreds wounded, and thousands ran howling into the woods. The Latin-Grammar-Master had a spare nightcap lent him, and a long-tail coat which he wore hind side before. He presented a ludicrous though pitiable appearance, and serve him right.

We now find Captain Boldheart, with this rescued wretch on board, standing off for other islands. At one of these, not a cannibal island, but a pork and vegetable one, he married (only in fun on his part) the King's daughter. Here he rested some time, receiving from the natives great quantities of precious stones, gold-dust, elephants' teeth, and sandal-wood, and getting very rich. This, too, though he almost every day made presents of enormous value to his men.

The ship being at length as full as she could hold of all sorts of valuable things, Boldheart gave orders to weigh the anchor, and turn the Beauty's head towards England. These orders were obeyed with three cheers, and ere the sun went down full many a hornpipe had been danced on deck by the uncouth though agile William.

We next find Captain Boldheart about three leagues off Madeira, surveying through his spy-glass a stranger of suspicious appearance making sail towards him. On his firing a gun ahead of her to bring her to, she ran up a flag, which he instantly recognised as the flag from the mast in the back garden at home.

Inferring from this, that his father had put to sea to seek his long-lost son, the captain sent his own boat on board the stranger, to inquire if this was so, and if so, whether his father's intentions were strictly honourable. The boat came back with a present of greens and fresh meat, and reported that the stranger was The Family, of twelve hundred tons, and had not only the captain's father on board, but also his mother, with the majority of his aunts and uncles, and all his cousins. It was further reported to Boldheart that the whole of these relations had expressed themselves in a becoming manner, and were anxious to embrace him and thank him for the glorious credit he had done them. Boldheart at once invited them to breakfast next morning on board the Beauty, and gave orders for a brilliant ball that should last all day.

It was in the course of the night that the captain discovered the hopelessness of reclaiming the Latin-Grammar-Master. That thankless traitor was found out, as the two ships lay near each other, communicating with The Family by signals, and offering to give up Boldheart. He was hanged at the yard-arm the first thing in the morning, after having it impressively pointed out to him by Boldheart that this was what spiters came to.

The meeting between the captain and his parents was attended with tears. His uncles and aunts would have attended their meeting with tears too, but he wasn't going to stand that. His cousins were very much astonished by the size of his ship and the discipline of his men, and were greatly overcome by the splendour of his uniform. He kindly conducted them round the vessel, and pointed out everything worthy of notice. He also fired his hundred guns, and found it amusing to witness their alarm.

The entertainment surpassed everything ever seen on board ship, and lasted from ten in the morning until seven the next morning. Only one disagreeable incident occured. Captain Boldheart found himself obliged to put his Cousin Tom in irons, for being disrespectful. On the boy's promising amendment, however, he was humanely released, after a few hours' close confinement.

Boldheart now took his mother down into the great cabin, and asked after the young lady with whom, it was well known to the world, he was in love. His mother replied that the object of his affections was then at school at Margate, for the benefit of sea-bathing (it was the month of September), but that she feared the young lady's friends were still opposed to the union. Boldheart at once resolved, if necessary, to bombard the town.

Taking the command of his ship with this intention, and putting all but fighting men on board The Family, with orders to that vessel to keep in company, Boldheart soon anchored in Margate Roads. Here he went ashore well armed, and attended by his boat's crew (at their head the faithful though ferocious William), and demanded to see the Mayor, who came out of his office.

'Dost know the name of yon ship, Mayor?' asked Boldheart, fiercely.

'No,' said the Mayor, rubbing his eyes, which he could scarce believe when he saw the goodly vessel riding at anchor.

'She is named the Beauty,' said the captain.

'Hah!' exclaimed the Mayor, with a start. 'And you, then, are Captain Boldheart?'

'The same.'

A pause ensued. The Mayor trembled.

'Now, Mayor,' said the captain, 'choose. Help me to my Bride, or be bombarded.'

The Mayor begged for two hours' grace, in which to make inquiries respecting the young lady. Boldheart accorded him but one, and during that one placed William Boozey sentry over him, with a drawn sword and instructions to accompany him wherever he went, and to run him through the body if he showed a sign of playing false.

At the end of the hour, the Mayor re-appeared more dead than alive, closely waited on by Boozey more alive than dead.

'Captain,' said the Mayor, 'I have ascertained that the young lady is going to bathe. Even now she waits her turn for a machine. The tide is low, though rising. I, in one of our town-boats, shall not be suspected. When she comes forth in her bathing dress into the shallow water from behind the hood of the machine, my boat shall intercept her and prevent her return. Do you the rest.'

'Mayor,' returned Captain Boldheart, 'thou hast saved thy town.'

The captain then signalled his boat to take him off, and steering her himself ordered her crew to row towards the bathing-ground, and there to rest upon their oars. All happened as had been arranged. His lovely bride came forth, the Mayor glided in behind her, she became confused and had floated out of her depth, when, with one skilful touch of the rudder and one quivering stroke from the boat's crew, her adoring Boldheart held her in his strong arms. There, her shrieks of terror were changed to cries of joy.

Before the Beauty could get under weigh, the hoisting of all the flags in the town and harbour, and the ringing of all the bells, announced to the brave Boldheart that he had nothing to fear. He therefore determined to be married on the spot, and signalled for a clergyman and clerk, who came off promptly in a sailing-boat named the Skylark. Another great entertainment was then given on board the Beauty, in the midst of which the Mayor was called out by a messenger. He returned with the news that Government had sent down to know whether Captain Boldheart, in acknowledgement of the great services he had done his country by being a Pirate, would consent to be made a Lieutenant-Colonel. For himself he would have spurned the worthless boon, but his Bride wished it and he consented.

Only one thing further happened before the good ship Family was dismissed, with rich presents to all on board. It is painful to record (but such is human nature in some cousins) that Captain Boldheart's unmannerly cousin Tom was actually tied up to receive three dozen with a rope's end 'for cheekyness and making games,' when Captain Boldheart's Lady begged for him and he was spared. The Beauty then refitted, and the Captain and his Bride departed for the Indian Ocean to enjoy themselves for evermore.

PART 4

Romance. From the Pen of Miss Nettie Ashford*

There is a country, which I will show you when I get into Maps, where the children have everything their own way. It is a most delightful country to live in. The grown-up people are obliged to obey the children, and are never allowed to sit up to supper,

* Aged half-past six.

except on their birthdays. The children order them to make jam and jelly and marmalade, and tarts and pies and puddings and all manner of pastry. If they say they won't, they are put in the corner till they do. They are sometimes allowed to have some, but when they have some, they generally have powders given them afterwards.

One of the inhabitants of this country, a truly sweet young creature of the name of Mrs Orange, had the misfortunte to be sadly plagued by her numerous family. Her parents required a great deal of looking after, and they had connexions and companions who were scarcely ever out of mischief. So Mrs Orange said to herself, 'I really cannot be troubled with these Torments any longer, I must put them all to school.'

Mrs Orange took off her pinafore, and dressed herself very nicely, and took up her baby, and went out to call upon another lady of the name of Mrs Lemon, who kept a Preparatory Establishment. Mrs Orange stood upon the scraper to pull at the bell, and gave a Ring-ting-ting.

Mrs Lemon's neat little housemaid, pulling up her socks as she came along the passage, answered the Ring-ting-ting.

'Good morning,' said Mrs Orange. 'Fine day. How do you do? Mrs Lemon at home?'

'Yes, ma'am.'

'Will you say Mrs Orange and baby?'

'Yes, ma'am. Walk in.'

Mrs Orange's baby was a very fine one, and real wax all over. Mrs Lemon's baby was leather and bran. However, when Mrs Lemon came into the drawing-room with her baby in her arms, Mrs Orange said politely, 'Good morning. Fine day. How do you do? And how is little Tootleum-Boots?'

'Well, she is but poorly. Cutting her teeth, ma'am,' said Mrs Lemon.

'Oh, indeed, ma'am!' said Mrs Orange 'No fits, I hope?'

'No, ma'am.'

'How many teeth has she, ma'am?'

'Five, ma'am.'

'My Emilia, ma'am, has eight,' said Mrs Orange. 'Shall we lay them on the mantelpiece side by side, while we converse?'

'By all means, ma'am,' said Mrs Lemon. 'Hem!'

'The first question is, ma'am,' said Mrs Orange – 'I don't bore you?'

'Not in the least, ma'am,' said Mrs Lemon. 'Far from it, I assure you.'

'Then pray *have* you,' said Mrs Orange, '*have* you any vacancies?'

'Yes, ma'am. How many might you require?'

'Why, the truth is, ma'am,' said Mrs Orange, 'I have come to the conclusion that my children' – O I forgot to say that they call the grown-up people, children, in that country – 'that my children are getting positively too much for me. Let me see. Two parents, two intimate friends of theirs, one godfather, two godmothers, and an aunt. *Have* you as many as eight vacancies?'

'I have just eight, ma'am,' said Mrs Lemon.

'Most fortunate! Terms moderate, I think?'

'Very moderate, ma'am.'

'Diet good, I believe?'

'Excellent, ma'am.'

'Unlimited?'

'Unlimited.'

'Most satisfactory! Corporal punishment dispensed with?'

'Why, we do occasionally shake,' said Mrs Lemon, 'and we have slapped. But only in extreme cases.'

'*Could* I, ma'am,' said Mrs Orange, '*could* I see the establishment?'

'With the greatest of pleasure, ma'am,' said Mrs Lemon.

Mrs Lemon took Mrs Orange into the school-room, where there were a number of pupils. 'Stand up, children!' said Mrs Lemon, and they all stood up.

Mrs Orange whispered to Mrs Lemon, 'There is a pale bald child with red whiskers, in disgrace. Might I ask what he has done?'

'Come here, White,' said Mrs Lemon, 'and tell this lady what you have been doing.'

'Betting on horses,' said White, sulkily.

'Are you sorry for it, you naughty child?' said Mrs Lemon.

'No,' said White. 'Sorry to lose, but shouldn't be sorry to win.'

'There's a vicious boy for you, ma'am,' said Mrs Lemon. 'Go along with you, sir. This is Brown, Mrs Orange. Oh, a sad case, Brown's! Never knows when he has had enough. Greedy. How is your gout, sir?'

'Bad,' said Brown.

'What else can you expect?' said Mrs Lemon. 'Your stomach is the size of two. Go and take exercise directly. Mrs Black, come here to me. Now here is a child, Mrs Orange, ma'am, who is always at play. She can't be kept at home a single day together; always gadding about and spoiling her clothes. Play, play, play, play, from morning to night, and to morning again. How can she expect to improve!'

'Don't expect to improve,' sulked Mrs Black. 'Don't want to.'

'There is a specimen of her temper, ma'am,' said Mrs Lemon. 'To see her when she is tearing about, neglecting everything else, you would suppose her to be at least good-humoured. But bless you, ma'am, she is as pert and as flouncing a minx as ever you met with in all your days!'

'You must have a great deal of trouble with them, ma'am,' said Mrs Orange.

'Ah! I have indeed, ma'am,' said Mrs Lemon. 'What with their tempers, what with their quarrels, what with their never knowing what's good for them, and what with their always wanting to domineer, deliver me from these unreasonable children!'

'Well, I wish you good morning, ma'am,' said Mrs Orange.

'Well, I wish you good morning, ma'am,' said Mrs Lemon.

So Mrs Orange took up her baby and went home, and told the family that plagued her so that they were all going to be sent to school. They said they didn't want to go to school, but she packed up their boxes and packed them off.

'Oh dear me, dear me! Rest and be thankful!' said Mrs Orange, throwing herself back in her little arm-chair. 'Those troublesome troubles are got rid of, please the Pigs!'

Just then another lady named Mrs Alicumpaine came calling at the street-door with a Ring-ting-ting.

'My dear Mrs Alicumpaine,' said Mrs Orange, 'how do you do? Pray stay to dinner. We have but a simple joint of sweet stuff, followed by a plain dish of bread and treacle, but if you will take us as you find us it will be *so* kind!'

'Don't mention it,' said Mrs Alicumpaine. 'I shall be too glad. But what do you think I have come for, ma'am? Guess, ma'am.'

'I really cannot guess, ma'am,' said Mrs Orange.

'Why, I am going to have a small juvenile party to-night,' said

Mrs Alicumpaine, 'and if you and Mr Orange and baby would
but join us, we should be complete.'

'More than charmed, I am sure!' said Mrs Orange.

'So kind of you!' said Mrs Alicumpaine. But I hope the
children won't bore you?'

'Dear things! Not at all,' said Mrs Orange. 'I dote upon them.'

Mr Orange here came home from the city, and he came too
with a Ring-ting-ting.

'James, love,' said Mrs Orange, 'you look tired. What has
been doing in the city to-day?'

'Trap bat and ball, my dear,' said Mr Orange, 'and it knocks
a man up.'

'That dreadfully anxious city, ma'am,' said Mrs Orange to
Mrs Alicumpaine; 'so wearing, is it not!'

'Oh, so trying!' said Mrs Alicumpaine. 'John has lately been
speculating in the peg-top ring, and I often say to him at night,
"John, *is* the result worth the wear and tear?"'

Dinner was ready by this time, so they sat down to dinner;
and while Mr Orange carved the joint of sweet-stuff, he said,
'It's a poor heart that never rejoices. Jane, go down to the cellar
and fetch a bottle of the Upest Ginger-beer.'

At tea-time Mr and Mrs Orange, and baby, and Mrs Alicumpaine, went off to Mrs Alicumpaine's house. The children had
not come yet, but the ball-room was ready for them, decorated
with paper flowers.

'How very sweet!' said Mrs Orange. 'The dear things! How
pleased they will be!'

'I don't care for children myself,' said Mr Orange, gaping.

'Not for girls?' said Mrs Alicumpaine. 'Come! You care for
girls.'

Mr Orange shook his head and gaped again. 'Frivolous and
vain, ma'am.'

'My dear James,' cried Mrs Orange, who had been peeping
about, 'do look here. Here's the supper for the darlings, ready
laid in the room behind the folding-doors. Here's their little
pickled salmon, I do declare! And here's their little salad, and
their little roast beef and fowls, and their little pastry, and their
wee, wee, wee, champagne!'

'Yes, I thought it best, ma'am,' said Mrs Alicumpaine, 'that
they should have their supper by themselves. Our table is in the
corner here, where the gentlemen can have their wineglass of

negus and their egg-sandwich, and their quiet game at beggar-my-neighbour, and look on. As for us, ma'am, we shall have quite enough to do to manage the company.'

'Oh, indeed you may say so. Quite enough, ma'am!' said Mrs Orange.

The company began to come. The first of them was a stout boy, with a white top-knot and spectacles. The housemaid brought him in and said, 'Compliments, and at what time was he to be fetched?' Mrs Alicumpaine said, 'Not a moment later than ten. How do you do, sir? Go and sit down.' Then a number of other children came; boys by themselves, and girls by themselves, and boys and girls together. They didn't behave at all well. Some of them looked through quizzing-glasses at others, and said, 'Who are those? Don't know them.' Some of them looked through quizzing-glasses at others, and said, 'How do?' Some of them had cups of tea or coffee handed to them by others, and said, 'Thanks! Much!' A good many boys stood about, and felt their shirt-collars. Four tiresome fat boys *would* stand in the doorway and talk about the newspapers, till Mrs Alicumpaine went to them and said, 'My dears, I really cannot allow you to prevent people from coming in. I shall be truly sorry to do it, but, if you put yourselves in everybody's way, I must positively send you home.' One boy, with a beard and a large white waistcoat, who stood straddling on the hearth-rug warming his coat-tails, *was* sent home. 'Highly incorrect, my dear,' said Mrs Alicumpaine, handing him out of the room, 'and I cannot permit it.'

There was a children's band – harp, cornet, and piano – and Mrs Alicumpaine and Mrs Orange bustled among the childen to persuade them to take partners and dance. But they were so obstinate! For quite a long time they would not be persuaded to take partners and dance. Most of the boys said, 'Thanks. Much. But not at present.' And most of the rest of the boys said, 'Thanks. Much. But never do.'

'Oh! These children are very wearing,' said Mrs Alicumpaine to Mrs Orange.

'Dear things! I dote upon them, but they ARE wearing,' said Mrs Orange to Mrs Alicumpaine.

At last they did begin in a slow and melancholy way to slide about to the music, though even then they wouldn't mind what they were told, but would have this partner, and wouldn't have

The Obstinate Boys

that partner, and showed temper about it. And they wouldn't smile, no not on any account they wouldn't; but when the music stopped, went round and round the room in dismal twos, as if everybody else was dead.

'Oh! It's very hard indeed to get these vexing children to be entertained,' said Mrs Alicumpaine to Mrs Orange.

'I dote upon the darlings, but it is hard,' said Mrs Orange to Mrs Alicumpaine.

They were trying children, that's the truth. First, they wouldn't sing when they were asked, and then, when everybody fully believed they wouldn't, they would. 'If you serve us so any more, my love,' said Mrs Alicumpaine to a tall child, with a good deal of white back, in mauve silk trimmed with lace, 'it will be my painful privilege to offer you a bed, and to send you to it immediately.'

The girls were so ridiculously dressed, too, that they were in rags before supper. How could the boys help treading on their trains? And yet when their trains were trodden on, they often showed temper again, and looked as black, they did! However, they all seemed to be pleased when Mrs Alicumpaine said, 'Supper is ready, children!' And they went crowding and pushing in, as if they had had dry bread for dinner.

'How are the children getting on?' said Mr Orange to Mrs Orange, when Mrs Orange came to look after baby. Mrs Orange had left Baby on a shelf near Mr Orange while he played at Beggar-my-Neighbour, and had asked him to keep his eye upon her now and then.

'Most charmingly, my dear!' said Mrs Orange. 'So droll to see their little flirtations and jealousies! Do come and look!'

'Much obliged to you, my dear,' said Mr Orange, 'but I don't care about children myself.'

So Mrs Orange, having seen that baby was safe, went back without Mr Orange to the room where the children were having supper.

'What are they doing now?' said Mrs Orange to Mrs Alicumpaine.

'They are making speeches and playing at Parliament,' said Mrs Alicumpaine to Mrs Orange.

On hearing this, Mrs Orange set off once more back again to Mr Orange, and said 'James dear, do come. The children are playing Parliament.'

'Thank you, my dear,' said Mr Orange, 'but I don't care about Parliament myself.'

So Mrs Orange went once again without Mr Orange to the room where the children were having supper, to see them playing at Parliament. And she found some of the boys crying 'Hear, hear, hear!' while other boys cried 'No, no!' and others 'Question!' 'Spoke!' and all sorts of nonsense that ever you heard. Then one of those tiresome fat boys who had stopped the doorway, told them he was on his legs (as if they couldn't see that he wasn't on his head, or on his anything else) to explain, and that with the permission of his honourable friend, if he would allow him to call him so (another tiresome boy bowed), he would proceed to explain. Then he went on for a long time in a sing-song (whatever he meant!), did this troublesome fat boy, about that he held in his hand a glass, and about that he had come down to that house that night to discharge what he would call a public duty, and about that on the present occasion he would lay his hand (his other hand) upon his heart, and would tell honourable gentlemen that he was about to open the door to general approval. Then he opened the door by saying 'To our hostess!' and everybody else said 'To our hostess!' and then there were cheers. Then another tiresome boy started up in sing-song, and then half a dozen noisy and nonsensical boys at once. But at last Mrs Alicumpaine said, 'I cannot have this din. Now, children, you have played at Parliament very nicely, but Parliament gets tiresome after a little while, and it's time you left off, for you will soon be fetched.'

After another dance (with more tearing to rags than before supper) they began to be fetched, and you will be very glad to be told that the tiresome fat boy who had been on his legs was walked off first without any ceremony. When they were all gone, poor Mrs Alicumpaine dropped upon a sofa and said to Mrs Orange, 'These children will be the death of me at last, ma'am, they will indeed!'

'I quite adore them, ma'am,' said Mrs Orange, 'but they DO want variety.'

Mr Orange got his hat, and Mrs Orange got her bonnet and her baby, and they set out to walk home. They had to pass Mrs Lemon's Preparatory Establishment on their way.

'I wonder, James dear,' said Mrs Orange, looking up at the window, 'whether the precious children are asleep!'

'I don't much care whether they are or not, myself,' said Mr Orange.

'James dear!'

'You dote upon them, you know,' said Mr Orange. 'That's another thing.'

'I do!' said Mrs Orange, rapturously. 'Oh I DO!'

'I don't,' said Mr Orange.

'But I was thinking, James love,' said Mrs Orange, pressing his arm, 'whether our dear good kind Mrs Lemon would like them to stay the holidays with her.'

'If she was paid for it, I dare say she would,' said Mr Orange.

'I adore them, James,' said Mrs Orange; 'but SUPPOSE we pay her then.'

This was what brought that country to such perfection, and made it such a delightful place to live in; the grown-up people (that would be in other countries) soon left off being allowed any holidays after Mr and Mrs Orange tried the experiment; and the children (that would be in other countries) kept them at school as long as ever they lived, and made them do whatever they were told.

THE LIFE OF OUR LORD

My dear children, I am very anxious that you should know something about the History of Jesus Christ. For everybody ought to know about Him. No one ever lived, who was so good, so kind, so gentle, and so sorry for all people who did wrong, or were in any way ill or miserable, as he was. And as he is now in Heaven, where we hope to go, and all to meet each other after we are dead, and there be happy always together, you never can think what a good place Heaven is, without knowing who he was and what he did.

He was born, a long long time ago – nearly Two Thousand years ago – at a place called Bethlehem. His father and mother lived in a city called Nazareth, but they were forced, by business, to travel to Bethlehem. His father's name was Joseph, and his mother's name was Mary. And the town being very full of people, also brought there by business, there was no room for Joseph and Mary in the Inn or in any house; so they went into a Stable to lodge, and in this stable Jesus Christ was born. There was no cradle or anything of that kind there, so Mary laid her pretty little boy in what is called the Manger, which is the place the horses eat out of. And there he fell asleep.

While he was asleep, some Shepherds who were watching Sheep in the Fields, saw an Angel from God, all light and beautiful, come moving over the grass towards Them. At first they were afraid and fell down and hid their faces. But it said 'There is a child born to-day in the City of Bethlehem near here, who will grow up to be so good that God will love him as his own son; and he will teach men to love one another; and his name will be Jesus Christ; and people will put that name in their prayers, because they will know God loves it, and will know that they should love it too.' And then the Angel told the Shepherds to go to that Stable, and look at that little child in the

Manger. Which they did; and they kneeled down by it in its sleep, and said 'God bless this child!'

Now the great place of all that country was Jerusalem – just as London is the great place in England – and at Jerusalem the King lived, whose name was King Herod. Some wise men came one day, from a country a long way off in the East, and said to the King 'We have seen a Star in the Sky, which teaches us to know that a child is born in Bethlehem who will live to be a man whom all people will love.' When King Herod heard this, he was jealous, for he was a wicked man. But he pretended not to be, and said to the wise men, 'Whereabouts is this child?' And the wise men said 'We don't know. But we think the Star will shew us; for the Star has been moving on before us, all the way here, and is now standing still in the sky.' Then Herod asked them to see if the Star would shew them where the child lived, and ordered them, if they found the child, to come back to him. So they went out, and the Star went on, over their heads a little way before them, until it stopped over the house where the child was. This was very wonderful, but God ordered it to be so.

When the Star stopped, the wise men went in, and saw the child with Mary his Mother. They loved him very much, and gave him some presents. Then they went away. But they did not go back to King Herod; for they thought he was jealous, though he had not said so. So they went away, by night, back into their own country. And an Angel came, and told Joseph and Mary to take the child into a Country called Egypt, or Herod would kill him. So they escaped too, in the night – the father, the mother, and the child – and arrived there, safely.

But when this cruel Herod found that the wise men did not come back to him, and that he could not, therefore, find out where this child, Jesus Christ, lived, he called his soldiers and captains to him, and told them to go and Kill all the children in his dominions that were not more than two years old. The wicked men did so. The mothers of the children ran up and down the streets with them in their arms trying to save them, and hide them in caves and cellars, but it was of no use. The soldiers with their swords killed all the children they could find. This dreadful murder was called the Murder of the Innocents. Because the little children were so innocent.

King Herod hoped that Jesus Christ was one of them. But He

was not, as you know, for He had escaped safely into Egypt. And he lived there, with his father and mother, until Bad King Herod died.

CHAPTER 2

When King Herod was dead, an angel came to Joseph again, and said he might now go to Jerusalem, and not be afraid for the child's sake. So Joseph and Mary, and her Son Jesus Christ (who are commonly called The Holy Family) travelled towards Jerusalem; but hearing on the way that King Herod's son was the new King, and fearing that he, too, might want to hurt the child, they turned out of the way, and went to live in Nazareth. They lived there, until Jesus Christ was twelve years old.

Then Joseph and Mary went to Jerusalem to attend a Religious Feast which used to be held in those days, in the Temple of Jerusalem, which was a great church or Cathedral; and they took Jesus Christ with them. And when the Feast was over, they travelled away from Jerusalem, back towards their own home in Nazareth, with a great many of their friends and neighbours. For people used, then, to travel a great many together, for fear of robbers; the roads not being so safe and well guarded as they are now, and travelling being much more difficult altogether, than it now is.

They travelled on, for a whole day, and never knew that Jesus Christ was not with them; for the company being so large, they thought he was somewhere among the people, though they did not see Him. But finding that he was not there, and fearing that he was lost, they turned back to Jerusalem in great anxiety to look for him. They found him, sitting in the Temple, talking about the goodness of God, and how we should all pray to him, with some learned men who were called Doctors. They were not what you understand by the word 'doctors' now; they did not attend sick people; they were scholars and clever men. And Jesus Christ shewed such knowledge in what he said to them, and in the questions he asked them, that they were all astonished.

He went, with Joseph and Mary, home to Nazareth, when

they had found him, and lived there until he was thirty or thirty-five years old.

At that time there was a very good man indeed, named John, who was the son of a woman named Elizabeth – the cousin of Mary. And people being wicked, and violent, and killing each other, and not minding their duty towards God, John (to teach them better) went about the country, preaching to them, and entreating them to be better men and women. And because he loved them more than himself, and didn't mind himself when he was doing them good, he was poorly dressed in the skin of a camel, and ate little but some insects called locusts, which he found as he travelled: and wild honey, which the bees left in the Hollow Trees. You never saw a locust, because they belong to that country near Jerusalem, which is a great way off. So do camels, but I think you have seen a camel? At all events they are brought over here, sometimes; and if you would like to see one, I will shew you one.

There was a River, not very far from Jerusalem, called the River Jordan; and in this water, John baptized those people who would come to him, and promise to be better. A great many people went to him in crowds. Jesus Christ went too. But when John saw him, John said, 'Why should I baptize you, who are so much better than I!' Jesus Christ made answer, 'Suffer it to be so now.' So John baptized him. And when he was baptized, the sky opened, and a beautiful bird like a dove came flying down, and the voice of God, speaking up in Heaven, was heard to say 'This is my beloved Son, in whom I am well pleased!'

Jesus Christ then went into a wild and lonely country called the Wilderness, and stayed there forty days and forty nights, praying that he might be of use to men and women, and teach them to be better, so that after their deaths, they might be happy in Heaven.

When he came out of the Wilderness, he began to cure sick people by only laying his hand upon them; for God had given him power to heal the sick, and to give sight to the blind, and to do many wonderful and solemn things of which I shall tell you more bye and bye, and which are called 'The Miracles' of Christ. I wish you would remember that word, because I shall use it again, and I should like you to know that it means something which is very wonderful and which could not be done without God's leave and assistance.

The first miracle which Jesus Christ did, was at a place called Cana, where he went to a Marriage-Feast with Mary his Mother. There was no wine; and Mary told him so. There were only six stone water-pots filled with water. But Jesus turned this water into wine, by only lifting up his hand; and all who were there, drank of it.

For God had given Jesus Christ the power to do such wonders; and he did them, that people might know he was not a common man, and might believe what he taught them, and also believe that God had sent him. And many people, hearing this, and hearing that he cured the sick, did begin to believe in him; and great crowds followed him in the streets and on the roads, wherever he went.

CHAPTER 3

That there might be some good men to go about with Him, teaching the people, Jesus Christ chose Twelve poor men to be his companions. These twelve are called *The apostles* or *Disciples*, and he chose them from among Poor Men, in order that the Poor might know – always after that; in all years to come – that Heaven was made for them as well as for the rich, and that God makes no difference between those who wear good clothes and those who go barefoot and in rags. The most miserable, the most ugly, deformed, wretched creatures that live, will be bright Angels in Heaven if they are good here on earth. Never forget this, when you are grown up. Never be proud or unkind, my dears, to any poor man, woman, or child. If they are bad, think that they would have been better, if they had had kind friends, and good homes, and had been better taught. So, always try to make them better by kind persuading words; and always try to teach them and relieve them if you can. And when people speak ill of the Poor and Miserable, think how Jesus Christ went among them and taught them, and thought them worthy of his care. And always pity them yourselves, and think as well of them as you can.

The names of the Twelve apostles were, Simon Peter, Andrew, James the son of Zebedee, John, Philip, Bartholomew, Thomas, Matthew, James the son of Alphaeus, Labbæus, Simon, and Judas Iscariot. This man afterwards betrayed Jesus Christ, as you will hear bye and bye.

The first four of these were poor fishermen, who were sitting in their boats by the seaside, mending their nets, when Christ passed by. He stopped, and went into Simon Peter's boat, and asked him if he had caught many fish. Peter said No; though they had worked all night with their nets, they had caught nothing. Christ said, 'let down the net again.' They did so; and it was immediately so full of fish, that it required the strength of many men (who came and helped them) to lift it out of the water, and even then it was very hard to do. This was another of the miracles of Jesus Christ.

Jesus then said 'Come with me.' And they followed him directly. And from that time the Twelve disciples or apostles were always with him.

As great crowds of people followed him, and wished to be taught, he went up into a Mountain and there preached to them, and gave them, from his own lips, the words of that Prayer, beginning 'Our father which art in Heaven,' that you say every night. It is called The Lord's Prayer, because it was first said by Jesus Christ, and because he commanded his disciples to pray in those words.

When he was come down from the Mountain, there came to him a man with a dreadful disease called the leprosy. It was common in those times, and those who were ill with it, were called lepers. This Leper fell at the feet of Jesus Christ, and said 'Lord! If thou wilt, thou can'st make me well!' Jesus, always full of compassion, stretched out his hand, and said 'I will! Be thou well!' and his disease went away, immediately, and he was cured.

Being followed, wherever he went, by great crowds of people, Jesus went, with his disciples, into a house, to rest. While he was sitting inside, some men brought upon a bed, a man who was very ill of what is called the Palsy, so that he trembled all over from head to foot, and could neither stand, nor move. But the crowd being all about the door and windows, and they not being able to get near Jesus Christ, these men climbed up to the roof of the house, which was a low one; and through the tiling at the top, let down the bed, with the sick man upon it, into the room where Jesus sat. When he saw him, Jesus, full of pity, said 'Arise! Take up thy bed, and go to thine own home!' And the man rose up and went away quite well; blessing him, and thanking God.

There was a Centurion too, or officer over the Soldiers, who came to him, and said, 'Lord! My servant lies at home in my house, very ill.' – Jesus Christ made answer, 'I will come and cure him.' But the Centurion said 'Lord! I am not worthy that Thou should'st come to my house. Say the word only, and I know he will be cured.' Then Jesus Christ, glad that the Centurion believed in him so truly, said 'Be it so!' And the servant became well, from that moment.

But of all the people who came to him, none were so full of grief and distress, as one man who was a Ruler or Magistrate over many people, and he wrung his hands, and cried, and said 'Oh Lord, my daughter – my beautiful, good, innocent little girl, is dead. Oh come to her, come to her, and lay Thy blessed hand upon her, and I know she will revive, and come to life again, and make me and her mother happy. Oh Lord we love her so, we love her so! And she is dead!'

Jesus Christ went out with him, and so did his disciples and went to his house, where the friends and neighbours were crying in the room where the poor dead little girl lay, and where there was soft music playing; as there used to be, in those days, when people died. Jesus Christ, looking on her, sorrowfully, said – to comfort her poor parents – 'She is not dead. She is asleep.' Then he commanded the room to be cleared of the people that were in it, and going to the dead child, took her by the hand, and she rose up, quite well, as if she had only been asleep. Oh what a sight it must have been to see her parents clasp her in their arms, and kiss her, and thank God, and Jesus Christ his son, for such great Mercy!

But he was always merciful and tender. And because he did such Good, and taught people how to love God and how to hope to go to Heaven after death, he was called *Our Saviour*.

There were, in that country where Our Saviour performed his Miracles, certain people who were called Pharisees. They were very proud, and believed that no people were good but themselves; and they were all afraid of Jesus Christ, because he taught the people better. So were the Jews, in general. Most of the Inhabitants of that country were Jews.

Our Saviour, walking once in the fields with his disciples on a Sunday (which the Jews called, and still call, the Sabbath) they gathered some ears of the corn that was growing there, to eat. This, the Pharisees said, was wrong; and in the same way, when our Saviour went into one of their churches – they were called Synagogues – and looked compassionately on a poor man who had his hand all withered and wasted away, these Pharisees said 'Is it right to cure people on a Sunday?' Our Saviour answered them by saying, 'If any of you had a sheep and it fell into a pit, would you not take it out, even though it happened on a Sunday? And how much better is a man than a sheep!' Then he said to the poor man, 'Stretch out thine hand!' And it was cured immediately, and was smooth and useful like the other. So Jesus Christ told them 'You may always do good, no matter what the day is.'

There was a city called Nain into which Our Saviour went soon after this, followed by great numbers of people, and especially by those who had sick relations, or friends, or children. For they brought sick people out into the streets and roads through which he passed, and cried out to him to touch them, and when he did, they became well. Going on, in the midst of this crowd, and near the Gate of the city, He met a funeral. It was the funeral of a young man, who was carried on what is called a Bier, which was open, as the custom was in that country, and is now in many parts of Italy. His poor mother followed the bier, and wept very much, for she had no other child. When Our Saviour saw her, he was touched to the heart to see her so sorry, and said 'Weep not!' Then, the bearers of the bier standing still, he walked up to it and touched it with his hand, and said 'Young Man! Arise.' The dead man, coming to life again at the sound of The Saviour's

Voice, rose up and began to speak. And Jesus Christ leaving him with his mother – Ah how happy they both were! – went away.

By this time the crowd was so very great that Jesus Christ went down to the waterside, to go in a boat, to a more retired place. And in the boat, He fell asleep, while his Disciples were sitting on the deck. While he was still sleeping a violent storm arose, so that the waves washed over the boat, and the howling wind so rocked and shook it, that they thought it would sink. In their fright the disciples awoke Our Saviour, and said 'Lord! Save us, or we are lost!' He stood up, and raising his arm, said to the rolling Sea and to the whistling wind, 'Peace! Be still!' And immediately it was calm and pleasant weather, and the boat went safely on, through the smooth waters.

When they came to the other side of the waters they had to pass a wild and lonely burying-ground that was outside the City to which they were going. All burying-grounds were outside cities in those times. In this place there was a dreadful madman who lived among the tombs, and houled all day and night, so that it made travellers afraid, to hear him. They had tried to chain him, but he broke his chains, he was so strong; and he would throw himself on the sharp stones, and cut himself in the most dreadful manner: crying and houling all the while. When this wretched man saw Jesus Christ a long way off, he cried out 'It is the son of God! Oh son of God, do not torment me!' Jesus, coming near him, perceived that he was torn by an Evil Spirit, and cast the madness out of him, and into a herd of swine (or pigs) who were feeding close by, and who directly ran headlong down a steep place leading to the sea and were dashed to pieces.

Now Herod, the son of that cruel King who murdered the Innocents, reigning over the people there, and hearing that Jesus Christ was doing these wonders, and was giving sight to the blind and causing the deaf to hear, and the dumb to speak, and the lame to walk, and that he was followed by multitudes and multitudes of people – Herod, hearing this, said 'This man is a companion and friend of John the Baptist.' John was the good man, you recollect, who wore a garment made of camel's hair, and ate wild honey. Herod had taken him Prisoner, because he taught and preached to the people; and had him then, locked up, in the prisons of his Palace.

*

While Herod was in this angry humour with John, his birthday came; and his daughter, Herodias, who was a fine dancer, danced before him, to please him. She pleased him so much that he swore an oath he would give her whatever she would ask him for. 'Then', said she, 'father, give me the head of John the Baptist in a charger.' For she hated John, and was a wicked, cruel woman.

The King was sorry, for though he had John prisoner, he did not wish to kill him; but having sworn that he would give her what she asked for, he sent some soldiers down into the Prison, with directions to cut off the head of John the Baptist, and give it to Herodias. This they did, and took it to her, as she had said, in a charger, which was a kind of dish. When Jesus Christ heard from the apostles of this cruel deed, he left that city, and went with them (after they had privately buried John's body in the night) to another place.

CHAPTER 5

One of the Pharisees begged Our Saviour to go into his house, and eat with him. And while our Saviour sat eating at the table, there crept into the room a woman of that city who had led a bad and sinful life, and was ashamed that the Son of God should see her; and yet she trusted so much to his goodness, and his compassion for all who, having done wrong were truly sorry for it in their hearts, that, by little and little, she went behind the seat on which he sat, and dropped down at his feet, and wetted them with her sorrowful tears; then she kissed them and dried them on her long hair, and rubbed them with some sweet-smelling ointment she had brought with her in a box. Her name was Mary Magdalene.

When the Pharisee saw that Jesus permitted this woman to touch Him, he said within himself that Jesus did not know how wicked she had been. But Jesus Christ, who knew his thoughts, said to him 'Simon' — for that was his name — 'if a man had debtors, one of whom owed him five hundred pence, and one of whom owed him only fifty pence, and he forgave them, both, their debts, which of those two debtors do you think would love him most?' Simon answered 'I suppose that one whom he forgave most.' Jesus told him he was right, and said 'As God forgives this woman so much sin, she will love Him, I hope, the more.' And he said to her, 'God forgives you!' The company who were present wondered that Jesus Christ had power to forgive sins, but God had given it to Him. And the woman thanking Him for all his mercy, went away.

We learn from this, that we must always forgive those who have done us any harm, when they come to us and say they are truly sorry for it. Even if they do not come and say so, we must still forgive them, and never hate them or be unkind to them, if we would hope that God will forgive us.

After this there was a great feast of the Jews, and Jesus Christ went to Jerusalem. There was, near the sheep market in that place, a pool, or pond, called Bethesda, having five gates to it; and at the time of the year when that feast took place great numbers of sick people and cripples went to this pool to bathe in it: believing that an Angel came and stirred the water, and that whoever went in first after the Angel had done so, was cured of any illness he or she had, whatever it might be. Among these poor persons, was one man who had been ill, thirty eight years; and he told Jesus Christ (who took pity on him when he saw him lying on his bed alone, with no one to help him) that he never could be dipped in the pool, because he was so weak and ill that he could not move to get there. Our Saviour said to him, 'take up thy bed and go away.' And he went away, quite well.

Many Jews saw this; and when they saw it, they hated Jesus Christ the more: knowing that the people, being taught and cured by him, would not believe their Priests, who told the people what was not true, and deceived them. So they said to one another that Jesus Christ should be killed, because he cured people on the Sabbath Day (which was against their strict law) and because he called himself the Son of God. And they tried to raise enemies against him, and to get the crowd in the streets to murder Him.

But the crowd followed Him wherever he went, blessing him, and praying to be taught and cured; for they knew He did nothing but Good. Jesus going with his disciples over a sea, called the Sea of Tiberias, and sitting with them on a hill-side,

saw great numbers of these poor people waiting below, and said
to the apostle Philip, 'Where shall we buy bread, that they may
eat and be refreshed, after their long journey?' Philip answered,
'Lord, two hundred pennyworth of bread would not be enough
for so many people, and we have none.' 'We have only', said
another apostle – Andrew, Simon Peter's brother – 'five small
barley loaves, and two little fish, belonging to a lad who is
among us. What are they, among so many!' Jesus Christ said,
'Let them all sit down!' They did; there being a great deal of
grass in that place. When they were all seated, Jesus took the
bread, and looked up to Heaven, and blessed it, and broke it,
and handed it in pieces to the apostles, who handed it to the
people. And of those five little loaves, and two fish, five thousand
men, besides women, and children, ate, and had enough; and
when they were all satisfied, there were gatherd up twelve
baskets full of what was left. This was another of the Miracles
of Jesus Christ.

Our Saviour then sent his disciples away in a boat, across the
water, and said he would follow them presently, when he had
dismissed the people. The people being gone, he remained by
himself to pray; so that the night came on, and the disciples
were still rowing on the water in their boat, wondering when
Christ would come. Late in the night, when the wind was
against them and the waves were running high, they saw Him
coming walking towards them on the water, as if it were dry
land. When they saw this, they were terrified, and cried out, but
Jesus said, 'It is I. Be not afraid!' Peter taking courage, said,
'Lord, if it be thou, tell me to come to thee upon the water.'
Jesus Christ said, 'Come!' Peter then walked towards Him, but
seeing the angry waves, and hearing the wind roar, he was
frightened and began to sink, and would have done so, but that
Jesus took him by the hand, and led him into the boat. Then, in
a moment, the wind went down; and the Disciples said to one
another, 'It is true! He is the Son of God!'

Jesus did many more miracles after this happened and cured the
sick in great numbers: making the lame walk, and the dumb
speak, and the blind see. And being again surrounded by a great
crowd who were faint and hungry, and had been with him for
three days eating little, he took from his disciples seven loaves

and a few fish, and again divided them among the people who were four thousand in number. They all ate, and had enough; and of what was left, there were gathered up seven baskets full.

He now divided the disciples, and sent them into many towns and villages, teaching the people, and giving them power to cure, in the name of God, all those who were ill. And at this time He began to tell them (for he knew what would happen) that he must one day go back to Jerusalem where he would suffer a great deal, and where he would certainly be put to Death. But he said to them that on the third day after he was dead, he would rise from the grave, and ascend to Heaven, where he would sit at the right hand of God, beseeching God's pardon to sinners.

CHAPTER 6

Six days after the last Miracle of the loaves and fish, Jesus Christ went up into a high Mountain, with only three of the Disciples – Peter, James, and John. And while he was speaking to them there, suddenly His face began to shine as if it were the Sun, and the robes he wore, which were white, glistened and shone like sparkling silver, and he stood before them like an angel. A bright cloud overshadowed them at the same time; and a voice, speaking from the cloud, was heard to say 'This is my beloved Son in whom I am well pleased. Hear ye him!' At which the three disciples fell on their knees and covered their faces: being afraid.

This is called the Transfiguration of our Saviour.

When they were come down from this mountain, and were among the people again, a man knelt at the feet of Jesus Christ, and said, 'Lord have mercy on my son, for he is mad and cannot help himself, and sometimes falls into the fire, and sometimes into the water, and covers himself with scars and sores. Some of Thy Disciples have tried to cure him, but could not.' Our Saviour cured the child immediately; and turning to his disciples told them they had not been able to cure him themselves, because they did not believe in Him so truly as he had hoped.

*

The Disciples asked him, 'Master, who is greatest in the King-dom of Heaven?' Jesus called a little child to him, and took him in his arms, and stood him among them, and answered, 'a child like this. I say unto you that none but those who are as humble as little children shall enter into Heaven. Whosoever shall receive one such little child in my name receiveth me. But whosoever hurts one of them, it were better for him that he had a millstone tied about his neck, and were drowned in the depths of the sea. The angels are all children.' Our Saviour loved the child, and loved all children. Yes, and all the world. No one ever loved all people, so well and so truly as He did.

Peter asked Him, 'Lord, how often shall I forgive any one who offends me? Seven times?' Our Saviour answered 'Seventy times seven times, and more than that. For how can you hope that God will forgive you, when you do wrong, unless you forgive all other people!'

And he told his disciples this Story – He said, there was once a Servant who owed his master a great deal of money, and could not pay it, at which the Master, being very angry, was going to have this servant sold for a Slave. But the servant kneeling down and begging his Master's pardon with great sorrow, the Master forgave him. Now this same servant had a fellow-servant who owed him a hundred pence, and instead of being kind and forgiving to this poor man, as his Master had been to him, he put him in prison for the debt. His master hearing of it, went to him, and said 'oh wicked Servant, I forgave you. Why did you not forgive your fellow-servant!' And because he had not done so, his Master turned him away with great misery. 'So,' said Our Saviour; 'how can you expect God to forgive you, if you do not forgive others!' This is the meaning of that part of the Lord's prayer, where we say 'forgive us our trespasses' – that word means faults – 'as we forgive them that trespass against us.'

And he told them another story, and said 'There was a certain Farmer once, who had a Vineyard, and he went out early in the morning, and agreed with some labourers to work there all day, for a Penny. And bye and bye, when it was later, he went out again and engaged some more labourers on the same terms; and bye and bye went out again; and so on, several times, until the afternoon. When the day was over, and they all came to be paid, those who had worked since morning complained that those who had not begun to work until late in the day had the same money as themselves, and they said it was not fair. But the Master said, 'Friend, I agreed with you for a Penny; and is it less money to you, because I give the same money to another man?'

Our Saviour meant to teach them by this, that people who have done good all their lives long, will go to Heaven after they are dead. But that people who have been wicked, because of their being miserable, or not having parents and friends to take care of them when young, and who are truly sorry for it, however late in their lives, and pray God to forgive them, will be forgiven and will go to Heaven to. He taught His disciples in these stories, because he knew the people liked to hear them, and would remember what He said better, if he said it in that way. They are called Parables – THE PARABLES OF OUR SAVIOUR; and I wish you to remember that word, as I shall soon have some more of these Parables to tell you about.

The people listened to all that our Saviour said, but were not agreed among themselves about Him. The Pharisees and Jews had spoken to some of them against Him, and some of them were inclined to do Him harm and even to murder Him. But they were afraid, as yet, to do Him any harm, because of His goodness, and His looking so divine and grand – although he was very simply dressed; almost like the poor people – that they could hardly bear to meet his eyes.

One morning, He was sitting in a place called the Mount of Olives, teaching the people who were all clustered round Him, listening and learning attentively, when a great noise was heard, and a crowd of Pharisees, and some other people like them, called Scribes, came running in, with great cries and shouts, dragging among them a woman who had done wrong, and they all cried out together, 'Master! Look at this woman. The law says she shall be pelted with stones until she is dead. But what say you? what say you?'

Jesus looked upon the noisy crowd attentively, and knew that they had come to make Him say the law was wrong and cruel; and that if He said so, they would make it a charge against Him and would kill him. They were ashamed and afraid as He looked into their faces, but they still cried out, 'Come! What say you Master? what say you?'

*

Jesus stooped down, and wrote with his finger in the sand on the ground. 'He that is without sin among you, let him throw the first stone at her.' As they read this, looking over one another's shoulders, and as He repeated the words to them, they went away, one by one, ashamed, until not a man of all the noisy crowd was left there; and Jesus Christ, and the woman, hiding her face in her hands, alone remained.

Then said Jesus Christ, 'Woman, where are thine accusers? Hath no man condemned Thee?' She answered, trembling, 'No, Lord!' Then said our Saviour, 'Neither do *I* condemn Thee. Go! and sin no more!'

CHAPTER 7

As Our Saviour sat teaching the people and answering their questions, a certain Lawyer stood up, and said 'Master what shall I do, that I may live again in happiness after I am dead?' Jesus said to him *'The first of all the commandments is, the Lord our God is one Lord: and Thou shalt love the Lord Thy God with all Thy heart, and all Thy Soul, and with all thy mind, and with all thy Strength. And the second is like unto it. Thou shalt love thy neighbour as thyself. There is none other commandment greater than these.'*

Then the Lawyer said 'But who *is* my neighbour? Tell me that I may know.' Jesus answered in this Parable:

'There was once a traveller,' he said, 'journeying from Jerusalem to Jericho, who fell among Thieves; and they robbed him of his clothes, and wounded him, and went away, leaving him half dead upon the road. A Priest, happening to pass that way, while the poor man lay there, saw him, but took no notice, and passed by, on the other side. Another man, a Levite, came that way, and also saw him; but he only looked at him for a moment, and then passed by, also. But a certain Samaritan who came travelling along that road, no sooner saw him than he had compassion on him, and dressed his wounds with oil and wine, and set him on the beast he rode himself, and took him to an Inn, and next morning took out of his pocket Two pence and gave them to the Landlord, saying "take care of him and whatever you may spend beyond this, in doing so, I will repay you when I come here again." —Now which of these three men,' said our Saviour to the Lawyer, 'do you think should be called the neighbour of him who fell among the Thieves?' The Lawyer said, 'The man who shewed compassion on him.' 'True,' replied our Saviour. 'Go Thou and do likewise! Be compassionate to all men. For all men are your neighbours and brothers.'

And he told them this Parable, of which the meaning is, that we are never to be proud, or think ourselves very good, before God, but are always to be humble. He said, 'when you are invited to a Feast or Wedding, do not sit down in the best place, lest some more honoured man should come, and claim that seat. But sit down in the lowest place, and a better will be offered you if you deserve it. For whosoever exalteth himself shall be abased, and whosoever humbleth himself shall be exalted.'

He also told them this Parable. –

'There was a certain man who prepared a great supper, and invited many people, and sent his Servant round to them when supper was ready to tell them they were waited for. Upon this, they made excuses. One said he had bought a piece of ground and must go to look at it. Another that he had bought five yoke of Oxen, and must go to try them. Another, that he was newly married, and could not come. When the Master of the house heard this, he was angry, and told the servant to go into the streets, and into the high roads, and among the hedges, and invite the poor, the lame, the maimed, and the blind to supper instead.'

The meaning of Our Saviour in telling them this Parable, was, that those who are too busy with their own profits and pleasures, to think of God and of doing good, will not find such favour with him as the sick and miserable.

It happened that our Saviour, being in the city of Jericho, saw, looking down upon him over the heads of the crowd, from a tree into which he had climbed for that purpose, a man named Zacchæus, who was regarded as a common kind of man, and a Sinner, but to whom Jesus Christ called out, as He passed along, that He would come and eat with him in his house that day. Those proud men, the Pharisees and Scribes, hearing this, muttered among themselves, and said 'he eats with Sinners.' In answer to them, Jesus related this Parable, which is usually called THE PARABLE OF THE PRODIGAL SON.

*

'There was once a Man', he told them, 'who had two sons: and the younger of them said one day, "Father, give me my share of your riches now, and let me do with it what I please?" The father granting his request, he travelled away with his money into a distant country, and soon spent it in riotous living.

'When he had spent all, there came a time, through all that country, of great public distress and famine, when there was no bread, and when the corn, and the grass, and all the things that grow in the ground were all dried up and blighted. The Prodigal Son fell into such distress and hunger, that he hired himself out as a servant to feed swine in the fields. And he would have been glad to eat, even the poor coarse husks that the swine were fed with, but his Master gave him none. In this distress, he said to himself "How many of my father's servants have bread enough, and to spare, while I perish with hunger! I will arise and go to my father, and will say unto him, Father! I have sinned against Heaven, and before thee, and am no more worthy to be called Thy Son!"

'And so he travelled back again, in great pain and sorrow and difficulty, to his father's house. When he was yet a great way off, his father saw him, and knew him in the midst of all his rags and misery, and ran towards him, and wept, and fell upon his neck, and kissed him. And he told his servants to clothe this poor repentant Son in the best robes, and to make a great feast to celebrate his return. Which was done; and they began to be merry.

'But the eldest Son, who had been in the field and knew nothing of his brother's return, coming to the house and hearing the music and Dancing, called to one of the Servants, and asked him what it meant. To this the Servant made answer that his brother had come home, and that his father was joyful because of his return. At this, the elder brother was angry and would not go into the house; so the father, hearing of it, came out to persuade him.

' "Father", said the elder brother, "you do not treat me justly, to shew so much joy for my younger brother's return. For these many years I have remained with you constantly, and have been true to you, yet you have never made a feast for me. But when my younger brother returns, who has been prodigal, and riotous, and spent his money in many bad ways, you are full of delight, and the whole house makes merry!" – "Son," returned the father, "you have always been with me, and all I have is yours. But we thought your brother dead, and he is alive. He was lost, and he is found; and it is natural and right that we should be merry for his unexpected return to his old home."'

By this, our Saviour meant to teach, that those who have done wrong and forgotten God, are always welcome to him and will always receive his mercy, if they will only return to Him in sorrow for the sin of which they have been guilty.

Now the Pharisees received these lessons from our Saviour, scornfully; for they were rich, and covetous, and thought themselves superior to all mankind. As a warning to them, Christ related this Parable: – OF DIVES AND LAZARUS.

'There was a certain rich man who was clothed in purple and fine linen, and fared sumptuously every day. And there was a certain beggar, named Lazarus, who was laid at his gate, full of sores, and desiring to be fed with the crumbs which fell from the rich man's table. Moreover, the dogs came and licked his sores.

'And it came to pass that the Beggar died, and was carried by the angels into Abraham's bosom – Abraham had been a very good man who lived many years before that time, and was then in Heaven. The rich man also died, and was buried. And in Hell, he lifted up his eyes, being in torments, and saw Abraham afar off, and Lazarus. And he cried and said, "Father Abraham have mercy on me, and send Lazarus that he may dip the tip of his finger in water and cool my tongue, for I am tormented in this flame." But Abraham said, "Son, remember that in thy life time thou receivedst good things, and likewise Lazarus evil things. But now, he is comforted, and thou art tormented!"'

And among other Parables, Christ said to these same Pharisees, because of their pride, That two men once went up into the Temple, to pray; of whom, one was a Pharisee, and one a Publican. The Pharisee said, 'God I thank Thee, that I am not unjust as other men are, or bad as this Publican is!' The Publican, standing afar off, would not lift up his eyes to Heaven, but struck his breast, and only said, 'God be merciful to me, a Sinner!' And God – our Saviour told them – would be merciful to that man rather than the other, and would be better pleased with his prayer, because he made it with a humble and a lowly heart.

The Pharisees were so angry at being taught these things, that they employed some spies to ask Our Saviour questions, and try to entrap Him into saying something which was against the Law. The Emperor of that country, who was called Cæsar, having commanded tribute-money to be regularly paid to him by the people, and being cruel against any one who disputed his right to it, these spies thought they might, perhaps, induce our Saviour to say it was an unjust payment, and so to bring himself under the Emperor's displeasure. Therefore, pretending to be very humble, they came to Him and said, 'Master you teach the word of God rightly, and do not respect persons on account of their wealth or high station. Tell us, is it lawful that we should pay tribute to Cæsar?'

Christ, who knew their thoughts, replied, 'Why do you ask? Shew me a penny.' They did so. 'Whose image, and whose name, is this upon it?' he asked them. They said 'Cæsar's.' 'Then,' said He, 'render unto Cæsar, the things that are Cæsar's.'

So they left him; very much enraged and disappointed that they could not entrap Him. But our Saviour knew their hearts and thoughts, as well as He knew that other men were conspiring against him, and that he would soon be put to Death.

As he was teaching them thus, he sat near the Public Treasury, where people as they passed along the street, were accustomed to drop money into a box for the poor; and many rich persons, passing while Jesus sat there, had put in a great deal of money. At last there came a poor Widow who dropped in two mites, each half a farthing in value, and then went quietly away. Jesus, seeing her do this as he rose to leave the place, called his disciples about him, and said to them that that poor widow had been more truly charitable than all the rest who had given money that day; for the others were rich and would never miss what they had given, but she was very poor, and had given those two mites which might have bought her bread to eat.

Let us never forget what the poor widow did, when we think we are charitable.

CHAPTER 8

There was a certain man named Lazarus of Bethany, who was taken very ill; and as he was the Brother of that Mary who had anointed Christ with ointment, and wiped his feet with her hair, she and her sister Martha sent to him in great trouble, saying, Lord, Lazarus whom you love is sick, and like to die.

Jesus did not go to them for two days after receiving this message; but when that time was past, he said to his Disciples, 'Lazarus is dead. Let us go to Bethany.' When they arrived there (it was a place very near to Jerusalem) they found, as Jesus had foretold, that Lazarus was dead, and had been dead and buried, four days.

When Martha heard that Jesus was coming, she rose up from among the people who had come to condole with her on her poor brother's death, and ran to meet him: leaving her sister Mary weeping, in the house. When Martha saw Him she burst into tears, and said 'Oh Lord if Thou had'st been here, my brother would not have died.' – 'Thy brother shall rise again,' returned Our Saviour. 'I know he will, and I believe he will, Lord, at the Resurrection on the Last Day,' said Martha.

Jesus said to her, 'I am the Resurrection and the Life. Dost Thou believe this?' She answered 'Yes Lord'; and running back to her sister Mary, told her that Christ was come. Mary hearing this, ran out, followed by all those who had been grieving with her in the house, and coming to the place where he was, fell down at his feet upon the ground and wept; and so did all the rest. Jesus was so full of compassion for their sorrow, that He wept too, as he said, 'where have you laid him?'—They said, 'Lord, come and see!'

He was buried in a cave; and there was a great stone laid upon it. When they all came to the Grave, Jesus ordered the stone to be rolled away, which was done. Then, after casting up his eyes, and thanking God, he said, in a loud and solemn voice, 'Lazarus, come forth!' and the dead man, Lazarus, restored to life, came out among the people, and went home with his sisters. At this sight, so awful and affecting, many of the people there believed that Christ was indeed the Son of God, come to instruct and save mankind. But others ran to tell the Pharisees; and from that day the Pharisees resolved among themselves – to prevent more people from believing in him, that Jesus should be killed. And they agreed among themselves – meeting in the Temple for that purpose – that if he came into Jerusalem before the Feast of the Passover, which was then approaching, he should be seized.

It was six days before the Passover, when Jesus raised Lazarus from the dead; and, at night, when they all sat at supper together, with Lazarus among them, Mary rose up, and took a pound of ointment (which was very precious and costly, and was called ointment of Spikenard) and anointed the feet of Jesus Christ with it, and, once again, wiped them on her hair; and the whole house was filled with the pleasant smell of the ointment. Judas Iscariot, one of the Disciples, pretended to be angry at this, and said that the ointment might have been sold for Three Hundred Pence, and the money given to the poor. But he only said so, in reality, because he carried the Purse, and was (unknown to the rest, at that time) a Thief, and wished to get all the money he could. He now began to plot for betraying Christ into the hands of the chief Priests.

The Feast of the Passover now drawing very near, Jesus Christ, with his disciples, moved forward towards Jerusalem. When they were come near to that city, He pointed to a village and told two of his disciples to go there, and they would find an ass, with a colt, tied to a tree, which they were to bring to Him. Finding these animals exactly as Jesus had described, they brought them away, and Jesus, riding on the ass, entered Jerusalem. An immense crowd of people collected round him as He went along, and throwing their robes on the ground, and cutting down green branches from the trees, and spreading them in His path, they shouted, and cried 'Hosanna to the Son of David!' (David had been a great King there) 'He comes in the name of the Lord! This is Jesus, the Prophet of Nazareth!' And when Jesus went into the Temple, and cast out the tables of the money-changers who wrongfully sat there, together with people who sold Doves; saying 'My father's house is a house of prayer, but ye have made it a den of Thieves!' – and when the people and children cried in the Temple 'This is Jesus the Prophet of Nazareth,' and would not be silenced – and when the blind and lame came flocking there in crowds, and were healed by his hand – the chief Priests, and Scribes, and Pharisees were filled with fear and hatred of Him. But Jesus continued to heal the sick, and to do good, and went and lodged at Bethany; a place that was very near the City of Jerusalem, but not within the walls.

One night, at that place, he rose from Supper at which he was seated with his Disciples, and taking a cloth and a basin of water, washed their feet. Simon Peter, one of the Disciples, would have prevented Him from washing his feet; but our Saviour told Him that He did this, in order that they, remembering it, might be always kind and gentle to one another, and might know no pride or ill-will among themselves.

Then, he became sad, and grieved, and looking round on the Disciples said, 'There is one here, who will betray me.' They cried out, one after another, 'Is it I, Lord!' – 'Is it I!' But he only answered, 'It is one of the Twelve that dippeth with me in the dish.' One of the disciples, whom Jesus loved, happening to be leaning on His breast at that moment listening to his words, Simon Peter beckoned to him that he should ask the name of this false man. Jesus answered 'It is he to whom I shall give a sop when I have dipped it in the dish.' And when he had dipped it, He gave it to Judas Iscariot, saying 'What thou doest, do quickly.' Which the other disciples did not understand, but which Judas knew to mean that Christ had read his bad thoughts.

So Judas, taking the sop, went out immediately. It was night, and he went straight to the chief Priests and said 'what will you give me, if I deliver him to you?' They agreed to give him thirty pieces of Silver; and for this, he undertook soon to betray into their hands, his Lord and Master Jesus Christ.

CHAPTER 9

The feast of the Passover being now almost come, Jesus said to two of his disciples, Peter and John, 'Go into the city of Jerusalem, and you will meet a man carrying a pitcher of water. Follow him home, and say to him, "the Master says where is the guest-chamber, where he can eat the Passover with his Disciples."

And he will shew you a large upper room, furnished. There, make ready the supper.'

The two disciples found that it happened as Jesus had said; and having met the man with the pitcher of water, and having followed him home, and having been shewn the room, they prepared the supper, and Jesus and the other ten apostles came at the usual time, and they all sat down to partake of it together.

It is always called The Last Supper, because this was the last time that Our Saviour ate and drank with his Disciples.

And he took bread from the table, and blessed it, and broke it, and gave it to them; and he took the cup of Wine, and blessed it, and drank, and gave it to them, saying 'Do this in remembrance of Me!' And when they had finished supper, and had sung a hymn, they went out into the Mount of Olives.

There, Jesus told them that he would be seized that night, and that they would all leave him alone and would think only of their own safety. Peter said, earnestly, he never would, for one. 'Before the cock crows,' returned Our Saviour, 'you will deny me thrice.' But Peter answered 'No Lord. Though I should die with Thee, I will never deny Thee.' And all the other Disciples said the same.

Jesus then led the way over a brook, called Cedron, into a garden that was called Gethsemane; and walked with three of the disciples into a retired part of the garden. Then he left them as he had left the others, together; saying 'Wait here, and watch!'—and went away and prayed by Himself, while they, being weary, fell asleep.

And Christ suffered great sorrow and distress of mind, in his prayers in that garden, because of the wickedness of the men of Jerusalem who were going to kill Him; and He shed tears before God, and was in deep and strong affliction.

When His prayers were finished, and He was comforted, He returned to the Disciples, and said 'Rise! let us be going! He is close at hand, who will betray me!'

Now, Judas knew that garden well, for Our Saviour had often walked there, with his Disciples; and, almost at the moment when Our Saviour said these words, he came there, accompanied by a strong guard of men and officers, which had been sent by the chief Priests and Pharisees. It being dark, they carried lanterns and torches. They were armed with swords and staves too; for they did not know but that the people would rise and defend Jesus Christ; and this had made them afraid to seize Him boldly in the day, when he sat teaching the people.

As the leader of this guard had never seen Jesus Christ and did not know him from the apostles, Judas had said to them, 'The man whom I kiss, will be he.' As he advanced to give this wicked kiss, Jesus said to the soldiers 'Whom do you seek?'—'Jesus of Nazareth,' they answered. 'Then,' said Our Saviour, 'I am He. Let my disciples here, go freely. I am He.' Which Judas confirmed, by saying 'Hail Master!' and kissing Him. Whereupon Jesus said, 'Judas, Thou betrayest me with a kiss!'

The guard then ran forward to seize Him. No one offered to protect Him, except Peter, who, having a sword, drew it, and cut off the right ear of the High Priest's Servant, who was one of them, and whose name was Malchus. But Jesus made him sheath his sword, and gave himself up. Then, all the disciples forsook Him, and fled; and there remained not one – not one – to bear Him company.

CHAPTER 10

After a short time, Peter and another Disciple took heart, and secretly followed the guard to the house of Caiaphas the High Priest, whither Jesus was taken, and where the Scribes and others were assembled to question Him. Peter stood at the door, but the other disciple, who was known to the High Priest, went in, and presently returning, asked the woman, who kept the door, to admit Peter too. She, looking at him said, 'Are you not one of the Disciples?' He said 'I am not.' So she let him in; and he stood before a fire that was there, warming himself, among the servants and officers who were crowded round it. For it was very cold.

Some of these men asked him the same question as the woman had done, and said 'Are you not one of the disciples?' He again denied it, and said, 'I am not.' One of them, who was related to that man whose ear Peter had cut off with his sword, said 'Did I not see you in the garden with him?' Peter again denied it with an oath, and said 'I do not know the man.' Immediately the cock crew, and Jesus turning round, looked stedfastly at Peter. Then Peter remembered what He had said – that before the cock crew, he would deny Him thrice – and went out, and wept bitterly.

Among other questions that were put to Jesus, the High Priest asked Him what He had taught the people. To which He answered that He had taught them in the open day, and in the open streets, and that the Priests should ask the people what they had learned of Him. One of the officers struck Jesus with his hand for this reply; and two false witnesses coming in, said they had heard Him say that He could destroy the Temple of God and build it again in three days. Jesus answered little; but the Scribes and Priests agreed that He was guilty of blasphemy, and should be put to death; and they spat upon, and beat him.

When Judas Iscariot saw that his Master was indeed condemned, he was so full of horror for what he had done, that he took the Thirty Pieces of Silver back to the chief Priests, and said 'I have betrayed innocent blood! I cannot keep it!' With those words, he threw the money down upon the floor, and rushing away, wild with despair, hanged himself. The rope, being weak, broke with the weight of his body, and it fell down on the ground, after Death, all bruised and burst, – a dreadful sight to see! The chief Priests, not knowing what else to do with the Thirty Pieces of Silver, bought a burying-place for strangers with it, the proper name of which was The Potters' Field. But the people called it The Field of Blood ever afterwards.

Jesus was taken from the High Priests to the Judgment Hall where Pontius Pilate, the Governor, sat, to administer Justice. Pilate (who was not a Jew) said to Him 'your own Nation, the Jews, and your own Priests have delivered you to me. What have you done?' Finding that He had done no harm, Pilate went out and told the Jews so; but they said 'He has been teaching the People what is not true and what is wrong; and he began to do so, long ago, in Galilee.' As Herod had the right to punish people who offended against the law in Galilee, Pilate said, 'I find no wrong in him. Let him be taken before Herod!'

They carried Him accordingly before Herod, where he sat surrounded by his stern soldiers and men in armour. And these laughed at Jesus, and dressed him, in mockery, in a fine robe, and sent him back to Pilate. And Pilate called the Priests and People together again, and said 'I find no wrong in this man; neither does Herod. He has done nothing to deserve death.' But they cried out, 'He has, he has! Yes, yes! Let him be killed!'

Pilate was troubled in his mind to hear them so clamorous against Jesus Christ. His wife, too, had dreamed all night about it, and sent to him upon the Judgment Seat saying 'Have nothing to do with that just man!' As it was the custom at the feast of the Passover to give some prisoner his liberty, Pilate endeavoured to persuade the people to ask for the release of Jesus. But they said (being very ignorant and passionate, and being told to do so, by the Priests) 'No no, we will not have him released. Release Barabbas, and let this man be crucified!'

Barabbas was a wicked criminal, in jail for his crimes, and in danger of being put to death.

Pilate, finding the people so determined against Jesus, delivered him to the soldiers to be scourged – that is, beaten. They plaited a crown of thorns, and put it on his head, and dressed Him in a purple robe, and spat upon him, and struck him with their hands, and said 'Hail, King of the Jews!' – remembering that the crowd had called him the Son of David when he entered into Jerusalem. And they ill-used him in many cruel ways; but Jesus bore it patiently, and only said 'Father! Forgive them! They know not what they do!'

Once more, Pilate brought Him out before the people, dressed in the purple robe and crown of thorns, and said 'Behold the man!' They cried out, savagely, 'Crucify him! Crucify him!' So did the chief Priests and officers. 'Take him and crucify him yourselves,' said Pilate. 'I find no fault in him.' But they cried out, 'He called himself the Son of God; and that by the Jewish Law is Death! And he called himself King of the Jews; and that is against the Roman Law, for we have no King but Cæsar, who is the Roman Emperor. If you let him go, you are not Cæsar's friend. Crucify him! Crucify him!'

When Pilate saw that he could not prevail with them, however hard he tried, he called for water, and washing his hands before the crowd, said, 'I am innocent of the blood of this just person.' Then he delivered Him to them to be crucified; and they, shouting and gathering round Him, and treating him (who still prayed for them to God) with cruelty and insult, took Him away.

CHAPTER II

That you may know what the People meant when they said 'Crucify him!' I must tell you that in those times, which were very cruel times indeed (let us thank God and Jesus Christ that they are past!) it was the custom to kill people who were sentenced to Death, by nailing them alive on a great wooden Cross, planted upright in the ground, and leaving them there, exposed to the Sun and Wind, and day and night, until they died of pain and thirst. It was the custom too, to make them walk to the place of execution, carrying the cross-piece of wood to which their hands were to be afterwards nailed; that their shame and suffering might be the greater.

Bearing his Cross, upon his shoulder, like the commonest and most wicked criminal, our blessed Saviour, Jesus Christ, surrounded by the persecuting crowd, went out of Jerusalem to a place called in the Hebrew language, Golgotha; that is, the place of a scull. And being come to a hill called Mount Calvary, they hammered cruel nails through his hands and feet and nailed him on the Cross, between two other crosses, on each of which a common thief was nailed in agony. Over His head, they fastened this writing 'Jesus of Nazareth, the King of the Jews' – in three languages; in Hebrew, in Greek, and in Latin.

Meantime, a guard of four soldiers, sitting on the ground, divided His clothes (which they had taken off) into four parcels for themselves, and cast lots for His coat, and sat there, gambling and talking, while He suffered. They offered him vinegar to drink, mixed with gall; and wine, mixed with myrrh; but he took none. And the wicked people who passed that way, mocked him, and said 'If Thou be the Son of God, come down from the Cross.' The Chief Priests also mocked Him, and said 'He came to save Sinners. Let him save himself!' One of the thieves too, railed at him, in his torture, and said, 'If Thou be Christ, save thyself, and us.' But the other Thief, who was penitent, said 'Lord! Remember me when Thou comest into Thy

Kingdom!' And Jesus answered, 'To-day, thou shalt be with me in Paradise.'

None were there, to take pity on Him, but one disciple and four women. God blessed those women for their true and tender hearts! They were, the mother of Jesus, his mother's sister, Mary, the wife of Cleophas, and Mary Magdalene who had twice dried his feet upon her hair. The disciple was he whom Jesus loved – John, who had leaned upon his breast and asked Him which was the Betrayer. When Jesus saw them standing at the foot of the Cross, He said to His mother that John would be her son, to comfort her when He was dead; and from that hour John was as a son to her, and loved her.

At about the sixth hour, a deep and terrible darkness came over all the land, and lasted until the ninth hour, when Jesus cried out, with a loud voice, 'My God, My God, why has Thou forsaken me!' The soldiers, hearing him, dipped a sponge in some vinegar, that was standing there, and fastening it to a long reed, put it up to His Mouth. When He had received it, He said 'It is finished!' – And crying 'Father! Into thy hands I commend my Spirit!' – died.

Then, there was a dreadful earthquake; and the Great wall of the Temple cracked; and the rocks were rent asunder. The guard, terrified at these sights, said to each other, 'Surely this was the Son of God!' – and the People who had been watching the cross from a distance (among whom were many women) smote upon their breasts, and went, fearfully and sadly, home.

The next day being the Sabbath, the Jews were anxious that the Bodies should be taken down at once, and made that request to Pilate. Therefore some soldiers came, and broke the legs of the two criminals to kill them; but coming to Jesus, and finding Him already dead, they only pierced his side with a spear. From the wound, there came out blood and water.

There was a good man named Joseph of Arimathea – a Jewish City – who believed in Christ, and going to Pilate privately (for fear of the Jews) begged that he might have the body. Pilate consenting, he and one Nicodemus rolled it in linen and spices – it was the custom of the Jews to prepare bodies for burial in that way – and buried it in a new tomb or sepulchre, which had been cut out of a rock in a garden near to the place of Crucifixion, and where no one had ever yet been buried. They then rolled a great stone to the mouth of the sepulchre, and left Mary Magdalene, and the other Mary, sitting there, watching it.

The Chief Priests and Pharisees remembering that Jesus Christ had said to his disciples that He would rise from the grave on the third day after His death, went to Pilate and prayed that the Sepulchre might be well taken care of until that day, lest the disciples should steal the Body, and afterwards say to the people that Christ was risen from the dead. Pilate agreeing to this, a guard of soldiers was set over it constantly, and the stone was sealed up besides. And so it remained, watched and sealed, until the third day; which was the first day of the week.

When that morning began to dawn, Mary Magdalene and the other Mary, and some other women, came to the Sepulchre, with some more spices which they had prepared. As they were saying to each other, 'How shall we roll away the stone?' the earth trembled and shook, and an angel, descending from Heaven, rolled it back, and then sat resting on it. His countenance was like lightning, and his garments were white as snow; and at sight of him, the men of the guard fainted away with fear, as if they were dead.

Mary Magdalene saw the stone rolled away, and waiting to see no more, ran to Peter and John who were coming towards the place, and said 'They have taken away the Lord and we know not where they have laid him!' They immediately ran to the Tomb, but John, being the faster of the two, outran the other, and got there first. He stooped down, and looked in, and saw the linen clothes in which the body had been wrapped, lying there; but he did not go in. When Peter came up, he went in, and saw the linen clothes lying in one place, and a napkin that had been bound about the head, in another. John also went in, then, and saw the same things. Then they went home, to tell the rest.

But Mary Magdalene remained outside the sepulchre, weeping. After a little time, she stooped down, and looked in, and saw Two angels, clothed in white, sitting where the body of Christ had lain. These said to her, 'Woman, why weepest Thou?' She answered, 'Because they have taken away my Lord, and I know not where they have laid him.' As she gave this answer, she turned round, and saw Jesus standing behind her, but did not then know Him. 'Woman,' said He, 'why weepest thou? what seekest thou?' She, supposing Him to be the gardener, replied, 'Sir! If thou hast borne my Lord hence, tell me where thou hast laid him, and I will take him away.' Jesus pronounced her name, 'Mary.' Then she knew him, and, starting, exclaimed 'Master!' – 'Touch me not,' said Christ; 'for I am not yet ascended to my Father; but go to my disciples, and say unto them, I ascend unto my Father, and your Father; and to my God, and to your God!'

Accordingly, Mary Magdalene went and told the Disciples that she had seen Christ, and what He had said to her; and with them she found the other women whom she had left at the Sepulchre when she had gone to call those two disciples Peter and John. These women told her and the rest, that they had seen at the Tomb two men in shining garments, at sight of whom they had been afraid, and had bent down, but who had told them that the Lord was risen; and also that as they came to tell this, they had seen Christ, on the way, and had held him by the feet, and worshipped Him. But these accounts seemed to the apostles at that time, as idle tales, and they did not believe them.

The soldiers of the guard too, when they recovered from their fainting-fit, and went to the Chief Priests to tell them what they had seen, were silenced with large sums of money, and were told by them to say that the Disciples had stolen the Body away while they were asleep.

But it happened that on that same day, Simon and Cleopas – Simon one of the twelve Apostles, and Cleopas one of the followers of Christ – were walking to a village called Emmaus, at some little distance from Jerusalem, and were talking, by the way, upon the death and resurrection of Christ, when they were joined by a stranger, who explained the Scriptures to them, and told them a great deal about God, so that they wondered at his knowledge. As the night was fast coming on when they reached the village, they asked this stranger to stay with them, which he consented to do. When they all three sat down to supper, he took some bread, and blessed it, and broke it as Christ had done at the Last Supper. Looking on him in wonder they found that his face was changed before them, and that it was Christ himself; and as they looked on him, he disappeared.

They instantly rose up, and returned to Jerusalem, and finding the disciples sitting together, told them what they had seen. While they were speaking, Jesus suddenly stood in the midst of all the company, and said 'Peace be unto ye!' Seeing that they were greatly frightened, he shewed them his hands and feet, and invited them to touch Him; and, to encourage them and give them time to recover themselves, he ate a piece of broiled fish and a piece of honeycomb before them all.

But Thomas, one of the Twelve Apostles, was not there, at that time; and when the rest said to him afterwards, 'we have seen the Lord!' he answered 'Except I shall see in his hands the print of the nails, and thrust my hand into his side, I will not believe!' At that moment, though the doors were all shut, Jesus again appeared, standing among them, and said 'Peace be unto you!' Then He said to Thomas, 'Reach hither thy finger, and behold my hands; and reach hither thy hand, and thrust it into my side; and be not faithless, but believing.' And Thomas answered, and said to him, 'My Lord and my God!' Then said Jesus, 'Thomas, because thou hast seen me, thou hast believed. Blessed are they that have not seen me, and yet have believed.'

After that time, Jesus Christ was seen by five hundred of his followers at once, and He remained with others of them forty days, teaching them, and instructing them to go forth into the world, and preach His gospel and religion; not minding what wicked men might do to them. And conducting his disciples at last, out of Jerusalem as far as Bethany, he blessed them, and ascended in a cloud to Heaven, and took His place at the right hand of God. And while they gazed into the bright blue sky where He had vanished, two white-robed angels appeared among them, and told them that as they had seen Christ ascend to Heaven, so He would, one day, come descending from it, to judge the World.

When Christ was seen no more, the Apostles began to teach the People as He had commanded them. And having chosen a new apostle, named Matthias, to replace the wicked Judas, they wandered into all countries, telling the People of Christ's Life and Death – and of His Crucifixion and Resurrection – and of the Lessons he had taught – and baptising them in Christ's name. And through the power He had given them they healed the sick, and gave sight to the Blind, and speech to the Dumb, and Hearing to the Deaf, as he had done. And Peter being thrown into Prison, was delivered from it, in the dead of night, by an Angel: and once, his words before God caused a man named Ananias, and his wife Sapphira, who had told a lie, to be struck down dead, upon the Earth.

Wherever they went, they were persecuted and cruelly treated; and one man named Saul who had held the clothes of some barbarous persons who pelted one of the Christians named Stephen, to death with stones, was always active in doing them harm. But God turned Saul's heart afterwards; for as he was travelling to Damascus to find out some Christians who were there, and drag them to prison, there shone about him a great light from Heaven; a voice cried, 'Saul, Saul, why persecutest thou me!' and he was struck down from his horse, by an invisible hand, in sight of all the guards and soldiers who were riding with him. When they raised him, they found that he was blind; and so he remained for three days, neither eating nor drinking, until one of the Christians (sent to him by an angel for that purpose) restored his sight in the name of Jesus Christ. After which, he became a Christian, and preached, and taught, and believed, with the apostles, and did great service.

They took the name of Christians from Our Saviour Christ, and carried Crosses as their sign, because upon a Cross He had suffered Death. The religions that were then in the World were false and brutal, and encouraged men to violence. Beasts, and even men, were killed in the churches, in the belief that the smell of their blood was pleasant to the Gods – there were supposed to be a great many Gods – and many most cruel and disgusting ceremonies prevailed. Yet, for all this, and though the Christian Religion was such a true, and kind, and good one, the Priests of the old Religions long persuaded the people to do all possible hurt to the Christians; and Christians were hanged, beheaded, burnt, buried alive, and devoured in Theatres by Wild Beasts for the public amusement, during many years. Nothing would silence them, or terrify them though; for they knew that if they did their duty, they would go to Heaven. So thousands upon thousands of Christians sprung up and taught the people and were cruelly killed, and were succeeded by other Christians, until the Religion gradually became the great religion of the World.

Remember! – It is Christianity TO DO GOOD always – even to those who do evil to us. It is Christianity to love our neighbour as ourself, and to do to all men as we would have them Do to us. It is Christianity to be gentle, merciful, and forgiving, and to keep those qualities quiet in our own hearts, and never make a boast of them, or of our prayers or of our love of God, but always to shew that we love Him by humbly trying to do right in everything. If we do this, and remember the life and lessons of Our Lord Jesus Christ, and try to act up to them, we may confidently hope that God will forgive us our sins and mistakes, and enable us to live and die in Peace.

THE END

DICKENS AND HIS CRITICS

George Saintsbury, 'Dickens', *Cambridge History of English Literature*, vol. XIII (1916). Saintsbury (1845–1933) was Regius Professor of Rhetoric and English Literature at Edinburgh 1895–1915.

> Of the deplorable *Child's History of England*, it is not necessary to say more than it is, perhaps, the capital instance of a man of genius, not tempted by the wellknown 'want of pence', or by anything except his own wilfulness, going far out of his way to write something for which he was (in everything but the possession of narrative faculty) absolutely disqualified. [p. 329]

Stephen Leacock, *Charles Dickens* (1933). Leacock (1869–1944), political economist and humorist, taught at McGill University.

> In some senses [*A Child's History of England*] is the most notable history of England that was ever written. It never obtained recognition as a manual either for the nursery, or the school. Nor was it suited to be such. In the first place, the proportion is all wrong. Dickens wrote at such length about early times that when he at last got to William of Orange and the opening of the eighteenth century, he had to end the book up in two pages. . . . But there were other objections to such a history in mid-Victorian England. It was far too out-spoken; it broke away from the tradition that children must only hear of the glories of history and the majesty of kingship and the pomp of royalty.
>
> . . . Dickens went out of his way to follow the picturesque by-paths of history, the striking stories and the telling incidents, without proper regard to their real importance. More than all, his own strange absorption with the horrors of crime and the cruelties of the criminal law led him to intrude them too brutally on the minds of his readers; at times it goes beyond the necessity of what is wholesome and becomes morbid. [pp. 140–1]

John Holloway, 'The Myth of England', *The Listener*, 15 May 1969. Holloway (1920–) was Professor of Modern English at Cambridge 1972–82.

> Dickens, in his *Child's History*, knew about the tradition of English radicalism. He gave three times as much space to Wat Tyler as the liberal historian Green was to do 20 years later, and he writes fully and sympathetically about John Ball, Jack Cade, the Lollards, Wycliffe and Robert Ket. He makes as much as Green of the Marian martyrs, he does justice to Hampden and Pym, he suitably denounces Claverhouse (ignored by Green), and spares a few lines for Oliver Plunkett and a paragraph for Algernon Sidney. Also he's not mealy-mouthed about rulers. . . . But it's not like that quite all the time. He notes Edward I's pitiless brutality, yet he speaks of his aggressive ambitions in the same breath as his having been 'a wise and great monarch'. He rather glamorises Crecy and the rest; he's too keen on Cromwell's overseas victories; he dramatises and a little sentimentalises the death of Charles I; and he very much sentimentalises the escape of Charles II after the battle of Worcester. The freedom part of the Myth had its allure for him, but the greatness part had a lot of allure too. Kings and their reigns gave him all his chapter-headings. [p. 671]

Peter Ackroyd, *Dickens* (1990). Ackroyd (1949–), Dickens's most recent biographer, has also written on Ezra Pound and T. S. Eliot.

> *A Child's History of England* is in many ways a melodramatic and theatrical account – in parts it is very close to the caricature tradition of Rowlandson and Hogarth – since Dickens had deliberately decided that his historical narrative must have 'a romantic and attractive air' in order to inveigle the children into reading it. But it is also very sharp and very opinionated; 'true', as Dickens said in a letter, and not 'genteel'. He was not interested in dictating the kind of book he satirised later in *Little Dorrit*: 'Even the said great personages dying in bed, making exemplary ends and sounding speeches; a polite history, more servile than their instruments, embalming them!' There is nothing polite about Dickens's own account of England's past and, from a reading of the volume, you would think the history of that country to be no more than a continuing 'battle of life'; a frenzied, active, heaving controversy which ends up in the death of a monarch only to begin all over again. In fact the book bears a strong resemblance to his two historical novels, *Barnaby Rudge* and *A Tale of Two*

Cities; it is essentially history as theatre, with crowds, confrontations, clashes, battles, death scenes and sundry noises off. [p. 584]

Janet L. Larson, *Dickens and the Broken Scripture* (Georgia, 1985). Janet Larson teaches at Rutgers University.

Had [*The Life of Our Lord*] been published in the author's lifetime, it would have brought down on his head the very controversy that his revised New Testament tries to settle. If his refusal to confess Jesus as 'Very God of very God' would have offended conservative Anglicans and evangelicals, the fourteen miracles he includes, climaxing with Christ's resurrection, would have amused the rationalists among his readers, although they might have been content enough with the moral parables Dickens retells in stressing Jesus' teaching ministry. Like William Ellery Channing abandoning some points of faith disproved by reason but not others, Dickens inadvertently courts the ironies of a Mr Facing-Both-Ways. He does not allow that Jesus is really divine (he only 'look[s]' so divine and grand), yet he credulously reports the miracles, the most powerful signs that Jesus is God; the forgiveness stories are particularly important, yet Dickens insists that heaven is the reward of Duty Done. The duty theme is paramount: John baptizes people who 'promise to be better'; the early Christians 'knew that if they did their duty, they would go to Heaven'; and Jesus is the exemplary human being who teaches us 'to DO GOOD always' so that we may be forgiven and 'live and die in Peace'. If one might expect this emphasis from a father to his children, one also hears in this reconstruction the voice of the Victorian who cannot believe in Bible promises of Christ's full atonement for sin, a religious mystery even adults 'can but imperfectly understand', and Unitarian sympathizers like Dickens not at all. [pp. 11–12]

F. J. Harvey Darton, *Children's Books in England* (3rd edn, Cambridge, 1982). Darton (1878–1936) was a historian of children's literature. This work, originally published in 1932, is still regarded as the finest work on pre-1900 children's books.

Holiday Romance, though quite jolly in a slightly sophisticated way, has most of the faults of jocular artifice. The alleged narrators, aged six and a half to nine, speak too often with a voice and a mind like those of Charles Dickens being playful in his fifty-sixth year. He pretends to take seriously, but laughs a little superciliously at, the tremendous trivialities of make-believe which are so real to childhood. The narrative is not devoid of some vulgar crudeness. But it does contain the right sort of properties. A colonel who is also a pirate, a magic fishbone, discomfited schoolmasters, cannibal savages singing an excellent anthem:

> Choo a choo a choo tooth.
>   Muntch, muntch, Nycey!
> Choo a choo a choo tooth.
>   Muntch, muntch. Nyce!

and mothers rejoicing (obviously) in the names of Mrs Alicumpaine and Mrs Orange: these are strained and overdone in the actual 'romance', but they have the root of the matter in them. Their presence as objects of both ridicule and sympathy so early as 1868 is remarkable. It is a waste of time to ridicule unknown things. [pp. 293–4]

SUGGESTIONS FOR FURTHER READING

John Forster's *Life of Charles Dickens* (3 vols, 1872–4), Edgar Johnson's *Charles Dickens: His Tragedy and Triumph* (2 vols, 1952) and Peter Ackroyd's *Dickens* (1990) all refer to the works below, though only Ackroyd covers *A Child's History* in any detail. Forster has interesting anecdotes about Dickens's religious attitudes and beliefs. Michael Patrick Hearn's essay on Dickens in *Writers for Children*, ed. Jane Bingham (New York, 1988), appraises all three works and discusses Dickens's own childhood reading.

A CHILD'S HISTORY OF ENGLAND

G. K. Chesterton, introduction to 1907 edition of the work in Everyman's Library, reprinted in *Chesterton on Dickens*, ed. M. Slater (1992): Writing before the development of critical and scholarly analysis of Dickens, Chesterton, always an enthusiastic Dickensian, approaches the work with sympathy and good sense, though well aware of its defects.

Philip Collins, *Dickens and Education* (1964): Chapter III, 'Dedicated to my Own Dear Children', discusses both *A Child's History* and *The Life of Our Lord*, but seems not to have seen the histories on which he assumes the first to have been based.

Rosemary Jann, 'Fact, Fiction, and Interpretation in *A Child's History of England*', *Dickens Quarterly* 4 (1987) pp. 199–205: a useful summary with some discussion of other juvenile histories.

HOLIDAY ROMANCE

F. J. Harvey Darton, *Children's Books in England* (3rd edn, revised by Brian Alderson, 1982): sets the work in its context.

THE LIFE OF OUR LORD

Sister Madonna Egan, CSJ, 'Telling "the Blessed History": Charles Dickens's *The Life of Our Lord*' (Ph.D., University of Minnesota, 1983): a thorough, scholarly investigation of the text in both manuscript and printed form which illuminatingly addresses the question of Dickens's religious beliefs, the use he made of the Gospels in writing the *Life*, and the way in which it relates to his published works.

Humphry House, *The Dickens World* (1941): Chapter v, 'Religion', is still the best general account of Dickens's religious beliefs and attitudes.

Janet L. Larson, *Dickens and the Broken Scripture* (1985): a study of the allusive use of the Bible in Dickens's novels.

N. C. Peyrouton, 'The Life of Our Lord: Some Notes of Explication', *The Dickensian* 59 (1963), pp. 102–12: a detailed study of both the theology and the literary style of this work.

Dennis Walder, *Dickens and Religion* (1981): interesting, but lacks sufficiently wide knowledge of the Victorian religious scene.

CLASSIC NOVELS
IN EVERYMAN

A SELECTION

The Way of All Flesh
SAMUEL BUTLER
A savagely funny odyssey from joyless duty to unbridled liberalism **£4.99**

Born in Exile
GEORGE GISSING
A rationalist's progress towards love and compromise in class-ridden Victorian England **£4.99**

David Copperfield
CHARLES DICKENS
One of Dickens's best-loved novels, brimming with humour **£3.99**

The Last Chronicle of Barset
ANTHONY TROLLOPE
Trollope's magnificent conclusion to his Barsetshire novels **£4.99**

He Knew He Was Right
ANTHONY TROLLOPE
Sexual jealousy, money and women's rights within marriage – a novel ahead of its time **£6.99**

Tess of the D'Urbervilles
THOMAS HARDY
The powerful, poetic classic of wronged innocence **£3.99**

Tom Jones
HENRY FIELDING
The wayward adventures of one of literatures most likeable heroes **£5.99**

Wuthering Heights and Poems
EMILY BRONTË
A powerful work of genius – one of the great masterpieces of literature **£3.50**

The Master of Ballantrae and Weir of Hermiston
R. L. STEVENSON
Together in one volume, two great novels of high adventure and family conflict **£4.99**

£5.99

AVAILABILITY
All books are available from your local bookshop or direct from
Littlehampton Book Services Cash Sales, 14 Eldon Way, Lineside Estate, Littlehampton, West Sussex BN17 7HE. PRICES ARE SUBJECT TO CHANGE.

To order any of the books, please enclose a cheque (in £ sterling) made payable to Littlehampton Book Services, or phone your order through with credit card details (Access, Visa or Mastercard) on 0903 721596 (24 hour answering service) stating card number and expiry date. Please add £1.25 for package and postage to the total value of your order.

In the USA, for further information and a complete catalogue call 1-800-526-2778.